PESIQTA deRAB KAHANA

Volume One
Pisqaot One Through Fourteen

Number 122
PESIQTA deRAB KAHANA
An Analytical Translation
Volume One
Pisqaot One Through Fourteen
Translated by
Jacob Neusner

PESIQTA deRAB KAHANA
An Analytical Translation

Volume One
Pisqaot One Through Fourteen

Translated by
Jacob Neusner

Scholars Press
Atlanta, Georgia

BM
517
.P34
E5
1987
v. 1

PESIQTA deRAB KAHANA
An Analytical Translation
Volume One
Pisqaot One Through Fourteen

©1987
Brown University

Library of Congress Cataloging in Publication Data

Pesikta de-Rav Kahana. English.
  Pesiqta deRab Kahana.

  (Brown Judaic studies ; no. 122-123)
  Bibliography: v.
  Includes index.
  Contents: pt. 1. Pisqaot one through fourteen. -- pt. 2.
Pisqaot fifteen through twenty-eight.
    1. Bible. O.T.--Sermons. 2. Jewish sermons.
I. Neusner, Jacob, 1932-   . II. Title. III. Series.
BM517.P34E5 1986   296.4'2   86-26042
ISBN 1-55540-072-8 (alk. paper : v. 1)

Printed in the United States of America
on acid-free paper

For

Bernard Mandelbaum

My teacher, friend,
and
co-worker

model of devotion to study of the Torah
and commitment to the service of the Jewish People
for an entire generation of
rabbis and teachers

and

Editor of
the authoritative Hebrew Edition of

PESIQTA DERAB KAHANA

Here is yours before you!

Contents

On the day that Moses completed *[the setting up of the Tabernacle, he anointed and consecrated it].*

(Num. 7:1)

When you lift up the head *[RSV: take the census] [of the people of Israel, then each shall give a ransom for himself to the Lord when you number them, that there be no plague among them when you number them].*

(Ex. 30:12)

Remember *[what the Amalekites did to you on your way out of Egypt, how they met you on the road when you were faint and weary and cut off your rear, which was lagging behind exhausted; they showed no fear of God. When the Lord your God gives you peace from your enemies on every side, in the land which he is giving you to occupy as your patrimony, you shall not fail to blot out the memory of the Amalekites from under heaven].*

(Deut. 25:17-19)

[Now the Lord said to Moses and to Aaron, '"This is the statute of the Torah which the Lord has commanded: Tell the people of Israel to bring you] a red heifer *[without defect, in which there is no blemish, and upon which a yoke has never come....And a man who is clean shall gather up the ashes of the heifer and deposit them outside the camp in a clean place; and they shall be kept for the congregation of the people of Israel for the water for impurity, for the removal of sin. And he who gathers the ashes of the heifer shall wash his clothes and be unclean until evening...He who touches the dead body of any person shall be unclean seven days; he shall cleanse himself with the water on the third day and on the seventh day and so be clean; but if he does not cleanse himself on the third day and on the seventh day he will not become clean. Whoever touches a dead person...and does not cleanse himself defiles the tabernacle of the Lord, and that person shall be cut off from Israel, because the water for impurity was not thrown upon him, he shall be unclean; his uncleanness is still on him"].*

(Num. 19:1-13, pass.)

[The Lord said to Moses and Aaron in the land of Egypt,] '"This month *[shall be for you the beginning of months; it shall be the first month of the year for you]"*.

(Ex. 12:1-2)

[The Lord spoke to Moses and said, Give this command to the Israelites:] See that you present my offerings, the food [for the food-offering of soothing odor, to me at the appointed time. Tell them: This is the food-offering which you shall present to the Lord: the regular daily whole-offering of two yearling rams without blemish. One you shall sacrifice in the morning and the second between dusk and dark].

(Num. 28:1-4)

And it came to pass at midnight [that the Lord smote all the firstborn in the land of Egypt, from the firstborn of Pharaoh who sat on his throne to the firstborn of the handmaiden behind the millstones, and all the firstborn of the cattle. And Pharaoh rose up in the night, he and all his servants and all the Egyptians, and there was a great cry in Egypt, for there was not a house where one was not dead. And he summoned Moses and Aaron by night and said, "Rise up, go forth from among my people, both you and the people of Israel, and go, serve the Lord as you have said. Take your flocks and your herds, as you have said, and be gone; and bless me also!]

(Ex. 12:29-32)

[When you enter the land which I give you and reap its harvest, you shall bring] the first sheaf [of your harvest to the priest. He shall present the sheaf as a special gift before the Lord on the day after the sabbath so as to gain acceptance for yourselves].

(Lev. 23:11)

When a bull or sheep or goat [is born, it shall remain seven days with its mother, and from the eighth day on, it shall be acceptable as an offering by fire to the Lord].

(Lev. 22:26)

[Year by year] you shall set aside a tithe [of all the produce of your seed, of everything that grows on the land. You shall eat it in the presence of the Lord your God in the place which he will choose as a dwelling for his name — the tithe of your corn and new wine and oil, and the firstborn of your cattle and sheep, so that for all time you may learn to fear the Lord your God].

(Deut. 14:22)

Now it came to pass that when Pharaoh let the people go, [God did not guide them by the road towards the Philistines, although that was the shortest; for he said, "The people may change their minds when they see war before them, and turn back to Egypt." So God made them go round by way of the wilderness towards the Red Sea, and the fifth generation of Israelites departed from Egypt].

(Exodus 13:17-18)

In the third month *[after Israel had left Egypt, they came to the wilderness of Sinai. They set out from Rephidim and entered the wilderness of Sinai, where they encamped, pitching their tent opposite the Mountain. Moses went up the mountain of God, and the Lord called to him from the mountain and said, "Speak thus to the house of Jacob and tell this to the sons of Israel: You have seen with your own eyes what I did to Egypt and how I have carried you on eagles' wings and brought you here to me. If only you will now listen to me and keep my covenant, then out of all peoples you shall become my special possession; for the whole earth is mine. You shall be my kingdom of priests, my holy nation"].*

(Exodus 19:1-6)

The words of Jeremiah *[son of Hilkiah, one of the priests at Anathoth in Benjamin. The word of the Lord came to him in the thirteenth year of the reign of Josiah son of Amon, king of Judah; also during the reign of Jehoiakim, son of Josiah, king of Judah, until the eleventh year of Zedekiah son of Josiah, king of Judah, was completed. In the fifth month the people of Jerusalem were carried away into exile].*

(Jer. 1:1-3)

Hear *[the word of the Lord, O House of Jacob, and all the families of the House of Israel. Thus says the Lord: "What wrong did your fathers find in me that they went far from me and went after worthlessness and became worthless? They did not say, 'Where is the Lord who brought us up from the Land of Egypt, who led us in the wilderness, in a land of deserts and pits, in a land of drought and deep darkness, in a land that none passes through, where no man dwells?'"]*

(Jer. 2:4-6)

Preface

This is the first complete and systematic translation of the authoritative and critical Pesiqta deRab Kahana, that is, the one published by Bernard Mandelbaum, *Pesikta de Rab Kahana. According to An Oxford Manuscript. With Variants from All Known Manuscripts and Genizoth Fragments and Parallel Passages. With Commentary and Introduction* (N.Y., 1962: The Jewish Theological Seminary of America) I-II. I have further followed Mandelbaum's notes and commentary. My translation aims at a most literal and analytical picture, in English, of Mandelbaum's Hebrew text. My primary goal is to give, in serviceable English, as literal but also as clear a picture as I can of the original Hebrew text. A test of my success will derive from the possibility of returning to, or envisioning, the Hebrew from the English. My translation, while meant to make sense in English, should pass that test. I mean further to make possible a systematic description of, and introduction to, the document, and the comparison of the document to others of its genus and species within the canon of the Judaism of the dual Torah, the classification of the document within its larger genus. These goals are accomplished in the introduction, which is given in Volume II of the project.

The prior English rendition, William G. (Gershon Zev) Braude and Israel J. Kapstein, *Pesikta de-Rab Kahana. R. Kahana's Compilation of Discourses for Sabbaths and Festal Days* (Philadelphia, 1975: Jewish Publication Society of America) is no translation at all. That is why this is in fact the first translation into English of the Hebrew text. There are three problems with the Braude and Kapstein rendition.

First, they have not *translated* the text that is before us. Let me explain. When I turned to the study of Pesiqta deRab Kahana for my larger study of the formation of Judaism, I found it useless, because it is far too much of a paraphrase, harmonizing and unifying what are really distinct and unrelated passages, solving textual problems by imputing verbiage with no counterpart in the Hebrew, and other exercises in circumlocution, to permit systematic analytical description and study of the document. That fact necessitated my rereading and fresh translation of the original Hebrew. That earlier version, while rich in stylistic originality and other merits of attractive rendition of the sense or the gist of the Hebrew, does not really translate the actual Hebrew text from one language into the other; proof is that reversing the process, moving out of English into Hebrew, leads us far away from the actual Hebrew text, which, out of the English, we can scarcely imagine. What they have done is not

a translation but a paraphrastic rendition, more of a literary and rabbinical than
an academic and scholarly translation. They do not address an academic audience
but a lay and literary one. So we cannot criticize them for not accomplishing
what they to begin with did not set out to do.

Not only is Braude and Kapstein's rendering not a translation, but there is a
second, still more compelling consideration to require a translation of the
document. They have not translated the best critical *text* of our document. In
fact it is difficult to know precisely what version or text, at any given point,
they do claim to translate. The Hebrew text on which Braude's and Kapstein's
translation is based *appears* to be eclectic,[1] therefore is not readily available to
scholars in general, rather than systematic and commonly accessible. I say
appears, because they do not explicitly state that it is Mandelbaum's, and their
English is commonly so loosely related to the Hebrew that we cannot guess
what other text, besides Mandelbaum's, they might have had in hand. In their
English translation of the work, Braude and Kapstein, the translators, do not
indicate what text is translated, and, while referring to Mandelbaum's edition as
"an admirable achievement," "superior to Buber's," "more accurately and more
amply edited," Braude and Kapstein do not allege that they have translated
Mandelbaum's text, beginning, middle, and end. I have done just that, so that
readers who wish to compare my translation to the original Hebrew can do so –
and improve on my rendering. Because of the paraphrastic approach to
translation chosen by the earlier translators, the differences between
Mandelbaum's text of Pesiqta deRab Kahana and the apparently-eclectic text
developed by Braude and Kapstein will not be easy to follow up. But where the
differences are substantive and considerable, they will be readily apparent. Let
me give a concrete example of what I believe is simple "overinterpretation," or
improving upon the Hebrew and imputing to it a sense – continuity, harmony,
cogency – that the Hebrew does not contain. It derives from the linkage of two
discourses I believe should stand independent of one another.

II:VI

1. A. R. Yudan opened discourse by citing the following verse of Scripture: *A
      good man's tongue is pure silver, the heart of the wicked is trash. [The
      lips of a good man teach many, but fools perish for want of sense]*
      (Prov. 10:20):
   B. *"A good man's tongue is pure silver* speaks of Jedo the prophet [2 Chr.
      9:29].
   C. *"...the heart of the wicked is trash* refers to Jeroboam [1 Kgs. 12:28-
      29)."
   D. *As Jeroboam stood by the altar to burn the sacrifice, a man of God from
      Judah, moved by the word of the Lord, appeared at Bethel. He inveighed
      against the altar in the Lord's name, crying out, "O altar, altar! [This is*

---

[1] I say "appears to be," because their rendition is so loosely tied to the Hebrew that I cannot
reconstruct the Hebrew out of the English.

the word of the Lord: 'Listen! A child shall be born to the house of David, named Josiah. He will sacrifice upon you the priests of the hill-shrines who make offerings upon you, and he will make human bones upon you.'" He gave a sign the same day: "This is the sign which the Lord has ordained: This altar will be rent in pieces and the ashes upon it will be spilt." When King Jeroboam heard the sentence which the man of God pronounced against the altar at Bethel, he pointed to him from the altar and said, "'Seize that man!" Immediately the hand which he had pointed at him became paralyzed, so that he could not draw it back. The altar too was rent in pieces and the ashes were spilt, in fulfilment of the sign that the man of God had given at the Lord's command] (1 Kgs. 13:1-5).

E. Why does it say, *altar, altar,* two times?

F. Said R. Abba bar Kahana, "One alludes to the altar in Beth El, the other to the altar in Dan."

G. And what was the prophet's proclamation? *"O altar, altar! This is the word of the Lord: 'Listen! A child shall be born to the house of David, named Josiah. He will sacrifice upon you the priests of the hill-shrines who make offerings upon you, and he will make human bones upon you.'"*

H. "The bones *of Jeroboam* will be burned on you" is not what is stated, but rather, *he will make human bones upon you.*

I. This teaches that he paid all due respect to the monarchy.

J. It is written, *When King Jeroboam heard the sentence which the man of God pronounced against the altar at Bethel, he pointed to him from the altar and said, 'Seize that man!'*

K. R. Huna in the name of R. Idi: "The Omnipresent had more concern for the honor owing to the righteous man than to the honor owing to himself. For when he [the king] was standing and offering a sacrifice to idolatry, his hand did not dry up. But when he put his hand against that righteous man [the prophet], then his hand dried up.

L. "So it is written: *Immediately the hand which he had pointed at him became paralyzed, so that he could not draw it back."*

M. *The king appealed to the man of God to pacify the Lord your God and pray for him that his hand might be restored. [The man of God did as he asked; his hand was restored and became as it had been before. Then the king said to the man of God, "Come home and take refreshment at my table and let me give you a present." But the man of God answered, "If you were to give me half your house, I would not enter it with you; I will eat and drink nothing in this place, for the Lord's command to me was to eat and drink nothing and not to go back by the way I came." So he went back another way; he did not return by the road he had taken to Bethel]* (1 Kgs. 13:6-10).

N. Two Amoras: one said, "The meaning of the reference to *the Lord your God* is, *your God,* not mine."

O. The other said, "By what sort of brazenness could he have called him, 'my God,' while he was standing and offering to an idol? Could he then have called him 'my God'?"

P. Nonetheless: *The man of God did as he asked; his hand was restored and became as it had been before.*

Q. What is the meaning of the statement, *as it had been before?*

R.   R. Berekhiah, R. Judah b. R. Simon in the name of R. Joshua b. Levi:
     "'Even though you beat a fool in the mortar of a craftsman, you will
     make nothing of him.' Just as, in the beginning, he would stand and
     make offerings to idolatry, so even afterward he would stand and make
     offerings to an idol."

2. A.   Another interpretation of *A good man's tongue is pure silver* refers to the
        Holy One, blessed be He, who chose the tongue of Moses and said, *When
        you raise up the head of the children of Israel* (Ex. 30:12).

The intersecting-verse reverts to the base-verse only at No. 2, while the far
more fully articulated exposition, No. 1, reads the intersecting-verse in the light
of an entirely unrelated matter. The problem of the translator, as Braude and
Kapstein see things, is to link No. 1 to No. 2, so establishing what is in their
mind a unitary *and also intelligible* text. Accordingly, Braude and Kapstein
translate the operative language of No. 2 as follows:

This is to say that the Holy One [not at all concerned with the respect
due to Him], saw to it that Moses chose words [as precious as choice
silver and as dazzling in the unexpected favor they showed to Israel]:
When Thou liftest the head tax from the children of Israel, [Thou also
liftest their heads].

What they have attempted is to link the two distinct compositions,
introducing the theme of the former into the latter, and, further, they have
imputed a meaning to No. 2 which I do not see in the text. My sense is that
they err by making more sense of the materials before us than the naked eye
discerns. This is a good example of what I maintain is simply a translation that
makes more sense than and so improves upon the original Hebrew.

My third reason to reject their work as translation is simply stated. I have
the strong sense that the document is not so accessible as they render it. They
find more sense in the Hebrew than I think can be demonstrated to be present.
So through paraphrase and imaginative renderings, they impute clarity,
ubiquitous continuity and even harmony, that the Hebrew does not provide,
solve problems that the Hebrew does not permit to be solved, and, in all, give us
rather more than, in the Hebrew, meets the eye. I prefer to give what I see and
to allow the reader in on the secret that not every word is equally clear, not every
statement equally accessible of sense and meaning, in the text as we presently
have it.

My fourth reason for rejecting the title "translation" to what we now have is
that the philosophy of translation rests on the premise that the "translators"
know more than the author of the text. If I may offer a single example of the
"philosophy" of paraphrase and revision grounded on knowledge of events
superior to that of the original narrator, that governs in Braude and Kapstein, it

is a simple footnote to the statement at Pisqa XI:XVIII.1A, translated by them
as follows:

> Wishing to buy corn, some donkey-drivers came to the city where dwelt
> Eleazar, son of R. Simeon [ben Yohai].

To the name, Eleazar, they append the following footnote (p. 218, n. 68):

> Since R. Eleazar had not yet become a scholar, the title "Rabbi" is
> deleted in the translation here and further on.

The premise of the footnote is that the story is told to represent "how things
really were" at a particular point in Eleazar's life; that this account of a real event
(involving the miraculous transport by Eleazar of a herd of asses from the ground
to the roof and back again!) must be made to conform to the facts; and that
Braude and Kapstein know the facts of Eleazar's life better than the hapless
narrator, whose account the latter-day translators will now correct. It would be
too harsh a judgment to call this charlatanism. Still the translator-revisers
apparently place their knowledge of the personal biography of Eleazar above that
of the text while at the same time gullibly believing every detail of the text.
But it is surely not a "revision" of the text that demands or even deserves the
title, "accurate translation."

That is not to suggest there is nothing to be learned from Braude and
Kapstein. The contrary is the case. I consulted the rendition of Kapstein and
Braude and used it wherever I could. I have consulted Braude and Kapstein at
every point, to take full advantage of their proposals where they seemed to me
compelling, and, where I have done so, both for word choices and for broader
matters of meaning, I have either cited them verbatim and so indicated or marked
the passage as follows [B&K, p. 00:]. In this way I am able to give full credit
to my predecessors. Where I do not concur with their rendering, I do not so
indicate, because my basic approach to translation is entirely different from
theirs, which, as I said, accounts for the necessity to retranslate the work in its
entirety.

The difference is more than a matter of taste or style in how one should
translate. It is whether one is translating at all when the translator imputes to
the text at hand a vast range of meanings and conceptions contributed only by
the later commentaries, or by the translator serving as commentator. Obviously,
every translation is also a commentary. But there seem to me limits to the sort
of commentary one provides in the guise of a translation, and because Braude and
Kapstein find no guidance in the restraints of the original language, they have
given us something other than a translation. It is a commentary in the form of a
paraphrase, something new and different, if, for purposes of academic study, not

terribly useful. Let me close with a brief contrast between their approach and mine.

Braude and Kapstein, p. 31, Pisqa **II:VII:**

> In the phrase *the head* (Exod. 30:12), so said R. Jose bar Hanina, it is intimated that Moses would bring back into Israel's midst the head – that is, the oldest one – of the Tribe Fathers. Who was that? Reuben, of course, of whom at the end of Moses' life, Moses was to say, *Let Reuben live:* [let his sin in lying with Bilhah be remembered no more] *and let his people be reckoned in the numbering [of Israel]* (Deut. 33:6).

At *[of Israel]* they add the following note: "See Rashi on Deut. 33:6, and Gen. 35:22."

My translation of the same passage is as follows:

2. A.   *[When you raise up] the head [of the children of Israel] [and take a census]* (Ex. 30:12).
  B.   Said R. Yose bar Haninah, "This statement served to provide an indication that [Moses] was going to draw near [restoring primacy to] the first of the tribes, and who is that? It is Reuben:
  C.   *"Let Reuben live* (Deut. 33:6)."

The first difference is in my insistence on giving, in English, only what is in the Hebrew.

The second, as I said, is that I follow a single, consistent text. Specifically, I believe that Mandelbaum's position that certain materials contained in only a single manuscript do not form part of Pesiqta deRab Kahana should be taken into account in presenting an English version of the same; Braude and Kapstein differ, and so translate sizable selections of materials that, from a critical viewpoint, enjoy only a dubious claim to a place in our document.

The third point of difference is in the paraphrastic harmonization of discrete pericopae, a constant feature of Braude's and Kapstein's translation to which I have already alluded. The following rendition seems to me not a translation at all (Braude and Kapstein, p. 18, Pisqa **I:VIII**):

> At the same time Moses was distraught but for a different reason. He said: The Holy spirit must have departed from me, and having come to rest upon the princes, [inspired them to bring the wagons and the oxen]. Whereupon the Holy One said: "Moses, if I had wanted the princes to bring their offerings, I would have asked you to tell them so. But what I now tell you is *Purchase; it is of them* (Num. 7:5): The idea of offerings came from the 'them' [referred to elsewhere in Scripture, and not from the princes]." Who, then, are meant by "them"? The Tribe of Issachar who gave the idea to the princes, the Tribe of whom Scripture says, *And of the children of Issachar came men who had understanding of the times* (1

Chron. 12:33). What is meant by *the times*? The right times for doing what should be done, according to R. Tanhuma; intercalary days and months, according to R. Jose bar Kasri. Concerning the tribe of Issachar, Chronicles goes on: *the heads of them were two hundred (ibid.),* implies that their brethren in Israel were to conduct themselves in keeping with the practical advice given them by Issachar. It was the Tribe of Issachar, then, [and not the holy spirit] which said to the princes: "This Tent of Meeting that you see being made–how is it to move about? Is it to fly in the air? Make wagons for it and carry its parts therein."

My translation is as follows:

I:VIII

4.   A.   *And the Lord spoke to Moses and said, [Accept these from them: they shall be used for the service of the tent of the presence"]:* (Num. 7:5):
     B.   What is the meaning of the word, *and said?*
     C.   R. Hoshaia taught, "The Holy One, blessed be He, said to Moses, 'Go and say to Israel words of praise and consolation.'
     D.   "Moses was afraid, saying, 'But is it not possible that the holy spirit and abandoned me and come to rest on the chiefs?'
     E.   "The Holy One said to him, 'Moses, had I wanted them to bring their offering, I should have said to you to 'say to them,' [so instructing them to do so], but *Take – it is from them [at their own volition, not by my inspiration]* (Num. 7:5) is the language that meaning, they did it on their own volition [and have not received the holy spirit].'"

5.   A.   And who gave them the good ideas [of making the gift]?
     B.   It was the tribe of Simeon who gave them the good idea, in line with this verse: *And of the children of Issachar came men who had understanding of the times* (1 Chr. 12:33).
     C.   What is the sense of *the times?*
     D.   R. Tanhuma said, "The ripe hour [*kairos*]."
     E.   R. Yose bar Qisri said, "Intercalating the calendar."
     F.   *They had two hundred heads* (1 Chr. 12:33):
     G.   This refers to the two hundred heads of sanhedrins that were produced by the tribe of Issachar.
     H.   *And all of their brethren were subject to their orders* (1 Chr. 12:33):
     I.   This teaches that the law would accord with their rulings.
     J.   They said to the community, "Is this tent of meeting which you are making going to fly in the air? Make wagons for it, which will bear it."

The differences are blatant. Readers who go to the Hebrew text will recognize the words I have translated, I believe with exact, meticulous concern for detail. I see many merits in the interpretative rendition of Braude and Kapstein; I believe their sense of the passage at hand has much to recommend it; it certainly joins what to me are discrete items. But while I maintain that Braude and Kapstein have given us a first-rate paraphrase, I find it self-evident that theirs is not a translation at all.

Let me give one further example by showing the effect upon their translation of their insistence that we have a seamless and unitary text, not a composite of diverse materials joined together, as seems to me blatantly obvious, by the ultimate compositors. For this purpose I give my translation alone, with reference to how Braude and Kapstein treat the matter.

I:II.

1. A. *King Solomon made a pavilion for himself* (Song 3:9) [The New English Bible: *The palanquin which King Solomon had made for himself was of wood from Lebanon. Its poles he made of silver, its head-rest of gold; its seat was of purple stuff, and its lining was of leather]:*

   B. *Pavilion* refers to the tent of meeting.

   C. *King Solomon made a... for himself:* he is the king to whom peace [*shalom/shelomoh*] belongs.

2. A. Said R. Judah bar Ilai, "[The matter may be compared to the case of] a king who had a little girl. Before she grew up and reached puberty, he would see her in the market place and chat with her, or in alleyways and chat with her. But when she grew up and reached puberty, he said, 'It is not fitting for the dignity of my daughter that I should talk with her in public. Make a pavilion for her, so that I may chat with her in the pavilion.'

   B. "So, to begin with: *When Israel was a child in Egypt, then in my love of him, I used to cry out* (Hos 11:1). In Egypt they saw me: *And I passed through the land of Israel* (Ex. 12:12). At the sea they saw me: *And Israel saw the great hand* (Ex. 14:31). At Sinai they saw me: *Face to face the Lord spoke with you* (Deut. 5:4).

   C. "But when they received the Torah, they became a fully-grown nation for me. So he said, 'It is not appropriate to the dignity of my children that I should speak with them in public. But make me a tabernacle, and I shall speak from the midst of the tabernacle.'

   D. "That is in line with this verse: *And when Moses entered the tent of the presence to speak with God, he heard the voice speaking from above the cover over the ark of the tokens from between the two cherubim: the voice spoke to him* (Num. 7:89)."

Seen by itself, No. 1 has no bearing upon the larger context, but it does provide a good exegesis of Song 3:9 in terms of the theme at hand, the tabernacle. The point of No. 2 is that the purpose of the tabernacle was to make possible appropriate communication between a mature Israel and God. Then the two items are simply distinct workings of the theme of the tabernacle, one appealing to Song 3:9, the other, Num. 7:89. But Braude and Kapstein so translate as to link the two:

King Solomon made Himself: that is, the King of the universe needing a means of private communication [with Israel] made it for himself. In explanation of the verse, R. Judah bar Ilai told the parable, etc.

The footnotes justify *made Himself*, referring to God, and *communicate* out of the letters of the word translated as peace, by appeal to allegedly pertinent parallels. I find myself puzzled by the mode of argument, all the more so, the result, since it seems to me little more than free association. Erudite and inventive but uncontrolled and farfetched, exercises of this sort will not detain us.

For analysis of the text, I therefore found that I had to provide a simple and reliable translation, and that is what I have done in this book for *pisqaot* 1-14, and shall present in the coming Volume II for *pisqaot* 15-28. Volume II will also contain an introduction to the document as a whole. That study will prepare the way for the comparison of one midrash-compilation to another, that is, *comparative midrash,* along the lines already explored in the following:

> *The Integrity of Leviticus Rabbah. The Problem of the Autonomy of a Rabbinic Document.* Chico, 1985: Scholars Press for Brown Judaic Studies.

> *Comparative Midrash: The Plan and Program of Genesis Rabbah and Leviticus Rabbah.* Atlanta, 1986: Scholars Press for Brown Judaic Studies.

> *Canon and Connection: Intertextuality in Judaism.* Lanham, 1986: University Press of America. *Studies in Judaism* Series.

> *Literature and Midrash: The Primacy of Documentary Discourse.* (In press.)

> *The Workings of Midrash. Major Trends in Rabbinic Bible Interpretation.* (In press.)

> *What is Midrash?* Philadelphia, 1988: Fortress Press.

For biblical verses, I commonly consulted The New English Bible translation or the Revised Standard Version, both of which I find admirable, and, on occasion, I have copied Braude and Kapstein's rendering, always so indicated; a few translations of scriptural verses are my own and free-hand.

Jacob Neusner

Program in Judaic Studies
Brown University
Providence, Rhode Island 02912-1826 U.S.A.

Acknowledgements

I express my thanks to both Dr. Bernard Mandelbaum and Provost Ray Scheindlin of The Jewish Theological Seminary of America for permission to translate the critical text produced by Dr. Mandelbaum and copyrighted by the Jewish Theological Seminary of America: © 1962: The Jewish Theological Seminary of America.

Professor Mandelbaum also offered me every encouragement, beyond the call of duty, and reviewed my translation for me. While he bears no responsibility for inadequacies that may remain, he generously contributed his guidance, and I am grateful.

Pisqa One

On the day that Moses completed *[the setting up of the Tabernacle,
he anointed and consecrated it]*
(Num. 7:1).

I:I

1. A. *I have come back to my garden, my sister, my bride* (Song 5:1):
   B. R. Azariah in the name of R. Simon said, "[The matter may be compared to the case of] a king who became angry at a noble woman and drove her out and expelled her from his palace. After some time he wanted to bring her back. She said, 'Let him renew in my behalf the earlier state of affairs, and then he may bring me back.'
   C. "So in former times the Holy One, blessed be He , would receive offerings from on high, as it is said, *And the Lord smelled the sweet odor* (Gen. 8:21). But now he will accept them down below."

2. A. *I have come back to my garden, my sister, my bride* (Song 5:1):
   B. Said R. Hanina, "The Torah teaches you proper conduct,
   C. "specifically, a groom should not go into the marriage canopy until the bride gives him permission to do so: *Let my beloved come into his garden* (Song 4:16), after which, *I have come back to my garden, my sister, my bride* (Song 5:1)."

3. A. R. Tanhum, son-in-law of R. Eleazar b. Abina, in the name of R. Simeon b. Yosni: "What is written is not, 'I have come into the garden,' but rather, *I have come back to my garden.* That is, 'to my [Mandelbaum:] canopy.'
   B. "That is to say, to the place in which the the principal [presence of God] had been located to begin with.
   C. "The principal locale of God's presence had been among the lower creatures, in line with this verse: *And they heard the sound of the Lord God walking about* (Gen. 3:8)."

4. A. *[And they heard the sound of the Lord God walking about* (Gen. 3:8):]
   Said R. Abba bar Kahana, "What is written is not merely 'going,' but 'walking about,' that is, 'walking away from.'"
   B. *And man and his wife hid* (Gen. 3:8):
   C. Said R. Aibu, "At that moment the first man's stature was cut down and diminished to one hundred cubits."

5. A. Said R. Isaac, "It is written, *The righteous will inherit the earth* (Ps. 47:29). Where will the wicked be? Will they fly in the air?

B. "Rather, the sense of the clause, *they shall dwell thereon in eternity* is, 'they shall bring the presence of God to dwell on the earth.'"

6. A. [Reverting to 3.C,] the principal locale of God's presence had been among the lower creatures, but when the first man sinned, it went up to the first firmament.

B. The generation of Enosh came along and sinned, and it went up from the first to the second.

C. The generation of the flood [came along and sinned], and it went up from the second to the third.

D. The generation of the dispersion [came along] and sinned, and it went up from the third to the fourth.

E. The Egyptians in the time of Abraham our father [came along] and sinned, and it went up from the fourth to the fifth.

F. The Sodomites [came along], and sinned, ...from the fifth to the sixth.

G. The Egyptians in the time of Moses...from the sixth to the seventh.

H. And, corresponding to them, seven righteous men came along and brought it back down to earth:

I. Abraham our father came along and acquired merit, and brought it down from the seventh to the sixth.

J. Isaac came along and acquired merit and brought it down from the sixth to the fifth.

K. Jacob came along and acquired merit and brought it down from the fifth to the fourth.

L. Levi came along and acquired merit and brought it down from the fourth to the third.

M. Kahath came along and acquired merit and brought it down from the third to the second.

N. Amram came along and acquired merit and brought it down from the second to the first.

O. Moses came along and acquired merit and brought it down to earth.

P. Therefore it is said, *On the day that Moses completed the setting up of the Tabernacle, he anointed and consecrated it* (Num. 7:1).

The selection of the intersecting-verse, Song 5:1, rests on the appearance of the letters KLT, meaning completed, but yielding also the word KLH, meaning bride. The exegete wishes to make the point that in building the tabernacle, Moses has brought God down to earth, 6.P. This he accomplishes by bringing the theme of "garden, bride" together with the theme of the union of God and Israel. The parable at 1.B then is entirely apt, since it wishes to introduce the notion of God's having become angry with humanity but then reconciled through Israel in the sacrificial cult. 1.B then refers to the fall from grace, with Israel as the noble spouse who insists that the earlier state of affairs be restored. C then makes explicit precisely what is in mind, a very effective introduction to the whole. No. 2 pursues the exegesis of the intersecting-verse, as does No. 3, the latter entirely apropos. Because of 3.C, Nos. 4 is tacked on; it continues the exegesis of the proof-text but has no bearing on the intersecting-verse. But No. 5 does – at least in its proposition, if not in its selection of proof-texts. No. 6

then brings us back to 3.C, citing the language of the prior component and then making the point of the whole quite explicit. Even with the obvious accretions at No. 4, 5, the whole hangs together and makes its point – the intersecting verse, Song 5:1, the base verse Num. 7:1 – in a cogent way.

I:II.

1. A. *King Solomon made a pavilion for himself* (Song 3:9) [The New English Bible: *The palanquin which King Solomon had made for himself was of wood from Lebanon. Its poles he made of silver, its head-rest of gold; its seat was of purple stuff, and its lining was of leather]:*
   B. *Pavilion* refers to the tent of meeting.
   C. *King Solomon made a... for himself:* he is the king to whom peace *[shalom/shelomoh]* belongs.

2. A. Said R. Judah bar Ilai, "[The matter may be compared to the case of] a king who had a little girl. Before she grew up and reached puberty, he would see her in the market place and chat with her, or in alleyways and chat with her. But when she grew up and reached puberty, he said, 'It is not fitting for the dignity of my daughter that I should talk with her in public. Make a pavilion for her, so that I may chat with her in the pavilion.'
   B. "So, to begin with: *When Israel was a child in Egypt, then in my love of him, I used to cry out* (Hos 11:1). In Egypt they saw me: *And I passed through the land of Israel* (Ex. 12:12). At the sea they saw me: *And Israel saw the great hand* (Ex. 14:31). At Sinai they saw me: *Face to face the Lord spoke with you* (Deut. 5:4).
   C. "But when they received the Torah, they became a fully-grown nation for me. So he said, 'It is not appropriate to the dignity of my children that I should speak with them in public. But make me a tabernacle, and I shall speak from the midst of the tabernacle.'
   D. "That is in line with this verse: *And when Moses entered the tent of the presence to speak with God, he heard the voice speaking from above the cover over the ark of the pact from between the two cherubim: the voice spoke to him* (Num. 7:89)."

3. A. *[The palanquin which King Solomon had made for himself was of wood from Lebanon. Its poles he made of silver, its head-rest of gold; its seat was of purple stuff, and its lining was of leather] ...was of wood from Lebanon. Make for the tabernacle planks of acacia wood as uprights* (Ex. 26:15).
   B. *Its poles he made of silver: The hooks and bands on the posts shall be of silver (Ex. 27:10).*
   C. *...its head-rest of gold: Overlay the planks with gold, make rings of gold on them to hold the bars* (Ex. 26:29).
   D. *...its seat was of purple stuff: Make a veil of finely woven linen and violet, purple, and scarlet yarn* (Ex. 26:31).
   E. *...and its lining was of leather:*
   F. R. Yudan says, "This refers to the merit accruing on account of the Torah and the righteous."

G. R. Azariah in the name of R. Judah bar Simon says, "This refers to the Presence of God."

4. A. Said R. Aha bar Kahana, "It is written, *And there I shall meet with you* (Ex. 25:22),

    B. "to teach that even what is on the outside of the ark-cover is not empty of God's presence."

5. A. A gentile asked Rabban Gamaliel, saying to him, "On what account did the Holy One, blessed be He, reveal himself to Moses in a bush?"

    B. He said to him, "If he had revealed himself to him in a carob tree or a fig tree, what might you have said?

    C. "It is so as to indicate that there is no place in the earth that is empty of God's presence."

6. A. R. Joshua of Sikhnin in the name of R. Levi: "To what may the tent of meeting be compared?

    B. "To an oceanside cave. The sea tide flows and engulfs the cave, which is filled by the sea, but the sea is not diminished.

    C. "So the tent of meeting is filled with the splendor of the presence of God."

    D. Therefore it is said, *On the day that Moses completed the setting up of the Tabernacle, he anointed and consecrated it* (Num. 7:1).

The introduction at I:II of Song 3:9, with the explanation that palanquin refers to the tent of meeting, accounts for the exposition of No. 3, which reads each phrase of that intersecting-verse in line with the proof-texts concerning the tent of meeting. Had I:II.1 been continued by No. 3, we should have a smoother statement of the main point. No. 4 seems to me to flow from No. 3's interest in the tent of meeting; the point of contact is with the viewpoint that God's presence was in the tent. Then No. 5 is tacked on for obvious reasons, a story that makes the same point as the exegesis. No. 6 goes over the matter yet again. The force of 6.D is derived only from its redactional function, which is to direct our attention back to our base-verse. But while the theme – the tent of meeting or tabernacle – has been worked out, the base-verse has not been discussed. Tacking it on is only for purpose of marking the finish of the discourse at hand.

I:III

1. A. [Continuing the exegesis of the successive verses of Song 3:9ff.] *Come out, daughters of Jerusalem, you daughters of Zion, come out and welcome King Solomon, wearing the crown with which his mother has crowned him, on his wedding day, on his day of joy* (Song 3:11) [Braude and Kapstein: *Go forth, O younglings whose name Zion indicates that you bear a sign]*:

    B. Sons who are marked [a play on the letters that stand for the word, *come out*] for me by the mark of circumcision, by not cutting the corners of the head [in line with Lev. 19:27], and by wearing show-fringes.

2. A. *[...and welcome] King Solomon:*
   B. The king to whom peace belongs.

3. A. Another interpretation: *and welcome King Solomon:*
   B. The King [meaning God] who brings peace through his deeds among his creatures.
   C. He made the fire make peace with our father Abraham, the sword with our father Isaac, the angel with our father Jacob.
   D. It is the king who brings peace among his creatures.
   E. Said R. Yohanan, *"Merciful dominion and fear are with him* (Job 25:2) [that is, are at peace with him]."
   F. Said R. Jacob of Kefar Hanan, *"Merciful dominion* refers to Michael, and *fear* to Gabriel.
   G. *"With him* means that they make peace with him and do not do injury to one another."
   H. Said R. Yohanan, "The sun has never laid eyes on the blemished part of the moon [the black side], nor does one star take precedence over another one, nor does a planet lay eyes on the one above it."
   I. Said Rabbi, "All of them traverse as it were a spiral staircase."

4. A. It is written, *Who lays the beams of your upper chambers in the waters, who makes the flaming fires your ministers* (Ps. 104:2-3):
   B. R. Simeon b. Yohai taught, "The firmament is of water, the stars of fire, and yet they dwell with one another and do not do injury to one another.
   C. "The firmament is of water and the angel is of fire, and yet they dwell with one another and do not do injury to one another."
   D. Said R. Abin, "It is not the end of the matter [that there is peace between] one angel and another. But even the angel himself is half fire and half water, and yet they make peace."
   E. The angel has five faces – *The angel's body was like beryl, his face as the appearance of lightning, his eyes as torches of fire, his arms and feet like in color to burnished brass, and the sound of his words like the sound of a roaring multitude* (Dan. 10:6) – [yet none does injury to the other].

5. A. *So there was hail and fire flashing continually amid the hail* (Ex. 9:24):
   B. R. Judah says, "There was a flask of hail filled with fire."
   C. R. Nehemiah said, "Fire and hail, mixed together."
   D. R. Hanin said, "In support of the position of R. Judah is the case of the pomegranate in the pulp of which seeds can be discerned."
   E. R. Hanin said, "As to R. Nehemiah's, it is the case of a crystal lamp in which are equivalent volumes of water and oil, which together keep the flame of the wick burning above the water and the oil."

6. A. *[So there was hail and fire flashing continually amid the hail* (Ex. 9:24)]: What is the meaning of *flashing continually?*
   B. Said R. Judah bar Simon, "Each one is dying in its [B&K, p. 10:] determination to carry out their mission."
   C. Said R. Aha, "[The matter may be compared to the case of] a king, who had two tough legions, who competed with one another, but when the

time to make war in behalf of the king came around, they made peace with one another.

D. "So is the case with the fire and hail, they compete with one another, but when the time has come to carry out the war of the Holy One, blessed be He, against the Egyptians, then: *So there was hail and fire flashing continually amid the hail* (Ex. 9:24) – one miracle within the other [more familiar one, namely, that the hail; and fire worked together]."

7. A. *[Come out, daughters of Jerusalem, you daughters of Zion, come out and welcome King Solomon,] wearing the crown with which his mother has crowned him, on his wedding day, [on his day of joy]* (Song 3:11):

   B. Said R. Isaac, "We have reviewed the entire Scripture and have not found evidence that Beth Sheba made a crown for her son, Solomon. This refers, rather, to the tent of meeting, which is crowned with blue and purple and scarlet."

8. A. Said R. Hunia, "R. Simeon b. Yohai asked R. Eleazar b. R. Yose, 'Is it possible that you have heard. from your father what was the crown with which his mother crowned him?'

   B. "He said to him, 'The matter may be compared to the case of a king who had a daughter, whom he loved even too much. He even went so far, in expressing his affection for her, as to call her, 'my sister.' He even went so far, in expressing his affection for her, as to call her, 'my mother.'

   C. "'So at the outset, the Holy One, blessed be He, expressed his affection for Israel by calling them, 'my daughter': *Hear, O daughter, and consider* (Ps. 45:11). Then he went so far, in expressing his affection for them, as to call them, 'my sister': *My sister, my bride* (Song 5:1). Then he went so far, in expressing his affection for them, as to call them, 'my mother': *Attend to me, O my people, and give ear to me, O my nation* (Is. 51:4). The letters that are read as 'my nation' may also be read as 'my mother.'"

   D. "R. Simeon b. Yohai stood and kissed him on his brow.

   E. "He said to him, 'Had I come only to hear this teaching, it would have been enough for me.'"

9. A. R. Joshua of Sikhnin taught in the name of R. Levi: "When the Holy One, blessed be He, said to Moses, 'Make me a tabernacle,' Moses might have brought four poles and spread over them [skins to make] the tabernacle. This teaches, therefore, that the Holy One, blessed be He, showed Moses on high red fire, green fire, black fire, and white fire.

   B. "He said to him, 'Make me a tabernacle.'

   C. "Moses said to the Holy One, blessed be he, 'Lord of the ages, where am I going to get red fire, green fire, black fire, or white fire?'

   D. "He said to him, *After the pattern which is shown to you on the mountain* (Ex. 25:40)."

10. A. R. Berekhiah in the name of R. Levi: "[The matter may be compared to the case of] a king who appeared to his household clothed in a garment [B&K, p. 11] covered entirely with precious stones.

    B. "He said to him, 'Make me one like this.'

C. "He said to him, 'My lord, O king, where am I going to get myself a garment made entirely of precious stones?'

D. "He said to him, 'You in accord with your raw materials and I in accord with my glory.'

E. "So said the Holy One, blessed be He, to Moses, 'Moses, if you make what belongs above down below, I shall leave my council up here and go down and reduce my Presence so as to be among you down there.'

F. "Just as up there: *seraphim are standing* (Is. 6:2), so down below: *boards of shittim-cedars are standing* (Ex. 26:15).

G. "Just as up there are stars, so down below are the clasps."

H. Said R. Hiyya bar Abba, "This teaches that the golden clasps in the tabernacle looked like the fixed stars of the firmament."

11. A. [*Come out, daughters of Jerusalem, you daughters of Zion, come out and welcome King Solomon, wearing the crown with which his mother has crowned him,] on his wedding day, [on his day of joy]* (Song 3:11):

B. ...*on his wedding day* [B&K, p. 12:] the day he entered the tent of meeting.

C. ...*on his day of joy:*

D. this refers to the tent of meeting.

E. Another interpretation of the phrase, *on his wedding day, on his day of joy* (Song 3:11):

F. ...*on his wedding day,* refers to the tent of meeting.

G. ...*on his day of joy* refers to the building of the eternal house.

H. Therefore it is said, *On the day that Moses completed the setting up of the Tabernacle, he anointed and consecrated it* (Num. 7:1).

The exegesis of Song 3:11 now receives attention in its own terms, our point of departure having been forgotten. No. 1 simply provides a play on one of the words of the verse under study. Nos. 2-6 proceed to work on the problem of the name of the king, Solomon. We have a striking and fresh approach at Nos. 2-3: the reference is now to God as King, and the name, Solomon, then is interpreted as God's function as bringing peace both among his holy creatures, the patriarchs and the angels, and also among the elements of natural creation. Both topics are introduced and then, at No. 4-6, the latter is worked out. God keeps water and fire working together and to do his bidding, they do not injure one another. The proof-text, Ex. 9:24, then leads us in its own direction, but at No. 6 discourse returns to the main point. No. 7 moves us on to a fresh issue, namely, Solomon himself. And now we see the connection between the passage and our broader theme, the tabernacle. The Temple is now compared to a crown. No. 8 pursues the interpretation of the same clause. But the point of interest is the clause, not the theme under broader discussion, so what we have is simply a repertoire of exegeses of the cited verse. No. 9 carries forward the theme of making the tabernacle. It makes the point that Moses was to replicate the colors he had seen on high. I see no connection to the preceding. It is an essentially fresh initiative. No. 10 continues along that same line, now making yet another point, which is that the tabernacle on earth was comparable to the abode of God in heaven. No. 11 brings us back to our original verse. We take up a clause by clause interpretation of the matter. 11.H is an editorial subscript, with no connection to the foregoing except the rather general thematic one. But the original interest in working on the theme of the building of the tabernacle as Israel's wedding day to God is well expressed, beginning to end.

I:IV

1. A. *Who has ever gone up to heaven and come down again? Who has cupped the wind in the hollow of his hands? Who has bound up the waters in the fold of his garment? Who has fixed the boundaries of the earth? What is his name or his son's name, if you know it?* (Prov. 30:4):

   B. *...Who has ever gone up to heaven:* this refers to the Holy One, blessed be He, as it is written, *God has gone up to the sound of the trumpet* (Ps. 37:6).

   C. *...and come down again: The Lord came down onto Mount Sinai* (Ex. 19:20).

   D. *...Who has cupped the wind in the hollow of his hands: In whose hand is the soul of all the living* (Job 12:10).

   E. *...Who has bound up the waters in the fold of his garment: He keeps the waters penned in dense cloud-masses* (Job 26:8).

   F. *...Who has fixed the boundaries of the earth: ...who kills and brings to life* (1 Sam. 2:6).

   G. *...What is his name:* his name is the Rock, his name is The Almighty, his name is The Lord of Hosts.

   H. *...or his son's name, if you know it: My son, my first born is Israel* (Ex. 4:22).

2. A. Another interpretation of the verse, *Who has ever gone up to heaven:* Who is the one whose prayer goes up to heaven and brings down rain?

   B. This is one who with his hands sets aside the tithes that he owes, who brings dew and rain into the world.

   C. *Who has cupped the wind in the hollow of his hands? Who has bound up the waters in the fold of his garment? Who has fixed the boundaries of the earth?* Who is the one whose prayer does not go up to heaven and bring down rain?

   D. This is one who with his hands does not set aside the tithes that he owes, who does not bring dew and rain into the world.

3. A. Another interpretation of the verse, *Who has ever gone up to heaven:*

   B. This refers to Elijah, concerning whom it is written, *And Elijah went up in a whirlwind to heaven* (2 Kgs. 2:11).

   C. *...and come down again: Go down with him, do not be afraid* (2 Kgs. 1:16).

   D. *Who has cupped the wind in the hollow of his hands: Lord, God of Israel, before whom I stand* (1 Kgs. 17:1).

   E. *Who has bound up the waters in the fold of his garment: And Elijah took his mantle and wrapped it together and smote the waters and they were divided* (1 Kgs. 2:8).

F. *Who has fixed the boundaries of the earth: And Elijah said, See your son lives* (1 Kgs. 17:23).

4. A. Another interpretation of the verse, *Who has ever gone up to heaven and come down again:*
    B. This refers to Moses, concerning whom it is written, *And Moses went up to God* (Ex. 19:3).
    C. *...and come down again: And Moses came down from the mountain* (Ex. 19:14).
    D. *Who has cupped the wind in the hollow of his hands: As soon as I have gone out of the city, I shall spread my hands out to the Lord* (Ex. 9:29).
    E. *Who has bound up the waters in the fold of his garment: The floods stood upright as a heap* (Ex. 15:8).
    F. *Who has fixed the boundaries of the earth:* this refers to the tent of meeting, as it is said, *On the day on which Moses completed setting up the tabernacle* (Num. 7:1) – for the entire world was set up with it.

5. A. R. Joshua b. Levi in the name of R. Simeon b. Yohai: "What is stated is not 'setting up the tabernacle [without the accusative particle, *et*],' but 'setting up + *the accusative particle* + the tabernacle,' [and since the inclusion of the accusative particle is taken to mean that the object is duplicated, we understand the sense to be that he set up a second tabernacle along with the first].
    B. "What was set up with it? It was the world that was set up with [the tabernacle, that is, the tabernacle represented the cosmos].
    C. "For until the tabernacle was set up, the world trembled, but after the tabernacle was set up, the world rested on firm foundations."
    D. Therefore it is said, *On the day that Moses completed the setting up of the Tabernacle, he anointed and consecrated it* (Num. 7:1).

The intersecting-verse, Prov. 30:4, is systematically applied to God, to tithing, then Elijah, finally Moses, at which point the exposition comes to a fine editorial conclusion. I cannot imagine a more representative example of the intersecting-verse/base-verse exposition. No. 5 is tacked on because it provides a valuable complement to the point of No. 4.

I:V

1. A. Another interpretation of the verse: *On the day that Moses completed the setting up of the Tabernacle, he anointed and consecrated it* (Num. 7:1):
    B. The letters translated as "completed" are so written that they be read "bridal," that is, on the day on which [Israel, the bride] entered the bridal canopy.

2. A. R. Eleazar and R. Samuel bar Nahmani:
    B. R. Eleazar says, *"On the day that Moses completed* means on the day on which he left up setting up the tabernacle day by day."
    C. It has been taught on Tannaite authority: Every day Moses would set up the tabernacle, and every morning he would make his offerings on it and then take it down. On the eighth day [to which reference is made in the

verse, *On the day that Moses completed the setting up of the Tabernacle, he anointed and consecrated it]* he set it up but did not take it down again.

D.   Said R. Zeira, "On the basis of this verse we learn the fact that an altar set up on the preceding night is invalid for the offering of sacrifices on the next day."

E.   R. Samuel bar Nahmani says, "Even on the eighth day he set it up and took it apart again."

F.   And how do we know about these dismantlings?

G.   It is in line with what R. Zeira said, *"On the day that Moses completed* means on the day on which he left off setting up the tabernacle day by day."

3.   A.   R. Eleazar and R. Yohanan:

B.   R. Eleazar said, *"On the day that Moses completed* means on the day on which demons ended their spell in the world.

C.   "What is the scriptural basis for that view?

D.   *"No evil thing will befall you, nor will any demon come near you* [B&K p. 15] *by reason of your tent* (Ps. 91:10) – on the day on which demons ended their spell in the world."

E.   Said R. Yohanan, "What need do I have to derive the lesson from another passage? Let us learn it from the very passage in which the matter occurs: *May the Lord bless you and keep you* (Num. 6:24) – keep you from demons."

4.   A.   R. Yohanan and R. Simeon b. Laqish:

B.   R. Yohanan said, *"On the day that Moses completed* means on the day on which on the day on which hatred came to an end in the world. For before the tabernacle was set up, there was hatred and envy, competition, contention, and strife in the world. But once the tabernacle was set up, love, affection, comradeship, righteousness, and peace came into the world.

C.   "What is the verse of scripture that so indicates?

D.   *"Let me hear the words of the Lord, are they not words of peace, peace to his people and his loyal servants and to all who turn and trust in him? Deliverance is near to those who worship him, so that glory may dwell in our land. Love and fidelity have come together, justice and peace join hands* (Ps. 85:8-10).

E.   Said R. Simeon b. Laqish, "What need do I have to derive the lesson from another passage? Let us learn it from the very passage in which the matter occurs: *and give you peace.*

5.   A.   *[On the day that Moses completed] the setting up of the Tabernacle, [he anointed and consecrated it]:*

B.   R. Joshua b. Levi in the name of R. Simeon b. Yohai: "What is stated is not 'setting up the tabernacle [without the accusative particle, *et*],' but 'setting up + *the accusative particle* + the tabernacle,' [and since the inclusion of the accusative particle is taken to mean that the object is duplicated, we understand the sense to be that he set up a second tabernacle along with the first].

C.   "What was set up with it? It was the world that was set up with [the tabernacle, that is, the tabernacle represented the cosmos].

D.   "For until the tabernacle was set up, the world trembled, but after the tabernacle was set up, the world rested on firm foundations."

We work our way through the clause, *on the day that Moses completed.* No. 1 goes over familiar ground. It is a valuable review of the point of stress, the meaning of the word *completed.* No. 2 refers to the claim that from day to day Moses would set up and take down the tent, until on the day at hand, he left it standing; so the "completed" bears the sense of ceasing to go through a former procedure. The word under study bears the further sense of "coming to an end," and therefore at Nos. 3, 4, we ask what came to an end when the tabernacle was set up. The matched units point to demons, on the one side, and hatred, on the other. No. 5 moves us along from the word KLT to the following set, *accusative + tabernacle.*

I:VI.

1.   A.   *[On the day that Moses completed the setting up of the Tabernacle], he anointed and consecrated it:*

     B.   Since it is written, *he anointed and consecrated it,* why does it also say, *he anointed them and consecrated them* (Num. 7:1)?

     C.   R. Aibu said, "R. Tahalipa of Caesarea, and R. Simeon:

     D.   "One of them said, 'After he had anointed each one, he then anointed all of them simultaneously.'

     E.   "The other said, *'And he anointed them* refers to an anointing in this world and another anointing in the world to come.'"

2.   A.   Along these same lines: *You shall couple the tent together* (Ex. 26:11), *You shall couple the curtains* (Ex. 26:6):

     B.   R. Judah and R. Levi, R. Tahalipa of Caesarea and R. Simeon b. Laqish:

     C.   One of them said, "Once he had coupled them all together, he went back and coupled them one by one."

     D.   The other said, *"You shall couple the curtains and it shall be one* meaning, one for measuring, one for anointing."

The exposition of the verse continues to occupy our attention, with the problem clear as stated.

I:VII.

1.   A.   *The chief men of Israel, heads of families – that is, the chiefs of the tribes, [who had assisted in preparing the detailed lists] came forward and brought their offering before the Lord* (Num. 7:2):

     B.   [(Following B&K, p. 16:) The word for *tribes* can mean *rods*, so we understand the meaning to be, they had exercised authority through rods] in Egypt.

     C.   *...who had assisted in preparing the detailed lists:* the standards.

2 . A. *...came forward and brought their offering before the Lord, six covered*
        wagons [and twelve oxen, one wagon from every two chiefs and from
        each one an ox] (Num. 7:2):
    B. The six corresponded to the six days of creation.
    C. The six corresponded to the six divisions of the Mishnah.
    D. The six corresponded to the six matriarchs: Sarah, Rebecca, Rachel,
        Leah, Bilhah, and Zilpah.
    E. Said R. Yohanan, "The six corresponded to the six religious duties that
        pertain to a king: *[1] He shall not have too many wives* (Deut. 17:17),
        [2] He shall not have too many horses (Deut. 17:16), *[3] He shall not*
        have too much silver and gold (Deut. 17:17), *[4] He shall not pervert*
        justice, [5] show favor, or [6] take bribes (Deut. 16:9)."

3 . A. The six corresponded to the six steps of the throne. How so?
    B. When he goes up to take his seat on the first step, the herald goes forth
        and proclaims, *He shall not have too many wives* (Deut. 17:17).
    C. When he goes up to take his seat on the second step, the herald goes
        forth and proclaims, *He shall not have too many horses* (Deut. 17:16).
    D. When he goes up to take his seat on the third step, the herald goes forth
        and proclaims, *He shall not have too much silver and gold* (Deut. 17:17).
    E. When he goes up to take his seat on the fourth step, the herald goes
        forth and proclaims, *He shall not pervert justice.*
    F. When he goes up to take his seat on the fifth step, the herald goes forth
        and proclaims, *...or show favor.*
    G. When he goes up to take his seat on the sixth, step, the herald goes
        forth and proclaims, *...or take bribes* (Deut. 16:9).
    H. When he comes to take his seat on the seventh step, he says, "Know
        before whom you take your seat."

4 . A. *And the top of the throne was round behind* (1 Kgs. 10:19):
    B. Said R. Aha, "It was like the throne of Moses."
    C. *And there were arms on either side of the throne by the place of the seat*
        (1 Kgs. 10:19):
    D. How so? There was a scepter of gold suspended from behind, with a dove
        on the top, and a crown of gold in the dove's mouth, and he would sit
        under it on the Sabbath, and it would touch but not quite touch.

5 . A. The six corresponded to the six firmaments.
    B. But are they not seven?
    C. Said R. Abia, "The one where the King dwells is royal property [not
        counted with what belongs to the world at large]."

We proceed with the detailed exposition of the verse at hand. The focus of
interest, after No. 1, is on the reason for bringing six wagons. The
explanations, Nos. 2 (+3-4), 5, relate to the creation of the world, the Torah, the
life of Israel, the religious duties of the king, and the universe above. The
underlying motif, the tabernacle as the point at which the supernatural world of
Israel meets the supernatural world of creation, is carried forward.

I:VIII.

1. A. *[...came forward and brought their offering before the Lord , six] covered [wagons and twelve oxen, one wagon from every two chiefs and from each one an ox]* (Num. 7:2):

   B. The word for covered wagons may be read to yield these meanings:

   C. like a lizard-skin [B&K, p. 17: "it signifies that the outer surface of the wagons' frames was as delicately reticulated as the skin of a lizard"];

   D. [and the same word may be read to indicate that the wagons were] decorated, or fully equipped.

   E. It has been taught in the name of R. Nehemiah, "They were like a bent bow."

2. A. *...twelve oxen, one wagon from every two chiefs... :*

   B. This indicates that two chiefs would together bring one wagon, while each tribe gave an ox.

3. A. *These they brought forward before the tabernacle* (Num. 7:3):

   B. This teaches that they turned them into their monetary value and sold them to the congregation at large [so that everyone had a share in the donation].

4. A. *And the Lord spoke to Moses and said, [Accept these from them: they shall be used for the service of the tent of the presence"]:* (Num. 7:45):

   B. What is the meaning of the word, *and said?*

   C. R. Hoshaia taught, "The Holy One, blessed be He, said to Moses, 'Go and say to Israel words of praise and consolation.'

   D. "Moses was afraid, saying, 'But is it not possible that the holy spirit has abandoned me and come to rest on the chiefs?'

   E. "The Holy One said to him, 'Moses, had I wanted them to bring their offering, I should have said to you to 'say to them,' [so instructing them to do so], but *Take – it is from them [at their own volition, not by my inspiration*] (Num. 7:5) is the language that meaning, they did it on their own volition [and have not received the holy spirit].'"

5. A. And who gave them the good ideas [of making the gift]?

   B. It was the tribe of Issachar who gave them the good idea, in line with this verse: *And of the children of Issachar came men who had understanding of the times* (1 Chr. 12:33).

   C. What is the sense of *the times?*

   D. R. Tanhuma said, "The ripe hour [*kairos*]."

   E. R. Yose bar Qisri said, "Intercalating the calendar."

   F. *They had two hundred heads* (1 Chr. 12:33):

   G. This refers to the two hundred heads of sanhedrins that were produced by the tribe of Issachar.

   H. *And all of their brethren were subject to their orders* (1 Chr. 12:33):

   I. This teaches that the law would accord with their rulings.

   J. They said to the community, "Is this tent of meeting which you are making going to fly in the air? Make wagons for it, which will bear it."

6. A. Moses was concerned, saying, "Is it possible that one of the wagons might break, or one of the oxen die, so that the offering of the chiefs might be invalid?"

    B. Said to Moses the Holy One, blessed be He, *They shall be used for the service of the tent of the presence* (Num. 7:5).

    C. "To them has been given a long-term existence."

7. A. How long did they live?

    B. R. Yudan in the name of R. Samuel bar Nahman, R. Hunia in the name of Bar Qappara, *"In Gilgal they sacrificed the oxen* (Hos. 12:12)."

    C. And where did they offer them up?

    D. R. Abba bar Kahana said, "In Nob they offered them up."

    E. R. Abbahu said, "In Gibeon they offered them up."

    F. R. Hama bar Hanina said, "In the eternal house [of Jerusalem] they offered them up."

    G. Said R. Levi, "A verse of Scripture supporting the view of R. Hama bar Hanina: *Solomon offered a sacrifice of peace offerings, which he slaughtered for the Lord, twenty two thousand oxen* (1 Kgs. 8:63)."

    H. It was taught in the name of R. Meir, "They endure even to now, and they never produced a stink, got old, or produced an invalidating blemish."

    I. Now that produces an argument *a fortiori*:

    J. If the oxen, who cleaved to the work of the making of the tent of meeting, were given an eternal existence, Israel, who cleave to the Holy One, blessed be He, how much the more so!

    K. *And you who cleave to the Lord your God are alive, all of you, this day* (Deut. 4:4).

The exegesis of the verse in its own terms leads us through the several phrases, No. 1, 2, 3. No. 4, continuing at No. 6, with an important complement at No. 5, goes on to its own interesting question. No. 7 serves No. 6 as No. 6 serves No. 5.

Pisqa Two

When you lift up the head *[RSV: take the census] [of the people of Israel,*
then each shall give a ransom for himself to the Lord
when you number them, that there be
no plague among them when you number them]
(Ex. 30:12).

II:I

1. A. *O Lord, how many are my foes! Many are rising against me; many are*
      saying of me, there is no help for him in God. Sela (Ps. 3:2-3):
   B. R. Samuel bar Immi and Rabbis:
   C. R. Samuel bar Immi interpreted the verse to speak of Doeg and
      Ahitophel:
   D. *"...many are saying of me,* refers to Doeg and Ahitophel. Why does he
      refer to them as 'many'?
   E. "For they formed a majority in Torah-study.
   F. *"...many are saying of me,* – They say to David, 'A man who has seized a
      ewe-lamb, killed the shepherd, and made Israelites fall by the sword –
      will he have salvation? *There is no help for him in God.'*
   G. "Said David, 'And you, O Lord, have concurred with them, writing in your
      Torah, saying, *The adulterer and the adulteress will surely die* (Lev.
      20:10).
   H. *"'But you, O Lord, are a shield about me* (Ps. 3:4): For you have formed a
      protection for me through the merit attained by my ancestors.
   I. *"'My glory* (Ps. 3:4): For your restored me to the throne.
   J. *"'And the lifter of my head* (Ps. 3:4): While I was liable to you to have
      my head removed, you raised my head through the prophet, Nathan, when
      he said to me, *Also the Lord has removed your sin and you will not die*
      (2 Sam. 12:13).'"
   K. And rabbis interpreted the verse to refer to the nations of the world:
   L. *"Many* – these are the nations of the world.
   M. "Why does he call them many? For it is written, *Ah the uproar of many*
      peoples (Is. 17:12).
   N. *"...many are saying of me:* this refers to Israel.
   O. "'A nation that heard from the mouth of its God at Mount Sinai, *You*
      shall have no other gods before me (Ex. 20:3), and yet after forty days
      said to the calf, *This is your god, O Israel* (Ex. 32:4) – will such a nation
      have salvation?
   P. "'*...there is no help for him in God. Sela.'* [so said the nations of the
      world].

Q.   "The Israelites said, 'And you, O Lord, have concurred with them, writing
     in your Torah, *'And you shall say, one who sacrifices to other gods will
     be utterly exterminated* (Ex. 22:19).'

R.   *"'But you, O Lord, are a shield about me* (Ps. 3:4): For you have afforded
     protection for us on account of the merit accrued by our ancestors.'

S.   *"'My glory* (Ps. 3:4): For you have brought your Presence to come to rest
     among us.

T.   *"'And the lifter of my head* (Ps. 3:4): While I was liable to you to have
     my head removed, you raised my head through Moses: *When you lift up
     the head [RSV: take the census] of the people of Israel, then each shall
     give a ransom for himself to the Lord when you number them, that there
     be no plague among them when you number them* (Ex. 30:12)."

The intersecting-verse, Ps. 3:3-4, is beautifully articulated, clause by clause,
in the two matched components of the exegesis, leading us back to the base-
verse cited at the end. The base-verse using the idiom, *lift up the head*, meaning
take the census, and the appearance of that same idiom at Ps. 3:3-4 accounts for
the selection of the intersecting-verse. The message of salvation then is
addressed to both the messiah-king, David, and also to Israel, with the point that,
while both committed sin, both were forgiven. As David was restored to his
throne, after suffering a penalty for his sin, so Israel's fortunes will take a turn
for the better despite the sin of the golden calf. In both cases the source of
salvation is the merit of the ancestors.

II:II

1. A.   R. Jacob bar Judah in the name of R. Jonathan of Bet Gubrin opened
         [discourse by citing the following intersecting-verse:] *"The way of a
         sluggard is overgrown with thorns, but the path of the upright is a level
         highway* (Prov. 15:19):

    B.   *"The way of a sluggard* refers to the wicked Esau.

    C.   *"...is overgrown with thorns:* for he is comparable to a hedge. If you
         take away [thorns] from one side, it pricks from the other. So too the
         wicked Esau [Rome] turns this way and that: 'Produce your poll tax,
         produce your share of the crop.' If one does not have the money, [the
         government then] imposes fines and penalties on him.

    D.   *"...but the path of the upright is a level highway* – this refers to the
         Holy One, blessed be He, concerning whom it is written, *The ways of the
         Lord are straight, and the righteous will walk in them* (Hos. 14:10).

    E.   "So he used appropriate language in telling Moses, *When you take the
         census of the people of Israel, then each shall give a ransom for himself
         to the Lord when you number them, that there be no plague among them
         when you number them* (Ex. 30:12)."

The intersecting-verse is interpreted clause by clause and then returns to the
base-verse at E. The link of E to the foregoing is not self-evident. Explaining
matters as they translate, Braude and Kapstein, p. 23, render the passage so as to
link E to the foregoing, "translating" as follows: "[He is the one who made it
easy for Israel to support the House of God by narrowing down their obligations

to a single head tax. And even with this single obligation, God is not demanding—indeed, he makes it an occasion for exalting Israel]: Moses was to say, *When thou dost accept the head tax from the children of Israel, Thou also liftest their heads.*" On the rendering, Moses was to say, they state: "Literally 'He so framed the words Moses was to utter [as to endow them with the promise of exaltation].' In order to provide an intelligible transition, however, between Jonathan's comment on Prov. 15:19 and Exod. 30:12, it is necessary to expand the cryptic original into 'He is the one who made it easy for Israel...Moses was to say.'" This of course is very clever, but I have for my part to state that I do not see any connection with E and the foregoing, and regard the citation of the base-verse as redactional and not substantive and propositional.

II:III

1. A. R. Jonathan opened discourse [by citing the following verse]: *"A man shall be brought low, all men shall be humbled; and how can they raise themselves* (Is. 2:9).
   B. *"A man shall be brought low* refers to Israel, concerning whom it is written, *You, my sheep, the sheep of my pasture, are man* (Ezek. 34:31).
   C. *"...all men shall be humbled refers to Moses,* concerning whom it is written, *And the man, Moses, was very humble* (Num. 12:3).
   D. "Said Moses before the Holy One, blessed be he, 'Lord of the ages, I know that the Israelites have bowed down to the calf, and I was humiliated. *And how can they raise themselves?'*
   E. "He said to him, 'I shall raise them up.'
   F. *"When you lift up the head [RSV: take the census] of the people of Israel, then each shall give a ransom for himself to the Lord when you number them, that there be no plague among them when you number them* (Ex. 30:12)."

The intersecting-verse joins more directly to the base-verse than in the preceding. Now we have a clear exercise in drawing lessons from the use of the word "raise," meaning, as we see, "lift up" and also "take the poll." The tendency is clearly to link the census to an act of forgiveness on God's part on account of the worship of the golden calf, with the further implication that the support of the tabernacle that is involved in the contribution of the half-shekel to the Temple commemorates God's forgiveness of sin; the Temple then is a mark of the reconciliation of God and Israel. The basic mode of thought of the exegetical authorship behind our materials is to ask about the connections between a passage and its context, fore and aft. That accounts for the persistent linkage between the sin of the calf and the taking of the census/raising of the head.

II:IV

1. A. R. Jonah of Bosrah opened discourse by citing the following verse: *For God is the judge, this one he brings low, that one he raises up* (Ps. 75:8).

2. A. A Roman lady asked R. Yose b. R. Halapta, saying to him, "In how many days did the Holy One, blessed be He, create his world?"

    B. He said to her, "In six days, as it is said, *In six days the Lord made...* (Ex. 31;17)."

    C. She said to him, "What has he been sitting and doing ever since then?"

    D. He said to her, "Making matches: 'the daughter of Mr. So-and-so is for Mr. Such and such,' 'the widow of Mr. So-and-so for Mr. Such-and-such,' 'the estate of Mr. So-and-so is to go to Mr. So-and-so.'"

    E. She said to him, "Is that all? Even I can do as much. How many slave boys and slave girls I have, and in one minute I can match them up."

    F. He said to her, "If it's so easy in your view, for the Holy One, blessed be He, it is as difficult as the splitting of the Red Sea."

    G. R. Yose b. R. Halapta left the woman and went his way.

    H. What did she do? She took a thousand slave boys and a thousand slave girls and set them up in rows and said, "Mr. So-and-so will marry Miss So-and-so," "Miss Such-and-such will marry Mr. So-and-So," and so she matched them up in a single night.

    I. In the morning they came to her, this one with a split head, that one with a black eye, the other with a broken leg.

    J. This one said, "I don't want that one," and that said, "I don't want this one."

    K. She sent and summoned R. Yose b. R. Halapta, saying to him, "Your Torah is true, correct, and praiseworthy. Everything you said was so."

    L. He said to her, "Didn't I say to you, 'If it's so easy in your view, for the Holy One, blessed be He, it is difficult, as the splitting of the Red Sea.'

    M. "What does the Holy One, blessed be He, do? He matches them together willy-nilly, even without their acknowledgement. That is in line with this verse: *He brings the unmarried to live in a married domesticity and brings out the prisoners in chains* (Ps. 68:7).

    N. "What is the meaning of *in chains*? It is composed of letters that may be read, 'With weeping' and 'with song,' for if one wants, he sings, and if he does not want, he weeps."

3. A. Said R. Berekhiah, "This is the language that R. Yose b. R. Halapta used in answering her:

    B. "The Holy One, blessed be He, sits and makes ladders, bringing one up and bringing another down, lowering one and raising another: *For God is the judge, this one he brings low, that one he raises up* (Ps. 75:8)."

4. A. R. Jonah of Bosra and Rabbis:

    B. Rabbis interpret the reference of the cited verse to *this one* [*For God is the judge, this one he brings low, that one he raises up* (Ps. 75:8)] to speak of Aaron,

    C. "in the sense that, by the word *this* he was brought down, and by the same word *this*, he was raised up.

    D. "By the word *this* he was brought down: *And I threw it into the fire, and this* calf came out (Ex. 32:24).

    E. "And by the word *this*, he was raised up: This *is the offering of Aaron and his sons* (Lev. 6:12)."

    F. R. Jonathan of Bosrah interpreted the same verse to speak of Israel:

G. "By the word *this* they were brought down, and by the word *this* they were raised up.

H. "By the word *this*, they were brought down: *For* this *man Moses...* (Ex. 32:1).

I. "And by the word *this* they were raised up: This *everyone who passes among those who are numbered shall give* (Ex. 30:13)."

That No. 1's introduction of the intersecting-verse is purely redactional is shown by No. 3, which is the point at which that verse plays a part. Prior to that point all we have, as No. 1, is simply the uninterpreted verse. Then it serves its purpose at No. 3. This means that the redactor has introduced No. 1 to provide an editorial entry into the story at hand, which is included whole, even though only No. 3 serves the larger editorial purpose at hand. No. 2 self-evidently is a set-piece item, joined to No. 1 before the entire composite was inserted here. Alternatively, No. 2 has been parachuted down by a remarkably incompetent redactor, who threw in whatevber he had relevant to the intersecting-verse, without asking whether it was pertinent. But then No. 3 is poorly expounded, being disproportionately modest in its exposition of its idea in comparison to No. 2. No. 4 then moves on to the continuation of the base-verse, interpreting a later clause in a way consistent with what has gone before. The same underlying motif, that the tabernacle is the point at which Israel is exalted, recurs.

II:V

1. A. *Righteousness raises a people to honor; lovingkindness is a disgrace to any nation [except Israel]* (Prov. 14:34):

   B. R. Eliezer, R. Joshua, and Rabbis:

   C. R. Eliezer says, *"Righteousness raises a people to honor* refers to Israel, while *lovingkindness is a disgrace to any nation* means, acts of lovingkindness are sins for the nations, for they take pride in them."

   D. R. Joshua says, *"Righteousness raises a people to honor* refers to Israel, while *lovingkindness is a disgrace to any nation* means, it is a pleasure for the nations of the world when the Israelites sin, for they go and subjugate them."

   E. Rabbis say, *"Righteousness raises a people to honor* refers to Israel, while *lovingkindness is a disgrace to any nation* means, the acts of lovingkindness which the nations carry out are a sin for them.

   F. "For so Daniel says to Nebuchadnezzer, *Break off your sins by almsgiving...that there may be a lengthening of your prosperity* (Dan. 4:24)."

   G. R. Eleazar b. Arakh says, *"Righteousness raises a people to honor* refers to Israel, but they are a sin for the nations of the world."

   H. Said Rabban Yohanan ben Zakkai, "I prefer the opinion of Eleazar b. Arakh to your opinion, for he assigns both righteousness and acts of lovingkindness to Israel and only sin to the nations of the world."

2. A. Abin bar Judah says, *"Righteousness raises a people to honor* refers to Israel, while *lovingkindness is a disgrace to any nation* means, the

Israelites receive acts of humiliation from the nations of the world when they commit a sin.

B. "For so Rab-shakeh said to Hezekiah, *Have I now come up without the Lord against this place to destroy it? The Lord said to me, Go up against this land and destroy it* (2 Kgs. 18:25).

C. "And Nebuzaradan said to Jeremiah, *The Lord has brought it and done according as he said because you have sinned against the Lord, therefore what he spoke has come upon you* (Jer. 40:3)."

3. A. R. Nehuniah b. Haqqaneh says, *"Righteousness raises a people to honor* refers to Israel, while *lovingkindness is a disgrace to any nation* means, 'The acts of lovingkindness which nations of the world do are a disgrace for Israel.'

B. "From whom do you derive that lesson? From the case of Mesha: *Mesha, king of Moab, was a* noked (2 Kgs. 3:4). What is the sense of *noked*? It is a shepherd.

C. *"He handed over to the king of Israel a hundred thousand fatted lambs and a hundred thousand wool-bearing rams* (2 Kgs. 3:4)."

D. What is the meaning of wool-bearing rams?

E. R. Abba bar Kahana said, "Unshorn."

F. What did he do? He assembled all the astrologers of his court and said to them, "Tell me: if I make war with any nation, will I conquer? If it is with these Jews, will they conquer me?"

G. They said to him, "[The answer to both questions is yes], on account of the merit accruing on account of one old man [whose merit they have] acquired."

H. He said to them, "And who is this old man?"

I. They said to him, "It is Abraham."

J. He said to them, "And what sort of deeds did he do?"

K. They said to him, "One only son was given to him at the age of one hundred years, and he offered him up as a sacrifice."

L. He said to them, "And did he actually offer him up?"

M. They said to him, "No."

N. He said to them, "If even though he did not offer him up, miracles were done for him, if he had offered him up, how much the more so! Now there is one man who has an only son, who is destined to rule in his place. He will go and offer him up, perhaps miracles will be done for him."

O. That is in line with this verse: *He took his firstborn son, who was to rule in his stead, and offered him up on the wall* (2 Kgs. 3:27).

P. What is written are letters that may be read not only on *the wall* but on *account of the sun.*

Q. This indicates that he worshipped the sun.

R. What is written in that passage? *And there came great anger on Israel* (2 Kgs. 3:27).

S. Said the Holy One, blessed be He, to Israel, "My children, the nations of the world, who do not know my power, rebel against me, but [how can] you, knowing my power, also rebel against me?"

T. Said R. Mana, "Were it not on account of the merit accruing to the wife of Obadiah, the Israelites from that moment would have been wiped out of the world. What did she do on that day? *Now there cried a certain woman of the wives of the sons of the prophets to Elisha, saying, Your servant, my husband [has died...you know that he was a man who feared the Lord...]* (2 Kgs. 4:1)."

4. A. R. Zeorah sent word to R. Zeira, "Have you heard about that pearl that R. Huna would provide as interpretation of this verse: *Righteousness raises a people to honor; lovingkindness is a disgrace to any nation* (Prov. 14:34)?"

    B. He said to him, *"Righteousness raises a people to honor* refers to Israel.

    C. "...*lovingkindness is a disgrace to any nation* (Prov. 14:34) means, [the merit accruing on account of] the acts of lovingkindness which the nations of the world carry out is stored up for them like the venom of a snake.

    D. "From whom do you learn that lesson? From the case of Merodach.

    E. "Merodach Baladan was accustomed to eat at the sixth hour and to sleep to the ninth [noon, mid-afternoon, respectively]. But when the orb of the sun went back in the time of Hezekiah *[This shall be your sign from the Lord...Watch the shadow cast by the sun on the stairway of Ahaz: I will bring backwards ten steps the shadow which has gone down on the stairway. And the sun went back ten steps on the stairway down which it had done* (Is. 38:8)], he went to sleep and woke up and found it was dawn.

    F. "He wanted to kill his entire staff. He said to them, 'You let me sleep the entire day and night.'

    G. "They said to him, 'My lord, it was in your usual time that you eat, and in your usual time that you slept, but it was the day that went backward.'

    H. "He said to them, 'Which god pushed the day back?'

    I. "They said to him, 'It was the God of Hezekiah who pushed it back.'

    J. "He said to them, 'And is any god greater than my god?'

    K. "They said to him, 'The God of Hezekiah is greater than your god.'

    L. "He immediately sent letters with a gift to Hezekiah.

    M. "That is in line with the statement of Isaiah: *At that time Merodach Baladan son of Baladan, king of Babylonia, sent letters and a gift to Hezekiah* (Is. 39:1).

    N. "What did he write in them? 'Peace to Hezekiah, peace to his God, peace to Jerusalem.'

    O. "But when the writing had already gone forth, he reconsidered the matter and said, 'I did not do things right. I gave precedence to the greeting of peace for Hezekiah over that for his God.'

    P. "He immediately arose from his throne and took three steps and got the letters back and wrote other letters in their place. What did he write in them? 'Peace be to the God of Hezekiah, peace be to Hezekiah, peace be to Jerusalem, the holy city.'

    Q. "Said to him the Holy One, blessed be He, 'You arose from your throne and took three steps on account of the honor owing to me. By your life, I shall hold up on your account three kings, world-monarchs, ruling from one end of the world to the other.

    R. "And who are they? Nebuchadnezzar, Evil-Merodach, and Belshazzar.

    S. "But when they want and blasphemed, the Holy One, blessed be He, wiped out their seed from the world and raised up others in their place."

5. A. And rabbis say, "*Righteousness raises a people to honor, and lovingkindness is a disgrace to any nation* (Prov. 14:34):

B. "On account of the contribution that the Israelites brought to the tent of meeting for the making of the tabernacle, a raising of the head was accorded to them through Moses: *When you raise the head of the children of Israel* (Ex. 30:2)."

The intersecting-verse, Prov. 14:34, is brought into contact with the base-verse only at the end. Righteousness is now understood in its sense of philanthropy, hence, the gifts that the Israelites brought led to the raising up to honor of the people of Israel through the building of the tabernacle. But, as usual, we first ring the changes on the sense of the verse on its own. In that setting we read the verse to contrast *people* with *nations*, Israel with the gentiles, and the theme of No. 1 is repeated. Israel's righteousness raises the people to honor; that of the gentiles humiliates them. No. 1 replicates, rather poorly, the model of Avot 2:8ff., in which Yohanan hears opinions of his five disciples, approving that of Eleazar b. Arakh over those of the others. The form is not fully worked out here, but the conventional message is clearly stated at H. No. 2 goes over the same ground, now finding an example of an act of lovingkindness paid by a gentile, that is, the message of Rab-shakeh to Hezekiah. No. 3 gives yet another example, Mesha of Moab. The contrast is remarkably apt. What Abraham did, Mesha did, so the act is the same, but not the consequence. No. 4 pursues the same contrast, now making the further point – entirely consonant with what has gone before – that when the gentiles acquire merit, that merit serves only to condemn and humiliate Israel. The three steps involved merit, which later on served to bring Israel down. What is interesting is how No. 5 completely changes the ground of exegesis, yielding a shift in the thrust of discourse in an entirely new direction.

II:VI

1. A. R. Yudan opened discourse by citing the following verse of Scripture: *A good man's tongue is pure silver, the heart of the wicked is trash. [The lips of a good man teach many, but fools perish for want of sense]* (Prov. 10:20):

B. "*A good man's tongue is pure silver* speaks of Jedo the prophet [2 Chr. 9:29].

C. "*...the heart of the wicked is trash* refers to Jeroboam [1 Kgs. 12:28-29)."

D. *As Jeroboam stood by the altar to burn the sacrifice, a man of God from Judah, moved by the word of the Lord, appeared at Bethel. He inveighed against the altar in the Lord's name, crying out, "O altar, altar! [This is the word of the Lord: 'Listen! A child shall be born to the house of David, named Josiah. He will sacrifice upon you the priests of the hill-shrines who make offerings upon you, and he will make human bones upon you.'" He gave a sign the same day: "This is the sign which the Lord has ordained: This altar will be rent in pieces and the ashes upon it will be spilt." When King Jeroboam heard the sentence which the man of God pronounced against the altar at Bethel, he pointed to him from the altar and said, "Seize that man!" Immediately the hand which he had pointed at him became paralyzed, so that he could not draw it back. The altar too was rent in pieces and the ashes were spilt, in fulfilment of the sign that the man of God had given at the Lord's command]* (1 Kgs. 13:1-5).

E. Why does it say, *altar, altar,* two times?

F. Said R. Abba bar Kahana, "One alludes to the altar in Beth El, the other to the altar in Dan."

G. And what was the prophet's proclamation? *"O altar, altar! This is the word of the Lord: 'Listen! A child shall be born to the house of David, named Josiah. He will sacrifice upon you the priests of the hill-shrines who make offerings upon you, and he will make human bones upon you.'"*

H. "The bones *of Jeroboam* will be burned on you" is not what is stated, but rather, *he will make human bones upon you.*

I. This teaches that he paid all due respect to the monarchy.

J. It is written, *When King Jeroboam heard the sentence which the man of God pronounced against the altar at Bethel, he pointed to him from the altar and said, 'Seize that man!'*

K. R. Huna in the name of R. Idi: "The Omnipresent had more concern for the honor owing to the righteous man than to the honor owing to himself. For when he [the king] was standing and offering a sacrifice to idolatry, his hand did not dry up. But when he put his hand against that righteous man [the prophet], then his hand dried up.

L. "So it is written: *Immediately the hand which he had pointed at him became paralyzed, so that he could not draw it back."*

M. *The king appealed to the man of God to pacify the Lord your God and pray for him that his hand might be restored. [The man of God did as he asked; his hand was restored and became as it had been before. Then the king said to the man of God, "Come home and take refreshment at my table and let me give you a present." But the man of God answered, "If you were to give me half your house, I would not enter it with you; I will eat and drink nothing in this place, for the Lord's command to me was to eat and drink nothing and not to go back by the way I came." So he went back another way; he did not return by the road he had taken to Bethel]* (1 Kgs. 13:6-10).

N. Two Amoras: one said, "The meaning of the reference to *the Lord your God* is, *your God,* not mine."

O. The other said, "By what sort of brazenness could he have called him, 'my God,' while he was standing and offering to an idol? Could he then have called him 'my God'?"

P. Nonetheless: *The man of God did as he asked; his hand was restored and became as it had been before.*

Q. What is the meaning of the statement, *as it had been before?*

R. R. Berekhiah, R. Judah b. R. Simon in the name of R. Joshua b. Levi: "'Even though you beat a fool in the mortar of a craftsman, you will make nothing of him.' Just as, in the beginning, he would stand and make offerings to idolatry, so even afterward he would stand and make offerings to an idol."

2 . A.   Another interpretation of *A good man's tongue is pure silver* refers to the
         Holy One, blessed be He, who chose the tongue of Moses and said, *When
         you raise up the head of the children of Israel* (Ex. 30:12).

The intersecting-verse reverts to the base-verse only at No. 2, while the far
more fully articulated exposition, No. 1, reads the intersecting-verse in the light
of an entirely unrelated matter. Yet the pertinence of No. 1 – the issue of the
right altar, that of the Lord, as against the wrong one – cannot be missed.

II:VII

1 . A.   What is written just prior to the passage under discussion? *Aaron shall
         make expiation with blood on its horns once a year; [with blood from
         the sin-offering of the yearly Expiation he shall do this for all time. It
         is most holy to the Lord]* (Ex. 30:120).
    B.   What follows? *When you raise up the head of the children of Israel [and
         take a census]* (Ex. 30:12).
    C.   What is written, however, are the letters that spell out the word meaning
         lend, as in the verse, *When you make a loan to another man, [do not
         enter his house to take a pledge from him. Wait outside, and the man
         whose creditor you are shall bring the pledge out to you]* (Deut. 24:10-
         11).
    D.   Said Moses before the Holy One, "Lord of the Ages, when the Israelites
         enjoy sufficient merit [through the effect of the actual sacrifices on the
         altar, which achieve atonement], let them be. But when [with the Temple
         in ruins] they do not enjoy sufficient merit, as it were, lend to them once
         in the year on the Day of Atonement [enough merit to get through the
         year] so that it will effect atonement for them [in the absence of the
         offerings of the cult]."
    E.   *For on this day will atonement be made for you* (Lev. 16:30).

2 . A.   *[When you raise up]* the head *[of the children of Israel] [and take a
         census]* (Ex. 30:12).
    B.   Said R. Yose bar Haninah, "This statement served to provide an
         indication that [Moses] was going to draw near [restoring primacy to] the
         first of the tribes, and who is that? It is Reuben:
    C.   *"Let Reuben live* (Deut. 33:6)."

3 . A.   *[When you raise up the head of]* the children of Israel *[and take a census]*
         (Ex. 30:12).
    B.   R. Yudan in the name of R. Samuel bar Nahman: "[The matter may be
         compared] to the case of a king who had underwear, about which he gave
         orders to his servant, saying to him, 'Shake it out, fold it up, take good
         care of it.'
    C.   "He said to him, 'My lord, King, of all the underwear that you have, you
         give me orders only about this one.'
    D.   He said to him, "It is because it cleaves to [fits firmly on] my body.'
    E.   "So Moses said to the Holy One, blessed be He, 'Lord of the ages, among
         the seventy sovereign nations that you have in your world, you give me
         orders only concerning Israel: *to the children of Israel you shall say,*
         (Lev. 20:2); *to the children of Israel speak* '(Ex. 30:31); *say to the*

children of Israel (Ex. 33:5); *speak to the children of Israel* (Ex. 31:134);
command the children of Israel (Lev. 24:2); *and you, command the
children of Israel* (Ex. 27:20); *when you take the count of the children of
Israel* (Ex. 30:12).

F.   "Said to him the Holy One, 'It is because they cleave to me.'

G.   "For it is written, *As the girdle cleaves to the loins of a man, so I have
     made all of the house of Israel cleave to me* (Jer. 13:11)."

4.   A.   Said R. Abin, "[The matter may be compared] to the case of a king who
          had a purple cloak, about which he gave orders to his servant, saying to
          him, 'Shake it out, fold it up, take good care of it.'

     B.   "He said to him, 'My lord, King, of all the purple cloaks that you have,
          you give me orders only about this one.'

     C.   "He said to him, 'That is because that is the one that I wore when I first
          was made king.'

     F.   "So Moses said to the Holy One, blessed be He, 'Lord of the ages, among
          the seventy sovereign nations that you have in your world, you give me
          orders only concerning Israel: *'to the children of Israel you shall say,*
          (Lev. 20:2); *to the children of Israel speak* (Ex. 30:31); *say to the
          children of Israel* (Ex. 33:5); *speak to the children of Israel* (Ex. 31:134);
          command the children of Israel (Lev. 24:2); *and you, command the
          children of Israel* (Ex. 27:20); *when you take the count of the children of
          Israel* (Ex. 30:12).'

     G.   "He said to him, 'It is because they declared me king at the sea, saying:
          The Lord will reign forever and ever (Ex. 15:18)."

5.   A.   Said R. Berekhiah, "The matter may be compared to the case of an elder
          who had a head-covering, concerning which he gave orders to his
          servant, saying to him, 'Shake it out, fold it up, take good care of it.'

     B.   "He said to him, 'My lord, elder, among all the head-coverings that you
          have, you give me orders only concerning this one.'

     C.   "He said to him, 'It is because this is the one in which I covered myself
          when I was first appointed an elder.'

     D.   "So Moses said to the Holy One, blessed be He, 'Lord of the ages, among
          the seventy sovereign nations that you have in your world, you give me
          orders only concerning Israel: *to the children of Israel you shall say,*
          (Lev. 20:2); *to the children of Israel speak* (Ex. 30:31); *say to the
          children of Israel* (Ex. 33:5); *speak to the children of Israel* (Ex. 31:13);
          command the children of Israel (Lev. 24:2); *and you, command the
          children of Israel* (Ex. 27:20); *when you take the count of the children of
          Israel* (Ex. 30:12).'

     E.   "He said to him, 'It is because they accepted the yoke of my dominion at
          Sinai, saying, *Whatever the Lord has spoken, we shall do and we shall
          hear* (Ex. 24:7)."

6.   A.   Said R. Yudan, "Come and see how much the Holy One, blessed be He,
          cherishes Israel, for he makes mention of them five times in a single
          verse:

     B.   *"I have given the Levites to Aaron and his sons, dedicated among the
          children of Israel to perform the service of the children of Israel in the
          tent of the presence and to make expiation for the children of Israel, and*

then no calamity will befall the children of Israel, when the children of
Israel come close to the sanctuary (Num. 8:19)."

7. A. R. Simeon bar Yohai taught on Tannaite authority, "The matter may be
        compared to the case of a king who handed his son over to his tutor, and
        gave orders to him, saying, '[See to it that] my son eats, drinks, goes to
        the school house, comes home from the school house.'
    B. "So the Holy One, blessed be He, yearns to make mention of Israel every
        moment."

8. A. Said R. Judah bar Simon, "The matter may be compared to one who was
        sitting and making a crown for the king. Someone came by and saw
        him. He said to him, 'What are you sitting and making?'
    B. "He said to him, 'A crown for the king.'
    C. "He said to him, 'As many emeralds as you can set into it, set; precious
        stones and pearls, set. For it is destined to be placed upon the head of
        the king.'
    D. "So the Holy One, blessed be He, said to Moses, 'Moses, as much praise
        as you can set forth for Israel before me, set forth; as much glory [as you
        can give them], give. For I am destined to be glorified through them:
        And he said to me, You are my servants, Israel, in whom I glorify myself
        (Is. 49:3)."

As the exposition shifts from the intersecting-verse/base-verse mode to the
simple exegesis of the base-verse, clause by clause, we begin a new sequence.
We start by asking about the context in which the base-verse occurs, and draw
the lesson give at No. 1. The appropriate message, already familiar, is that the
census is linked to the altar. Israel is beloved, and in the taking of the census,
God has provided for the age in which the altar is no more. That is the powerful
message of No. 1, entirely congruent with the interest in altar-stories pursued at
No. 6. I do not see the pertinence of No. 2, but its interest in the clause by
clause exegesis of the verse accounts for the inclusion of the passage here. Nos.
3, 4, and 5 go over the same parable three times. The main point is that God
expresses his love for Israel by giving many commandments concerning them.
The particular point of relevance, however, is not expressed: it is that God
counts them one by one, cherishing each one – just as in the census. That is the
unstated premise of the redactor who has selected the materials for the exposition
of his base-verse. No. 6 goes over the same ground, but is hardly particular to
this context. No. 7 is tacked on, but it is not fully worked out. No. 8 then
makes the same point in a different context. So the principle of selection is
propositional. Once the redactor has chosen his message, to be imputed to his
base-verse (or a clause in it), he then proceeds to assemble pertinent materials,
whether or not those materials intersect with his base-verse in some concrete
way, e.g., in language or image. The abstract proposition, never expressed,
always predominates in which is a catalogue of examples of an unstated
proposition.

II:VIII

1. A. *[The Lord spoke to Moses and said, "When you number the Israelites]
   according to their number"* (Ex. 30:12):
   B. Said R. Joshua bar Nehemiah, "Said the Holy One, blessed be He, to
   Moses, 'Moses, Go, count Israel.'
   C. "Moses said before the Holy One, blessed be He, 'Lord of all ages, it is
   written, *And your seed will be like the dust of the earth* (Gen. 28:14),
   And I shall multiply your seed like the stars of the heaven (Gen. 26:4),
   And the number of the children of Israel will be like the sand of the sea
   (Hos. 2:1), and yet you say to me, 'Go, count Israel''"!
   D. "He said to him, 'Moses, it is not as you are thinking. But if you want
   to master the exact number of the Israelites, take the first letters of the
   tribes' names, and you will know their count. The R in the name of
   Reuben stands for two hundred thousand, the S of Simeon, three hundred
   thousand, the N of Naftali, fifty thousand, the Y [in the Hebrew] of
   Judah, Joseph, and Issachar, thirty thousand, the Z of Zebulun, seven
   thousand, the D of Dan, four thousand, the G of Gad, three thousand, the
   B of Benjamin, two thousand, the A of Asher, one thousand. So you
   come up with five hundred ninety-seven thousand.'
   E. "As to the other three thousand [of the anticipated 600,000]?
   F. "They are those who fell in the time of the golden calf: *And the children
   of Levite acted in accord with the word of Moses, and of the people on
   that day three thousand men fell* (Ex. 32:28)."

2. A. R. Menahama in the name of R. Bibi: "The matter may be compared to
   the case of a king who had a flock. Wolves broke in on the flock and
   ravaged it. Said the king to the shepherd, 'Count up my flock, so as to
   know how many have been lost.'
   B "So said the Holy One, blessed be He, 'Count up the Israelites to know
   how many they have lost.'"

3. A. In ten passages the Israelites are subjected to a census.
   B. Once when they went down to Egypt: *Your fathers came down with
   seventy souls* (Deut. 10:22).'
   C. Once when they came up: *And they journeyed from Raamses to Sukkoth
   six hundred thousand men on foot* (Ex. 12;37).
   D. Twice in the Book of Numbers, once in the passage of the standards
   [Num. 2:2], once in the division of the land [Num. 26:19-56].
   E. Twice in the time of Saul: *Saul counted them by lambs* (1 Sam. 15:4),
   And he counted them by pebbles (1 Sam. 11:8).
   F. When they were rich, he counted them by lambs, and when they were
   poor, by pebbles.
   G. Once in the time of David: *And Joab took the census of the count of the
   people* (2 Sam. 25:9).
   H. If a census, why a count, and if a count, why a census? But in fact he
   had two counts, large and small. The smaller he showed to David, the
   larger he did not show to David, as it is said, *And Joab took the census
   of the count of the people.*
   I. Once in the time of Ezra: *...the whole community together was forty
   thousand* (Ezra 2:64).

J.   And once in the age to come: *The flocks will again pass under the hands of him who counts them* (Jer. 33:13).

K.   And the present case as well: *When you number the Israelites* (Ex. 30:12).

The thematic exposition turns to the matter of the census itself, that is, the next words in the verse under discussion. The opening point, No. 1, draws a range of pertinent passages into a single cogent picture. This approach forms the counterpart to the prior one, which addresses the issue of the context, fore and aft, of the base-verse. No. 2 does the same, with its allusion to the ones killed in the aftermath of the golden calf. No. 3 then provides a catalogue of pertinent parallels, an appendix of a thematic character. I see no proposition in the catalogue of No. 3.

II:IX

1.   A.   R. Menahama and R. Bibi and R. Hiyya the Elder in the name of R. Eliezer bar Jacob: "The Israelites are compared to sand.

     B.   "Just as in the case of sand, if you make a hole in it at night, in the morning you find it is filled up, so all of the thousands of Israelites lost in the time of David were made up in the time of Solomon.

     C.   "For it is said, *Judah and Israel are as many as the sand* (1 Kgs. 4:20)."

2.   A.   R. Eliezer in the name of R. Yose b. Zimra, "Whenever the Israelites were counted on account of need, they did not lose, but if it was not necessary, they lost in numbers.

     B.   "When was it for need? In the time of Moses.

     C.   "When was it not for need? In the time of David."

     D.   R. Samuel bar Nahmani in the name of R. Jonathan: *"They will give every man a ransom for his soul* (Ex. 30:12) in the time of Moses.

     E.   *"That there be no plague among them when you count them* (Ex. 30:12) in the time of David."

This looks like a miscellany. No. 1 fits only because of its theme. No. 2 then proceeds to an exegesis of the base-verse.

II:X

1.   A.   This *they shall give, as each man crosses over to those already counted [he shall give half a shekel by the sacred standard as a contribution to the Lord. Everyone from twenty years old and upward who has crossed over to those already counted shall give a contribution to the Lord. The rich man shall give no more than the half-shekel and the poor man shall give no less, when you give the contribution to the Lord to make expiation for your lives]* (Ex. 30:13-15):

     B.   Said R. Meir, "[God] took out a kind of coin made of fire from underneath his throne of glory and showed it to Moses, saying, This *they shall give.*"

2.   A.   *...as each man crosses... :*

B.   R. Judah and R. Nehemiah:

C.   R. Judah says, "Whoever crossed the Red Sea will give it."

D.   R. Nehemiah says, "[B&K, p. 35:] Whoever is a lay member of the congregation."

3.   A.   *A half shekel:*

B.   R. Judah and R. Nehemiah:

C.   R. Judah says, "Since they had sinned when the day had half gone by, let them give a half shekel."

D.   R. Nehemiah says, "Since they had sinned at the sixth hour of the day, they give a half shekel. For the shekel is made up of six grains."

E.   R. Joshua bar Nehemiah in the name of Rabban Yohanan b. Zakkai: "Since the Israelites had violated the Ten Commandments, therefore let each of them give ten *gerahs*."

4.   A.   R. Berekhiah and R. Levi in the name of R. Simeon b. Laqish: "Because they had sold the firstborn [Joseph] of Rachel for twenty pieces of silver, therefore let each one of them redeem his firstborn son with a payment of twenty pieces of silver."

5.   A.   R. Phineas in the name of R. Levi says, "Because they had sold the firstborn of Rachel for twenty pieces of silver, and each one received a *teba* [half shekel] as his share, therefore let each one of them give as his shekel a *teba*."

6.   A.   R. Judah bar Simon in the name of R. Yohanan: "There were three statements that Moses heard from the mouth of the Almighty, on account of which he was astounded and recoiled.

B.   "When he said to him, *And they shall make me a sanctuary [and I shall dwell among them]* (Ex. 25:8), said Moses before the Holy One, blessed be He, 'Lord of the ages, lo, the heavens and the heavens above the heavens cannot hold you, and yet you yourself have said, *And they shall make me a sanctuary [and I shall dwell among them].'*

C.   "Said to him the Holy One, blessed be He, 'Moses, it is not the way you are thinking. But there will be twenty boards' breadth at the north, twenty at the south, eight at the west, and I shall descend and shrink my Presence among you below.'

D.   "That is in line with this verse of Scripture: *And I shall meet you there* (Ex. 25:20).

E.   "When he said to him, *My food which is presented to me for offerings made by fire [you shall observe to offer to me]* (Num. 28:2), said Moses before the Holy One, blessed be He, 'Lord of the ages, if I collect all of the wild beasts in the world, will they produce one offering [that would be adequate as a meal for you]?

F.   "'If I collect all the wood in the world, will it prove sufficient for one offering,' as it is said, *Lebanon is not enough for altar fire, nor the beasts thereof sufficient for burnt-offerings* (Is. 40:16).

G.   "Said to him the Holy One, blessed be He, "Moses, it is not the way you are thinking. But: *You shall say to them, This is the offering made by fire [he lambs of the first year without blemish, two day by day]* (Num.

28:3), and not two at a time but one in the morning and one at dusk, as it is said, *One lamb you will prepare in the morning, and the other you will prepare at dusk* (Num. 28:4).'

H.   "And when he said to him, *When you give the contribution to the Lord to make expiation for your lives* (Ex. 30:15), said Moses before the Holy One, blessed be He, 'Lord of the ages, who can give redemption-money for his soul?

I.   "'*One brother cannot redeem another* (Ps. 49:8), *for too costly is the redemption of men's souls* (Ps. 49:9).'

J.   "Said the Holy One, blessed be He, to Moses, 'It is not the way you are thinking. But: This *they shall give* – something like *this* [namely, the half-shekel coin] they shall give.'"

7. A.   R. Huna in the name of Rab, *"Almighty – we cannot find him out, great one in strength* (Job 37:23): we have not yet found out the strength of the Holy One, blessed be He, for the Holy One, blessed be He, does not impose burdens on Israel. [He accepts only a half-shekel.]

    B.   "And when Moses heard this, he began to praise Israel, saying, *Happy is the people whose God is the Lord, happy is the people for whom such is the case* (Ps. 144:15). *Happy is the one whose help is the God of Jacob* (Ps. 146:5)."

The concluding composition works through the end of the pertinent passage of Scripture. The language is interpreted, clause by clause. No. 1 takes up the reference to *this*. The meaning is that God showed Moses the coin he required. No. 2 explains who is to give the poll tax. No. 3 explains the meaning of the half-shekel. I am puzzled by No. 4, though No. 5 seems to me to account for the inclusion of the foregoing. No. 6 then provides a composite of three cases in which God's requirements are shown to be moderate indeed, scarcely commensurate to God's glory, and No. 7 then goes over the same matter.

Pisqa Three

Remember *[what the Amalekites did to you on your way out of Egypt, how they met you on the road when you were faint and weary and cut off your rear, which was lagging behind exhausted; they showed no fear of God. When the Lord your God gives you peace from your enemies on every side, in the land which he is giving you to occupy as your patrimony, you shall not fail to blot out the memory of the Amalekites from under heaven]*
(Deut. 25:17-19).

III:I[1]

1. A. Remember *[what the Amalekites did to you on your way out of Egypt, how they met you on the road when you were faint and weary and cut off your rear, which was lagging behind exhausted; they showed no fear of God. When the Lord your God gives you peace from your enemies on every side, in the land which he is giving you to occupy as your patrimony, you shall not fail to blot out the memory of the Amalekites from under heaven]* (Deut. 25:17-19).

   B. *May the sins of his forefathers be remembered [and his mother's wickedness never be wiped out! May they remain on record before the Lord but may he extinguish their name from the earth]* (Ps. 109:14-15).

   C. [Since Ps. 109:17 refers to one's not delighting in the blessing, and since, as we shall see, Amalek is identified with Esau, we assume that the cited passage refers to Esau, who rejected the birthright, and so ask:] now were the *forebears* of Esau wicked? Were they not utterly righteous? Abraham, after all, was his grandfather, Isaac his father,

   D. and yet you say, *May the sins of his forefathers be remembered!*

   E. But [the sense is,] the sin that he committed was against his forefathers.

   F. And what is the sin that he committed against his forefathers?

   G. You find that Isaac represented Abraham. Now Isaac lived a hundred and eighty years, while Abraham lived only one hundred seventy-five years. [We shall now see that the loss of those five years to Abraham's loss is attributed to the behavior of Esau.]

   H. R. Yudan in the name of R. Aibu, R. Phineas in the name of R. Levi: "In the five years that were withheld from the life of Abraham, Esau, that wicked man, committed two severe transgressions. He had sexual relations with a betrothed maiden, and he committed murder. [Abraham then was taken away five years earlier than he should have been, so that

---

[1] I follow Mandelbaum in omitting the materials printed on his pp. 35-36. He regards them as not part of Pesiqta, and I translate beginning on p. 37, starting with the pericope he marks as No. 1.

he would not have to witness these sins, and Isaac suffered in like manner on that same account.]

I. "That is in line with this verse: *Esau came from the field* (Gen. 25:29), and the word *field* stands only for *a betrothed maiden*, as it is said, *and if it is in the field that the man found the betrothed maiden* (Deut. 22:25).

J. *"And he was tired* (Gen. 25:29), and the word *tired* stands only for *murder,* as it is said, *For my soul is tired like the soul of a murderer* (Jer. 4:31)."

K. R. Zakkai the Elder says, "He also had stolen."

L. [Resuming the discourse broken off at H:] said the Holy One, blessed be He, "I promised Abraham, *And you shall come to your fathers in peace* (Gen. 15:15). Would it be a good old age for this man to see his son's son fornicating, murdering, and stealing? Is that good old age? It is better for that righteous man to be gathered up in peace: *For your lovingkindness is better than life* (Ps. 63:4)."

M. And what is the sin that he committed against his father? He caused his eyes to weaken.

N. On the basis of that case, they have said: "Whoever brings up a wicked son or a wicked disciple in the end will suffer from weak eyes."

O. The case of the wicked son derives from our father, Isaac: *And when Isaac got old, his eyes grew so weak that he could not see* (Gen. 27:1).

P. Why? Because he had raised a wicked son, Esau.

Q. The rule of the wicked disciple comes from the case of Ahiah the Shilonite: *And Ahiah the Shilonite could not see, because his eyes had grown weak on account of old age* (1 Kgs. 14:4).

R. Why? Because he had raised a wicked disciple. And who was it? It was Jeroboam son of Nabat, who committed sin and who caused the Israelites to sin. Therefore his eyes grew dim.

2. A. What was the sin that he committed against his mother [to whom reference is made in the intersecting-verse, *...and his mother's wickedness never be wiped out*]?

B. R. Tanhum bar Abun and R. Judah and R. Nehemiah and rabbis:

C. R. Judah says, "When he was coming out of his mother's womb, he cut off her uterus, so that she should not give birth again. That is in line with this verse of Scripture [in the translation of Braude and Kapstein]: *Because he pursued his brother with a sword, he destroyed the womb whence he came* (Amos 1:11)."

D. Said R. Berekhiah, "You should not conclude that it was merely [adventitious, that is,] because he was coming forth from his mother's womb, but as he was coming out of his mother's womb, his fist was [deliberately] stretched out toward [his brother, and this was intentional]. What verse of Scripture so indicates? [In the translation of Braude and Kapstein:] *The wicked have a fist from the womb, liars go astray as soon as they are born* (Ps. 58:4)."

E. R. Nehemiah says, "He caused her not to produce the twelve tribes."

F. For R. Huna said, "Rebecca was worthy of producing all the twelve tribes, a fact indicated by this verse: *And the Lord said to her, Two nations are in your womb* (Gen. 25:23). Lo, there are two. *And two peoples will separate from your belly* (Gen. 25:23), thus four. *One people shall be stronger than the other* – so six; *the elder shall serve the younger* – eight; *And when her days to be delivered were fulfilled, behold there were twins in her womb*, then ten; *And the first came forth..and after that came forth his brother...* – twelve in all."

G. There are those who prove the same proposition from this verse of Scripture: *If this is the way my childbearing is to go, why should I bear this* (Gen. 25:22). The word for *this* is composed of the letters Z and H, the numerical value of which is seven and five, respectively, thus twelve.

H. And rabbis say, "[Esau] caused her bier not to be carried out in public. You find that when Rebecca died, people said, 'Who is going to go forth before the bier? Abraham is dead, Isaac is blind and stays at home, Jacob has fled before Esau. Will the wicked Esau be permitted to go forth before her bier?' People will say, 'Cursed be the teats that suckled that one.'

I. "What did they do? They brought out her bier by night [without public display]."

J. Said R. Yose bar Haninah, "And since her bier was not carried out in public, Scripture too dealt with her death only obliquely: *Deborah, Rebecca's nurse died...and was buried below Beth-el under the oak, which was called allon-bacuth [bacuth* being understood to mean weeping] (Gen. 35:8)."

K. What is the meaning of *allon*?

L. R. Simeon bar Nahman in the name of R. Jonathan, "It is a word in Greek, meaning, *another*."

M. [Hence the sense of the name of the oak is, *another* weeping. The first, then, was for Rebecca. So it is only obliquely that we learn that she had died, as is made clear in the immediately-following verse of Scripture.] While Jacob was sitting and observing the lamentation for his nurse-maid, news came to him about his mother: *God appeared to Jacob again when he came from Paddan-aram and blessed him* (Gen. 35:9).

N. What is the blessing that he bestowed on him?

O. R. Aha in the name of R. Jonathan, "It was the blessing that is bestowed upon mourners."

3. A. Said the Holy One, "His father could have paid him back with evil, his mother could have paid him back with evil, his brother [Jacob] could have paid him back with evil, his grandfather could have paid him back with evil. Now you [Israel] pay him back with evil, so shall I pay him back with evil.

B. "You make mention of his name down below, and I shall wipe out his name up above: *May they remain on record before the Lord but may he extinguish their name from the earth.*

C. "*Remember what the Amalekites did to you.*"

We have a perfect rendition of the intersecting-verse/base-verse form, begun with the base-verse at 1.A only because we stand at the head of a complete *pisqa.* Otherwise we should not expect to begin with the base-verse, and the other instances do not do so. The base-verse tells Israel to remember Amalek. The statement of Ps. 109:13 is that one is to remember the wicked. The wicked person who is to be remembered in the cited Psalm is Esau, and, it follows, Esau is the same as Amalek. That is the unstated premise on which all else

rests. That is, the supposition is that Esau is the same as Amalek, and the cited
verse speaks of Esau. The rest follows in a point by point exposition of the
intersecting-verse, showing the sins of Esau against his grandfather, father, and
mother. Now the main point comes at the end. Jacob did not pay Esau back for
the evil that he had committed, though he had every right to do so, and neither
did Abraham, Isaac, or Rebecca. But the task of Israel is to make mention of
Amalek's name, down below, thus remembering the sins of Amalek down
below, while God, on high, will wipe out the name and remembrance of
Amalek=Esau=Rome. Jacob-Israel's rival and nemesis, Esau, thus will receive
his just reward from God, and the task of Israel is to keep alive the memory, the
name of Amalek. The exposition of No. 1 contributes to the conclusion by
proving that Abraham had every right to pay back Esau for the evil that he had
done. But Abraham did not do so. In resignation, he simply died a few years
before he should have. Isaac did nothing; he went blind and did not see. Jacob,
of course, did nothing; he fled. Rebecca did nothing; she suffered the indignity
of a secret burial, rather than having Esau the principal at her cortege. So Nos.
1, 2 give us the preparation for the conclusion reached at No. 3. Even though
enriched by diverse pieces of information preserved in their own language, the
passage hangs together beautifully. Every detail of the exposition of the
intersecting-verse contributes to the conclusion at which the intersecting-verse
meets the base-verse. I cannot imagine a more perfect version of this form.

III:II

1. A. R. Tanhum bar Hanilai opened [discourse by citing the following
   intersecting-verse]: *"Your memorials shall be like unto ashes, your
   eminences to eminences of clay* [New English Bible: *your pompous talk
   is dust and ashes, your defenses will crumble like clay*] [Braude and
   Kapstein, p. 46: *Your acts of remembering Amalek, followed by
   repentance for your sins, will be like 'ashes,' but when you deserve
   visitation [for sin], visitation in 'clay' shall be your punishment]* (Job
   13:12).
   B. "Said the Holy One, blessed be He, to Israel [with reference to the verse's
   statement about *memorials*, that is, acts of remembering], "As to those
   two acts of remembrance that I inscribed for you in Scripture, be
   meticulous about them: *Blot out the memory of Amalek* (Deut. 25:19),
   For I shall certainly blot out the memory of Amalek (Ex. 17:14).
   C. *"'...shall be like unto ashes*: that is, are comparable to ashes. If you
   have acquired merit, lo, you are the children of Abraham, the one who
   compared himself to ashes: *For I am dust and ashes* (Gen. 18:27). And if
   not: *your eminences to eminences of clay,* that is, prepare yourselves for
   the subjugation of Egypt. For what is written with respect to Egypt:
   They embittered their lives with hard work in clay (Ex. 1:14)."

The intersecting-verse makes the same point in a different way, namely, in
the merit of Israel's remembering Amalek, God will redeem them. But there is
now a condition, which is provided by the intersecting-verse. One has to be like
Abraham, like ashes; not like clay, that is, embittered by the hard work in clay

in the subjugation to Egypt. That seems to me the point of the composition, which addresses the theme of remembering Amalek, but does not, in a formal sense, bring us back to the base-verse at hand.

III:III

1. A. R. Judah in the name of R. Aibu opened discourse by citing the following verse of Scripture: *"Do not behave like horse or mule, unreasoning creatures, whose course must be checked with bit and bridle. [Many are the torments of the ungodly; but unfailing love enfolds him who trusts in the Lord]* (Ps. 32:9-10).

   B. "Six matters have been stated with reference to a horse: it eats a lot, excretes a little, loves fornication, loves war, despises sleep, and displays arrogance."

   C. And some say, "In battle it also kills its owner."

   D. [Continuing A:] *"Do not behave like horse:* as to a horse, when you bridle it, it kicks, when you pat it, it kicks, when you ornament it, it kicks, when you feed it barley, it kicks.

   E. "If you do not get near it, it kicks.

   F. "You should not be like that. Rather, be conscientious about responding to good with good, and responding to evil with evil.

   G. "Paying back good with good: *You will not abominate the Edomites* (Deut. 23:8).

   H. "Paying back evil with evil: *Remember what Amalek did to you* (Deut. 25:17)."

The intersecting-verse is drawn directly into alignment with the base-verse, and the message of the former is applied to the latter. The intersecting-verse has therefore supplied a parable permitting the main point of the base-verse to be stated.

III:IV

1. A. R. Banai in the name of R. Huna commenced discourse by citing the following verse: *"A false balance is an abomination to the Lord [but a just weight is his delight. When pride comes, then comes disgrace]* (Prov. 11:1-2)."

   B. Said R. Banai in the name of R. Huna, "If you have seen a generation, the measures of which are perverted, know that the government is going to come and declare war against that generation. What verse of Scripture so indicates? *A false balance is an abomination to the Lord.* And what is written immediately following? *When pride comes, then comes disgrace* [Braude and Kapstein: *The insolent (kingdom) will come and bring humiliation (to Israel)]*."

2. A. R. Berekhiah in the name of R. Abba bar Kahana, "It is written: *Shall I acquit the man with wicked scales and with a bag of deceitful weights* (Micah 6:11).

   B. *"Shall I acquit the man with wicked scales:* is it possible even to imagine that God would acquit one with perverted scales? But: *a bag of deceitful weights* [means, even in your own bag, they will remain deceitful weights [Mandelbaum, p. 43, n. to 1. 4)]."

3 . A. Said R. Levi, "So Moses gave an indication to Israel in the Torah: *You will not have in your bag a large stone and a small one, you will not have in your house two ephah-measures, one large, one small* (Deut. 25:13-14).

   B. "If you have done so, know that the government is going to come and declare war against that generation. What verse of Scripture so indicates? *A false balance is an abomination to the Lord.*

   C. And what is written immediately following [Deut. 25:13-14]? *Remember what Amalek did to you* (Deut. 25:17)."

The point of intersection with the base-verse comes only at No. 3. The text is not ideal, particularly at 2.B. No. 1 makes its point with respect to the intersecting-verse alone, but, as we see, No. 3 can do its work only in the aftermath of the point at hand. So, overall, it seems to me the composition is meant to be cogent. Then No. 2 appears to be intruded, since it deals with neither the intersecting-verse nor the base-verse. If we read No. 3 as continuous with No. 1, by contrast, the passage proves cogent, beginning to end. The source of the exegetical idea is the juxtaposition of verses, which, as we have seen, commonly stimulates the imagination of our authorship to insight into the verse under study. That of course is nothing but a variation of the basic interest in how one verse opens up the meaning of some other, that is, the intersecting-verse/base-verse construction that dominates in the opening pericopes of each *pisqa.*

III:V

1 . A. R. Levi commenced discourse by citing the following verse of Scripture: *"You have rebuked the nations, you have destroyed the wicked, you have blotted out their name forever and ever* (Ps. 9:5):

   B. *"You have rebuked the nations* refers to Amalek, concerning whom it is written: *Amalek was the first of the gentiles* (Num. 24:20).

   C. *"...you have destroyed the wicked,* refers to the wicked Esau, concerning whom it is written, *Edom shall be called the border of wickedness* (Mal. 1:4).

   D. "If one would say to you, even Jacob is covered by that statement, say to him, *you have destroyed the wicked,* [which cannot possibly speak of Jacob, for] what is written is not wicked ones, in the plural, but the wicked one, in the singular, which refers to the wicked Esau.

   E. *"...you have blotted out their name forever and ever:* [this speaks of Amalek, as it is said,] *Blot out the remembrance of Amalek* (Deut. 25:17)."

The intersecting-verse is simply linked to the base-verse, which is now Deut. 25:17, because the reference to the blotting out of the name invites that identification. The established interest in Esau/Edom and Amalek recurs. The composition is a simple one, which repeats the main theme.

III: VI

1. A. *Return sevenfold into the bosom of our neighbors the taunts with which they have taunted you, O Lord* (Ps. 79:12):

   B. R. Judah bar Guria said, "Let what they did to us in respect to the circumcision, which was assigned to the bosom of Abraham, be remembered against them."

   C. This accords with that which R. Hinenah bar Silqah, R. Joshua of Sikhnin, and R. Levi in the name of R. Yohanan said, "What were the members of the household of Amalek doing? They cut off the circumcised penises of the Israelites and tossing them upward, saying, 'Is this what you have chosen? Here is what you have chosen!'"

2. A. And R. Joshua b. Levi: "Let what they did to us with respect to the Torah be remembered against them.

   B. "For concerning the Torah it is written: *It is refined seven times* (Ps. 12:7). So: *Return sevenfold into the bosom of our neighbors the taunts with which they have taunted you, O Lord* (Ps. 79:12)."

3. A. Rabbis say, "Let what they did to us with regard to the sanctuary, which is set in the bosom of the world, be remembered against them [for they razed the Temple to its foundations, which are at the bosom of the earth (Braude and Kapstein, p. 48)]."

   B. For R. Huna said, *"From the bottom of the ground [bosom of the earth,* so Braude and Kapstein, p. 48] *to the lower settle shall be two cubits* (Ez. 43:14)."

4. A. Now Samuel came along and paid them back: *Samuel cut Agag apart before the Lord in Gilgal* (1 Sam. 15:33).

   B. What did he do to him?

   C. R. Abba bar Kahana said, "He chopped off his flesh in small bits, the size of an olive's bulk, and fed it to the ostriches:

   D. *"Pieces of his body shall be devoured, yes, the firstborn of death shall devour pieces of his flesh* (Job 18:13).

   E. "He chose for him a bitter form of death."

   F. And rabbis say, "He set up four stakes in the ground and tied him on them.

   G. "[Agag] was saying, *'Surely the most bitter of deaths is at hand* (1 Sam. 15:32).

   H. "'Do people put princes to death in such a way, with so harsh a form of death?'"

5. A. R. Samuel bar Abidimi said, "They judged him in accord with the law of the nations of the world, that is, without appropriately cross-examined testimony of witnesses, and without an admonition in advance."

   B. R. Isaac said, "They castrated him: *Samuel said, As your sword has made women childless, so shall your mother be childless among women* (1

Sam. 15:33), reading the word for *mother* as if the letters meant *penis*, hence, the penis of that man [shall not produce children]."

6. A. Said R. Levi, "So in the Torah Moses gave an indication of the same matter to Israel: *When men fight with one another and the wife of the one draws near to rescue her husband from the hand of him who is beating him and puts out her hand and seizes him by the private parts, then you shall cut off her hand; your eye shall have no pity* (Deut. 25:11-12).

   B. "What is written thereafter: *Remember what Amalek did to you on the way as you came out of Egypt* (Deut. 25:17)."

This is on the surface a rather meandering passage, which only at the end joins the theme of remembrance to the topic of Amalek. The compositor aims at a systematic linking of the several themes of Deut. 25 to the matter of Amalek, and that leads him to review the matter at hand. On the surface it seems farfetched, because the tight linking of intersecting-verse to base-verse is loosened. But the form in fact is tightly disciplined and joins three generative verses: the intersecting-verse, Ps. 79:12, the base-verse, Deut. 25:17, and the contextual verse, linked through the intersecting- to the base-verse, which we see is Deut. 25:11-12. In accord with this complex composition, therefore, we move from the intersecting-verse – *returning sevenfold into the bosom of our neighbors* – in a protracted course. Despite the slow progress, once more the unity of the whole strikes most compellingly. For the theme of No. 1 is the matter of circumcision, and that same theme is introduced at the end. The Amalekites cut off the Israelites' penises, and the prophet, Samuel, did the same; then the final intrusion of the matter of Deut. 25:11-12 produces no surprise, because we are prepared for it. Nos. 2 and 3 continue closely with No. 1's main theme, paying them back for what they did, and then lead us right into No. 4, how the Amalekites, through Agag, were paid back. No. 6 then presents a stunning and appropriate statement of the whole.

III:VII

1. A. *Remember [what Amalek did to you on the way as you came out of Egypt]* (Deut. 25:17):

   B. Said R. Berekhiah, "You say to us, 'Remember'! You do the remembering. For we are often forgetful, but you, who are never forgetful, you are the one to do the remembering *of what Amalek did to you on the way as* you *came out of Egypt* (Deut. 25:17)."

2. A. *[Remember] what [Amalek] did to you [on the way as you came out of Egypt]* (Deut. 25:17):

   B. Said R. Isaac, "Did he do it to us and not to you? *Remember, O Lord, against the children of Edom, the day of Jerusalem [the day they said, raze it, raze it]* (Ps. 137:7)."

3 . A. *[Remember, O Lord, against the children of Edom, the day of Jerusalem the day they said,] raze it, raze it* (Ps. 137:7):

   B. R. Abba bar Kahana said, "The meaning of the Hebrew word translated *raze it* follows the sense of the same word as it occurs in the following verse: *The broad walls of Babylon shall be utterly razed* (Jer. 51:58)."

   C. R. Levi said, "The meaning of the Hebrew word translated *raze* it should be rendered as *empty it, empty it,* for it follows the sense of the same word as it occurs in the following verse: *She hastened and emptied her pitcher into the trough* (Gen. 24:20)."

   D. In the view of R. Abba bar Kahana, who holds that the word means *raze it, raze it,* the sense is that they went down to the very foundations, to the base.

   E. In the view of R. Levi, who holds that the word means, *empty it out, empty it out,* the sense is that they cut away the foundations, taking them away.

We shift to a different exegetical mode, namely, the phrase by phrase interpretation of the base-verse in its own terms, beginning with the first word of the verse, *Remember.* No. 1 makes the point that God has to do the remembering too. No. 2 justifies it: what Amalek did, he did to God, not only to Israel. No. 3 introduces the destruction of Jerusalem, which involves God as much as Israel, and then explains the language of the verse. We see that the cited verse in no way serves as an intersecting-verse; it is merely a proof-text for the proposition announced in the preceding passage.

III:VIII

1 . A. *[Remember what] the Amalekites [did to you on your way out of Egypt, how they met you on the road when you were faint and weary and cut off your rear, which was lagging behind exhausted; they showed no fear of God. When the Lord your God gives you peace from your enemies on every side, in the land which he is giving you to occupy as your patrimony, you shall not fail to blot out the memory of the Amalekites from under heaven]* (Deut. 25:17-19):

   B. The word for Amalek is to be divided into two components, bearing the meanings *am,* people, and *yeleq,* locust.

   C. It flew down like the *zahla*-locust.

   D. Another interpretation: the nation of Amalek came down to lick up the blood of Israel like a dog.

2 . A. R. Levi in the name of R. Simeon b. Halapta: "To what may Amalek be compared? To a fly that was lusting for an open wound.

   B. "So Amalek was lusting after Israel like a dog."

3 . A. It was taught in the name of R. Nathan,"Four hundred *parasangs* did Amalek leap in coming to make war against Israel at Rephidim.

There is a slight problem with No. 2, since B has nothing to do with A. The rest of the passage moves smoothly in its exposition of the name of Amalek.

III:IX

1. A. Remember *[what the Amalekites did to you] on your way out of Egypt, how they met you on the road when you were faint and weary and cut off your rear, which was lagging behind exhausted; they showed no fear of God. When the Lord your God gives you peace from your enemies on every side, in the land which he is giving you to occupy as your patrimony, you shall not fail to blot out the memory of the Amalekites from under heaven]* (Deut. 25:17-19):

    B. Said R. Levi, "They came against you on the way like highwaymen.

    C. "The matter may be compared to the case of a king who had a vineyard, and he surrounded it with a wall and the king put in the vineyard a vicious dog.

    D. "Said the king, 'The dog will bite anyone who comes and breaks through the wall.'

    E. "Then the son of the king came along and broke through the wall, and the dog bit him.

    F. "Whenever the king wanted to remind the son about the sin that he had committed in the vineyard, he said to him, 'Remember how the dog bit you.'

    G. "So whenever the Holy One, blessed be He, wanted to remind the Israelites of the sin that they had committed in Rephidim, saying, *Whether God is in our midst or not* (Ex. 17:7), he says to them, *Remember what Amalek did to you* (Deut. 25:17)."

The net effect is to link the several passages concerning Amalek into a single account, a tendency we have observed in respect to Deut. 25 now affecting the reading of Ex. 17. The result is a solid piece of explanation of how the details all form a single cogent point.

III:X

1. A. Remember *[what the Amalekites did to you on your way out of Egypt, how they met you on the road when you were faint and weary and cut off your rear, which was lagging behind exhausted; they showed no fear of God. When the Lord your God gives you peace from your enemies on every side, in the land which he is giving you to occupy as your patrimony, you shall not fail to blot out the memory of the Amalekites from under heaven]* (Deut. 25:17-19):

    B. R. Judah, R. Nehemiah, and rabbis:

    C. R. Judah said, "The letters for words, *how they met you,* can be read, *how they made you unclean* [Mandelbaum: through pederasty], in line with this verse, in which the same letters bear that meaning: *Any man who is not clean because of a seminal emission by night* (Deut. 23:11)."

    D. R. Nehemiah says, "The letters for words, *how they met you,* can be read to mean *read,* thus: They read up on you.

E. "What did Amalek do? He went into the archives in Egypt and took the volumes of genealogies of the tribes which were located there in their names. He came and stood outside of the cloud and announced, 'Reuben, Simeon, Levi, Judah, I am your brother. Come out, for I want to do business with you.'

F. "When one of them came out, he would kill him."

G. Rabbis say, "The letters for words, *how they met you*, can be read to mean, to *cool*, that is, he made them look cold [and not heated up for battle and good fighters] before the nations of the world."

H. Said R. Hunia, "The matter may be compared to the case of a scalding-hot bath, into which no one could dip himself. One son of Beeliel came along and jumped in; even though he was burned, he made it appear cool for others [who followed him in and got burned].

I. "So when the Israelites had gone forth from Egypt, fear of them fell upon all the nations of the world: *Then were the chiefs of Edom frightened...terror and dread fell on them* (Ex. 15:15-16).

J. "But when Amalek attacked them and made war against them, even though he got his from them, he made them look cold before the nations of the world."

The three possible meanings of the word translated *met you* are worked out. The first resorts to the sense of seminal emission, as explained by Mandelbaum; the second imputes a silent A, hence, QRA, *read*; and the third emphasizes the sense of cool, in the meaning of, not spirited but lethargic, hence, Amalek's minor success made the Israelites look unprepared, laconic and not warlike. The basic intent remains the same, namely, the word by word exposition of the base-verse.

III:XI

1. A. Remember *[what the Amalekites did to you on your way out of Egypt, how they met you on the road when you were faint and weary] and cut off your rear, which was lagging behind exhausted; they showed no fear of God. When the Lord your God gives you peace from your enemies on every side, in the land which he is giving you to occupy as your patrimony, you shall not fail to blot out the memory of the Amalekites from under heaven]* (Deut. 25:17-19):

B. [The word, *how he cut off your rear*, means] how we smote you with a blow to the "tail" [penis].

C. This accords with that which R. Hinenah bar Silqah, R. Joshua of Sikhnin, and R. Levi in the name of R. Yohanan said, "What were the members of the household of Amalek doing? They cut off the circumcised penises of the Israelites and tossing them upward, saying, 'Is this what you have chosen? Here is what you have chosen!'"

D. For the Israelites did not know about the character of the "branch": *Lo, they put the branch to their nose* (Ez. 8:17).

E. When Amalek came along, he taught it to them.

F. From whom had he learned it? From our forefather Esau: *Is he not rightly named Jacob* (Gen. 27:36).

G. He cleared his throat and produced the "branch" [penis, as a gesture of disrespect].

The clarification of the clauses proceeds, all the time emphasizing the character of Amalek as sexually depraved.

III:XII

1. A. Remember *[what the Amalekites did to you on your way out of Egypt, how they met you on the road when you were faint and weary and cut off your rear, which was lagging behind exhausted; they showed no fear of God. When the Lord your God gives you peace from your enemies on every side, in the land which he is giving you to occupy as your patrimony, you shall not fail to blot out the memory of the Amalekites from under heaven]* (Deut. 25:17-19):
   B. R. Judah, R. Nehemiah, and rabbis:
   C. R. Judah said, "Whoever hung back was cut off."
   D. R. Nehemiah said, "Whomever the cloud expelled was cut off."
   E. Rabbis say, "This refers to the tribe of Dan, which the cloud expelled.
   F. "For all of them worshipped idolatry."

2. A. Another interpretation of the clause: *...[when you were faint and weary and cut off your rear,] which was lagging behind exhausted:*
   B. Said R. Isaac, "All those who were whispering *in your rear* [against you, that is, against God, as will now be spelled out]."

3. A. R. Judah, R. Nehemiah, and Rabbis:
   B. R. Judah said, "They said, 'If he is the lord of all his works as he is lord over us, we shall worship him, and if not, we shall rebel against him.'"
   C. R. Nehemiah said, "They said, 'If he provides our food the way a king does in his capital, so that the city lacks nothing, we shall worship him, and if not, we shall rebel against him.'"
   D. And rabbis say, "They said, 'If we reflect in our hearts and he knows what we are thinking, we shall serve him, and if not, we shall rebel against him.'"

4. A. R. Berekhiah in the name of R. Levi: "In their hearts they would reflect, and the Holy One would give them what they wanted.
   B. "What verse of Scripture shows it? *And in their hearts they tested God, asking food for their soul* (Ps. 78:18). What then is written there? *And they ate and were most sated because he brought them what they craved* (Ps. 78:29)."

The next clause produces a familiar mode of interpretation. No. 2, carried forward at No. 3, takes the *in your rear* to mean, *against you,* and the rest follows.

III:XIII

1. A.   Remember *[what the Amalekites did to you on your way out of Egypt,*
          how they met you on the road] when you were faint and weary [and cut
          off your rear, which was lagging behind exhausted; they showed no fear
          of God. When the Lord your God gives you peace from your enemies on
          every side, in the land which he is giving you to occupy as your
          patrimony, you shall not fail to blot out the memory of the Amalekites
          from under heaven] (Deut. 25:17-19):

    B.   ...*faint*: from thirst.

    C.   ...*and weary*: from the journey.

2. A.   ...*they showed no fear of God:*   R. Phineas in the name of R. Samuel bar
          Nahman, "There is a tradition concerning the narrative that the seed of
          Esau will fall only by the hand of the sons of Rachel.

    B.   *"Surely the youngest of the flock shall drag them* (Jer. 49:20).

    C.   "Why does he refer to them as the youngest of the flock? Because they
          were the youngest of all the tribes.

    D.   "[Now we shall see the connection to the downfall of
          Esau=Amalek=Rome:] This one is called a youth, and that one is called
          young.

    E.   "This one is called a youth: *And he was a youth* (Gen. 37:2).

    F.   "And that one is called young: *Lo, I have made you the youngest among*
          the nations (Ob. 1:2).

    G.   "This one [Esau] grew up between two righteous men and did not act like
          them, and that one [Joseph] grew up between two wicked men and did not
          act like them.

    H.   "Let this one come and fall by the hand of the other.

    I.   "This one showed concern for the honor owing to his master, and that
          one treated with disdain the honor owning to his master.

    J.   "Let this one come and fall by the hand of the other.

    L.   "In connection with this one it is written, *And he did not fear God* (Deut.
          25:18), and in connection with that one it is written, *And I fear God*
          (Gen. 42:18).

    M.   "Let this one come and fall by the hand of that one."

No. 1 deals with the first part of the clause, No. 2 the second. The reference
to not fearing God precipitates the inclusion of the theme of how that one will
fall by the hand of one who did fear God, with the consequence interest in the
contrast of Joseph and Esau=Amalek. The contrast of the salvation of Israel and
the downfall of Israel's enemies, with the details of one forming an exact
counterpart and opposite to those of the other, recurs throughout our
documment.

III:XIV

1. A.   ...*When the Lord your God gives you peace from your enemies on every*
          side, in the land which he is giving you to occupy as your patrimony,
          you shall not fail to blot out the memory of the Amalekites from under
          heaven (Deut. 25:17-19):

B.   R. Azariah, R. Judah bar Simon in the name of R. Judah bar Ilai: "When the Israelites entered the Land, they were commanded in three matters: to appoint a king, to build the chosen house, *And they shall make me a sanctuary* (Ex. 25:8), and to wipe out the memory of Amalek."

The passage is formally flawed, lacking as it does the requisite proof-texts. It is not particular to the exposition of the verse at hand and makes its own point independent of that verse.

III:XV

1.   A.   R. Joshua b. Levi in the name of R. Alexandri: "One verse of Scripture says, *You shall not fail to blot out the memory of the Amalekites from under heaven* (Deut. 25:17-19), and another verse of Scripture says, *For I shall surely wipe out the memory of Amalek* (Ex. 17:14).

     B.   "How can both verses be carried out? [Either Israel will do it or God will do it.]

     C.   "Before Amalek laid his hand on God's throne [with reference to *And Moses built an altar and called the name of it, The Lord is my banner, saying, 'A hand upon the throne of the Lord. The Lord will have war with Amalek from generation to generation'* (Ex. 17:15-16)], *You shall not fail to blot out the memory of the Amalekites*.

     D.   "After he had laid hands on God's throne, *For I shall surely wipe out the memory of Amalek*. [God is victim of Amalek, as much as Israel is.]

     E.   "Now is it really possible for a mortal to lay hands on the throne of the Holy One, blessed be He?

     F.   "But because he was going to destroy Jerusalem, concerning which it is written, *At that time Jerusalem will be called the throne of the Lord* (Jer. 50:17), therefore: *For I shall surely wipe out the memory of Amalek* (Ex. 17:14)."

The recurrent polemic that God is involved in the war against Amalek because Amalek makes war against God reappears here. The two pertinent verses are harmonized and shown not to go over the same ground. This is a mark that we near the end of the exposition of the base-verse, Deut. 25:17, and move on to another base-verse, Ex. 17:15-17.

III:XVI

1.   A.   *[And Moses built an altar and called the name of it, The Lord is my banner,] saying, 'A hand upon the throne of the Lord. The Lord will have war with Amalek from generation to generation'* (Ex. 17:15-16):

     B.   It was taught in the name of R. Ilai: "The Holy One, blessed be He, took an oath: 'By my right hand, by my right hand, by my throne, by my throne, if proselytes come from any of the nations of the world, I shall accept them, but if they come from the seed of Amalek I shall never accept them.'

     C.   "And so was the case with David: *And David said to the youth who told him [that Saul and Jonathan had died], Where do you come from? And he said, I am the son of an Amalekite convert* (2 Sam. 1:13)."

     D.   Said R. Isaac, "He was Doeg the Edomite."

E.   [Continuing C:] *"And David said to him, Your blood be upon your own head* (2 Sam. 1:16)."

F.   Said R. Isaac, "What is written is, *your bloods*, meaning, he said to him, 'You [Doeg] have shed much blood in Nob, city of the priests.'"

2. A.   *...from generation to generation* (Ex. 17:15-16):

   B.   Said the Holy One, blessed be He, "From one generation to the next I am after him, for generations."

3. A.   [Continuing No. 2:] R. Eliezer, R. Joshua, and R. Yose:

   B.   R. Eliezer says, "It was from the generation of Moses to the generation of Samuel [but not beyond that point]."

   C.   R. Joshua says, "It was from the generation of Samuel to the generation of Mordecai and Esther."

   D.   R. Yose says, "It was from the generation of Mordecai and Esther to the generation of the Messiah-King, which is three generations."

   E.   And how do we know that to the generation of the Messiah-King it is three generations? As it is written, *They will fear you while the sun endures, and as long as the moon, a generation, generations* (Ps. 72:5).

   F.   *A generation* – one, then *generations* – two, lo, three in all.

4. A.   R. Berekhiah in the name of R. Abba bar Kahana: "So long as the seed of Amalek endures in the world, it is as if a wing covers the face [of God].

   B.   "When the seed of Amalek perishes from the world, *Your teacher shall not hide himself any more, but your eyes shall see your teacher* (Is. 30:20)."

5. A.   R. Levi in the name of R. Huna bar Hanina: "So long as the seed of Amalek endures in the world, the Name of God is not whole, and the throne is not whole. When the seed of Amalek perishes from the world, the Name of God is whole, and the throne is whole.

   B.   "What verse of Scripture indicates it?

   C.   *"The enemy have vanished in everlasting ruins, their cities you have rooted out, the very memory of them has perished* (Ps. 9:6).

   D.   "What is written immediately therefore: *But the Lord sits enthroned for ever, he has established his throne for judgment, [and he judges the world with righteousness righteousness, he judges the peoples with equity]* (Ps. 9:7-8)."

No. 1 makes its own point, that the sense of "from generation to generation" is that no proselytes will ever be accepted from Amalekites. No. 2 proceeds to amplify the statement of Scripture about the coming generations of the Amalekites. No. 3 glosses No. 2. Nos. 4 and 5 conclude with more general thematic statements. The pertinence of the proof-text, Ps. 9:6, is the allusion to the very memory of the enemy, and the rest follows. The conclusion is satisfying, since it draws us back to the point at which we began.

Pisqa Four

[Now the Lord said to Moses and to Aaron, "This is the statute of the Torah which the Lord has commanded: Tell the people of Israel to bring you] a red heifer [without defect, in which there is no blemish, and upon which a yoke has never come....And a man who is clean shall gather up the ashes of the heifer and deposit them outside the camp in a clean place; and they shall be kept for the congregation of the people of Israel for the water for impurity, for the removal of sin. And he who gathers the ashes of the heifer shall wash his clothes and be unclean until evening...He who touches the dead body of any person shall be unclean seven days; he shall cleanse himself with the water on the third day and on the seventh day and so be clean; but if he does not cleanse himself on the third day and on the seventh day he will not become clean. Whoever touches a dead person...and does not cleanse himself defiles the tabernacle of the Lord, and that person shall be cut off from Israel, because the water for impurity was not thrown upon him, he shall be unclean; his uncleanness is still on him"]

(Num. 19:1-13, pass.).

IV:I

1. A. *Who can bring forth something clean out of something unclean? Is it not the one?* (Job 14:4) [that is, the one God]:
   B. for examples [of bringing the clean out of the unclean]: Abraham from Terah, Hezekiah from Ahaz, Mordecai from Shimei, Israel from the nations, the world to come from this world.
   C. Who has done so? Who has commanded so? Who has decreed so? Is it not the one, is it not the Unique One of the world?

2. A. There we have learned: **If a white spot the size of a bean [is on a person's flesh], he is unclean. But if it flowered throughout the person's body, he is clean** [M. Neg. 8:2].
   B. Who has done so? Who has commanded so? Who has decreed so? Is it not the one, is it not the Unique One of the world?

3. A. There we have learned: **In the case of a woman whose fetus has died in her womb, if the midwife stuck in her hand and touched it, the midwife is unclean with an uncleanness that lasts for seven days [by reason of touching the corpse], while the woman remains in a state of cleanness until the offspring comes forth** [M. Hul. 4:3]. While the corpse is in the "house," [that is, the womb, the woman's body], it is clean, but when it comes forth therefrom, lo, it is unclean.

B. Who has done so? Who has commanded so? Who has decreed so? Is it not the one, is it not the Unique One of the world?

4. A. And we have learned there: **All those who are engaged in the work of preparing the ashes of the red cow from beginning to end impart uncleanness to clothing** [M. Par. 4:4], while the cow itself effects purification.
   B. [Supply:] Who has done so? Who has commanded so? Who has decreed so? Is it not the one, is it not the Unique One of the world?

5. A. Said the Holy One, blessed be He, "An ordinance have I ordained, a decree have I made, and you have no right to transgress my decrees: *Now the Lord said to Moses and to Aaron, 'This is the statute of the Torah which the Lord has commanded: [Tell the people of Israel to bring you a red heifer without defect, in which there is no blemish, and upon which a yoke has never come....And a man who is clean shall gather up the ashes of the heifer and deposit them outside the camp in a clean place; and they shall be kept for the congregation of the people of Israel for the water for impurity, for the removal of sin. And he who gathers the ashes of the heifer shall wash his clothes and be unclean until evening...He who touches the dead body of any person shall be unclean seven days; he shall cleanse himself with the water on the third day and on the seventh day and so be clean; but if he does not cleanse himself on the third day and on the seventh day he will not become clean. Whoever touches a dead person...and does not cleanse himself defiles the tabernacle of the Lord, and that person shall be cut off from Israel, because the water for impurity was not thrown upon him, he shall be unclean; his uncleanness is still on him]* (Num. 19:1-13, pass.).

We have a unitary composition which announces its proposition through the intersecting-verse and draws the whole to a close at its profoundly cogent conclusion. The paradox is that while uncleanness is associated with the rite of burning the red cow, the product of the rite, the ashes that are mixed with the water to make purification-water, effects purification. The paradox opens with historical examples, No. 1, and then proceeds to instances drawn from purity-law, Nos. 2, 3, 4, reaching the climax and conclusion of the base-verse at No. 5. I cannot imagine a more perfect example of the form, since the choice of the intersecting-verse is readily explained and assuredly does make possible the point important to the compositor or author. The intruded liturgy does not affect the basic form, intersecting-verse/base-verse.

IV:II

1. A. R. Tanhum b. R. Hanilai opened discourse by citing the following verse of Scripture: *"The sayings of the Lord are pure sayings* (Ps. 12:7).
   B. "The sayings of the Lord are sayings, but the sayings of mortals are not.
   C. "Under ordinary circumstances, when a mortal king comes into a town and the townsfolk laud him, if their praise pleases him, he says to them, 'Tomorrow I am going to build public baths and bathhouses for you,

tomorrow I am going to bring a water pipe for fresh water for you.' Then he goes to sleep and does not wake up in the morning.

D. "So where is he and where are his sayings?

E. "But the Holy One, blessed be He, is not like that.

F. "Rather: *The Lord God is truth* (Jer. 10:10)."

G. What is the meaning of truth?

H. Said R. Abin, "It means that *he is the living God and eternal king* (Jer. 10:10)."

2. A. *The sayings of the Lord are pure* (Ps. 12:7):

B. R. Yudan in the name of R. Isaac, R. Berekhiah in the name of R. Eleazar, R. Jacob of Kefar Hanin in the name of R. Joshua b. Levi: "We find that Scripture rearranged two or three words as a circumlocution in the Torah so as not to bring an unseemly word out of God's mouth.

C. "That is in line with the following verse of Scripture: *Of every clean beast you will take for yourself seven, male and female, and from every beast that is not clean* (Gen. 7:2).

D. "'And from every unclean beast' is not what is written here, but rather, *Of every beast that is not clean, two, male and female* (Gen. 7:2)."

E. Said R. Yudan b. R. Manasseh, "Even when Scripture came to introduce the marks of unclean beasts, Scripture commenced only with the marks of clean beasts, as in the following cases:

F. "'The camel, because it does not part the hoof' is not what is written here, but rather, *Because it chews the cud but does not*...(Lev. 11:4).

G. "'The rock badger, because it does not part the hoof' is not what is written here, but rather, *Because it chews the cud but does not*.. (Lev. 11:5).

H. "'The hare, because it does not part the hoof,' is not what is written here, but rather *Because it chews the cud but does not*.. (Lev. 11:6).

I. "'The pig, because it does not chew the cud' is not what is written here, but rather, *Because it chews the cud but does not*.. (Lev. 11:7)."

3. A. R. Yose of Malehayya and R. Joshua of Sikhnin in the name of R. Levi: "Children in David's time, before they had tasted the taste of sin [reaching sexual maturity] were able to expound the Torah in forty-nine different ways to reach a decision on uncleanness and in forty-nine different ways to reach a decision on cleanness.

B. "And David prayed for them: *You O Lord protect them* (Ps. 122:7). Preserve their learning in their heart.

C. *"Protect them forever from this generation* (Ps. 12:7). From the generation that deserves destruction."

4. A. And after all this praise [for their achievements, and David's prayer for them], that generation of disciples went out to war and fell.

B. It was because there were renegades among them.

C. That is in line with what David says, *My soul is in the midst of lions, I lie down among them that are aflame, sons of men whose teeth are spears and arrows, their tongues sharp swords* (Ps. 57:4).

D. *My soul is in the midst of lions* refers to Abner and Amasa, who were lions in the Torah.

E. *I lie down among them that are aflame* refers to Doeg and Ahitophel, who were burning up with gossip.

F. *Sons of men whose teeth are spears and arrows* refers to the men of Keilah: *Will the men of Keilah hand me over* (1 Sam. 32:11).

G. *Their tongues are sharp swords* refers to the Ziphites: *When the Ziphites came and said to Saul, Does David not hide himself with us* (1 Sam. 23:19).

H. At that moment said David, "Now what is the presence of God doing in the world? *Be exalted, O God, above the heavens* (Ps. 57:5). Remove your Presence from their midst!"

I. But the generation of Ahab, even though it was made up of idolators, because there were no renegades among them, would go out to war and won.

J. That is in line with what Obadiah said to Elijah: *Has it not been told my lord what I did when Jezebel killed the prophets of the Lord, how I hid a hundred men of the Lord's prophets by fifties in a cave and fed them with bread and water?* (1 Kgs. 18:13).

K. If bread, why water? This teaches that it was harder to bring water than bread.

L. Elijah announced on Mount Carmel, saying, *And I alone remain as a prophet to the Lord* (1 Kgs. 18:23).

M. Now the entire people knew full well [that there are other prophets who had survived] but they did not reveal it to the king.

5. A. Said R. Samuel bar Nahman, "They said to the snake, 'On what account are you commonly found among fences?'

B. "He said to them, 'Because I broke down the fence of the world [causing man to sin].'

C. "'On what account do you go along with your tongue on the ground?'

D. "He said to them, 'Because my tongue made it happen to me.'

E. "They said to him, 'Now what pleasure do you have form it all? A lion tramples but also devours the prey, a wolf tears but also devours, while you bite and kill but do not devour what you kill.'

F. "He said to them, *Does the snake bite without a charm* (Qoh. 10:11)? Is it possible that I do anything that was not commanded to me from on high?'

G. "'And on what account do you bite a single limb, while all the limbs feel it?'

H. "He said to them, 'Now are you saying that to me? Speak to the slanderer, who says something here and kills his victim in Rome, says something in Rome and kills his victim at the other end of the world.'"

6. A. And why is the slanderer called "the third party"?

B. Because he kills three: the one who speaks slander, the one who receives it, and the one about whom it is said.

C. But in the time of Saul, slander killed four: Doeg, who said it, Saul, who received it, Abimelech, about whom it was said, and Abner.

D. And why was Abner killed?

E. R. Joshua b. Levi said, "Because he made a joke out of the shedding of the blood of young men.

F. "That is in line with this verse of Scripture: *And Abner said to Joab, let the young men get up and play before us* (1Sam. 2:14)."

G. R. Simeon b. Laqish said, "Because he put his name before David's name.

H. "That is in line with this verse of Scripture: *And Abner sent messengers to David right away, saying, Whose is the land* (1 Sam. 3:12).

I. "He wrote, 'From Abner to David.'"

J. Rabbis say, "It was because he did not wait for Saul to become reconciled with David.

K. "That is in line with the following verse of Scripture: *Moreover, my father, see, yes, see the skirt of your robe in my hand* (1 Sam. 24:112). Abner said to him, 'What do you want of this man's boasting! The cloth was caught in a thornbush.'

L. *"When they came within the barricade, he said to him, 'Will you not answer, Abner* (1 Sam. 26:14)."

M. And there are those who say, "It was because he had had the power to protest against Saul in regard to Nob, the city of priests, and he did not do so."

7. A. R. Hanan bar Pazzi interpreted the cited verse *[The sayings of the Lord are pure sayings* (Ps. 12:7)] to apply to the pericope of the Red Cow, which contains seven times seven [references to matters of purification, thus:]

B. seven times is the red cow mentioned, seven times the burning, seven times the sprinkling, seven times the laundering of garments, seven times the matter of uncleanness, seven times the matter of cleanness, seven times the matter of priests.

C. And if someone should say to you that in fact they are lacking [in not mentioning the priests seven times,] say to him, "Moses and Aaron count."

D. *Now the Lord said to Moses and to Aaron, This is the statute of the law which the Lord has commanded* (Num. 19:1-13, pass.).

The entire passage, until No. 7, serves Leviticus Rabbah **XXVI:I-II**, which deals with Lev. 21:1, *And the Lord said to Moses, Speak to the priests.* The focus there is on the purity of speech, hence the reliability of God's statements, the importance of circumlocution in Scripture, the evil of sinful speech such as gossip. Only at No. 7, which has no counterpart in Lev. R., do we reach our base-verse. And then the intersecting-verse and the base-verse meet quite nicely, since the former points up an important trait in the latter. I would be inclined to see everything else as part of the freight attached to the intersecting-verse prior to its inclusion in the present passage, which in my judgment means that materials used for Leviticus Rabbah had attained final formulation before they were adapted for inclusion in Pesiqta deRab Kahana. That is assuredly the case in the matter of the intersecting-verse before us.

IV:III

1. A. R. Isaac opened discourse by citing this verse: "*All this have I proved in wisdom; I say, Would I could get wisdom,*" *yet it is far from me* (Qoh. 7:29).

   B. "It is written, *God gave Solomon wisdom and understanding in large measure...even as the sand that is on the seashore* (1 Kgs. 5:9)."

   C. R. Levi and rabbis:

   D. Rabbis say, "He gave him as much wisdom as all the rest of Israel had put together."

   E. Said R. Levi, "Just as the sand serves as the fence for the sea, so wisdom served as the fence for Solomon."

   F. A proverb says, If you have acquired knowledge, what do you lack, if you lack knowledge, what do you have?

   G. Such a one is a city that is breached and without a wall,

   H. *Like a city broken down and without a wall, so is he whose spirit is without restraint* (Prov. 25:28).

2. A. It is written, *Solomon's wisdom excelled the wisdom of all the children of the east* (1 Kgs. 5:10).

   B. What constituted *the wisdom of the children of the east*?

   C. For they were well informed about the stars and clever at {Braude & Kapstein, p. 65:] ornithomancy.

3. A. Said Rabban Simeon b. Gamaliel, "On three counts I admire the children of the east:

   B. "because they do not put a kiss on the mouth but on the hand,

   C. "because they do not bite at a piece of bread but cut it with a knife,

   D. "because they take counsel only in a broad place [where none can overhear],

   E. "as it is said concerning our father, Jacob, *And Jacob sent and called Rachel and Leah to the field, to his flock* (Gen. 31:4), a broad place."

4. A. *Solomon's wisdom excelled all the wisdom of Egypt* (1 Kgs. 5:10):

   B. What constituted *the wisdom of Egypt*?

   C. You find that when Solomon planned to build the house of the sanctuary, he sent to Pharaoh Neccho, saying to him, "Send me craftsmen, for a salary. For I am planning to build the house of the sanctuary."

   D. What did he do?

   E. He gathered all the astrologers of his court, who looked into the matter and picked out those men who were going to die in that year, and those he sent to him [collecting their wage for work not in fact carried out].

   F. And when they came to Solomon, he looked into the matter through the Holy Spirit, realizing that they were going to die in that year, and he gave them shrouds and sent them back to him.

   G. He sent and wrote to him, saying to him, "Did you not have enough shrouds in Egypt to bury your dead? Here are they, here are their shrouds."

5. A. *He was wiser than all man* (1 Kgs. 5:11):

B. [Since the verse uses for man the word *Adam*, we conclude that] this refers to the first Man.

C. And what constituted the wisdom of the first Man?

D. You find that when the Holy One, blessed be He, planned to create the first Man, he took counsel with the ministering angels, saying to them, *"Shall we make man"* (Gen. 1:26).

E. They said to him, *"Lord of the ages, what is man that you remember him, and the son of man that you think of him* (Ps. 8:5)."

F. He said to them, "This man whom I am planning to create in my world has wisdom greater than yours."

G. What did he do? He collected all the domesticated beasts and the wild beasts and fowl and brought them before them and said to them, "What are the names of these?"

H. But they did not know.

I. When he created the first Man, he collected all the domesticated beasts and the wild beasts and fowl and brought them them and said to him, "What are the names of these?"

J. He said, "This one it is proper to call, 'horse,' and that one it is proper to call, 'lion,' and that one it is proper to call, 'camel,' and that one it is proper to call, 'ox,' and that one it is proper to call, 'eagle,' and that one it is proper to call, 'ass.'"

K. That is in line with this verse: *And Man assigned names to all domesticated beasts and wild beasts and fowl* (Gen. 2:20).

L. He said to him, "And as to you, what is your name?"

M. He said to him, "Man."

N. He said to him, "Why?"

O. He said to him, "Because I have been created from the earth [*adam, adamah*, respectively]."

P. He said to him, "And what is my name?

Q. He said to him, "The Lord,"

R. He said to him, "Why?"

S. He said to him, "For you are the Lord over all those things that you have created."

6. A. Said R. Aha, "Said the Holy One, blessed be He, *'I am the Lord, that is my name* (Is. 42:8).

   B. "'That is the name that the first Man gave to me, that is the name for which I stipulated to myself, that is the name for which I stipulated with the ministering angels.'"

7. A. *[Solomon was wiser than] Ethan the Ezrahite [and Heman and Calcol and Darda the sons of Mahol]* (1 Kgs. 5:11):

   B. *Ethan* is the same as our father, Abraham, as it is written, *A maskil of Ethan the Ezrahite* (Ps. 89:1).

   C. *Heman* [trustworthy] is the same as Moses, *Not so is my servant Moses, he is trusted in all my house* (Num. 12:7).

   D. *Calcol* [the provider] is the same as Joseph, *And Joseph provided for his father* (Gen. 47:12).

   E. The Egyptians said, "Is it not so that this slave has become king over us merely because of his wisdom?"

F. What did they do? They took seventy slips and wrote on them words in seventy languages and threw them before him, and he would read each one in its original language.

G. And not only so, but he also spoke Hebrew, which *they* could not understand.

H. That is in line with this verse of Scripture: *A testimony of Joseph, that is his name, when he went forth to rule Egypt. I understand what is written* (Ps. 81:6).

E. *Darda* is the same as the generation of the wilderness.

F. Why does he call that generation *Darda*? Because they were all filled with knowledge (*deah*).

G. *The sons of Mahol*: these are the Israelites, sons whom the Presence of God forgave on account of the sin of the making of the calf.

8. A. *He uttered three thousand proverbs, [and his songs numbered a thousand and five. He discoursed of trees, from the cedar of Lebanon down to the marjoram that grows out of the wall, of beasts and birds, of reptiles and fishes. Men of all races came to listen to the wisdom of Solomon, and from all the kings of the earth who had heard of his wisdom he received gifts]* (1 Kgs. 4:32-34):

B. Said R. Samuel bar Nahman, "We have reviewed the whole of Scripture and have found that Solomon prophesied only about eight hundred verses, and yet you say, *He uttered three thousand proverbs*?

C. "This teaches that each and every verse of Scripture that he prophesied contains two or three reasons, in line with this verse: *As an earring of gold and also as an ornament of gold, so is the wise reprover* (Prov. 25:12)."

D. And rabbis say, "There were three thousand parables for each verse, a thousand and five reasons for each parable. What is written is not, 'And the song of Solomon,' but rather, *'And its application'* [yielding a thousand and five reasons behind each of the parables]."

9. A. *[He uttered three thousand proverbs, and his songs numbered a thousand and five.] He discoursed on trees, [from the cedar of Lebanon down to the marjoram that grows out of the wall, of beasts and birds, of reptiles and fishes. Men of all races came to listen to the wisdom of Solomon, and from all the kings of the earth who had heard of his wisdom he received gifts]* (1 Kgs. 4:32-34):

B. Is it possible for a person to speak on trees *[from the cedar of Lebanon down to the marjoram that grows out of the wall]?*

C. [The point is that he derived lessons from trees, for example,] Solomon said, "On what account is one afflicted with the skin-disease [described at Leviticus 13-14] purified by the use of a branch from the highest of the high and the lowest of the low [that is, cedar and hyssop, respectively]? It is to indicate that just as this man has raised himself up like a cedar and so has been smitten by the cedar [with the skin-ailment] and now has humbled himself like the hyssop, let him be healed by the hyssop."

10. A. *...of beasts and birds, of reptiles and fishes*:

B. Now is it possible for a person to speak on domesticated beasts and fowl?

C. Said Solomon, "On what account is a beast permitted [for Israelite use] only if it is properly slaughtered as to two indicators of fitness [both the windpipe and the gullet having to be properly cut], while, in the case of fowl, only a single such indicator is required [either the windpipe or the gullet has to be properly cut]?

D. "But as to the domesticated beast, it was created from dry land, while in the case of the fowl, one verse of Scripture indicates that it was from dry land, and another, from the sea.

E. "One verse of Scripture indicates that it was from dry land: *And the Lord God created from the earth all beasts of the field* (Gen. 2:19).

F. "Another verse of Scripture indicates that it was from the sea: *And God said, Let the waters swarm* (Gen. 1:20)."

11. A. Bar Qappara says, "Fowl were created from sea mud."

B. R. Abun in the name of Samuel of Cappodocia: "Nonetheless, the feet of the chicken are like [Braude and Kapstein, p. 69:] the scale-covered skin of fish [and so fowl are considered fish-like]."

12. A. *...of reptiles and fishes*:

B. Now is it possible for a person to speak on reptiles and fishes?

C. Said Solomon, "On what account is it the rule that as to the eight creeping things that are listed in the Torah, one who hunts them and does injury to them is liable [to compensate the owner for his loss], but as to all other abominated things and creeping things, one who does injury to them is exempt from liability?

C. "Because the former have valuable hides."

13. A. *...and fishes*:

B. Now is it possible for a person to speak on fishes?

C. Said Solomon, Why is it the rule that domesticated cattle, wild beasts, and fowl, all have to be subjected to a proper act of slaughter, while fish do not have to be properly slaughtered [but may be eaten even if they expire on their own]?" [This question is answered in the pericope that follows.]

14. A. Jacob of Kefar Naborayya gave a ruling in Tyre that fish require an act of proper slaughter.

B. R. Haggai heard and sent and had him brought before him.

C. He said to him, "Where did you learn this rule?"

D. He said to him, "From that which is written: *And God said, Let the waters swarm with living things, the wild beast and fowl* (Gen. 1:20). Just as fowl requires an act of slaughter, so fish should be subjected to slaughter."

E. He said, "Bend over, to receive your beating [for presenting an improper ruling]."

F. He said to him, "Is someone who has given a teaching of the Torah going to be flogged?"

G. He said to him, "The verse of the Torah is inappropriate. [You did not give a valid ruling.]"

H. He said to him, "And which one is appropriate?"

I. He said to him, "This verse of Scripture: *Shall the flocks and the herds be slaughtered for them? Or shall all the fish of the sea be gathered for them?* (Num. 11:22).

J. "What is written is not, 'Shall all the fish of the sea be slaughtered for them,' but, *shall all the fish of the sea be gathered for them?* "

K. He said to him, "Administer your strokes, for it is an appropriate flogging."

15. A. Jacob of Kefar Naborayya gave a ruling in Tyre that the son of a gentile woman may be circumcised on the Sabbath [as though he were an Israelite, on account of whom one sets aside the prohibitions of the Sabbath in order to effect the circumcision].

B. R. Haggai heard and sent and had him brought before him.

C. He said to him, "Where did you learn this rule?"

D. He said to him, "From that which is written: *They declared their pedigrees after their families, by their fathers' household* [so the child of a Jewish man and a gentile woman is valid as an Israelite, since he is given the status of the father, not the mother] (Num. 1:18). And it is written, *On the eighth day will every male be circumcised* (Gen. 17:12)."

E. He said, "Bend over, to receive your beating [for presenting an improper ruling]."

F. He said to him, "Is someone who has given a teaching of the Torah going to be flogged?"

G. He said to him, "The verse of the Torah is inappropriate. [You did not give a valid ruling.]"

H. He said to him, "And which one is appropriate?"

I. He said, "First bend over, then listen."

J. He said to him, "If a gentile should come to you and say to you, 'I want to be made into a Jew, on condition that I be circumcised on the Sabbath day or on the Day of Atonement, will they profane those days on his account?"

K. He said to him, "No, they do not profane those days on his account, but only on account of the son of an Israelite."

L. He said to him, "And what verse of Scripture applies? *Now therefore let us make a covenant with our God to put away all the wives and such as are born of them according to the counsel of the Lord* (Ezra 10:3) [so the children are in the status of the mother, therefore gentile]."

M. He said to him, "Are you going to administer a flogging to me because of what is taught [not in the Torah but in a book in the category of mere] tradition?"

M. He said to him, "It is written in that same passage, *And it is treated like the Torah* (Ezra 10:3)."

N. He said to him, "In accord with which [passage of] the Torah?"

O. He said to him, "It is in line with this teaching of R,. Yohanan in the name of R. Simeon b. Yohai: *'Neither shall you make marriages with them, your daughter you shall not give to his son* (Deut. 7:3). Why so? *For he will turn away your son from following me* (Deut. 7:4). 'Your son' born of a Israelite woman is called *your son* , but 'your son' born of a gentile woman is not called *your son.*'"

P. He said to him, "Administer your strokes, for it is an appropriate flogging."

16. A. Said Solomon, "I have fully grasped all of these other matters, but as to the passage about the Red Cow, when I came to it, I investigated it and studied it, but *I say, 'Would I could get wisdom,' yet it is far from me* (Qoh 7:29)."

This pastiche of materials pertinent to the wisdom of Solomon ends up with the theme of our pericope, but hardly contributes to its exposition. For the only point that the compositor makes is that while Solomon was very wise, he could not understand the rules at hand and explain them. No. 1, 15 form an intersecting-verse/base-verse composition. The rest of the materials go their own way, for the entire passage centers on the theme of Solomon's wisdom and merely proves the proposition that Solomon was wise. We have no reference to the intersecting-verse, Qoh. 7:29, until the very end. Here again we deal with a form different from the intersecting-verse/base-verse pattern. The theme, not the exegesis of verses, whether primary or secondary, predominates. No. 1 then works not on the intersecting-verse but on a proof-text cited separately from that verse, 1 Kgs. 5:9. Nos. 2-15 expound another set of such verses, 1 Kgs. 5:10ff.

IV:IV

1. A. *Who is wise enough for all this? Who knows the meaning of anything? Wisdom lights up a man's face, [and the strength of his face is changed]* (Qoh 8:1):
   B. *Who is wise enough for all this:* this refers to the Holy One, blessed be He, concerning whom it is written: *The Lord by wisdom founded the earth, by understanding he established the heavens* (Prov. 3:19).
   C. *Who knows the meaning of anything:* for he explained the meaning of the Torah to Israel.

2. A. *Wisdom lights up a man's face:*
   B. Said R. Yudan, "Great is the power of the prophets, who compare the likeness of the Almighty above to the likeness of man.
   C. "[For example:] *And I heard the voice of a man between the banks of Ulai* (Dan;. 8:16)."
   D. Said R. Judah b. R. Simon, "[To prove that point] there are still better verses of Scripture than that one: *And upon the likeness of the throne was the likeness of the appearance of a man* (Ez. 1:26).
   E. "*And the strength of his face is changed* (Qoh. 8:1), for it is changed on account of Israel from that of the attribute of strict justice to that of the attribute of mercy."

3. A. Another comment on the verse: *Who is wise enough for all this? [Who knows the meaning of anything? Wisdom lights up a man's face, and the strength of his face is changed]* (Qoh 8:1):
   B. *Who is wise enough for all this:* this speaks of the first Man.
   C. For it is written, *You seal most accurate, full of wisdom and perfect in beauty* (Ez. 28:12).
   D. *And who knows the meaning of anything:* for he explained the names of every creature: *And Man assigned names* (Gen. 2:20).

E. *Wisdom lights up a man's face:*

F. R. Levi in the name of R. Simeon b. Menassia: "The round part of the first Man's heal outshone the orb of the sun.

G. "And do not find that fact surprising, for in ordinary practice a person makes for himself two salvers, one for himself and one for a member of his household. Which of the two is the finer? Is it not his own?

H. "So the first Man was created for the service of the Holy One, blessed be He, while the orb of the sun was created only for the service of the created world.

I. "Is it not an argument *a fortiori* that the round part of the first Man's heal outshone the orb of the sun.

J. "And the countenance of his face all the more so!"

4. A. R. Levi in the name of R. Hamah bar Hanina: "Thirteen marriage canopies did the Holy One, blessed be He, weave for him in the Garden of Eden.

B. "That is in line with this verse of Scripture: *You were in Eden, the Garden of God, every kind of precious stone was your covering: the carnelian, the topaz, and the emerald, the beryl, the onyx, and the jasper, the sapphire, the carbuncle, and the smaragd, and gold* (Ez. 28;13)."

C. R. Simeon b. Laqish says, "There were eleven."

D. Rabbis say, "There were ten."

E. But there is no dispute among them.

F. One who maintains that there were thirteen treats *each precious stone, every kind*, and *was your covering* to encompass three more.

G. The one who maintains that there were eleven counts the phrase, *every kind of precious stone*, to indicate there was one more.

H. And the one who counts ten treats *every precious stone* as a general clause.

5. A. Now despite all of this glory: *For you are dust and to dust you return* (Gen. 3:19).

B. *...and the strength of his face is changed:*

C. When he said to him, *The woman whom* you *gave me...* (Gen. 3:12), then the Holy One, blessed be He, changed his face and drove him out of the Garden of Eden.

D. For it is written, *You change his face and send him away* (Job 14:20).

E. And Scripture states, *The Lord God sent him away from the Garden of Eden* (Gen. 3:23).

6. A. Another comment on the verse: *Who is wise enough for all this? [Who knows the meaning of anything? Wisdom lights up a man's face, and the strength of his face is changed]* (Qoh 8:1):

B. *Who is wise enough for all this*: this speaks of Israel,

C. concerning whom it is written, *Surely this great nation is a wise and understanding people* (Deut. 4:6).

D. *And who knows the meaning of anything*: for they know how to explain the Torah in forty-nine ways to reach a ruling for uncleanness, and in forty-nine ways to reach a conclusion in favor of cleanness.

E. *Wisdom lights up a man's face:*

F.   R. Zakkai of Sheab in the name of R. Samuel bar Nahman, "You find that, when the Israelites stood at Mount Sinai and said, *All which the Lord has spoken we shall do and hear* (Ex. 24:7), he imparted to them part of the splendor of the Presence of God above.

G.   "That is in line with this verse of Scripture: *And your renown went forth among the nations for your beauty, for it was perfect, through my splendor which I placed on you* (Ez. 16:14).

H.   "But when they made the statement to that thing: *This is your god, O Israel* (Ex. 32:4,) they turned into the enemies of the Holy One, blessed be He.

I.   "That is in line with this verse of Scripture: *...and the strength of his face is changed.*

J.   "The letters for the word *changed* may be read *hated.*

K.   "Then the Holy One, blessed be He, changed [his plans] for them: *Therefore like man you will die, and like one of the princes you will fall* (Ps. 82:7)."

7.   A.   Another comment on the verse: *Who is wise enough for all this? [Who knows the meaning of anything? Wisdom lights up a man's face, And the strength of his face is changed]* (Qoh 8:1):

B.   *Who is wise enough for all this*: this speaks of a disciple of sages.

C.   *And who knows the meaning of anything*: when he knows how to explain the Mishnah-passage that is his.

D.   *Wisdom lights up a man's face:* when he receives a question and answers it properly.

F.   *...and the strength of his face is changed:* when he receives a question and cannot answer it correctly.

8.   A.   Rabbi was in session and teaching, "How do we know that one cannot effect a valid exchange of one beast for another in the case of a firstling [so that if one says, 'This beast is in the place of that beast,' the first beast, of which he made the statement, is unaffected and does not enter the status of the firstling]?"

B.   Bar Pedaiah's face lit up.

C.   [Rabbi said,] "This one knows the sense of that which I am here in session and teaching."

9.   A.   A gentile saw that the face of R. Judah bar Ilai was shining and said, "As to this man, one of the following three rules applies to him:

B.   "Either he is lending at usurious interest, or he's raising pigs, or he has drunk wine."

C.   R. Judah bar Ilai heard the statement and said, "May that man's wind burst, for none of those categories applies to me.

D.   "I assuredly do not lend at usurious interest, for it is written, *You shall not lend interest to your brother, interest of money, interest of food, interest of anything that is lent on interest* (Deut. 23:20).

E.   "I certainly do not raise pigs, for it is forbidden for any Israelite to raise pigs, for we have learned in the Mishnah: **An Israelite may not raise pigs anywhere** (M. Baba Qamma 7:7).

F.   "And I do not drink wine, for merely on account of the four cups of wine which I drink on the night of Passover, I have to hold my head from Passover to Pentecost."

G.   (R. Mana has to hold his head on that same account from Passover to Tabernacles.)

H.   He said to him, "Then why is your face glowing?"

I.   He said to him, "It is the Torah that illuminates me.

J.   "For it is written, *Wisdom lights up a man's face.*"

10. A.   R. Abbahu went to Caesarea and he came from there with his face glowing.

B.   His disciples saw him. They went and told R. Yohanan, "Lo, R. Abbahu has found a treasure."

C.   He said to them, "Why so?"

D.   They said to him, "Because his face is glowing."

E.   He said to them, "Perhaps he has learned a new teaching of the Torah."

F.   He went to him. He said to him, "What new teaching of the Torah has you learned?"

G.   He said to him, "An ancient passage of the Tosefta has been stated."

H.   He recited in his regard: *Wisdom lights up a man's face.*

11. A.   Another comment on the verse: *Who is wise enough for all this? [Who knows the meaning of anything? Wisdom lights up a man's face, And the strength of his face is changed]* (Qoh 8:1):

B.   *Who is wise enough for all this*: this speaks of Moses, concerning whom it is written, *A wise man scales the city of the mighty [and brings down the strength [that is, the Torah] wherein it trusts]* (Prov. 21:22).

C.   *And who knows the meaning of anything*: for he explained the Torah to Israel.

D.   *Wisdom lights up a man's face:*

E.   R. Mani of Sheab, R. Joshua of Sikhnin in the name of R. Levi: "Concerning each item that the Holy One, blessed be He, discussed with Moses, he told him about how it becomes unclean and how it may be made clean. When he reached the passage, *Speak to the priests* (Lev. 21:1), he said to him, 'Lord of the ages, If a priest should become unclean, how will he be made clean?' But he did not reply to him.

F.   "At that moment our lord Moses's face grew dark, in line with this verse: *and the strength of his face is changed.*

G.   "But when he reached the passage concerning the red cow, the Holy One, blessed be He, said to him, 'Moses, as to that statement that I made to you, *Speak to the priests* (Lev. 21:1), on which occasion you said to me, "'Lord of the ages, If a priest should become unclean, how will he be made clean?" and I gave you no answer – this is the means by which he will be made clean:

H.   *"For such uncleanness they shall take some of the ash from the burnt mass of the sin offering and add fresh water to it in a utensil* (Num. 19:17).

I.   "And what then is that answer [that God gave to Moses]? *That is the ordinance of the Torah* (Num. 19:2)."

The basic pattern in the interpretation of the intersecting-verse is to point to a case in which someone had wisdom but acted unwisely. The wisdom is demonstrated through reference to the capacity to explain a difficult matter. Then the person subject to description is said to have sinned, his face changed, and God changed his plans for that person. The form of intersecting-verse/base-verse is followed, since we fully work out the intersecting-verse, assigning a range of settings to which it applies, and then bring the intersecting-verse back to the base-verse. No. 1 links admirably with the concluding passage. The verse speaks of God, who has the wisdom to explain to Moses the sense of the rite of the red cow. No. 2 is not a very smooth exposition. But once we reach No. 3, we follow the path without many turnings: the first Man, is shown first in glory, then in his fall, and then the same pattern applies to Israel. There is a fair amount of intruded material. The disciple of the sages does not follow the pattern, for the point of the exposition shifts. The sole important observation now is that the disciple of the sages glows through his study of the Torah. That has no bearing on the point the compositor wishes to make, and the entire set of materials, Nos. 7-10, is inserted solely because of the notion that *Wisdom lights up a man's face.* As I said, Moses recovers the basic pattern. But the point made earlier of the first Man and Israel, that is, the sin that causes *the strength of his face to be changed,* no longer pertains. So at the climax and conclusion of No. 11 we see a shift in the exegetical pattern imputed to the intersecting-verse as we recover the base-verse.

IV:V

1. A. *Moses and Aaron among his priests, and Samuel among those who call on his name, [called to the Lord and he answered. He spoke to them in a pillar of cloud; they followed his teaching and kept the statute that he gave them]* (Ps. 99:6-7):

    B. R. Yudan in the name of R. Joseph bar Judah, R. Berekhiah in the name of R. Joshua b. Qorhah: "During all those forty years that the Israelites spent in the wilderness, Moses did not refrain from serving in the high priesthood.

    C. "That is in line with this verse of Scripture: *Moses and Aaron among his priests, and Samuel among those who call on his name.*"

    D. R. Berekhiah in the name of R. Simeon derived the same fact from this verse: "*And the sons of Amram, Aaron and Moses, and Aaron was separated, that he should be sanctified as most holy* (1 Chr. 23:13).

    E. "What follows immediately afterward? *And Moses, man of God. But his sons were assigned to the tribe of Levi* (1 Chr. 23:14)."

2. A. Said R. Eleazar bar Joseph, "It is quite clear to us that in the wilderness Moses served in the white garments."

    B. Said R. Tanhum bar Yudan, and it has been taught on Tannaite authority, "All the seven days of dedication [of the tabernacle] Moses served in the high priesthood, and the Presence of God did not come to rest on his account. When Aaron came and served in the high priesthood, however, the Presence of God came to rest on his account.

C. "That is in line with this verse: *For on this day the Lord has appeared to you* (Lev. 9:4)."

3. A. *...called to the Lord and he answered:*

B. this one called and was answered, and that one called and was answered.

C. *He spoke to them in a pillar of cloud:*

D. We find in the case of Moses that he spoke with him in a cloud, for it is written, *And the Lord came down in a cloud and stood* (Ex. 34:5). *And the Lord came down in a cloud and spoke* (Num. 11:25).

E. In the case of Aaron he spoke with him in a pillar of cloud: *And the Lord came down in a pillar of cloud and stood at the tent of meeting and called Aaron* (Num. 12:5).

F. But in the case of Samuel, we have found no such case.

G. And where have we heard of such an instance? *And they answered them and said, he is; behold he is before you* (1 Sam. 9:12).

H. R. Yudan in the name of R. Mari bar Jacob: "The women said to them, 'Do you not see the cloud that is affixed above his courtyard? This is only the cloud, concerning which it is written, *And so it was when the cloud was upon the tabernacle* (Num. 9:20).'"

4. A. *...they followed his teaching and kept the statute that he gave them:*

B. We have heard in the case of Moses that the Torah was written in his name: *Remember the Torah of Moses, my servant* (Malachi 3:22).

C. And we have heard the same in the case of Samuel, that a book was written for him, as it is written, *And he wrote in a book and laid it before the Lord* (1 Sam. 10:25).

D. But in the case of Aaron, we have found no such matter.

E. This teaches that a particular passage was given to him, that it not depart from him or his sons or his sons' sons forever for all generations, and what is that? It is the passage beginning: *This is the statute of the Torah* (Num. 19:2).

On the surface the intersecting-verse returns to the base-verse only in a casual way, hardly illuminating the issue of the base-verse except in one aspect: that the rite of burning the cow is for the express requirement of the priesthood. What is not noted is that at Num. 19:1 the passage assigns the revelation to *both* Moses and Aaron. That may have won the attention of the exegete. Then we are told that the two were equal – both serving as high priests, so No. 1, which leads us to No. 2's point that Aaron's service was superior. The matched set at Nos. 3, 4 then leads us to the desired conclusion. The intersecting-verse therefore allows us to point up the equality of the priesthood in the present passage, which is implicit at Num. 19:1.

IV:VI

1. A. R. Joshua of Sikhnin in the name of R. Levi: "There are four matters concerning which the impulse to do evil brings doubts, and in the case of all of them, the word *statute* occurs. These are they: the rules governing the prohibition of marrying a brother's wife, the prohibition

of mixed species, the rule governing the goat that is sent forth [on the Day of Atonement] and the rule governing the red cow.

B. "As to the matter of the brother's wife: *You will not uncover the nakedness of your brother's wife* (Lev. 18:16). But it is also written, *Her levir will have sexual relations [and take her as his wife]* (Deut. 25:5). When the brother is alive, she is forbidden, but when he dies without children, she is permitted to her, and in that case the word *statute* occurs: *You will guard my statutes and my judgments, which one will do and live* (Lev. 18:5).

C. "As to the matter of mixed species: *You will not wear mixed species [wool and linen together]* (Deut. 22:11), but the case of a woolen cloak bearing linen show-fringes is one in which it is permitted to do just that. And in that case too the word *statute* occurs: *You will keep my statutes* (Lev. 19:19).

D. "As to the matter of the goat that is sent away: *The one who sends the goat to Azazel shall wash his clothes* (Lev. 16:26). The goat itself effects atonement for others [yet imparts uncleanness]. And in that regard, the word *statute* occurs: *And you shall have this rule as an eternal statute* (Lev. 16:29).

E. "And as to the red cow: there we have learned in the Mishnah, **All those who are occupied with the work of burning the red cow from beginning to end impart uncleanness to clothing.** The cow's ashes themselves effect purification for the unclean [and yet those who burn the cow are unclean]. And the word *statute* occurs in context: *This is the statute of the Torah* (Num. 19:23)."

The composition is not particular to our base-verse, and it makes the point already introduced at the very outset, namely, the paradox involved in the uncleanness of a rite which effects cleanness. But the proposition is broader, namely, the appearance of the word *statute* indicates that a matter is beyond rational explanation.

IV:VII

1. A. *...Tell the people of Israel to bring you a red heifer [without defect, in which there is no blemish, and upon which a yoke has never come]:*

B. Lulianus bar Tiberias in the name of R. Isaac: "[Braude & Kapstein, p. 79, citing E. E. Urbach:] "You initiate the rite."

2. A. R. Azariah said in the name of R. Isaac, and R. Yose bar Hanina: "Said to him the Holy One, blessed be He, Moses, to you I am revealing the duties of burning the red cow, but to others they will stand as a *statute* [lacking all explanation]."

B. For R. Huna said, *"At the set time which I appoint, I will judge with equity* (Ps. 75:2). *And it shall come to pass in that day that there shall be not light but heavy clouds and thick ones* (Zech. 14:6). The word for *thick ones* is written so as to be read [Braude and Kapstein, p. 79:], *perspicuous* thus matters which are hidden from you in this world are destined to be as clear as crystal to you.

C. "That is in line with this verse of Scripture: *I will bring the blind in a way that they have not know. I will make darkness light before them...These things I have done* (Is. 42:16).

D. "What is written is not, 'These things I shall do,' but, *These things I have done, and I shall not abandon them* (Is. 42:16).

E. "I have already done them for Rabbi Aqiba and his colleagues [explaining to him secrets of the Torah]."

F. For R. Aha said, "Matters which were not revealed to Moses at Sinai were revealed to R. Aqiba and his colleagues.

G. *"And his eye sees every precious thing* (Job 28:10) – this is R. Aqiba."

3. A. *[...Tell the people of Israel to bring you a red heifer:]* Said R. Yose bar Hanina, "[In saying, *bring you,*] he gave an indication that all the red cows will ultimately be null, but yours will endure."

B. R. Aha in the name of R. Yose bar Haninah: "When Moses went up to the highest heaven, he heard the voice of the Holy One, blessed be He, in session and engaged in teaching the passage of the red cow, saying a law in the name of the authority who laid it down: **R. Eliezer says, 'A heifer whose neck is broken is to be a year old and a red cow, two years old'** [M. Par. 1:1].

C. "Moses said before the Holy One, blessed be He, 'Lord of the ages, 'All beings above and below are in your dominion, and yet you go into session and teach a law in the name of the authority who laid it down!'

D. "Said to him the Holy One, blessed be He, 'Moses, a righteous man is destined to arise in my world and destined to open discourse with the passage on the red cow: **R. Eliezer says, 'A heifer whose neck is broken is to be a year old and a red cow, two years old'** [M. Par. 1:1].'

E. "He said before him, 'Lord of the ages, may it please you that such a one come from my loins.'

F. "He said to him, 'By your life, he will come from your loins.'

G. "That is in line with this verse of Scripture: *And the name of one of them was Eliezer* (Ex. 18:4). And the name of that distinguished figure was Eliezer."

4. A. There we have learned in the Mishnah: **Abba Saul says, "As to the ramp for the cow [to be brought to the altar,] the high priests made it out of their own funds. One of them would not bring out the red cow that he was going to prepare on the ramp belonging to his fellow. But he would destroy the old one and go and build a new one out of his own resources"** [M. Sheq. 4:2].

B. R. Aha in the name of R. Hanina: "He would spend more than sixty talents of gold."

C. And lo, it has been taught on Tannaite authority: **Simeon the Righteous prepared two red cows, and it was not on the ramp that he brought out the first of the two that he brought out the second** [cf. M. Sheq. 4:3].

D. Can you say of that righteous man that he was so wasteful?

E. R. Abun in the name of R. Eleazar: "It was on account of the meticulous rules applying to the red cow [that he did so]."

5. A. A gentile asked Rabban Yohanan ben Zakkai, saying to him, "These rites that you carry out look like witchcraft. You bring a cow and slaughter it, burn it, crush the remains, take the dust, and if one of you contracts corpse uncleanness, you sprinkle on him two or three times and say to him, 'You are clean.'"

   B. He said to him, "Has a wandering spirit never entered you?"

   C. He said to him, "No."

   D. He said to him, "And have you ever seen someone into whom a wandering spirit entered?"

   E. He said to him, "Yes."

   F. He said to him, "And what do you do?"

   G. He said to him, "People bring roots and smoke them under him and sprinkle water on the spirit and it flees."

   H. He said to him, "And should your ears not hear what your mouth speaks? So this spirit is the spirit of uncleanness, as it is written, *I will cause prophets as well as the spirit of uncleanness to flee from the land* (Zech. 13:2)."

   I. After the man had gone his way, his disciples said to him, "My lord, this one you have pushed off with a mere reed. To us what will you reply?"

   J. He said to them, "By your lives! It is not the corpse that imparts uncleanness nor the water that effects cleanness. But it is a decree of the Holy One, blessed be He.

   K. "Said the Holy One, blessed be He, 'A statute have I enacted, a decree have I made, and you are not at liberty to transgress my decree: *This is the* statute *of the Torah* (Num. 19:1).'"

I see a mere pastiche of thematically related materials, not a systematic exegesis of the cited verse. Following Urbach, we read No. 1 to mean that it was Moses who was to initiate the rite first of all. No. 2 reverts to the basic message, which is that the rite is essentially without rhyme or reason. Now the point is made that at some point in the future someone will understand it. But no clear effort is made to follow up on that matter. We are simply referred to Aqiba. 3.A seems to me a singleton. 3.B then returns to the prior theme, the capacity of later generations to make sense of the rite. But the substance of discourse diverges; now the point is that Eliezer bears the name of one of Moses's sons. No. 4 is utterly miscellaneous, with no connections fore or aft. No. 5 also is parachuted down, restating the point that the whole rite is nonsensical, a decree of God to be accepted without reasoned inquiry.

IV:VIII

1. A. On what account are the animals used for all other offerings to be males, while, in this case, the animal is a female?

   B. Said R. Aibu, "The matter may be compared to the case of a slave girl's son who took a crap in the royal palace.

   C. "Said the king, 'Let his mother come and wipe up the shit that her nursling made.'

   D. "So said the Holy One, blessed be He, 'Let the red cow come and effect atonement for the sin of making the golden calf.'"

The miscellany continues, a working through of the details of Scripture without pretense at an exegetical interest.

IV:IX

1. A,. ...*a heifer:* this refers to Egypt: *Egypt is a very fair heifer* (Jer. 46:20).
   B. ...*red:* this refers to Babylonia: *You are the head of gold* (Dan. 2:38).
   C. ...*without defect:* this refers to Media.
   D. Said R. Hiyya bar Abba, "The kings of Media were without fault. The sole complaint that the Holy One, blessed be He, has against them is idolatry, which, in any case, they inherited from their ancestors."
   E. ...*in which there is no blemish:* this refers to Greece.
   F. When Alexander of Macedonia saw Simeon the Righteous, he stood on his feet and said, "Blessed be the God of Simeon the Righteous."
   G. His courtiers said to him, "Are you standing up before a Jew?"
   H. He said to them, "When I go into battle, I see his face and conquer."
   I. ...*and upon which a yoke has never come:* this refers to the wicked Edom, which did not accept upon itself the yoke of the Holy One, blessed be He.
   J. And it was not sufficient for Edom that it did not accept upon itself the yoke, but it also blasphemed and cursed and said, *Whom do I have in heaven* (Ps. 73:25).

2. A. *You shall give it to Eleazar the priest, [and it shall be taken outside the camp and slaughtered to the east of it. Eleazar the priest shall take some of the blood on his finger and sprinkle it seven times toward the front of the Tent of the Presence. The cow shall be burnt in his sight, skin, flesh and blood, together with the offal. The priest shall then take cedar-wood, marjoram, and scarlet thread and throw them into the heart of the fire in which the cow is burning]* (Num. 19:3-6). *Eleazar:* [the name means] "God, who is a priest, helps."
   B. ...*and it shall be taken outside the camp:* for [God] is going to push [Edom's] priest outside of the pale [of his encampment].
   C. ...*and slaughtered to the east of it:* For the Lord has a sacrifice in Bosrah [place of refuge of the prince of Edom (Braude and Kapstein, p. 83, n. 110)] *and a great slaughter in the land of Edom* (Is. 34:6).
   D. Said R. Berekhiah, 'The slaughter of a great one will take place in the land of Edom."
   E. ...*The cow shall be burnt in his sight:*
   F. *The fourth beast...was handed over to be burned with fire* (Dan. 7:11).
   G. ...*skin, flesh and blood, together with the offal:*
   H. [Edom, together with] its dukes, its hyparchs, and its generals.
   I. *Your wealth, your staple wares, your imports, your sailors and your helmsmen, your caulkers, your merchants, and your warriors, all your ship's company, all who were with you were flung into the sea on the day of your disaster; at the cries of your helmsmen the troubled waters tossed* (Ez. 27:27-28):
   J. Said R. Samuel bar R. Isaac, "*All your ship's company* encompasses even those who had been of my company and had gone and joined your company – even they *were flung into the sea on the day of your disaster.*"

This stunning word-for-word exegesis of the base-verse now reads the entire passage in light of Israel's history among the empires, here five, including Egypt, but ordinarily, four, Babylonia, Media, Greece, then Rome=Edom – as always, last and worst, different from the others, but, also, the empire that comes immediately prior to the salvation of Israel. The concluding point, that Israelites who had gone over to Edom will be enveloped in Edom's coming disaster, cannot be missed, since it is the goal of the whole reading. No. 1 assembles the conventional repertoire of items on the first three (here: four) monarchies. The intent, as I said, is to underline the egregious character of the fourth. The red cow symbolizes all four, the uncleanness out of which purity – Israel's coming salvation – will emerge. The yoke of 1.I need not be read too literally, e.g., as the yoke of the commandments. No. 2 then moves forward, leaving behind the other kingdoms and concentrating on Edom=Rome, to make the point at the end. **IV:IX** cannot be read in isolation from **IV:X**, which completes the point with a powerful complement.

IV:X

1. A,. Another matter: *...a heifer:* this refers to Israel: *For like a stubborn heifer Israel was stubborn* (Hos. 4:16).

   B. *...red:* this refers to Israel: *...were redder than rubies* (Lam. 4:7).

   C. *...without defect:* this refers to Israel: *My dove, my perfect one, is unique* (Song 6:9).

   D. *...in which there is no blemish:* this refers to Israel: *You were all fair, my love, and there was no blemish in you* (Song 4:7).

   E. *...and upon which a yoke has never come:* this refers to Israel. in the generation of Jeremiah, which did not accept the yoke of the Holy One, blessed be He.

   F. *You shall give it to Eleazar the priest:* this refers to Jeremiah, *one of the priests of Anatoth* (Jer. 1:1).

   G. *...and it shall be taken outside the camp: Nebuchadnezzar ...carried the people away to Babylonia* (Ezra 5:12).

   H. *...and slaughtered to the east of it: And the sons of Zedekiah he slaughtered before him* (2 Kgs. 25:7).

   I. *The cow shall be burnt in his sight: He burned the house of the Lord and the house of the king* (2 Kgs. 25:9).

   J. *...skin, flesh and blood, together with the offal: And all of the houses of Jerusalem, and the entire great house, he burned with fire* (2 Kgs. 25:9).

   K. Why is it called the great house? This is the study-house of Rabban Yohanan ben Zakkai, in which the greatness of the Holy One, blessed be He, was expounded.

   L. *...shall take [some of the blood on his finger and sprinkle it seven times toward the front of the Tent of the Presence]:* this refers to Nebuchadnezzar, the evil man.

   M. *...cedar-wood, marjoram, and scarlet thread [and throw them into the heart of the fire in which the cow is burning]* (Num. 19:3-6): this refers to Hananiah, Mishael, and Azariah.

N.   *...and throw them into the heart of the fire in which the cow is burning:
      The flame of fire slew those men* (Dan. 3:22).

O.   *[Then a man who is clean] shall collect [the ashes of the cow]* (Num.
      19:9): this refers to the Holy One, blessed be He: *He will lift up a
      standard to the nations and collect the scattered ones of Israel* (Is.
      11:12).

P.   *[Then] a man who is clean shall collect [the ashes of the cow and deposit
      them outside the camp in a clean place]* (Num. 19:9): this refers to the
      Holy One, blessed be He, for it is written, *The Lord is a man of war* (Ex.
      15:3).

Q.   *[Then a man] who is clean [shall collect [the ashes of the cow and
      deposit them outside the camp in a clean place]* (Num. 19:9): this refers
      to the Holy One, blessed be He, as it is written, *You who have eyes too
      pure to look at evil* (Hab. 1:13).

R.   *...the ashes of the cow:* this refers to Israel's exiles.

S.   *...and deposit them outside the camp in a clean place:* this refers to
      Jerusalem, which is clean.

T.   *They shall be reserved for use by the community of Israel in the water of
      ritual purification; for the cow is a sin-offering* (Num. 19:9): this is
      because, in this age, decisions of uncleanness and rites of purification
      rest upon the instructions of the priest, but in the age to come, the Holy
      One, blessed be He, is destined to effect Israel's purification, as it is
      written, *I shall sprinkle on you water that purifies* (Ez. 36:25).

The complete and systematic exegesis is fully exposed, since the first go-
around pertained to the other empires of the history of humanity, and the second
read the rite in light of Israel's salvation. The presentation of Israel as
counterpart to Rome is exact and corresponds in detail. The point is that the
destruction of the Temple and of Jerusalem effected the purification of Israel as
the burning of the red cow produces purification-water, and in history, as in
nature, we look for the counterpart in the age to come as in supernature. Hence
God will purify Israel through the historical rite of the burning of Jerusalem:
purification out of the impure.

Pisqa Five

[The Lord said to Moses and Aaron in the land of Egypt,] "This month *[shall be for you the beginning of months; it shall be the first month of the year for you]"*
(Ex. 12:1-2).

V:I

1. A. *He appointed the moon for [lunar] seasons, yet the sun knows its coming* (Ps. 104:19):

   B Said R. Yohanan, "Only the orb of the sun was created for the purpose of giving light.

   C. *"Let there be light* (Gen. 1:14):

   D. "What is written is *light* [in the singular].

   E. "If so, why was the moon created? It was for the signification of the seasons, specifically so that, through [regular sightings of the moon, Israelites would] sanctify new months and years."

   F. R. Shila of Kefar Tamarata in the name of R. Yohanan: "Nonetheless: *The sun knows its coming* (Ps. 104:19). On the basis of that statement, we have the following rule: people count the advent of the new moon only once the sun has set."

   G. [Proving the foregoing proposition,] Yusta, an associate, in the name of R. Berekhiah: "*And they traveled from Raamses in the first month on the fifteenth day of the month* (Num. 33:3). Now if one counts only by the month, up to this point there had been only fourteen [Genesis Rabbah 6:1: thirteen] sunsets. [Freedman, *Genesis Rabbah*, p. 41, n. 4: This is based on the tradition that the Nisan – the first month – in which the Exodus took place fell on a Thursday, while the actual new moon occurred after midday on the preceding Wednesday. It is further assumed that, when this happens, the moon is not visible until the second evening following, i.e., the evening of Friday. Hence if we counted time solely from when the new moon is visible, then by the Thursday on which they left, a fortnight after, there would only have been thirteen sunsets. Since, however, it is called the *fifteenth* of the month, we see that the month was calculated from the first sunset after the new moon.]

   F. "One must therefore conclude that one counts the beginning of the month only from sunset."

2. A. R. Azariah in the name of R. Hanina: "Only the orb of the sun was created for the purpose of giving light.

   B. *"Let there be light* (Gen. 1:14):

   C. "What is written is *light* [in the singular].

   D. "If so, why was the moon created at all?

    E.   "The Holy One, blessed be He, foresaw that the nations of the world were going to make [the heavenly bodies] into gods. Said the Holy One, blessed be He, 'Now if they are two and contradict one another, and nonetheless, the nations of the world treat them as gods, if they are only one, how much the more so [will the nations of the world find reason to worship the heavenly body]!'"

    F.   R. Berekhiah in the name of R. Simon: "Both of them were created in order to give light, as it is said, *And they shall serve for light* (Gen. 1:14)."

3. A.   *And they shall serve as lights* (Gen. 1:15). *And God put them in the firmament of the heaven* (Gen. 1:17). *And they shall serve as signs and for seasons* (Gen. 1:14).

    B.   *And they shall serve as signs* (Gen. 1:14) refers to Sabbaths, for it is written, *For it is a sign for you* (Ex. 31:13).

    C.   *And for seasons* refers to the three pilgrim festivals.

    D.   *And for days* refers to new months.

    E.   *And years* refers to the sanctification of years.

    F.   Indicating in all that the nations of the world will follow a solar calendar, and Israel, a lunar one:

    G.   *The Lord said to Moses and Aaron in the land of Egypt, "This month shall be for you the beginning of months; it shall be the first month of the year for you"* (Ex. 12:1-2).

What captures interest in the base-verse is the reference to month, that is, new moon, and the stress that it is the new moon that marks the beginning of the months and the years. The further theme, to appear shortly, joins the new moon's appearance to the coming redemption, and further identifies the month of the original redemption, the Exodus, as the month of the final redemption. That of course is Nisan, the month in which Passover falls. Accordingly, the first of the two themes at hand – the importance of the lunar calendar – makes its appearance now, and the second, the association of redemption with the new moon of Nisan, will shortly make its appearance. This composition serves at Genesis Rabbah 6:1 and only at the end makes its contribution to the exegesis of Ex. 12:1-2. The intersection is merely thematic; there is no interest in the base-verses, which at Genesis Rabbah 6:1 do not occur anyhow. Nos. 1, 2 work out the implications of the intersecting-verse, which introduces the view that, while the sun is meant to give light, the moon serves some other purpose. That other purpose is for Israel's calendar, as we see at the end. We see the view, which is Yohanan's, is contradicted at the end by Berekhiah. The force of the intersecting-verse is not merely to illuminate the base-verse but to propose a syllogism in connection with the theme at hand, which, autonomous of the exegetical task, is subject to discussion and dispute on its own. So the syllogism has been (re)cast in exegetical form. But it remains a syllogistic argument. No. 3 is a narrowly exegetical exercise and the contrast then is probative.

V:II

1. A. *Great things have you done, O Lord my God; your wonderful purposes are all for our good; none can compare with you; I would proclaim them and speak of them, but they are more than I can tell* (Prov. 40:5):

   B. R. Hinenah bar Papa says two [teachings in respect to the cited verse]: "All those wonders and plans which you made so that our father, Abraham, would accept the subjugation of Israel to the nations were *for our good,* for our sake, so that we might endure in the world."

   C. Simeon bar Abba in the name of R. Yohanan: "Four things did the Holy One, blessed be He, show to our father, Abraham: the Torah, the sacrifices, Gehenna, and the rule of the kingdoms.

   D. "The Torah: *...and a flaming torch passed between these pieces* (Gen. 15:17).

   E. "Sacrifices: *And he said to him, Take for me a heifer divided into three parts* (Gen. 15:9).

   F. "Gehenna: *behold a smoking fire pot.*

   G. "The rule of the kingdoms: *Lo, dread, a great darkness* (Gen. 15:12)."

   H. "The Holy One, blessed be He, said to our father, Abraham, 'So long as your descendants are occupied with the former two, they will be saved from the latter two. If they abandon the former two of them, they will be judged by the other two.

   I. "'So long as they are occupied with study of the Torah and performance of the sacrifices, they will be saved from Gehenna and from the rule of the kingdoms.

   J. "'But [God says to Abraham] in the future the house of the sanctuary is destined to be destroyed and the sacrifices nullified. What is your preference? Do you want your children to go down into Gehenna or to be subjugated to the four kingdoms?'"

   K. R. Hinena bar Pappa said, "Abraham himself chose the subjugation to the four kingdoms.

   L. "What is the scriptural basis for that view? *How should one chase a thousand and two put ten thousand to flight, except their rock had given them over* (Deut. 32:30). That statement concerning the rock refers only to Abraham, as it is said, *Look at the rock from which you were hewn* (Is. 51:1)..

   M. *"But the Lord delivered them up* (Deut. 32:30) teaches that God then approved what he had chosen."

2. A. R. Berekhiah in the name of R. Levi: "Now Abraham sat and puzzled all that day, saying, 'Which should I choose, Gehenna or subjugation to the kingdoms? The one is worse than the other.?'

   B. "Said the Holy One, blessed be He, to him, 'Abraham, how long are you going to sit in puzzlement? Choose without delay.' That is in line with this verse: *On* that day *the Lord made a covenant with Abram saying* (Gen. 15:18)."

   C. What is the meaning of, *saying?*

   D. R. Hinena bar Pappa said, "Abraham chose for himself the subjugation to the four kingdoms."

   E. We have reached the dispute of R. Yudan and R. Idi and R. Hama bar Haninah said in the name of a single sage in the name of Rabbi: "The

Holy One, blessed be He, [not Abraham] chose the subjugation to the four kingdoms for him, in line with the following verse of Scripture: *You have caused men to ride over our heads* (Ps. 66:12). That is to say, *you have made ride over our heads various nations, and it is as though we went through fire and through water* (Ps. 66:21)."

3. A. R. Hinenah bar Papa said a further teaching.

   B. R. Hinenah bar Papa says: "All those wonders and plans which you made were so that a man might desire his wife.

   C. "What is the Scripture basis for that view? *And Adam knew his wife again* (Gen. 4:25).

   D. "What is the meaning of *again*? The lust for sexual relations that he had was augmented [so explaining the meaning of the word *again*].

   E. "In the past, if he did not see her, he did not lust after her. Now, whether or not he saw her, he desired her."

   F. R. Abba bar Yudan in the name of R. Aha: "This is an indication for commercial travelers and for sailors to remember their wives and come home as quickly as they can."

4. A. R. Simon said, "'All those wonders and plans which you made were so that the nations of the world would not accept your Torah.

   B. "'Now was it not perfectly obvious to you that the nations of the world were not going to accept your Torah?'

   C. "Why did it appear as though he were making the circuit of the nations? It was so as to double the reward that was coming to us."

5. A. For R. Simeon said, "*...your wonderful purposes are all for our good:* for all those two thousand four hundred forty eight years before the Israelites had gone forth from Egypt, the Holy One, blessed be He, was sitting and making calculations, intercalating the years, sanctifing the years, celebrating the new months. When the Israelites went forth from Egypt, he handed the task over to them.

   B. "That is in line with this verse of Scripture: *The Lord said to Moses and Aaron in the land of Egypt, saying, ["This month shall be for you the beginning of months; it shall be the first month of the year for you"]* (Ex. 12:1-2).

   C. "What is the meaning of *saying*? He said to them, From now on, lo, these are given over to you: *this month shall be for you the beginning of months; it shall be the first month of the year for you.*"

The intersecting-verse raises the issue of how God's purposes are all for our good. The possibilities are worked out in such a way that, in the end, Israel's command of the calendar becomes a marked of exceptional favor. No. 1 introduces the matter of the subjugation to the nations, which now is *for our good.* Abraham and God chose precisely the situation in which Israel now found itself. No. 2 carries forward that same topic, now moving away from the intersecting-verse but making the established point. No. 3 then deals with the first Man. No. 4 addresses the distinguishing mark of Israel, its possession of the Torah. It is difficult to make sense of No. 4 as we now have it; it seems to lack a referent. What wonders and plans Simeon has in mind are not at all clear. But No. 5 leads us back to our base-verse, and now we have a clear route to Abraham's choice of subjugation to the nations, first Egypt, now Edom. Israel is in charge of the movement of the seasons, sanctifying the new moon and recognizing the course of the planets in the heavens. That dominion endures even now. The sun and moon travel their circuits in the heaven under the supervision of Israel, a considerable consolation in the present circumstance.

V:III

1. A. *Hope deferred makes the heart sick, [but a desire fulfilled is a tree of life. He who despises the word brings destruction on himself, but he who respects the commandments will be rewarded. The teaching of the wise is a fountain of life, that one may avoid the snares of death]* (Prov. 13:12-14):

    B. R. Hiyya bar Ba opened discourse by citing the verse: *"Hope deferred makes the heart sick* – this refers to one who betrothes a woman and takes her as his wife only after delay.

    C. *"...but a desire fulfilled is a tree of life* – this refers to one who betrothes a woman and takes her as his wife right away."

2. A. Another interpretation: *"Hope deferred makes the heart sick* – this refers to David, who was anointed and then ruled only after two years had passed.

    B. *"...but a desire fulfilled is a tree of life* – this refers to Saul, who was anointed and then ruled right away.

    C. On account of what merit [did Saul have that good fortune]?

    D. On account of the merit accruing for the good deeds which were to his credit, for he was humble and modest.

    E. For he ate his ordinary food [not deriving from his share of an animal sacrificed in the Temple, for example] in a state of cultic cleanness [as if he were eating holy food deriving from his share of an offering made in the Temple].

    F. And, further, he would spend his own funds so as to protect the funds of Israel.

    G. And he treated as equal the honor owing to his servant with the honor owing to himself.

    H. Judah bar Nahman in the name of R. Simeon b. Laqish: "For he was one who was subject to study of the Torah: *By me [the Torah speaks] princes rule* (Prov. 18:16). *By me kings rule* [and Saul ruled through his study of the Torah] (Prov. 8:15)."

3. A. R. Ishmael taught on Tannaite authority, "Before a man has sinned, people pay him reverence and awe. Once he has sinned, they impose on him reverence and awe.

    B. "Thus, before the first man had sinned, he would hear [God's] voice in an workaday way. After he had sinned, he heard the same voice as something strange. Before he had sinned, the first man heard God's voice and would stand on his feet: *And they heard the sound of God walking in the garden in the heat of the day* (Gen. 3:8). After he had sinned, he heard the voice of God and hid: *And man and his wife hid* (Gen. 3:8)."

C.   Said R. Aibu, "At that moment the height of the first Man was cut down and he became a hundred cubits high."

D.   [Ishmael continues:] "Before the Israelites sinned, what is written in their regard? *And the appearance of the glory of the Lord was like a consuming fire on the top of the mountain before the eyes of the children of Israel* (Ex. 24:17)."

E.   Said R. Abba bar Kahana, "There were seven veils of fire, one covering the next, and the Israelites gazed and did not fear or take fright."

F.   "But when they had sinned, even on the face of the intercessor [Moses] they could not look: *And Aaron and all the children of Israel feared...to come near* (Ex. 34:40)."

4.   A.   R. Phineas bar Abun in the name of R. Hanin: "Also the intercessor felt the sin: *Kings of hosts do flee, do flee* (Ps. 68:13)." [This is now explained.]

B.   R. Yudan in the name of R. Aibu says, "'Angels of hosts' is not what is written here, but what is written is *Kings of hosts,* the kings of the angels, even Michael, even Gabriel, were not able to look upon the face of Moses.

C.   "But after the Israelites had sinned, even on the faces of lesser angels Moses could not gaze: *For I was in dread of anger and hot wrath* (Deut. 9:19)."

5.   A.   Before the deed of David [with Bath Sheba] took place, what is written? *For David: The Lord is my light and my salvation, of whom shall I be afraid?* (Ps. 27:1).

B.   But after that deed took place, what is written? *I will come upon him while he is weary and weak-handed* (2 Sam. 17:2).

6.   A.   Before Solomon sinned, he could rule over demons and demonesses: *I got for myself...Adam's progeny, demons and demonesses* (Qoh. 2:8).

B.   What is the sense of *demons and demonesses*? For he ruled over demons and demonesses.

C.   But after he had sinned, he brought sixty mighty men to guard his bed: *Lo, the bed of Solomon, with sixty mighty men around it, all of them holding a sword and veterans of war* (Song 3:7-8).

7.   A.   Before Saul had sinned, what is written concerning him? *And when Saul had taken dominion over Israel, he fought against all his enemies on every side, against Moab, against the Ammonites, against Edom, against the kings of Zobah, and against the Philistines; wherever he turned he put them to the worse* (1 Sam. 14:47).

B.   After he had sinned what is written concerning him? *And Saul saw the camp of the Philistines and was afraid* (1 Sam. 28:5).

8.   A.   Another interpretation of the verse *"Hope deferred makes the heart sick:*

B.   Said R. Hiyya bar Abba, "This refers to the Israelites before they were redeemed.

C. "You find that when Moses came to the Israelites and said to them, 'The Holy One, blessed be He, has said to me, *Go, say to Israel, I have surely remembered you,* (Ex. 3:16), they said to him, 'Moses, our lord, it is still a mere remembering! *What is my strength, that I should wait? And what is my end, that I should be patient? Is my strength the strength of stones, or is my flesh bronze? [In truth I have no help in me, and any resources is driven from me]* (Job 6:11-13).

D. "'Is our strength the strength of stones? is our flesh made of bronze?'

E. "But when he said to him, 'This month you will be redeemed,' they said, 'That is a good sign.'

F. "...*but a desire fulfilled is a tree of life: This month shall be for you the beginning of months; it shall be the first month of the year for you"* (Ex. 12:1-2).

The extensive treatment of the intersecting-verse does not prepare us for the final clarification of the base-verse at No. 8, and that is because the composite bears a heavy and inappropriate accretion of useless material. The point is that when Moses made his announcement that in the cited month of Nisan, the Israelites would be redeemed, that marked the end of hope deferred and the beginning of the desire fulfilled. But nothing has prepared us for that excellent conclusion. No. 1 gives a straightforward application of the verse. No. 2 brings us to David and Saul. The intrusion of Nos. 3-7 is not easy to explain, except as a secondary amplification on the theme of Saul. The first Man, the Israelites, Moses, David, Saul all are examples of the affect of sin, which takes a proud person and humbles him. We see, therefore, a vast insertion of irrelevant materials. No,. 8 then brings us back to the point at issue, and we have to regard the rest of the composite as a rather mindless amplification of a minor point – the mere mention of Saul! The basic intent, however, in introducing the intersecting-verse is striking and well executed at the end.

V:IV

1. A. Judah bar Nahman in the name of R. Simeon b. Laqish opened discourse by citing the following verse of Scripture: *"Oh send out your light and your truth; let them lead me, let them bring me to your holy hill and to your dwelling. [Then I will go to the altar of God, to God my exceeding joy; and I will praise you with the lyre, O God, my God]* (Ps. 43:3-4).

    B. "...*send out your light* refers to Moses: *And Moses did not know that his face was glistening with beams of light* (Ex. 34:29).

    C. "...*and your truth* refers to Aaron, *The Torah of truth was in his mouth* (Malachi 2:7).

    D. *"Your truth and light be with your holy one* (Deut. 33:8)."

    E. And there are those who reverse matters:

    F. "...*send out your light* refers to Aaron: *Your truth and light be with your holy one* (Deut. 33:8).

    G. "...*and your truth* refers to Moses, *Not so is my servant Moses, in all my household the most trustworthy* (Num. 12:7)."

2. A. Said R. Isaac, "Even at the sea Moses foresaw that he was not going to enter the Land of Israel: *She keeps her eye on the doings of her household* (Prov. 31:27).

   B. "What is written in the pertinent passage is not, 'you will bring it and plant it,' but rather, *You brought them in and planted them* (Ex. 15:17).

   C. "Yet it is written: *...let them lead me, let them bring me to your holy hill and to your dwelling.*

   D. "This refers to the scribes of the Land of Israel, who are as holy as the Land of Israel itself."

3. A. Another comment on the verse: *Oh send out your light and your truth; [let them lead me, let them bring me to your holy hill and to your dwelling. Then I will go to the altar of God, to God my exceeding joy; and I will praise you with the lyre, O God, my God]* (Ps. 43:3-4).

   B. *...send out your light* refers to Moses and Aaron, through whom the Holy One, blessed be He, sent light to Israel to redeem them from Israel.

   C. When did this take place?

   D. In this month: *This month for you is the first of the months* (Ex. 12:2).

A long sequence of wide-ranging passages about redemption, each ending, "When did this take place? In this month: *This month for you is the first of the months* (Ex. 12:2), now begins. A particular point of contact between the "illustrative" passage and the topic at hand, Ex. 12:2, never is specified. The general theme of redemption in Nisan than accounts for pretty much everything that follows; in no way can we regard the exercise as mainly exegetical. In fact it is a syllogistic exposition, through innumerable examples, of the single fact that redemption takes place "in this month." No. 1 sets the stage for No. 3, with No. 2 a secondary expansion of No. 1. Specifically, we apply the intersecting-verse to Moses, then to Aaron, then to both. But how the intersecting-verse opens the base-verse to a deeper meaning is not self-evident, since, as I said, the reversion to the base-verse seems artificial and mechanical. On the basis of this case one could revert to the any base-verse one wished. The theme, however, is clearly conventional – that is to say, syllogistic: redemption on the first of the months. And that is I believe what has guided the authorship at hand which wishes to read each of the base-verses as another instance in the unfolding of Israel's redemption.

V:V

1. A. R. Levi opened discourse by citing the following verse: *And you shall be holy to me [because I the Lord am holy. I have made a clear separation between you and the heathen, that you may belong to me]* (Lev. 20:26).

   B. R. Yudan in the name of R. Hama bar Hanina, R. Berekhiah in the name of R. Abbahu: "Had it been stated, 'And I shall separate the nations of the world from you,' the nations of the world would have had no standing. But what it says is, *I have made a clear separation between you and the heathen.*

C. "It is like someone who sorts out the good grain from the bad, choosing and coming back and choosing again.

D. "If he chooses the bad from the good, he makes a choice and does not go back and make a further selection."

2. A. [Reverting to 1.A:] said R. Levi, "In all their deeds the Israelites are different from the nations of the world, in their manner of ploughing, sowing, reaping, making sheaves, threshing, working at the threshing floor and at the wine press, counting and reckoning the calendar:

B. "As to ploughing: *You will not plough with an ox and and ass together* (Deut. 22:10).

C. "...sowing: *You will now sow your vineyard with mixed seeds* (Lev. 22:9).

D. "...reaping: *You will not gather the gleaning of your harvest* (Lev. 19:9).

E. "...making sheaves: *And the forgotten sheaf in the field you will not recover* (Deut. 24:12).

F. "...threshing: *You will not muzzle an ox in its threshing* (Deut. 25:4).

G. "...working at the threshing floor and at the wine press: *You will provide liberally [for the Hebrew servant] out of your threshing floor and wine press* (Deut. 15:14).

H. "...counting and reckoning the calendar: The nations of the world reckon by the sun, and Israel by the moon: *This month will be for you the first of the months* (Ex. 12:2).

The inclusion of our base-verse is in a syllogism that on its own makes its main point. The base-verse simply supplies another fact for the larger proposition at hand. The point is familiar.

V:VI

1. A. *I sleep by my heart is awake. Listen! My beloved is knocking: "Open to me, my sister, my dearest, my dove, my perfect one, for my head is drenched with dew, my locks with the moisture of the night"* (Song 5:2):

B. Said the community of Israel before the Holy One, blessed be He, "While *I am asleep* at the house of the sanctuary [because it is destroyed], *my heart is awake* in the houses of assembly and study.

C. "*I am asleep* as to the offerings, but *my heart is awake* as to the religious duties and acts of righteousness.

D. "*I am asleep* as to religious duties, but *my heart is nonetheless awake* to carry them out.

E. "*I am asleep* as to the end, but *my heart is awake* as to redemption.

F. "*I am asleep* as to redemption, but *the heart* of the Holy One, blessed be He, *is awake* to redeem us."

2. A. Said R. Hiyya bar Abba, "How do we know that the Holy One is called 'the heart of Israel'?

B. "On the basis of this verse: *Rock of my heart and my portion is God forever* (Ps. 73:26)."

3. A. *...My beloved is knocking* refers to Moses: *And Moses said, Thus said the Lord, At about midnight I shall go out in the midst of Egypt* (Ex. 11:4).

    B. *Open to me:* said R. Yose, "Said the Holy One, blessed be He, *'Open to me* [a hole] as small as the eye of a needle, and I shall open to you a gate so large that troops and siege-engines can go through it.'"

    C. *...my sister:* [God speaks:] *"My sister* – in Egypt, for they became my kin through two religious duties, the blood of the Passover-offering and the blood of circumcision."

    D. *...my dearest* – at the sea, for they showed their love for me at the sea, *And they said, the Lord will reign forever and ever* (Ex. 15:19).

    E. *...my dove – my dove* at Marah, where through receiving commandments they become distinguished for me like a dove.

    F. *...my perfect one – My perfect one* at Sinai, for they became pure at Sinai: *And they said, all that the Lord has spoken we shall do and we shall hear* (Ex. 24:7)."

    G. R. Yannai said, "My twin, for I am not greater than they, nor they than I."

    H. R. Joshua of Sikhnin said in the name of R. Levi, "Just as in the case of twins, if one of them gets a headache, the other one feels it, so said the Holy One, blessed be He, *'I am with him in trouble* (Ps. 91:15)."

    I. *..for my head is drenched with dew. The heavens dropped dew* (Judges 5:4).

    J. *...my locks with the moisture of the night: Yes, the clouds dropped water* (Judges 5:4).

    K. When is this the case? In this month: *This month is for you the first of the months* (Ex. 12:2).

The pattern is the same as before: an extended disquisition on a theme remote from our base-verse, ending with an artificial and unprepared for introduction of the base-verse. The sole relevant point is that the beginning of God's relationship to Israel is with the first of the months. Nothing else pertains. But the proposition, that God and Israel share one and the same destiny, on its own is stunning.

V:VII

1. A. *Hark! My beloved! Here he comes, bounding over the mountains, leaping over the hills. [My beloved is like a gazelle, or a young wild goat: there he stands outside our wall, peeking in at the windows, glancing through the lattice. My beloved answered, he said to me, Rise up, my darling; my fairest, come away. For now the winter is past, the rains are over and gone; the flowers appear in the countryside; the time is coming when the birds will sing, and the turtle-dove's cooing will be heard in our land; when the green figs will ripen on the fig-trees and the vines give forth their fragrance. Rise up my darling, my fairest, come away]* (Song 2:8-10):

    B. R. Judah, R. Nehemiah [below, No. 2], and rabbis [below, No. 3]:

    C. R. Judah says, *"Hark! My beloved! Here he comes* refers to Moses.

D.   "When Moses came and said to Israel, 'In this month you will be
     redeemed,' they said to him, 'Moses, our lord, how are we going to be
     redeemed?   Did not the Holy One, blessed be He, say to our father,
     Abraham, *"your descendants will be sojourners in a land that is not theirs
     and they will be slaves there, and they will be oppressed for four hundred
     years"* (Gen. 15:13)?   And is it not the case that we have to our account
     only two hundred and ten years [of slavery in Egypt]?'

E.   "He said to them, 'Since he wants to redeem you, he does not pay
     attention to your accounts.   But *bounding over the mountains, leaping
     over the hills* means that he is skipping over foreordained calculations of
     the end and over all reckonings and times.

F.   "'In this month you will be redeemed: *This month is for you the
     beginning of months* (Ex. 12:2).'"

2. A.   R. Nehemiah says, *"Hark! My beloved! Here he comes* refers to Moses.

    B.   "When Moses came and said to Israel, 'In this month you will be
         redeemed,' they said to him, 'Moses, our lord, how are we going to be
         redeemed?   And the land of Egypt is filled with the filth of idolatry that
         belongs to us.'

    C.   "He said to them, 'Since he wants to redeem you, he does not pay
         attention to your idolatry.   But he goes *bounding over the mountains,
         leaping over the hills,* and hills refers to idolatry, in line with this
         verse: *On the tops of mountains they make sacrifices and in hills they
         offer incense* (Hos. 4:12).'"

3. A.   Rabbis say, *"Hark! My beloved! Here he comes* refers to Moses.

    B.   "When Moses came and said to Israel, 'In this month you will be
         redeemed,' they said to him, 'Moses, our lord, how are we going to be
         redeemed?   And we have no good deeds to our credit.'

    C.   "He said to them, 'Since he wants to redeem you, he does not pay
         attention to your wicked deeds.   But to whom does he pay attention?   To
         the righteous who are among you, for example, Amram and his court.

    D.   "For *hills and mountains* refers only to courts, in line with this verse:
         That I may go and seek out upon the mountains (Judges 11:37)."

4. A.   Said R. Yudan, "As to slavery and sojourning in a land that is not theirs,
         *...that your descendants will be sojourners in a land that is not theirs and
         they will be slaves there, and they will be oppressed for four hundred
         years,*

    B.   "including even the years that they were at ease [cf. Braude and Kapstein,
         p. 101]."

5. A.   R. Yudan in the name of R. Eliezer son of R. Yose the Galilean, R.
         Hunah in the name of R. Eliezer b. Jacob: *"Hark! My beloved! Here he
         comes* refers to the messiah-king.

    B.   "When he came and said to Israel, 'In this month you will be redeemed,'
         they said to him, 'Messiah-king, our lord, how are we going to be
         redeemed?   Did not the Holy One, blessed be He, say that he would make
         us slaves among the seventy nations?'

C. "And he answered them with two replies, saying to them, 'If one of you has gone into exile to Barbaria and one to Sarmatia, it is as if all of you had gone into exile.'

D, "'Furthermore, this wicked government drafts soldiers from each nation. If one Samaritan comes and is drafted, it is as if the whole of his nation has been subjugated. If one Ethiopian comes and is drafted, it is as if the whole of his nation has been subjugated.

E. "'In this month you will be redeemed,' *This month is for you the beginning of months* (Ex. 12:2)."

The mélange of themes – Israel's love-affair with God, expressed in the Song of Songs, Israel's redemption from Egypt, Israel's redemption in the near future, the subjugation to the wicked kingdom, and the importance of the month of Nisan – is worked out as before. But the choice of the intersecting-verse is fully vindicated at No. 1. God can choose the time of redemption, skipping over all obstacles. As we shall see, the exposition of the intersecting-verse runs on and on, since we take full account of the entire pericope of Scripture, beginning to end. But the choice is fully validated. The return to the base-verse is natural and appropriate. The stress now is that God is not bound by prior calculations, but can do as he likes, God can overlook Israel's failings, and God finds in Israel's righteous ample reason for redeeming the whole nation (No. 1, 2, 3). No. 4 is a brief appendix to No. 1. Then No. 5 resumes the discussion, now with a powerful application to the present. We now continue with the exposition of the intersecting-verse. The reversion to the base-verse will not again prove so natural and compelling.

V:VIII

1. A. *My beloved is like a gazelle, or a young wild goat: [there he stands outside our wall, peeking in at the windows, glancing through the lattice. My beloved answered, he said to me, Rise up, my darling; my fairest, come away]* (Song 2:8-10):

   B. *My beloved is like a gazelle:* said R. Isaac, "You say to us, 'Come hither. Come hither to us, for you come to us first.'" [Braude and Kapstein, p. 101: The word for *beloved*, when separated into two parts, makes two Greek words, standing for *come hither* and *God*, so in the first part, 'You O God say to us, Come hither,' and in the second part, Israel replies, 'God, you come to us before we stir.']"

2. A. *[My beloved is like a gazelle:]* Said R. Isaac,"Just as a gazelle skips and jumps from tree to tree, hut to hut, fence to fence, so the Holy One, blessed be He, skipped from Egypt to the Sea, from the sea to Sinai.

   B. "In Egypt they saw him: *And I shall pass through through the land of Egypt on that night* (Ex. 12:12).

   C. "At the sea they saw him: *And Israel saw the great hand* (Ex. 14:32).

   D. "At Sinai they saw him: *And the Lord spoke from Sinai, he came and shown from Seir to him* (Deut. 32:2)."

3. A. *...or a young wild goat:*

B.   R. Yose b. R. Haninah said, "Like the young of a gazelle."

4. A.   *...there he stands outside our wall:*
    B.   *For on the third day the Lord came down before the eyes of the entire people* (Ex. 19:11).
    C.   *...peeking in at the windows:*
    D.   *And the Lord came down* (Ex. 19:20).
    E.   *...glancing through the lattice:*
    F.   When he said, *I am the Lord your God* (Ex. 20:23),
    G.   *My beloved answered, he said to me:*
    I.   What did he say to me? *I am the Lord your God* (Ex. 20:23).

5. A.   *[My beloved is like a gazelle:]* Said R. Isaac,"Just as a gazelle skips and jumps from tree to tree, hut to hut, fence to fence, so the Holy One, blessed be He, skips from one synagogue to another, one study-house to another.
    B.   "On what account? So as to bless Israel.
    C.   "On account of whose merit? On account of the merit of Abraham, who remained seated at the oak of Mamre [where he was praying and studying].
    D.   "That is in line with this verse of Scripture: *And the Lord appeared to him at the oak of Mamre, when he was sitting down at the door of the tent* (Gen. 18:1)."

6. A.   *[As he sat at the door of his tent in the heat of the day* (Gen. 18:1)]:
    B.   R. Berekhiah in the name of R. Levi: "What is written is *he sat* [and not in the progressive tent, while he *was sitting*]. When the Holy One, blessed be He, appeared to him, our father Abraham tried to stand.
    C.   "Said the Holy One, blessed be He, to him, 'Remain seated.' Our father Abraham sat down.
    D.   "Said the Holy One, blessed be He, to him, '[You thereby serve as a model for your children.]   Abraham, whenever your children enter synagogues and school houses, they may sit while my Glory remains standing.
    D.   "'What text of Scripture so indicates? *God stands in the congregation of God* (Ps. 82:1)."

7. A.   R. Haggai in the name of R. Isaac: "What is written is not standing but 'stationed at his post' [Freedman, *Genesis Rabbah ad loc.*:], which is to say, 'ready,'
    B.   "[Genesis Rabbah adds:] in line with this verse: *You shall be stationed on the rock* (Ex. 33:21)."

8. A.   R. Samuel b. R. Hiyya b. R. Yudan in the name of R. Haninah: "In response to each and every statement of praise with which Israel praises the Holy One, blessed be He, he brings his Presence to rest on them.
    B.   "What is the text that makes that point? *You are holy, O you who are enthroned upon the praises of Israel* (Ps. 22:4)."

9. A. *...or a young wild goat:*
    B. R. Yose b. R. Haninah said, "Like the young of a gazelle."

10. A. *...there he stands outside our wall:* outside the walls of synagogues and school houses.
    B. *...peeking in at the windows:* from among the shoulders of the priests.
    C.. *...glancing through the lattice:* from among the entwined fingers of the priests.
    D. *...My beloved answered, he said:* What did he say to me? *May the Lord bless you and keep you* (Num. 24:6).

11. A. Another interpretation of the verse: *My beloved is like a gazelle:*
    B. Said R. Isaac, "Just as a gazelle appears and goes and disappears, so the first messiah [Moses] appeared to them and then went and disappeared from their sight."
    C. How long did he disappear from sight?
    D. Judah b. Rabbi says, "Three months, in line with this verse of Scripture: *They met Moses and Aaron standing to meet them* (Ex. 5:20)."

12. A. *...or a young wild goat:*
    B. R. Yose b. R. Haninah said, "Like the young of a gazelle."

13. A. *...there he stands outside our wall:* outside the walls of the Western wall of the house of the sanctuary, which will never be destroyed.
    B. *...peeking in at the windows:* through the merit of the patriarchs.
    C.. *...glancing through the lattice:* through the merit of the matriarchs.
    D. This serves to teach you that just as there is a difference between a window and a lattice, so there is a difference between the merit of the patriarchs and the merit of the matriarchs.

14. A. R. Berekhiah in the name of R. Levi, "Like the first redeemer, so will the final redeemer be:
    B. "Just as the first redeemer appeared to them and then went and disappeared from them, so the final redeemer will appear to them and then go and disappear from them."
    C. And how long will he disappear from them?
    D. R. Tanhumah in the name of R. Hama bar Hoshaia, R. Menahema in the name of R. Hama bar Hanina: "Forty-five days, in line with this verse of Scripture: *From the time when the regular offering is abolished and 'the abomination of desolation' is set up, there shall be an interval of one thousand two hundred and ninety days. Happy the man who waits and lives to see the completion of one thousand three hundred and thirty-five days* [a difference of forty-five days] (Dan. 12:11-12)."
    E. "As to the forty-five days that remain over the figure given in the earlier verse, what are they? They are the forty-five days on which the Messiah, having appeared to them, will go and disappear from them."
    F. Where will he lead them?'
    G. Some say, "To the wilderness of Judea," and some, "To the wilderness of Sihon and Og."

H. That is in line with this verse of Scripture: *Therefore I will seduce Israel and bring her into the wilderness* (Hos. 2:16).

I. He who believes in him will eat saltwort and the roots of the broom and live, for *in the wilderness they pick saltwort with wormwood and the roots of the broom are their food* (Job 30:4).

J. And he who does not believe in him will go to the nations of the world, who will kill him.

K. Said R. Isaac bar Marian, "At the end of forty-five days the Holy One, blessed be He, will appear to them and bring down manna.

L. "Why? *For there is nothing new under the sun* (Qoh. 1:9).

M. "What is the pertinent scriptural verse? *I am the Lord your God from the land of Egypt; I will make you dwell in tents again as in the days of the festival* (Hos. 12:10)."

The systematic exegesis of the intersecting-verse continues, now without the slightest pretense of interest in the base-verse. The messianic focus of the present composition is all that joins the passage to our context. And much that is given seems miscellaneous, a set of diverse materials on a single theme. We review the redemption of Israel from Egypt, No. 2, for the reason made explicit at the end: the first redemption is the model for the second redemption. The form for the whole is shown at Nos. 2-4, a form repeated with minor variations later on. The obvious insertions, Nos. 6-8, provide the necessary appendix as indicated. Nos. 9-10 move from the redemption of Israel from Egypt to Israel today, in the synagogues and school houses. Then, at Nos. 11-13, we complete the matter. No. 14 then adds its appendix of episodic information.

V:IX

1. A. *My beloved answered, he said to me, [Rise up, my darling; my fairest, come away. For now the winter is past, the rains are over and gone; the flowers appear in the countryside; the time is coming when the birds will sing, and the turtle-dove's cooing will be heard in our land; when the green figs will ripen on the fig-trees and the vines give forth their fragrance. Rise up my darling, my fairest, come away]* (Song 2:8-10):

    B. Said R. Azariah, "Is not 'answering' the same thing as 'saying'?

    C. "*He answered me* through Moses, *and said to me,* through Aaron."

    D. What did he say to me?

    E. *Rise up:* bestir yourself.

    F. *...my darling:* daughter of Abraham, who made me beloved in my world.

    G. *...my fairest:* daughter of Isaac, who made me beautiful in my world, when his father bound him on the altar.

    H. *...come away:* daughter of Jacob, who listened to his father and his mother: *And Jacob listened to his father and his mother* (Gen. 28:17).

    I. *For now the winter is past:* this refers to the four hundred years that were decreed for our fathers to spend in Egypt.

    J. *...the rains are over and gone:* this refers to the two hundred and ten years.

2 . A. Another interpretation: *For now the winter is past:* this refers to the two hundred ten years.

   B. *...the rains are over and gone:* this refers to the subjugation.

3 . A. Are not the rain and the winter the same thing?

   B Said R. Tanhuma, "The principal trouble of the winter is the rain [which lasts eighty-six days], the principal [and truly difficult] part of the subjugation of Israel was only the eighty-six years from the time that Miriam was born."

   C. And why was she called Miriam?

   D. Said R. Isaac, "It is a name that contains the meaning of bitterness, in line with this verse: *And they embittered their lives with hard work and with mortar* (Ex. 1:14)."

4 . A. *...the flowers appear in the countryside:* this refers to Moses and Aaron.

   B. *...the time is coming when the birds will sing:* the time for the foreskin [to be properly cut off] has come.

   C. The time for the Egyptians to be cut off has come.

   D. The time for the idolatry to be removed from the world has come: *And against all the gods of Egypt I shall execute judgment, I am the Lord* (Ex. 12:2).

   E. The time for the sea to be split has come: *And the waters split open* (Ex. 14:21).

   F. The time for the recitation of the Song at the Sea has come: *Then Moses sang* (Ex. 15:1).

   G. The time for the Torah to be given has come: *The Lord is my strength and my song* (Ex. 15:2).

   H. Said R. Bibi: "[The appropriate text is this one:] *Your statutes have become my songs* (Ps. 119:54)."

   I. Said R. Tanhuma, "The time for the Israelites to make a song for the Holy One, blessed be He, has come: *The Lord is my strength and my song* (Ex. 15:2)."

5 . A. *...and the turtle-dove's cooing will be heard in our land:*

   B. Said R. Yohanan, "[Since the word for turtle dove uses letters that may yield *guide*, we read:] 'the voice of the good guide is heard in our land.' This refers to Moses: And Moses said, *Thus said the Lord, At about midnight* (Ex. 11:4)."

6 . A. *...when the green figs will ripen on the fig-trees:*

   B. This refers to the three days of darkness, on which the wicked of Israel perished.

7 . A. *...and the vines give forth their fragrance:*

   B. This refers to those who remained, who repented and were accepted.

   C. Moses said to them, "All this wonderful fragrance is coming from you, and you are sitting here! *Rise up my darling, my fairest, come away.*"

8. A. *My beloved answered, he said to me, [Rise up, my darling; my fairest, come away. For now the winter is past, the rains are over and gone; the flowers appear in the countryside; the time is coming when the birds will sing, and the turtle-dove's cooing will be heart in our land; when the green figs will ripen on the fig-trees and the vines give forth their fragrance. Rise up my darling, my fairest, come away]* (Song 2:8-10):

   B. Said R. Azariah, "Is not 'answering' the same thing as 'saying'?

   C. "*He answered me* through Joshua, *and said to me,* through Eleazar."

   D. What did he say to me? *Rise up, my darling; my fairest, come away'*

   E. *For now the winter is past:* this refers to the forty years that the Israelites spent in the wilderness..

   J. *...the rains are over and gone:* this refers to the thirty-eight years [after the rejection of the Land], in which anger was poured out on Israel [and the generation of the wilderness was left to die out].

   K. *...the flowers appear in the countryside:* this refers to the spies: *One representative, one representative for each tribe* (Num. 34:18).

   L. *...the time is coming when the birds will sing:* the time for the foreskin [to be properly cut off] has come.

   M. The time for the Canaanites to be cut off has come.

   N. The time for the Land of Israel to be cut up has come: *Among these you will cut up the land* (Num. 26:53).

   O. *...and the turtle-dove's cooing will be heard in our land:*

   P. Said R. Yohanan, "[Since the word for turtle-dove uses letters that may yield *guide*, we read:] 'the voice of the good guide is heard in our land.' This refers to Joshua: *And Joshua commanded the officers of the people, saying* (Josh. 1:10)."

   Q. *...when the green figs will ripen on the fig-trees:*

   R. This refers to the baskets of first fruits.

   S. *...and the vines give forth their fragrance:*

   T. This refers to the drink-offerings.

9. A. *My beloved answered, he said to me, [Rise up, my darling; my fairest, come away. For now the winter is past, the rains are over and gone; the flowers appear in the countryside; the time is coming when the birds will sing, and the turtle-dove's cooing will be heart in our land; when the green figs will ripen on the fig-trees and the vines give forth their fragrance. Rise up my darling, my fairest, come away]* (Song 2:8-10):

   B. Said R. Azariah, "Is not 'answering' the same thing as 'saying'?

   C. "*He answered me* through Daniel, *and said to me,* through Ezra."

   D. What did he say to me? *Rise up, my darling; my fairest, come away.*

   E. *For now the winter is past:* this refers to the seventy years of the dominion of Babylonia.

   F. *...the rains are over and gone:* this refers to the fifty-two years of the dominion of Media.

10. A. Another interpretation: *For now the winter is past:* this refers to the seventy years that the Israelites spent in exile.

    B. But were they not merely fifty-two years?

    C. Said R. Levi, "Eighteen years were taken off the total, for every eighteen years an echo would go forth and resound in the palace of

Nebuchadnezzar, saying to him, Wicked servant, go forth with the sword against the house of your master, for the children of your master do not obey him."

11. A. ...*the rains are over and gone:* this refers to the subjugation.
    B. ...*the flowers appear in the countryside:* for instance, Daniel and his colleagues, Mordecai and his colleagues, Ezra and his colleagues.
    C. ...*the time is coming when the birds will sing:* the time for the foreskin [to be properly cut off] has come.
    D. The time for the wicked to be broken has come: *The Lord has broken the staff of the wicked* (Is. 14:5).
    E. The time for Babylonians to be removed has come.
    F. The time for the house of the sanctuary to be rebuilt has come: *Greater will be the glory of the second house* (Haggai 2:9).
    G. ...*and the turtle-dove's cooing will be heard in our land:*
    H. Said R. Yohanan, "[Since the word for turtle-dove uses letters that may yield guide, we read:] 'the voice of the good guide is heard in our land.' This refers to Cyrus: *Thus said Cyrus, king of Persia, All the nations of the world...*(Ezra 1:2)."
    I. ...*when the green figs will ripen on the fig-trees:*
    J. This speaks of the baskets of first fruits.
    K. ...*and the vines give forth their fragrance:*
    L. This refers to the drink-offerings.
    M. Moses said to them, "All this wonderful fragrance is coming from you, and you are sitting here! *Rise up my darling, my fairest, come away."*

12. A. *My beloved answered, he said to me, [Rise up, my darling; my fairest, come away. For now the winter is past, the rains are over and gone; the flowers appear in the countryside; the time is coming when the birds will sing, and the turtle-dove's cooing will be heart in our land; when the green figs will ripen on the fig-trees and the vines give forth their fragrance. Rise up my darling, my fairest, come away]* (Song 2:8-10):
    B. Said R. Azariah, "Is not 'answering' the same thing as 'saying'?
    C. *"He answered me* through Elijah, *and said to me,* through the messiah-king."
    D. What did he say to me? *Rise up, my darling; my fairest, come away.*
    E. *For now the winter is past:*
    F. Said R. Azariah, "This refers to the wicked kingdom, which misled people.
    G. "That is in line with the following: *When your brother, son of your mother, misleads you* (Deut. 13:7)."
    H. ...*the rains are over and gone:* this refers to the subjugation [to Rome].
    I. ...*the flowers appear in the countryside:*
    J. Said R. Isaac, "It is written, *The Lord showed me four craftsmen* (Zech. 2:3). These are they: Elijah, the messiah-king, Melchisedek, and the anointed for war."
    K. ...*the time is coming when the birds will sing:* the time for the foreskin [to be properly cut off] has come.
    L. The time for the Egyptians to be cut off has come.

M. The time for the wicked to be broken has come: *The Lord has broken the staff of the wicked* (Is. 14:5).

N. The time for the wicked kingdom to be uprooted from the world has come.

O. The time for the revelation of the kingdom of heaven has come: *The Lord shall be king over all the earth* (Zech. 14:9).

P. *...and the turtle-dove's cooing will be heard in our land:*

Q. Said R. Yohanan, "[Since the word for turtle dove uses letters that may yield *guide*, we read:] 'the voice of the good guide is heard in our land.' This refers to the messiah king: *How beautiful on the hills are the feet of the bringer of glad tidings* (Is. 52:7)."

S. *...when the green figs will ripen on the fig-trees:*

T. Said R. Hiyya bar Abba, "Close to the days of the messiah a great thing will happen, and the wicked will perish in it.

U. "*...and the vines give forth their fragrance:*

V. "This refers to those who remained: *And those who remained in Zion, and the remnant in Jerusalem, will be holy* (Is. 4:3)."

13. A. And rabbis say, "In the septennate in which the son of David comes, in the first of the seven year spell, *I shall cause it to rain on one town and not on another* (Amos 4:7).

B. "In the second, the arrows of famine will be sent forth.

C. "In the third there will be a great famine, and men, women, and children will die in it, and the Torah will be forgotten in Israel.

D. "In the fourth, there will be a famine which is not really a famine, and plenty which is not plentiful.

E. "In the fifth year, there will be great plenty, and people will eat and drink and rejoice, and the Torah will again be renewed.

F. "In the sixth there will be great thunders.

G. "In the seventh there will be wars.

H. "And at the end of the seventh year of that septennate, the son of David will come."

I. Said R. Abbaye, "How many septennates have there been like this one, and yet he has not come."

J. But matters accord with what R. Yohanan said, "In the generation in which the son of David comes, disciples of sages will perish, and those that remain will have faint vision, with suffering and sighing, and terrible troubles will come on the people, and harsh decrees will be renewed. Before the first such decree is carried out, another will be brought along and joined to it."

K. Said R. Abun, "In the generation in which the son of David comes, the meeting place will be turned over to prostitution, the Galilee will be destroyed, Gablan will be desolate, and the Galileans will make the rounds from town to town and find no comfort.

L. "Truthful men will be gathered up, and the truth will be fenced in and go its way."

M. Where will it go?

N. A member of the household of R. Yannai said, "It will go and dwell in small flocks in the wilderness, in line with this verse of Scripture: *Truth shall be among bands* (Is. 59:15)."

O.   Said R. Nehorai, "In the generation in which the son of David comes,
      youths will humiliate old men, sages will rise before youths, a slave girl
      will abuse her mistress, a daughter-in-law her mother-in-law, a man's
      enemies will be his own householders, a son will not be ashamed for his
      father, the wisdom of scribes will turn rotten, the vine will give its fruit
      but wine will be expensive."

P.   Said R. Abba bar Kahana, "The son of David will come only to a
      generation which is liable for total extermination."

Q.   Said R. Yannai, "The son of David will come only to a generation the
      principal leaders of which are like dogs."

R.   Said R. Levi, "If you see one generation after another blaspheming, look
      for the footsteps of the messiah-king.

S.   "What verse of Scripture indicates it? *Remember Lord the taunts hurled at
      your servant, how I have borne in my heart the calumnies of the nations;
      so have your enemies taunted us, O Lord, taunted the successors of your
      anointed king* (Ps. 89:51).

T.   "What follows? *Blessed is the Lord for ever, amen, amen* (Ps. 89:52)."

The systematic work on Song 2:8-10 is completed in a highly formalized
exercise. We apply the verse to the following messianic figures in succession:
Moses and Aaron and the redemption from Egypt, Nos. 1-7, Joshua and Eleazar,
No. 8, thus the conquest of the Land; Ezra and Daniel, Nos. 9-11, thus the return
to the Land; Elijah and the messiah-king, No. 12+13, an appendix of familiar
materials (cf. B. San. 97a). The message is clear from the topics chosen to
illuminate the transaction described by the verse between God and Israel: a love
affair brought to its fulfilment in the messianic rule. Our "base-verse" has long
since been forgotten.

V:X

1.   A.   R. Jonah opened discourse by citing this verse of Scripture: *So I got her
            back for fifteen pieces of silver, a homer of barley, [and a measure of
            wine; and I said to her, Many a long day you shall live in my house and
            not play the wanton and have no intercourse with a man, nor I with you.
            For the Israelites shall live many a long day without king or prince,
            without sacrifice or sacred pillar, without image or household gods, but
            after that they will again seek the Lord their God and David their king
            and turn anxiously to the Lord for his bounty in days to come]* (Hos. 3:2-
            5).

      B.   Said R. Yohanan, *"So I got her back* for me, *for fifteen pieces of silver*,
            lo, fifteen; *and for a homer of barley*, lo, thirty, and *a half-homer of
            barley*, lo, sixty.

      C.   "This refers to the sixty religious duties that Moses inscribed for us in
            the Torah."

      D.   For R. Yohanan said in the name of R. Simeon b. Yohai, "There were
            three passages that Moses wrote for us in the Torah, in each one of
            which there are sixty religious duties, and these are they:

      E.   "the passage concerning the Passover offering, that concerning torts, and
            that concerning Holy Things."

F. R. Levi in the name of R. Shilah of Kefar Tamratah, "There are seventy in each."

G. Said R. Tanhumah, "They really do not differ. One who treats the passage concerning the Passover-offering as containing seventy religious duties treats it as encompassing the passage on the phylacteries. One who treats the passage on torts as containing seventy religious duties maintains that it encompasses the passage covering the year of release. One who treats the passage of Holy Things as including seventy religious duties encompasses with it the passage on *orlah*-fruit."

2. A. Another interpretation of the verse, *so I got her back for fifteen pieces of silver:*

B. Lo, the reference to fifteen pieces of silver brings us to the fifteenth day of Nisan.

C. When is this? It is in this month: *This month is for you the beginning of months* (Ex. 12:2).

The intersecting-verse is drawn to the base-verse by an artificial means familiar from earlier passage and in no way illuminates the base-verse. The deeper pertinence, of course, derives from Israel's redemption in the stated month, which is coherent with the theme of the exegesis of the verses in Song as God's love for Israel. Israel is like Hosea's wife, hence the passage at hand completes the foregoing. We cannot doubt that the final composition – meaning the selection and arrangement of diverse materials into a single syllogism – derives from a single authorship, which wishes to make its own cogent statement and has succeeded in doing so.

V:XI

1. A. *This month is for you [the first of months, you shall make it the first month of the year]* (Ex. 12:2):

B. [Reading the letters for *month* to sound like the word, *innovation:*] R. Berekhiah in the name of R. Yudan b. R. Simeon: "Said the Holy One, blessed be He, to Israel, 'There will be an innovation as to redemption for you in the age to come.

C. "'In the past I never redeemed one nation from the midst of another nation, but now I am going to redeem one nation from the midst of another nation.'

D. "That is in line with this verse of Scripture: *Has God tried to go and take for himself a nation from the midst of another nation* (Deut. 4:34)."

2. A. R. Joshua bar Nehemiah in the name of R. Yohanan bar Pazzi: "'A nation from the midst of a people' is not written here, nor do we find, 'a people from the midst of a nation,' but *a nation from the midst of a nation* [like itself, that is, in precisely the same classification].

B. "For the Egyptians were uncircumcised and the Israelites also were uncircumcised. The Egyptians grew ceremonial locks, and so did the Israelites.

C. "Therefore by the rule of strict justice, the Israelites ought not to have been redeemed from Egypt."

D. Said R. Samuel bar Nahmani, "If the Holy One, blessed be He, had not
bound himself by an oath, the Israelites in fact would never have been
redeemed from Egypt.

E. *"Therefore say to the children of Israel, I am the Lord, and I shall take
you out of the burdens of Egypt* (Ex. 6:6).

F. "The language, [*I am the Lord*] therefore, refers only to an oath, as it is
said, *Therefore I take an oath concerning the house of Eli* (1 Sam. 3:4)."

3. A. Said R. Berekhiah, *"You have redeemed your people with your arm* (Ps.
77:16) – with naked power.

B. Said R. Yudan, "From the phrase, *To go and take a nation from the midst
of another nation*, to the phrase *great terrors* (Deut. 4:34) are seventy-
two letters.

C. "Should you claim there are more, you should deduct from the count the
last reference to *nation* [Egypt], which does not count."

D. R. Abin said, "It was for the sake of his name that he redeemed them, and
the name of the Holy One, blessed be He, consists of seventy-two
letters."

4. A. [*"This month is for you [the first of months, you shall make it the first
month of the year]* (Ex. 12:2)]: Said R. Joshua b. Levi, "The matter may
be compared to the case of a king whose son was taken captive, and he
put on [the garb of] vengeance and went and redeemed his son, and he
said, 'Count the years of my reign as beginning from the time of the
redemption of my son.'

B. "So said the Holy One, blessed be He, 'Count the years of my reign as
beginning from the time of the Exodus from Egypt.'"

5. A. [*"This month is for you [the first of months, you shall make it the first
month of the year]* (Ex. 12:2)]: R. Levi in the name of R. Hama bar
Hanina said, "The matter may be compared to the case of a king who
married many wives, but he did not write for them either a marriage
license or the dates of the marriage.

B. "But when he married a woman of good family and the daughter of noble
parents, he wrote for her a marriage license and wrote the date of the
marriage.

C. "So too of all the women whom Ahasuerus married, he did not write for
any one of them either a marriage license or the date of the marriage.
But when he married Esther, the daughter of a good family and of noble
lineage, he wrote for her both a marriage license and the date of the
marriage.

D. "He wrote for her a marriage license: *On the tenth month, the month of
Tebeth* (Est. 2:16).

E. "And he wrote for her the date of the marriage: *In the seventh year of his
reign* (Est. 2:16)."

We move on to the exegesis of the base-verse, now essentially in its own
terms as to word-choice and contents. No. 1 takes up the word *month*, which
can be read as new, with the result that is given. Nos. 2 and 3 carry forward the
exegesis of the proof-text of No. 1 and so form an extended appendix. Nos. 4, 5

then explain why the month has been chosen as the first of the months, a very persuasive explanation at that. It is the month in which Israel is redeemed, and the two parables, No. 4 and No. 5, then explain the rest. But No. 5 clearly serves another setting entirely, and it does not fit into this context so well as No. 4.

V:XII

1. A. Said R. Berekhiah, *"This month is for you [the first of months, you shall make it the first month of the year]* (Ex. 12:2):
   B. "[The waxing and waning of the moon serve] as an omen for you.
   C. *"The seed of David...shall be established for ever as the moon* (Ps. 89:38):
   D. "Like the moon, which is full and then obscured.
   E. "If you have merit, lo, you will count days like the moon's waxing, but if you do not have merit, then you will count days like the moon's waning.
   F. "Abraham, Isaac, Jacob, Judah, Perez, Hezron, Ram, Aminadab, Nachshon, Salman, Boaz, Obed, Jesse, David, Solomon:
   G. *"Then Solomon sat on the throne of the Lord as king* (1 Chr. 29:23) – [all provide cases of counting days as] the moon when it is waxing.
   H. "Lo, in these cases the count was like the waning moon: Rehoboam, Abijah, Assa, Jehoshaphat, Jehoram, Ahaziah, Joash, Amaziah, Uzziah, Jothan, Ahaz, Hezekiah, Manasseh, Ammon, Josiah, and Zedekiah: *He blinded the eyes of Zedekiah* (2 Kgs. 25:7) – lo, [all these give us cases of] counting the days like the moon in its waning.

The exegesis of the word for month, identifying it with the moon, then joins the moon's waxing and waning to Israel's history and explains the whole by reference to merit. This is a strikingly cogent exegesis of the base-verse in terms of its own word choices.

V:XIII

1. A. *This month is for you [the first of months, you shall make it the first month of the year]* (Ex. 12:2):
   B. *...for you* means that it is handed over to you.
   C. Said R. Joshua b. Levi, "The matter may be compared to the case of a king who had a clock. When his son grew up, he handed over to him his clock."
   D. Said R. Yose bar Haninah, "The matter may be compared to the case of a king who had a watchtower. When his son grew up, he handed over to him his watchtower."
   E. Said R. Aha, "The matter may be compared to the case of a king who had a ring. When his son grew up, he handed over to him his ring."
   F. Said R. Isaac, "It may be compared to the case of a king who had many treasuries, and there was a key for each one of them. When his son grew up, he handed over to him all the keys."
   G. Said R. Hiyya bar Abba, "The matter may be compared to a carpenter who had tools. When his son grew up, he handed over to him the tools of his trade."

H. And rabbis say, "The matter may be compared to the case of a physician who had a case of medicines. When his son grew up, he handed over to him his medicine case."

2. A. R. Hoshaiah taught on Tannaite authority, "The court below made a decree saying, 'Today is the new year.'

   B. "Said the Holy One, blessed be He, to the ministering angels: 'Set up a platform, let the attorneys go up, let the clerks go up, for the court below has made a decree, saying, "Today is the New Year."'

   C. "If the witnesses [to the appearance of the new moon of Tishre] delayed in coming, or the court decided to intercalate the year on the next day [so that that day would not be the new year], the Holy One, blessed be He, says to the ministering angels, 'Take away the platform, take away the advocates and take away the clerks, for the court below has made a decree saying, "Tomorrow [not today] is the New Year."'

   D. "What verse of Scripture proves this point? *For it is a statute for Israel, a judgment of the God of Jacob* (Ps. 81:5).

   E. "If it is not *a statute for Israel*, it is – as it were – also not *a judgment of the God of Jacob.*"

3. A. R. Phineas, R. Hezekiah in the name of R. Simon: "All the ministering angels assemble with the Holy One, blessed be He, saying to him, 'Lord of the ages, when will it be the New Year?'

   B. "And he says to them, 'Me do you ask? You and I shall ask the court down below.'

   C. "What verse of Scripture proves this point? *For the Lord our God is near whenever* we *call to him* (Deut. 4:7).

   D. "And *we* call to him only on the set feasts, in line with this verse of Scripture: *These are the set feasts of the Lord, the holy convocations [which* you *shall proclaim]* (Lev. 23:4)."

   E. R. Qerispa in the name of R. Yohanan, "In the past: *These are the set feasts of the Lord.* But from now on: *which* you *shall proclaim:*

   F. "He said to them, 'If *you* proclaim them, they are my set feasts, and if not, they are not my set feasts.'"

We move on to the possessive: *for you.* The main point is announced at No. 1, presented in an implicit way at No. 2, and then given full articulation at No. 3. The declaration of the new moon – and the calendar that depends on it – is in the hands of Israel. God has handed the matter over to Israel at the beginning of redemption. The basic idea is well expressed and assuredly rests on the base-verse.

V:XIV

1. A. *This month is for you [the first of months, you shall make it the first month of the year]* (Ex. 12:2):

   B. You count by it, but the nations of the world will not count by it. [They use the solar calendar, you the lunar one.]

2. A. R. Levi in the name of R. Yose b. R. Ilai: "It is merely natural that someone who presently is great should count by what is great, and someone who presently is small should count by what is small.

   B. "Accordingly, Esau [Rome] counts by the sun, because it is great, while Jacob [Israel] counts by the moon, for it is small."

   C. Said R. Nahman, "That really is a good omen. Esau counts by the sun, because it is great. But just as the sun rules by day but does not rule by night, so the wicked Esau rules in this world but not in the world to come.

   D. "Jacob counts by the moon, which is small, and just as the moon rules by night and also by day [making its appearance both by night and by day], so too will Jacob rule in this world and in the world to come."

   E. R. Nahman said, "So long as the light of the great luminary glows splendidly in the world, the light of the lesser luminary is not going to be noted. Once the light of the great light sets, then the light of the lesser one shines forth.

   F. "So too, as long as the light of the wicked Esau lasts, the light of Jacob will not be seen. Once the light of the wicked Esau sets, then the light of Jacob will shine forth.

   G. "That is in line with this verse: *Arise, shine [for behold, darkness shall cover the earth, and gross darkness the peoples, but upon you the Lord will arise, and his glory shall be seen upon you]* (Is. 60:1)."

3. A. R. Simeon b. Yohai taught on Tannaite authority, "In three matters Moses had difficulty. The Holy One, blessed be He, showed him – as it were – with his finger: the candelabrum, the creeping things, and the moon.

   B. "As to the candelabrum: This *is the work of the candlestick* (Num. 8:4).

   C. "The creeping things: This *is what is unclean for you among the creeping things that creep on the earth* (Lev. 11:29).

   D. "The moon: This *month is for you [the first of months]* (Ex. 12:2)."

We remain focused upon the dative of possession, for you, and Nos. 1, 2 go over that point. Israel, but not the nations, calculate the calendar through the moon. No. 2 makes the recurrent point about the eschatological significance of that fact. No. 3 moves on to the next word, this, explaining why the demonstrative is used.

V:XV

1. A. R. Simlai, and it has been taught in the name of R. Samuel, "Every month on the beginning of which the [Braude and Kapstein, p. 116:] the conjunction of the new moon does not take place before noon, one cannot see [the moon] before evening."

   B. R. Samuel bar Yeba, R. Aha in the name of R. Samuel bar Nahman: "In the year in which the Israelites went forth, the beginning of the lunar month and the vernal equinox coincided [*sic!*]"

2. A [Explaining the procedure for receiving testimony of the appearance of the new moon, with reference to the demonstrative statement, *This*

month (=moon) is for you] R. Hiyya bar Ba in the name of R. Yohanan:
"The Holy One, blessed be He, cloaked himself in a cloak bearing fringes
and put Moses on one side and Aaron on the other, calling Michael and
Gabriel [to demonstrate the procedure for receiving testimony on the
appearance of the new moon]. He appointed them messengers to
proclaim the new moon and said to them, 'On what side did you see the
moon? Was it before the sun or after the sun? Was it to the north or to
the south? How high was it? Where was it inclining? How thick was
the cresent?'

B. "He said to them, 'This is the procedure, as you see it here, is the way in
which people should intercalate the year down below: through an elder,
with witnesses, through the use of a cloak bearing show-fringes.'"

No. 1 seems to make the point that the new moon on the occasion on
which the Israelites went out of Egypt coincided with the vernal equinox (March
21), which is not possible. On that basis Braude and Kapstein reject what we
have and choose to translate: "began on the same day of the week." But the sages
at hand seem to wish to say that it was a miracle. No. 2 reverts to the stress on
this moon, indicating that in so stating matters, God was explaining to Moses
the proper procedure for receiving testimony as to the appearance of the new
moon.

V:XVI

1. A. *[This month is for you [the first of months, you shall make it the first
month of the year]* (Ex. 12:2):] R. Nahman and R. Eleazar b. R. Yose and
R. Aha:

B. One of them said, "[Reading the letters for month to sound like the word,
innovation:] "Said the Holy One, blessed be He, to Israel, 'There will be
an innovation as to redemption for you in the age to come.'"

C. The other said, "It will be an innovation as to the age to come that you
will have here.

D. "Just as, in the age to come, *Then the eyes of the blind will be opened*
(Is. 35:5), so now, *And all the people saw the sounds* (Ex. 20:18).

E, "Just as in the age to come, *The ears of the deaf will be unstopped* (Is.
35:5), so here, *And they said, Everything which the Lord has spoken we
shall do and we shall hear* (Ex. 24:7).

F, "Just as in the age to come, *Then the lamb will skip like a ram* (Is.
35:6), so now, *Moses brought forth the people out of the camp to meet
God and they stood below the mountain* (Ex. 19:17).

G. "Just as in the age to come, *The tongue of the dumb shall sing* (Is.
35:6), so here: *All the people sang together* (Ex. 19:8).

The earlier tendency to compare the coming redemption to the redemption
from Egypt is now made still more concrete. Each detail of Isaiah's vision is
applied to the account of the Exodus from Egypt. The innovation that bears the
point is from C forward.

V:XVII

1. A. *Speak to the whole community of Israel and say to them, On the tenth day of this month [let each man take a lamb or a kid for his family, one for each household, but if a household is too small for one lamb or one kid then the man and his nearest neighbor may take one between them. They shall share the cost, taking into account both the number of persons and the amount each of them eats. Your lamb or kid must be without blemish, a yearling male. You may take equally a sheep or a goat. You must have it in safe keeping until the fourteenth day of this month, and then all the assembled community of Israel shall slaughter the victim between dusk and dark. They must take some of the blood and smear it on the two doorposts and on the lintel of every house in which they eat the lamb. On that night they shall eat the flesh roast on the fire; they shall eat it with unleavened cakes and bitter herbs. You are not to eat any of it raw or even boiled in water, but roasted, head, shins, and entrails. You shall not leave any of it till morning; if anything is left over until morning, it must be destroyed by fire]* (Ex. 12:1-10):

   B. Said R. Yohanan, "Is the lamb not suitable only when taken from the fold? Why say to designate it on the tenth day, [even though it will not be used until the fourteenth, four days later]?

   C. "This teaches that the lambs were tied up to the Israelites' beds from the tenth day, and the Egyptians would come in and see them and [realizing what was about to happen,] their souls would expire."

2. A. R. Hiyya son of R. Ada of Jaffa: *"[Moses summoned all the elders of Israel and said to them,] Draw out and get sheep for your families and slaughter the Passover* (Ex. 12:21):

   B. "The requirement is that each one of you draw out the god of an Egyptian and slaughter it in his presence, [Braude and Kapstein, p. 118: even as the Egyptian...speaks up in protest].'"

3. A. R. Helbo in the name of R. Yohanan: "Here you say, *On the tenth day of this month* (Ex. 12:3), and later on: *The people went up from the Jordan on the tenth day* (Joshua 4:19)."

   B. R. Hiyya in the name of R. Yohanan: "The act of taking the lamb is what sustained the Israelites at the Jordan, and the act of eating it is what protected them in the days of Haman.

   C. "*And they shall eat the meat on that night* (Ex. 12:8). *On that night the sleep of the king was troubled* (Est. 6:1)."

4. A. R. Berekhiah in the name of R. Abbahu: "Nahum the son of R. Simai in Tarsus gave this exposition: "...*let each man take [a lamb or a kid for his family, one for each household]* – the *man* here is the Holy One, blessed be He, as it is said, *The Lord is a man of war* (Ex. 15:3).

   B. "[Since the meaning is that they must "take" the Holy One, blessed be He, we ask:] with what does one acquire him? With the two daily continual offerings [one in the morning, the other at dusk,] *a lamb for the house of the fathers, a lamb for the house of the fathers* (Ex. 12:3)"

5. A. Said R. Yudan in the name of R. Simon, "No one ever spent the night in Jerusalem while still bearing sin. How so? The daily whole-offering of

then morning would effect atonement for the sins that had been committed overnight, and the daily whole-offering of dusk would effect atonement for the transgressions that had been committed by day.

B. "In consequence, no one ever spent the night in Jerusalem while still bearing sin.

C. "What is the verse of Scripture that makes that point? *Righteousness will spend the night in it* (Is. 1:21)."

Nos. 1, 2 links the preparations of the slaughter of the lamb as a Passover offering to the punishment of the Egyptians for their idolatry. No. 1 sets the stage for No. 2. No. 3 then broadens the frame of reference still further. The merit acquired on the occasion of the first Passover sustained the Israelites at two further crises, as shown. No. 4 draws the parallel between the Passover and the daily whole-offering, morning and night, and at this point Braude and Kapstein insert Ex. 29:39: *The one lamb you offer in the morning, the other at dusk,* at which point they further read, *The one lamb in the ancestral House, the other lamb in that House, in the Temple,* which they give as Ex. 12:3. None of this is in Mandelbaum's text, but it does clarify the passage. No. 5 forms an appendix to No. 4. The daily whole-offering effect atonement for sins of the community.

V:XVIII

1. A. [Interpreting the combination of the word for *month*, as new, hence, renewal, and the word for *first*, in the verse, *This month is for you the first of months, you shall make it the first month of the year]*, R. Berekhiah in the name of R. Isaac: *"New* (Ex. 12:3): Renew your deeds, for [otherwise] the head and *first* of all will come.

   B. "The *first* is Nebuchadnezzar, the wicked, of whom it is written: *You are the head of gold* (Dan. 2:38).

   C. "The *first* is the wicked Esau, of whom it is written, *The first came forth red* (Gen. 25:25).

   D. "Who will exact vengeance for you from the first? It is the first: *I the Lord am the first and the last, I am he* (Is. 41:4).

   E. "Who will exact vengeance for you from Media [Haman]? [It is the kingdom mentioned when the cited verse speaks of] *the tenth,* [at Ex. 12:3]."

2. A. Said R. Abin, "The *ten* alludes to [the ten thousand talents of silver to be paid to Ahasuerus] by Haman and his ten sons.

   B. "Who will exact vengeance for you from them?

   C. "The two guardians, Mordecai and Esther, Mordecai on the outside, Esther on the inside.

   D. "Who will exact vengeance for you from Greece? The sons of the Hasmoneans, who offered the two daily whole-offerings every day.

   E. "Who will exact vengeance for you from Edom? Natronah.

   F. *"And he shall serve as a guard for you to the fourteenth day of the month* (Ex. 12:6)."

3. A. [Reverting back to the verse cited above, *"The first came forth red"* (Gen. 25:25):] said the Holy One, blessed be He, "His father called him the greater: *And he called Esau, his son, the greater* (Gen. 27:1).

   B. "And his mother called him the greater: *Rebecca took the clothing of Esau, her son, the greater* (Gen. 27:15).

   C. "But I shall call him the lesser: *And lo, I have made you least among the nations* (Ob. 1:2).

   D. "Since they call him the greater, in accord with the size of the ox is the measure of the slaughterer: *The Lord has a sacrifice in Bosrah, a great slaughter in the land of Edom* (Is. 34:6)."

   E. Said R. Berekhiah, "[We read the verse:] 'There will be a great slaughterer in the land of Edom' [namely, God himself]."

The eschatological reading of the matter of Ex. 12:2ff. brings us to the two who are called first, Nebuchadnezzar and Esau, and that accounts for No. 1. No. 2 then raises the question of redemption: who will save Israel and punish the oppressor. That the passage is not particular to our setting is clear, since at No. 1 no one has referred to Haman, Mordecai, and Esther. But the goal, as always, is Edom, and that requires us to ring the changes on the four monarchies. The climax comes at No. 3: God himself will exact punishment of Edom/Rome.

V:XIX

1. A. [Continuing the account of the punishment of Edom:] *You are not to eat any of it raw* – that is, not merely half-cooked, or merely *or even boiled in water, but roasted, head, shins, and entrails.*

   B. [Edom, together with] its dukes, its hyparchs, and its generals.

   C. *Your wealth, your staple wares, your imports, your sailors and your helmsmen, your caulkers, your merchants, and your warriors, all your ship's company, all who were with you were flung into the sea on the day of your disaster; at the cries of your helmsmen the troubled waters tossed* (Ez. 27:27-28):

   D. Said R. Samuel bar R. Isaac, *"All your ship's company* encompasses even those who had been of my company and had gone and joined your company – even they *were flung into the sea on the day of your disaster."*

2. A. *This is the way in which you must eat it: you shall have your belt fastened, your sandals on your feet and your staff in your hand, and you must eat in urgent haste. It is the Lord's Passover* (Ex. 12:11):

   B. Said R. Samuel bar Nahman, "Since in this world, *you must eat in urgent haste,* in the world to come what is written?

   C. *"But you shall not come out* in urgent haste *nor leave like fugitives; for the Lord will march at your head, your rearguard will be Israel's God* (Is. 52:12)."

The exposition of the verse brings us back to IV:IX, which treats the same specification in the same way, and with the same effect: the eschatologization of the theme. No. 2 then applies the fixed notion that the exodus serves as model and counterpart to the final redemption.

Pisqa Six

[The Lord spoke to Moses and said, Give this command to the Israelites:] See that you present my offerings, the food *[for the food-offering of soothing odor, to me at the appointed time. Tell them: This is the food-offering which you shall present to the Lord: the regular daily whole-offering of two yearling rams without blemish. One you shall sacrifice in the morning and the second between dusk and dark]*
(Num. 28:1-4).

VI:I

1. A. *If I were hungry, I would not tell you, for the world and all that is in it are mine. [Shall I eat the flesh of your bulls or drink the blood of he-goats? Offer to God the sacrifice of thanksgiving and pay your vows to the Most High. If you call upon me in time of trouble, I will come to your rescue and you shall honor me]* (Ps. 50:12-15):

    B. Said R. Simon, "There are thirteen traits of a merciful character that are stated in writing concerning the Holy One, blessed be He.

    C. "That is in line with this verse of Scripture: *The Lord passed by before him and proclaimed, The Lord, the Lord, God, merciful and gracious, long-suffering and abundant in goodness and truth; keeping mercy unto the thousandth generation, forgiving iniquity, transgression, and sin, who will be no means clear* (Ex. 34:6-7).

    D. "Now is there a merciful person who would hand over his food to a cruel person [who would have to slaughter a beast so as to feed him]?

    E. "One has to conclude: *If I were hungry, I would not tell you.*"

2. A. Said R. Judah bar Simon, "Said the Holy One, blessed be He, 'There are ten beasts that are clean that I have handed over to you [as valid for eating], three that are subject to your dominion, and seven that are not subject to your dominion.

    B. "'Which are the ones that are subject to your dominion? *The ox, sheep, and he-goat* (Deut. 14:4).

    C. "'Which are the ones not subject to your dominion? *The hart, gazelle, roebuck, wild goat, ibex, antelope, and mountain sheep* (Deut. 14:5).

    D. "'Now [in connection with the sacrificial cult] have I imposed on you the trouble of going hunting in hills and mountains to bring before me an offering of one of those that are not in your dominion?

    E. "'Have I not said to you only to bring what is in your dominion and what is nourished at your stall?'

    F. "Thus: *If I were hungry, I would not tell you.*"

3. A. Said R. Isaac, "It is written, *[The Lord spoke to Moses and said, Give this command to the Israelites:] See that you present my offerings, the food for the food-offering of soothing odor, to me at the appointed time. [Tell them: This is the food-offering which you shall present to the Lord: the regular daily whole-offering of two yearling rams without blemish. One you shall sacrifice in the morning and the second between dusk and dark]* (Num. 28:1-4).

   B. "Now is there any consideration of eating and drinking before Me?

   C. "Should you wish to take the position that indeed there is a consideration of eating and drinking before me, derive evidence to the contrary from my angels, derive evidence to the contrary from my ministers: *...who makes the winds your messengers, and flames of fire your servants* (Ps. 104:4).

   D. "Whence then do they draw sustenance? From the splendor of the Presence of God.

   E. "For it is written, *In the light of the presence of the King they live* (Prov. 16:15)."

   F. R. Haggai in the name of R. Isaac: *"You have made heaven, the heaven of heavens...the host...and you keep them alive* (Neh. 9:6), meaning, you provide them with livelihood [Leon Nemoy, cited by Braude and Kapstein, p. 125, n. 4]."

4. A. Said R. Simeon b. Laqish, "It is written, *This was the regular whole-offering made at Mount Sinai, a soothing odor, a food-offering to the Lord* (Num. 28:6).

   B. "[God says,] 'Now is there any consideration of eating and drinking before Me?

   C. "'Should you wish to take the position that indeed there is a consideration of eating and drinking before me, derive evidence to the contrary from Moses, concerning whom it is written, *And he was there with the Lord for forty days and forty nights. Bread he did not eat, and water he did not drink* (Ex. 34:28).

   D. "'Did he see me eating or drinking?

   E. "'Now that fact yields an argument *a fortiori*: now if Moses, who went forth as my agent, did not eat bread or drink water for forty days, is there going to be any consideration of eating and drinking before me?'

   F. "Thus: *If I were hungry, I would not tell you.*"

5. A. Said R. Hiyya bar Ba, "Things that I have created do not need [to derive sustenance] from things that I have created, am I going to require sustenance from things that I have created?

   B. "Have you ever in your life heard someone say, 'Give plenty of wine to this vine, for it produces a great deal of wine'?

   C. "Have you ever in your life heard someone say, 'Give plenty of oil to this olive tree, for it produces a great deal of oil'?

   D. "Things that I have created do not need [to derive sustenance] from things that I have created, am I going to require sustenance from things that I have created?

   E. "Thus: *If I were hungry, I would not tell you.*"

6. A. Said R. Yannai, "Under ordinary circumstances if someone passes though the flood of a river, is it possible for him to drink a mere two or three *logs* of water? [Surely not. He will have to drink much more to be satisfied.]

   B. "[God speaks:] 'But as for Me, I have written that a mere single *log* of your wine shall I drink, and from that I shall derive full pleasure and satisfaction.'"

   C. R. Hiyya taught on Tannaite authority, *'The wine for the proper drink-offering shall be a quarter of a hin for each ram; you are to pour out this strong drink in the holy place as an offering to the Lord* (Num. 28:7).

   D. "This statement bears the sense of drinking to full pleasure, satisfaction, and even inebriation."

7. A. Yose bar Menassia in the name of R. Simeon b. Laqish, "When the libation was poured out, the stoppers [of the altar's drains] had to be stopped up [Braude and Kapstein, p. 126: so that the wine overflowing the altar would make it appear that God could not swallow the wine fast enough]."

   B. Said R. Yose bar Bun, "The rule contained in the statement made by R. Simeon b. Laqish is essential to the proper conduct of the rite [and if the drains are not stopped up, the libation offering is invalid and must be repeated]."

8. A. [God speaks:] "I assigned to you the provision of a single beast, and you could not carry out the order. [How then are you going to find the resources actually to feed me? It is beyond your capacity to do so.]'

   B. "And what is that? It is *the Behemoth on a thousand hills* (Ps. 50:10)."

   C. R. Yohanan, R. Simeon b. Laqish, and rabbis:

   D. R. Yohanan said, "It is a single beast, which crouches on a thousand hills, and the thousand hills produce fodder, which it eats. What verse of Scripture so indicates? *Now behold Behemoth which I made...Surely the mountains bring him forth food* (Job 40:15)."

   E. R. Simeon b. Laqish said, "It is a single beast, which crouches on a thousand hills, and the thousand hills produce all sorts of food for the meals of the righteous in the coming age.

   F. "What verse of Scripture so indicates? *Flocks shall range over Sharon and the Vale of Achor be a pasture for cattle; they shall belong to my people who seek me* (Is. 65:10)."

   G. Rabbis said, "It is a single beast, which crouches on a thousand hills, and the thousand hills produce cattle, which it eats.

   H. "And what text of Scripture makes that point? *And all beasts of the field play there* (Job 40:20)."

   I. But can cattle eat other cattle?

   J. Said R. Tanhuma, *"Great are the works of our God* (Ps. 111:2), how curious are the works of the Holy One, blessed be He."

   K. And whence does it drink?

   L. It was taught on Tannaite authority: R. Joshua b. Levi said, "Whatever the Jordan river collects in six months it swallows up in a single gulp.

M.   "What verse of Scripture indicates it? *If the river is in spate, he is not scared, he sprawls at his ease as the Jordan flows to his mouth* (Job 40:23)."

N.   Rabbis say, "Whatever the Jordan river collects in twelve months it swallows up in a single gulp.

O.   "What verse of Scripture indicates it? *He sprawls at his ease as the Jordan flows to his mouth* (Job 40:23).

P.   "And that suffices merely to wet his whistle."

Q.   R. Huna in the name of R. Yose: "It is not even enough to wet his whistle."

R.   Then whence does it drink?

S.   R. Simeon b. Yohai taught on Tannaite authority, *"And a river flowed out of Eden* (Gen. 2:10), and its name is Yubal, and from there it drinks, as it is said, *That spreads out its roots by Yubal* (Jer. 17:8)."

T.   It was taught on Tannaite authority in the name of R. Meir, *"But ask now the Behemoth* (Job 12:7) – this is *the Behemoth of the thousand hills* (Ps. 50:10), *and the fowl of the heaven will tell you* (Job 12:7), that is the ziz-bird (Ps. 50:10), *or speak to the earth that it tell you* (Job 12:8) – this refers to the Garden of Eden. Or *let the fish of the sea tell you* (Job 12:8) – this refers to Leviathan.

U.   *"Who does not know among all these that the hand of the Lord has done this* (Job 12:9)."

9.   A.   "I gave you a single king, and you could not provide for him. [How then are you going to find the resources actually to feed me? It is beyond your capacity to do so.] And who was that? It was Solomon, son of David."

     B.   *The bread required by Solomon in a single day was thirty kors of fine flower and sixty kors of meal* (1 Kgs. 5:2).

     C.   Said R. Samuel bar R. Isaac, "These were kinds of snacks. But as to his regular meal, no person could provide it: *Ten fat oxen* (1 Kgs 5:3), fattened with fodder, *and twenty oxen out of the pasture and a hundred sheep* (1 Kgs 5:3), also out of the pasture; *and harts, gazelles, roebucks, and fatted fowl* (1 Kgs. 5:3)."

     D.   What are these fatted fowl?

     E.   R. Berekhiah in the name of R. Judah said, "They were fowl raised in a vivarium."

     F.   And rabbis say, "It is a very large bird, of high quality, much praised, which would go up and be served on the table of Solomon every day."

     G.   Said R. Judah bar Zebida, "Solomon had a thousand wives, and every one of them made a meal of the same dimensions as this meal. Each thought that he might dine with her.

     H.   "Thus: *If I were hungry, I would not tell you.*"

10. A.   "One mere captive I handed over to you, and you could barely sustain him too. [How then are you going to find the resources actually to feed me? It is beyond your capacity to do so.]"

     B.   And who was that? It was Nehemiah, the governor:

     C.   *Now that which was prepared for one day was one ox and six choice sheep, also fowls were prepared for me, and once in ten days store of all sorts of wine; yet for all this I demanded not the usual fare provided for the governor, because the service was heavy upon this people* (Neh. 5:18).

D.   What is *the usual fare provided for the governor?*

E.   Huna bar Yekko said, "[Braude and Kapstein, p. 114:] It means gourmet food carefully cooked in vessels standing upon tripods."

F.   "Thus: *If I were hungry, I would not tell you.*"

11. A.   It has been taught on Tannaite authority: **The incense is brought only after the meal** (M. Ber. 6:6).

B.   Now is it not the case that the sole enjoyment that the guests derive from the incense is the scent?

C.   Thus said the Holy One blessed be He, "My children, among all the offerings that you offer before me, I derive pleasure from you only because of the scent: *the food for the food-offering of soothing odor, to me at the appointed time.*

The exposition of the intersecting-verse, No. 1, works itself out at Nos. 1ff. The point of No. 1 is somewhat odd, since, of course, the sacrificial cult does involve an act of slaughter. No. 2 makes a more pertinent observation, which is that the cult involves only accessible animals, entirely within the control of the Israelite. No. 3 reverts to the base-verse and raises the important question contributed by the original intersecting-verse. We have therefore to regard No. 3 as an appendix to the foregoing. No. 4 then takes up the same question, still with the focus on the base-verse. The exposition of that verse is now thematic, in line with the requirement of the intersecting-verse, which, for its part, is well-chosen. No. 5 goes over the intersecting-verse from yet another angle, making the same points as before. No. 6 makes a different point, which is that the requirement of the daily offering is minimal. But that basic point has already registered in the emphasis on how easy it is to get the animals needed for God's daily meal. No. 7 covers the same ground. No. 8 begins the sustained point that even if God had wanted man to provide his meals, man could not do it. Man could not even provide the food for the single beast, Behemoth, nor for a single king, Solomon, nor for a single captive (that is, son of the Exile), namely, Nehemiah. "How then are you going to find the resources actually to feed me? It is beyond your capacity to do so." That topic having entered, it defines the sequence of discourse to follow. The point that man cannot feed that enormous beast is worked out in detail; but it is made only by indirection. The materials at hand provide information that leads to such a conclusion, but the conclusion is not made explicit. Once the point enters, at 8.A, what follows works things out along quite distinct lines. No. 9 then makes the same point, that man really cannot do what God should require – were God to impose the appropriate requirements. And the same goes for No. 10. No. 11 seems to me miscellaneous. It simply reverts to a clause of the base-verse.

VI:II

1. A. *A righteous man eats his fill, [but the wicked go hungry]* (Prov. 13:25):
   B. This refers to Eliezer, our father Abraham's servant, as it is said, *Please let me have a little water to drink from your pitcher* (Gen. 24:17) — one sip.
   C. *...but the wicked go hungry:*
   D. This refers to the wicked Esau, who said to our father, Jacob, *Let me swallow some of that red pottage, for I am famished* (Gen. 28:30).

2. A. *[And Esau said to Jacob, Let me swallow some of that red pottage, for I am famished* (Gen. 25:30):]
   B. Said R. Isaac bar Zeira, "That wicked man opened up his mouth like a camel. He said to him, 'I'll open up my mouth, and you just toss in the food.'
   C. "That is in line with what we have learned in the Mishnah: **People may not stuff a camel or force food on it, but may toss food into its mouth** [M. Shab. 24:3]."

3. A. Another interpretation of the verse, *A righteous man eats his fill:*
   B. This refers to Ruth the Moabite, in regard to whom it is written, *She ate, was satisfied, and left food over* (Ruth 2:14).
   C. Said R. Isaac, "You have two possibilities: either a blessing comes to rest through a righteous man, or a blessing comes to rest through the womb of a righteous woman.
   D. "On the basis of the verse of Scripture, *She ate, was satisfied, and left food over*, one must conclude that a blessing comes to rest through the womb of a righteous woman."
   E. *...but the wicked go hungry:*
   F. This refers to the nations of the world.

4. A. Said R. Meir, "Dosetai of Kokhba asked me, saying to me, "What is the meaning of the statement, *'...but the wicked go hungry?'*
   B. "I said to him, 'There was a gentile in our town, who made a banquet for all the elders of the town, and invited me along with them. He set before us everything that the Holy One, blessed be He, had created on the six days of creation, and his table lacked only soft-shelled nuts alone.
   C. "What did he do? He took the tray from before us, which was worth six talents of silver, and broke it.
   D. "I said to him, 'On what account did you do this? [Why are you so angry?]'
   E. "He said to me, 'My lord, you say that we own this world, and you own the world to come. If we don't do the eating now, when are we going to eat [of every good thing that has ever been created]?'
   F. "I recited in his regard, *...but the wicked go hungry.*"

5. A. Another interpretation of the verse, *A righteous man eats his fill, [but the wicked go hungry]* (Prov. 13:25):
   B. This refers to Hezekiah, King of Judah.

C. They say concerning Hezekiah, King of Judah, that [a mere] two bunches of vegetables and a *litra* of meat did they set before him every day.

D. And the Israelites ridiculed him, saying, "Is this a king? *And they rejoiced over Rezin and Remaliah's son* (Is. 8:6). But Rezin, son of Remaliah, is really worthy of dominion."

E. That is in line with this verse of Scripture: *Because this people has refused the waters of Shiloah that run slowly and rejoice with Rezin and Remaliah's son* (Is. 8:6).

F. What is the sense of *slowly*?

G. Bar Qappara said, "We have made the circuit of the whole of Scripture and have not found a place that bears the name spelled by the letters translated *slowly*.

H. "But this refers to Hezekiah, King of Judah, who would purify the Israelites through a purification-bath containing the correct volume of water, forty *seahs*, the number signified by the letters that spell the word for slowly."

I. Said the Holy One, blessed be He, "You praise eating? *Behold the Lord brings up the waters of the River, mighty and many, even the king of Assyria and all his glory, and he shall come up over all his channels and go over all his bands and devour you as would a glutton* (Is. 8:7)."

6. A. *...but the wicked go hungry:* this refers to Mesha.

B. *Mesha, king of Moab, was a* noked (2 Kgs. 3:4). What is the sense of *noked*? It is a shepherd.

C. *"He handed over to the king of Israel a hundred thousand fatted lambs and a hundred thousand wool-bearing rams* (2 Kgs. 3:4)."

D. What is the meaning of wool-bearing rams?

E. R. Abba bar Kahana said, "Unshorn."

7. A. Another interpretation of the verse, *A righteous man eats his fill, [but the wicked go hungry]* (Prov. 13:25):

B. This refers to the kings of Israel and the kings of the House of David.

C. *...but the wicked go hungry* are the kings of the East:

D. R. Yudan and R. Hunah:

E. R. Yudan said, "A hundred sheep would be served to each one every day."

F. R. Hunah said, "A thousand sheep were served to each one every day."

8. A. Another interpretation of the verse, *A righteous man eats his fill* (Prov. 13:25):

B. this refers to the Holy One, blessed be He.

C. Thus said the Holy One blessed be He, "My children, among all the offerings that you offer before me, I derive pleasure from you only because of the scent: *the food for the food-offering of soothing odor, to me at the appointed time."*

God does not need the food of the offerings; at most he enjoys the scent. The same point is made as before at **VI:I.11**: what God gets out of the offering is not nourishment but merely the pleasure of the scent of the offerings. God does not eat; but he does smell. The exegesis of Prov. 13:25, however, proceeds along its own line, contrasting Eliezer and Esau, Ruth and the nations of the world, Hezekiah and Mesha, Israel's kings and the kings of the East, and then God – with no contrast at all.

VI:III

1. A.   *You have commanded your precepts to be kept diligently* (Ps. 119:4):
    B.   Where did he give this commandment? In the book of Numbers. [Braude and Kapstein, p. 132: *"In Numbers you did again ordain...* Where did God again ordain? In the Book of Numbers."]
    C.   What did he command?
    D.   *To be kept diligently* (Ps. 119:4): *The Lord spoke to Moses and said, Give this command to the Israelites: See that you present my offerings, the food for the food-offering of soothing odor, to me at the appointed time.*
    E.   That is the same passage that has already occurred [at Ex. 29:38-42] and now recurs, so why has it been stated a second time?
    F.   R. Yudan, R. Nehemiah, and rabbis:
    G.   R. Yudan said, "Since the Israelites thought, 'In the past there was the practice of making journeys, and there was the practice of offering daily whole-offerings. Now that the journeying is over, the daily whole-offerings also are over.'
    H.   "Said the Holy One, blessed be He, to Moses, 'Go, say to Israel that they should continue the practice of offering daily whole-offerings.'"
    I.   R. Nehemiah said, "Since the Israelites were treating the daily whole offering lightly, said the Holy One, blessed be He, to Moses, 'Go, tell Israel not to treat the daily whole-offerings lightly.'"
    J.   Rabbis said, "[The reason for the repetition is that] one statement serves for instruction, the other for actual practice."

2. A.   R. Aha in the name of R. Hanina: "It was so that the Israelites should not say, 'In the past we offered sacrifices and so were engaged [in studying about] them, but now that we do not offer them any more, we also need not study about them any longer.'
    B.   "Said the Holy One, blessed be He, to them, 'Since you engage in studying about them, it is as if you have actually carried them out.'"

3. A.   R. Huna made two statements.
    B.   R. Huna said, "All of the exiles will be gathered together only on account of the study of Mishnah-teachings.
    C.   "What verse of Scripture makes that point? *Even when they recount [Mishnah-teachings] among the gentiles, then I shall gather them together* (Hos. 8:10)."
    D.   R. Huna made a second statement.
    E.   R. Huna said, "*From the rising of the sun even to the setting of the sun my name is great among the nations, and in every place offerings are presented to my name, even pure-offerings* (Malachi 1:11). Now is it the case that a pure-offering is made in Babylonia?
    F.   "Said the Holy One, blessed be He, 'Since you engage in the study of the matter, it is as if you offered it up.'"

4. A. Samuel said, *"And if they are ashamed of all that they have done, show them the form of the house and the fashion of it, the goings out and the comings in that pertain to it, and all its forms, and write it in their sight, that they may keep the whole form of it* (Ez. 43:11).

   B. "Now is there such a thing as the form of the house at this time?

   C. "But said the Holy One, blessed be He, if you are engaged in the study of the matter, it is as if you were building it.'"

5. A. Said R. Yose, "On what account do they begin instruction of children with the Torah of the Priests [the book of Leviticus]?

   B. "Rather let them begin instruction them with the book of Genesis.

   C. "But the Holy One, blessed be He, said, 'Just as the offerings [described in the book of Leviticus] are pure, so children are pure. Let the pure come and engage in the study of matters that are pure.'"

6. A. R. Abba bar Kahana and R. Hanin, both of them in the name of R. Azariah of Kefar Hitayya: "[The matter may be compared to the case of] a king who had two cooks. The first of the two made a meal for him, and he ate it and liked it. The second made a meal for him, and he ate it and liked it.

   B. "Now we should not know which of the two he liked more, except that, since he ordered the second, telling him to make a meal like the one he had prepared, we know that it was the second meal that he liked more.

   C. "So too Noah made an offering and it pleased God: *And the Lord smelled the sweet savor* (Gen. 8:21).

   D. "And Israel made an offering to him, and it pleased the Holy One, blessed be He.

   E. "But we do not know which of the two he preferred.

   F "On the basis of his orders to Israel, saying to them, *See that you present my offerings, the food for the food-offering of soothing odor, to me at the appointed time,* we know that he preferred the offering of Israel [to that of Noah, hence the offering of Israel is preferable to the offering of the nations of the world]."

7. A. R. Abin made two statements.

   B. R. Abin said, "The matter may be compared to the case of a king who was reclining at his banquet, and they brought him the first dish, which he ate and found pleasing. They brought him the second, which he ate and found pleasing. He began to wipe the dish.

   C. *"I will offer you burnt-offerings which are to be wiped off* (Ps. 66:15), like offerings that are to be wiped off I shall offer you, like someone who wipes the plate clean."

   D. R. Abin made a second statement:

   E. "The matter may be compared to a king who was making a journey and came to the first stockade and ate and drank there. Then he came to the second stockade and ate and drank there and spent the night there.

   F. "So it is here. Why does the Scripture repeat concerning the burnt-offering: *This is the Torah of the burnt offering* (Lev. 3:5), *It is the burnt-offering* (Lev. 6:2)? It is to teach that the whole of the burnt-offering is burned up on the fires [yielding no parts to the priests]."

The exegesis moves from text to context. We have two statements of the same matter, in Numbers and in Exodus, as indicated at No. 1. Why is the passage repeated? No. 1 presents a systematic composition on that question, No. 2 on another. No. 3 serves as an appendix to No. 2, on the importance of studying the sacrifices. But No. 3 obviously ignores our setting, since it is interested in the Mishnah-study in general, not the study of the laws of the sacrifices in particular. No. 4 goes on with the same point. No. 5 then provides yet another appendix, this one on the study of the book of Leviticus, with its substantial corpus of laws on sacrifice. No. 6 opens a new inquiry, this time into the larger theme of the comparison of offerings. It has no place here, but is attached to No. 7. That item is particular to Leviticus 6:2, but it concerns the same question we have here, namely, the repetition of statements about sacrifices, this timed Lev. 3:5, 6:2. So Nos. 6, 7 are tacked on because of the congruence of the question, not the pertinence of the proposition.

VI:IV

1. A. *...the regular daily whole-offering of two yearling rams without blemish:*
   B. [Explaining the selection of the lambs,] the House of Shammai and the House of Hillel [offered opinions as follows:]
   C. The House of Shammai say, "Lambs are chosen because the letters that spell the word for lamb can also be read to mean that 'they cover up the sins of Israel,' as you read in Scripture: *He will turn again and have compassion upon us, he will put our iniquities out of sight* (Micah 7:19)."
   D. And the House of Hillel say, "Lambs are selected because the letters of the word lamb can yield the sound for the word, *clean,* for they clean up the sins of Israel.
   E. "That is in line with this verse of Scripture: *If your sins are like scarlet, they will be washed clean like wool* (Is. 1:18)."
   F. Ben Azzai says, *"...the regular daily whole-offering of two yearling rams without blemish* are specified because they wash away the sins of Israel and turn them into an infant a year old."

2. A. *[...the regular daily whole-offering of] two [yearling rams without blemish. One you shall sacrifice in the morning and the second between dusk and dark]:*
   B. *Two a day* on account of [the sins of] the day.
   C. *Two a day* to serve as intercessor for that day: *They shall be mine, says the Lord of hosts, on the day that I do this, even my own treasure, and I will spare them, as a man spares his son who serves him* (Malachi 3:17).
   D. *Two a day* meaning that they should be slaughtered in correspondence to that day in particular.
   E. *Two a day* meaning that one should know in advance which has been designated to be slaughtered in the morning and which at dusk.

3. A. *...a daily whole-offering:*
   B. Said R. Yudan in the name of R. Simon, "No one ever spent the night in Jerusalem while still bearing sin. How so? The daily whole-offering of

the morning would effect atonement for the sins that had been committed overnight, and the daily whole-offering of dusk would effect atonement for the transgressions that had been committed by day.

C. "In consequence, no one ever spent the night in Jerusalem while still bearing sin.

D. "And what verse of Scripture makes that point? *Righteousness will spend the night in it* (Is. 1:21)."

4. A. R. Judah bar Simon in the name of R. Yohanan: "There were three statements that Moses heard from the mouth of the Almighty, on account of which he was astounded and recoiled.

B. "When he said to him, *And they shall make me a sanctuary [and I shall dwell among them]* (Ex. 25:8), said Moses before the Holy One, blessed be He, 'Lord of the age, lo, the heavens and the heavens above the heavens cannot hold you, and yet you yourself have said, *And they shall make me a sanctuary [and I shall dwell among them]* .'

C. "Said to him the Holy One, blessed be He, 'Moses, it is not the way you are thinking. But there will be twenty boards' breadth at the north, twenty at the south, eight at the west, and I shall descend and shrink my Presence among you below.'

D. "That is in line with this verse of Scripture: *And I shall meet you there* (Ex. 25:20).

E. "When he said to him, *My food which is presented to me for offerings made by fire [you shall observe to offer to me]* (Num. 28:2), said Moses before the Holy One, blessed be He, 'Lord of the age, if I collect all of the wild beasts in the world, will they produce one offering [that would be adequate as a meal for you]?

F. "'If I collect all the wood in the world, will it prove sufficient for one offering,' as it is said, *Lebanon is not enough for altar fire, nor the beasts thereof sufficient for burnt-offerings* (Is. 40:16).

G. "Said to him the Holy One, blessed be He, "Moses, it is not the way you are thinking. But: *You shall say to them, This is the offering made by fire [the lambs of the first year without blemish, two day by day]* (Num. 28:3), and not two at a time but one in the morning and one at dusk, as it is said, *One lamb you will prepare in the morning, and the other you will prepare at dusk* (Num. 28:4).'

H. "And when he said to him, *When you give the contribution to the Lord to make expiation for your lives* (Ex. 30:15), said Moses before the Holy One, blessed be He, 'Lord of the age, who can give redemption-money for his soul?

I. "'*One brother cannot redeem another* (Ps. 49:8), *for too costly is the redemption of men's souls* (Ps. 49:9).'

J. "Said the Holy One, blessed be He, to Moses, 'It is not the way you are thinking. But: *This they shall give* – something like this [namely, the half-shekel coin] they shall give"

The exegesis of the base-verse accounts for the miscellany with which our *pisqa* draws to a close. But the point is cogent. The daily whole-offering effects atonement for sins of the preceding day. No. 1 makes that point in one way, No. 2 in another. Deriving from elsewhere, No. 3, bearing in its wake No. 4, says the same thing yet a third time. So the miscellany is a composite but makes a single point in a strong way.

Pisqa Seven

And it came to pass at midnight *[that the Lord smote all the firstborn in the land of Egypt, from the firstborn of Pharaoh who sat on his throne to the firstborn of the handmaiden behind the millstones, and all the firstborn of the cattle. And Pharaoh rose up in the night, he and all his servants and all the Egyptians, and there was a great cry in Egypt, for there was not a house where one was not dead. And he summoned Moses and Aaron by night and said, "Rise up, go forth from among my people, both you and the people of Israel, and go, serve the Lord as you have said. Take your flocks and your herds, as you have said, and be gone; and bless me also!]*

(Ex. 12:29-32).

VII:I

1. A. R. Tanhum of Jaffa in the name of R. Nunayya of Caesarea opened discourse by citing the following verse: *"But when I thought how to understand this, it seemed to me a wearisome task* (Ps. 73:16).

   B. "Said David, 'No one can reckon the exact moment of midnight except for the Holy One, blessed be He, but, as for me, *But when I thought how to understand this, it seemed to me a wearisome task.*

   C. "For no creature can reckon the exact moment except for him, for it is said: *And it came to pass at midnight [that the Lord smote all the firstborn in the land of Egypt, from the firstborn of Pharaoh who sat on his throne to the firstborn of the handmaiden behind the millstones, and all the firstborn of the cattle. And Pharaoh rose up in the night, he and all his servants and all the Egyptians, and there was a great cry in Egypt, for there was not a house where one was not dead. And he summoned Moses and Aaron by night and said, "Rise up, go forth from among my people, both you and the people of Israel, and go, serve the Lord as you have said. Take your flocks and your herds, as you have said, and be gone; and bless me also!]* (Ex. 12:29-32)."

The intersecting-verse serves to underline what the exegete finds interesting in the base-verse, God's precise timing of events, which only God can have accomplished.

VII:II

1. A. R. Aha opened discourse by citing this verse: *I am the Lord, the Lord is my name; I will not give my glory to another god, nor my praise to any idol* (Is. 42:8).

   B. *I am the Lord, the Lord is my name:* said R. Aha, "Said the Holy One, blessed be He, 'I am the Lord, the Lord is my name.*

- 111 -

C. "'That is the name that was given to me by the first Man.
D. "'That is my name, concerning which I made a stipulation with myself.
    That is the name concerning which I stipulated between the angels and
    myself.'"

2. A. *...I will not give my glory to another god, nor my praise to any idol* (Is.
       42:8):
   B. R. Menahema said in the name of R. Abin, "This refers to the shades."

3. A. R. Nehemiah in the name of R. Mina said, "No creature except for the
       Holy One, blessed be He, can distinguish between the drop of sperm that
       produces a firstborn and one that does not.
   B. "But as for me, *But when I thought how to understand this, it seemed to
       me a wearisome task.*
   C. "For no creature can reckon the exact moment except for him, for it is
       said: *And it came to pass at midnight [that the Lord smote all the
       firstborn in the land of Egypt.*"

There is a clear problem in the text of No. 3, which further leaves me
puzzled about the relevance of the intersecting-verse. I cannot put things
together into a cogent statement.

VII:III

1. A. *I make my servants' prophecies come true and give effect to my
       messengers' designs. I say of Jerusalem, "She shall be inhabited once
       more," and of the cities of Judah, "They shall be rebuilt, all their ruins I
       will restore"* (Is. 44:26):
   B. R. Berekhiah in the name of R. Levi: "If someone can *make my servants'
       prophecies come true and give effect to my messengers' designs,* do we
       not know that he will *say of Jerusalem, 'She shall be inhabited once
       more,' and of the cities of Judah, 'They shall be rebuilt, all their ruins I
       will restore'''*?
   C. "But the point is this: an angel appeared to Jacob, our father, and *said to
       him, What is your name? And he said, Jacob. And he said, Your name
       will not longer be Jacob, but Israel* (Gen. 32:28-29).
   D. "Then the Holy One, blessed be He, appeared to our father, Jacob, so as
       to confirm the decree of that angel: *And God said to him, Your name is
       Jacob* (Gen. 35:9, 10).
   E. "As to Jerusalem, since all of the prophets prophesied that Jerusalem
       would be rebuilt, how much the more so [will God confirm what his
       prophets have said]!"

2. A. Another interpretation of the verse: *I make my servants' prophecies come
       true and give effect to my messengers' designs. I say of Jerusalem, "She
       shall be inhabited once more," and of the cities of Judah, "They shall be
       rebuilt, all their ruins I will restore"* (Is. 44:26):
   B. *I make my servants' prophecies come true* refers to Moses: *Not so is my
       servant Moses* (Num. 12:7).

C. ...*and give effect to my messengers' designs* refers to Moses: *He sent an angel and brought us out of Egypt* (Num. 20:16).

D. Said the Holy One, blessed be He, to Moses, *Go, say to Israel, I shall pass through the land of Egypt on that night* (Ex. 12:12)."

E. Moses went and told Israel: *Thus said the Lord,* At midnight *I shall go forth through Egypt* (Ex. 11:4).

F. [Noting that Moses had specified the exact time,] said the Holy One, blessed be He, "I have already made a promise to Moses, saying to him, *Not so is my servant, Moses. In my entire household he is faithful* (Num. 12:7). Shall my servant, Moses, turn out to be a bluffer?

G. "But what has Moses said? *At midnight I shall go forth through Egypt.*

H. "So I shall do it at midnight: *and it came to pass* at midnight *[that the Lord smote all the firstborn in the land of Egypt, from the firstborn of Pharaoh who sat on his throne to the firstborn of the captive who was in the dungeon, and all the firstborn of the cattle.]"*

Now we have a fine rendition of the intersecting-verse/base-verse exegesis, and the intersecting-verse provides a powerful light on the base-verse. No. 1 reads the intersecting-verse in its own terms, registering the point that God is reliable in backing up the angel's changing of Jacob's name, so all the more so in rebuilding Jerusalem. This yields the occasion to make the same point on God's confirming Moses's statement, even when it went beyond what God, for his part, had said. That a close reading of the verses in hand has taken place is obvious.

VII:IV

1. A. *At midnight I rise to give you thanks for the justice of your decrees. I keep company with all who fear you, with all who follow your precepts. The earth is full of your never-failing love; O Lord, teach me your statutes* (Ps. 119:62-64):

    B. R. Phineas in the name of R. Eleazar bar Menahem: "What would David do?

    C. "He would take a psaltery and a harp and put them at his pillow and get up at midnight and play on them.

    D. "And the sages of Israel would hear the sound and say, 'Now if King David is occupied with Torah-study, how much the more so should we!'

    E. "It came about that all of Israel would occupy themselves in the study of Torah."

2. A. Said R. Levi, "There was a window by the bed of David, open to the north, and the harp was suspended at it, and as the north went blew at midnight, it would rush through the harp, and the harp would give forth sound on its own, in line with this verse: *When the instrument played* (2 Kgs. 3:5).

    B. "What it says is not, 'when David played...,' but, *When the instrument played.*

    C. "This indicates that the harp would give forth sound on its own."

    D. "And the sages of Israel would hear the sound and say, 'Now if King David is occupied with Torah-study, how much the more so should we!'

E.   "It came about that all of Israel would occupy themselves in the study of Torah."

3 .   A.   *[...and it came to pass at midnight that the Lord smote all the firstborn in the land of Egypt, from the firstborn of Pharaoh who sat on his throne to the firstborn of the captive who was in the dungeon, and all the firstborn of the cattle:]* That is in line with what David said: *[My heart is steadfast, O God, my heart is steadfast. I will sing and raise a psalm;] awake, my glory, awake, lute and harp, I will awake at dawn of day* (Ps. 57:7-8).

B.   "I will awake my glory before the glory of my creator, my glory is nothing before the glory of my creator."

C.   *I will awake at dawn of day:* "I will awake the dawn, and the dawn will not wake me up."

D.   But his impulse to do evil roused him and said to him, "David, ordinarily dawn wakes up kings, but you say, *I will awake at dawn of day!* Kings usually sleep to the third hour, but you say, *At midnight I rise to give you thanks for the justice of your decrees.*"

4 .   A.   What is the meaning of *the justice of your decrees*?

B.   [Thanks are due for] the decree of judgment that you carried out against the wicked Pharaoh, and the justice that you did with our elder, Sarah.

C   That is in line with this verse: *And the Lord afflicted Pharaoh with great plagues* (Gen. 12:17).

5 .   A.   Another interpretation of *the justice of your decrees*:

B.   [David said,] "[Thanks are due for] the decree of judgment that you carried out against the nations of the world [Ammon and Moab], and the justice that you did with our ancestor and our ancestress [reference here is to Boaz and Ruth].

C.   "For if he [Boaz] had [Braude and Kapstein, p. 143:] slipped into her as she lay at his feet, whence would I have had my origin?

D.   "Instead you set a blessing into his heart, so he said, *Blessed are you of the Lord, my daughter* (Ruth 3:10)."

6 .   A.   Another interpretation of *the justice of your decrees*:

B.   [Thanks are due for] the decree of judgment that you carried out against the Egyptians in Egypt.

C.   And for the righteousness that you carried out with our forefathers in Egypt.

D.   For they had to their credit only two religious duties on account of which they should be redeemed, the blood of the Passover-offering and the blood of circumcision.

E.   That is in line with this verse: *And I passed over you and I saw you wallowing in your bloods, and I said to you, In your bloods, live* (Ez. 16:6).

F.   *In your bloods:* the blood of the Passover-offering and the blood of circumcision.

The intersecting-verse, No. 1, is chosen because of its reference to midnight. But the opening clause of that verse is not the point of contact with our theme, God's redemption at midnight. Rather, we first work our way through the theme of events at midnight, No. 1-3, and then proceed, Nos. 4-6, to the point of intersection, which is the contrast between the justice done to Israel and the decrees of punishment issued against the nations. The net effect is not so strong because of the diversity of materials assembled in the treatment of the base-verse, some of them on one part of that verse, some on the other. And the climactic unit at the end has forgotten the base-verse altogether! But the point the compositor wishes to make is entirely exposed.

VII:V

1. A. Said R. Simeon b. Yohai, "Moses did not know how to calculate split seconds, let alone minutes or hours, of the night. But the Holy One, blessed be He, knows how to calculate split seconds, let alone minutes and hours, can stay within the rule even by a hair's breadth."

   B. [Mandelbaum, p. 125, n. to l. 13:] Therefore it is written, *...and it came to pass at midnight [that the Lord smote all the firstborn in the land of Egypt, from the firstborn of Pharaoh who sat on his throne to the firstborn of the captive who was in the dungeon, and all the firstborn of the cattle.]*

2. A. Who divided the night?

   B. R. Benjamin bar Japheth in the name of R. Yohanan: "The night divided itself up on its own."

   C. Rabbis say, "Its creator divided it."

3. A. Here you read: *And it came to pass at midnight* (Ex. 12:29) and elsewhere: *And he divided the night for them* (Gen. 14:15).

   B. Said R. Tanhuma, "[God said,] 'Your father went forth with me at midnight, so I shall go forth with his children at midnight.'"

   C. Rabbis say, "Said the Holy One, blessed be He, 'Your father went forth with me last night to midnight, so I shall go forth with his children from midnight to the morning.'"

4. A. Said R. Yohanan, "The angelic prince who protects the Egyptians will fall only by day.

   B. "What verse of Scripture so indicates? *Daylight shall fail in Tahpanhes, when I break the yoke of Egypt there; [then her boasted might shall be subdued; a cloud shall cover her, and her daughters shall go into captivity. Thus I will execute judgment on Egypt, and they shall know that I am the Lord]* (Ez. 30:18-19)."

   C. "And Scripture further states, *On that day there shall be five cities in the land of Egypt speaking the language [of Canaan and swearing allegiance to the Lord of Hosts, and one of them shall be called the City of the Sun]* (Is. 19:18)."

   D. What are these five cities?

   E. R. Hilkiah in the name of R. Simon says, "No, which is Alexandria, Noph, which is Memphis, Tehaphnehes, which is Hophnias, the city of

the sherds, which is [Braude and Kapstein, p. 145:] Ostracena, and the
city of the sun, which is Heliopolis.

5. A. Said Rabban Yohanan b. Zakkai, "We have found that both night and day
        are called day, for it is written, *And there was evening, and there was*
        morning, one day (Gen. 1:5)."
    B. R. Joshua bar Nehemiah derived the same proposition from this verse:
        "Also the night will not be too dark for you, and the night will glow
        like the day, darkness like light (Ps. 139:12).
    C. "[God says,] 'That is darkness which is light for me, and night so far as
        mortals are concerned.'"
    D. That yields the conclusion that on that very day the firstborn of the
        Egyptians died.
    E. How did it work out? They were smitten with a death-dealing blow in the
        evening, then writhed all night, and in the morning died.
    F. What verse of Scripture indicates it? "We have all died" is not what it
        says, but rather, *We are all dying,* that is to say, breathing our last.
    G. That is in line with this verse: *On the day on which I smote every*
        firstborn (Num. 3:13), and, further, *On the day on which I sanctified to*
        me every firstborn (Num. 8:17).
    H. On this basis you must conclude that on the day on which the firstborn
        of the Egyptians died, *I sanctified to me every firstborn [of Israel].*

We review the exegesis of the elements of our base-verse. The point of No.
1 is familiar. God alone could calculate the hours of the night with the
exactitude claimed by the verse before us. No. 2 carries forward the same theme.
No. 3 links the redemption in Egypt to the merit of the fathers. I cannot explain
the pertinence of No. 4, but it does flow into No. 5, which explains the sequence
by which the firstborn were killed.

VII:VI

1. A. *...the Lord smote all the firstborn in the land of Egypt* (Ex. 12:29):
    B. When the verse refers to a *firstborn,* it adds, *all* the firstborn,
        encompassing the firstborn of a man and the firstborn of a woman, the
        firstborn of a male and the firstborn of a female.
    C. How so? If a man had sexual relations with ten women and then they
        produced ten sons, it would turn out that all of them were firstborn of
        women.
    D. If ten men had sexual relations with one woman and she produced ten
        sons, all of them would turn out to be the firstborn of males.
    E. But take note of a case in which there was a household in which was no
        firstborn either for a male or for a female? How then can I apply to that
        house the verse: *...for there was not a house where one was not dead?*
    F. Said R. Abba bar Aha, "Then the one in charge of the household would
        die. That is in line with this verse: *Shimri the one in charge, for though*
        he was not firstborn, nonetheless his father put him in charge (1 Chr.
        26:10)."

2. A.   It was taught on Tannaite authority in the name of R. Nathan, "On the day on which a firstborn of one of them died, he would make an icon of him in the house. On that day [on which the firstborn was killed,] it too was smashed up, shattered, and scattered.

   B.   It was as hard for the parent as if on that very day he had buried the firstborn himself.

3. A.   Said R. Yudan, "Since the Egyptians would bury their dead in their houses, the dogs would come in through the burial niches [better: sewer pipes] and pull out the bones of the firstborn among the dead and play with them.

   B.   "It was as hard for the parent as if on that very day he had buried the firstborn himself."

The amplification of the base-verse proceeds, now with the exercise in explaining the sense of the encompassing adjective, *all*. The result is at No. 1. Nos. 2, 3 do not contribute to the exegesis of the base-verse but enrich the context in which the overall theme is worked out.

VII:VII

1. A.   *...from the firstborn of Pharaoh [who sat on his throne even to the firstborn of the maidservant who is behind the mill, and all the firstborn of the cattle]* (Ex. 12:29):

   B.   On the basis of that statement [read as *from the firstborn, Pharaoh*] it follows that Pharaoh himself was a firstborn.

2. A.   All of the firstborn came to their fathers, saying to them, "Since Moses has said, *And every firstborn will die* (Ex. 11:5), all the things that he has said against this people have come upon them. But now go and let these Hebrews go from among you, and if you do not do so, lo, this people is going to die."

   B.   They said, "Each one of us has ten sons. Let one of them die, and let what these Hebrews say not come to pass."

   C.   They said, "The sole remedy for the matter is for us to go to Pharaoh, for he is a firstborn. He may have mercy on his own life and let these Hebrews go away from among us."

   D.   They went to Pharaoh, saying to him, "Since Moses has said, *And every firstborn will die* (Ex. 11:5), all the things that he has said against this people have come upon them. But now go and let these Hebrews go from among you, and if you do not do so, lo, this people is going to die."

   E.   He said, "Go and beat the humps of these people. I have said, 'It is my life *or* the lives of these Hebrews!' And you say this!"

   F.   The firstborn went and killed sixty myriads of their fathers.

   G.   That is in line with this verse: *To the one who smote Egypt through their firstborn* (Ps. 136:10).

   H.   What is written is not, "To the one who smote the Egyptians in Egypt," but, *To the one who smote the Egyptians* through *their firstborn*, [for] the firstborn killed their fathers, in the number of sixty myriads.

3 . A. R. Abun in the name of R. Judah b. Pazzi said, "Batyah, the daughter of
       Pharaoh, was a firstborn. On account of what merit was she saved? It
       was through the prayer of Moses.

   B. "For it is written: *She perceives that her merchandise is profitable. Her
       lamp does not go out at night* (Prov. 31:18).

   C. "The reference to night calls to mind the verse: *It is a watch night for
       the Lord* (Ex. 12:42)."

The exposition of the theme of the firstborn continues. No. 1 is a
singleton, based on the verse at hand. No. 2, by contrast, pursues the theme,
but not in a close reading of our base-verse. No. 3 is tacked on, I should think
as an appendix to No. 2.

VII:VIII

1 . A. *[...from the firstborn of Pharaoh who sat on his throne] even to the
       firstborn of the maidservant who is behind the mill, [and all the firstborn
       of the cattle]* (Ex. 11:5):

   B. R. Huna and R. Aha in the name of R. Eleazar son of R. Yose the
       Galileans, "Even the handmaiden who were lashed to the millstones
       would say, 'We take pleasure in our subjugation, so long as the Israelites
       also are subjugated.'"

   C. Said R. Judah b. Pazzi, "There is a traditional narrative that this was with
       reference to Seah, daughter of Asher, for when she came down to Egypt,
       they had lashed her to the millstones."

The amplification of the cited verse now gives us a reason for the
punishment inflicted on the slaves, and that issue continues to receive attention
in the next pericope.

VII:IX

1 . A. *...and all the firstborn of the cattle:*

   B. If man had sinned, what sin had beasts done?

   C. It was because the Egyptians bow down to the ram.

   D. It was so that the Egyptian would not have occasion to say, "Our god
       [the ram] has brought this punishment on us. Our god is strong, for it
       has stood up for itself. Our god is strong, because the punishment did
       not touch it."

The question raised at **VII:VIII** is asked once again, with an equally
compelling answer.

VII:X

1 . A. R. Huna and R. Joshua bar Abin, son-in-law of R. Levi, in the name of
       R. Levi: "The Merciful God does not touch lives first of all [but exacts
       vengeance on property]. From whom do you learn that fact? From Job:
       *A messenger came to Job and said, The oxen were plowing and the asses
       feeding beside them* (Job 1:14)."

   B. What is the meaning of, *and the asses feeding beside them*?

C. Said R. Hama, "A model of the order of the world to come was made for him, in line with this verse: *Behold, the days are coming, says the Lord, when the one who ploughs shall overtake the one who reaps* (Amos 9:13). [Mendelbaum: That is, corn will ripen within moments after the seed is planted, so that browing animals will follow in the tracks of the plowing animals.]"

D. Said R. Abba bar Kahana, "[With reference to the verse, *The Sabeans made a raid and took the oxen and the asses away, yes, they smote the servants with the edge of the sword* (Job 1:15),] they went out of Kefar Kerinos and went through the whole of Ublin, and when they came to Migdal Sebayya, they died."

E. Said R. Hama, [In the verse,*And I alone have escaped* (Job 1:15),] the word *alone* bears the sense of *solely*, that is, he alone escaped [only with his life], but was himself broken and beaten."

F. Said R. Yudan, *"And I alone have escaped to tell you* (Job 1:15) means that 'the sole purpose for which I escaped was to *tell* you,' at which point he died.

G. "That is in line with this verse: *While he was still speaking, there came another and said, The fire of God fell from heaven and burned up the sheep and the servants and consumed them; and I alone have escaped to tell you. While he was speaking there came another and said, The Chaldaeans formed three companies and made a raid upon the camels and took them and slew the servants with the edge of the sword and I alone have escaped to tell you.* (Job 1:14-17)."

H. When Job heard this news, he forthwith began to collect a troop to make war against them [but then he changed his mind, as will now be explained]. That is in line with this verse: *Because I stood in great fear of the multitude, and the contempt of families terrified me, so that I kept silence and did not go out of doors* (Job 31:34)."

I. Said Job [in gathering his troops], "This nation is the most contemptible of all nations: *Behold the land of the Chaldaeans – the people that was a no-people* (Is. 23:13). Would that it had never come into existence. Does that people think that it can frighten me?"

J. But when people told him, *"The fire of God fell from heaven,* he said, "If it is from Heaven, what can I do."

K. Forthwith: *...so that I kept silence and did not go out of doors.*

L. And then: *And he took a potsherd with which to scrape himself and sat among the ashes* (Job 2:8).

2. A. [The same proposition derives from the case] also of Mahlon and Chilion. First their horses, camels, and asses died, and then he died,

B. as it is said: *And Elimelech, Naomi's husband, died* (Ruth 1:3), then the two sons: *Mahlon and Chilian died, both of them* (Ruth 1:5). [Delete: And then she died.]

3. A. So too is the rule applying to skin-ailments which affect man.

B. **First of all, it begins on his house, and, if the man repents, the affected stone has only to be removed:** *They shall dismantle the stones* **(Lev. 14:40). If the man does not repent, then the whole house has to be dismantled:** *And he will dismantle the house* **(Lev. 14:45). And then it** affects his clothing. If he repents, the clothing has to be ripped: *And he shall tear the affected patch out of the garment or the hide or from the warp or from the woof* (Lev. 13:56). If he does not repent, then the clothing has to be burned: *And he will burn the clothing* (Lev. 13:52). Then it affects his body. If he repents, it goes away, and he departs, and if not, it comes back on him: *And he shall sit solitary, his dwelling will be outside of the camp* (Lev. 13:46) [T. Neg. 6:4].

4. A. So too is the rule as to the events in Egypt:
   B. First the measure of justice affected their property: *He smote their vines and their fig trees* (Ps. 105:33).
   C. Then: *He gave over their cattle to the hail and their flocks to fiery bolts of lightning* (Ps. 78:48).
   D. Then at the end: *He smote all the firstborn of Egypt* (Ps. 78:51).

The syllogism that God punishes property, then persons, is worked out through a sequence of cases, ending with ours. The exegesis of the verse and theme therefore does not define the principle of cogency, rather the proof of the stated proposition.

VII:XI

1. A. R. Levi bar Zechariah in the name of R. Berekhiah: "It was with the arts of royal siege-warfare that God came against them.
   B. "First of all, [a besieging army] shuts up their water supply, then he brings against them thunders of war, then he shoots arrows, then he brings troops, then he storms them, then he pours burning oil, then he throws great stones against them, then he brings against them scaling troops, then he captures them, then he takes out their greatest figure and kills him.
   C. "[So too is the order of God's siege of Egypt:] first he shut up their water supply: *He turned their rivers into blood* (Ps. 78:44).
   D. "Then he brought against them thunders of war: This refers to the frogs.
   E. (Said R. Yose bar Hanina, "The croaking was worse for them than the frogs themselves.")
   F. "Then he shot arrows: This refers to the lice.
   G. "Then he brought troops: This refers to the swarms of wild beasts.
   H. "Then he starved them out: *A very heavy murrain* (Ex. 9:3).
   I. "Then he poured burning oil: This refers to the boils.
   J. "Then he threw great stones against them: This refers to the hail.
   K. "Then he brought against them scaling troops: This refers to the locusts.
   L. "Then he captured them: this refers to the darkness.
   M. "Then he took out their greatest figure and killed him: This refers to the killing of the firstborn."

2. A. R. Levi, son-in-law of R. Zechariah, in the name of R. Berekhiah said, "*As at the news concerning Egypt, so they shall be startled at the fall of the adversary* (Is. 23:5)."

B. Said R. Eliezer, "Whenever the name of Tyre is written in Scripture, if it is written out [with all of the letters], then it refers to the province of Tyre. Where it is written without all of its letters [and so appears identical to the word for enemy], the reference of Scripture is to Rome. [So the sense of the verse is that Rome will receive its appropriate reward.]"

3. A. [Resuming the discussion begun at No. 1 with the information just now given:] R. Levi in the name of R. Hama bar Hanina: "He who exacted vengeance from the former [oppressor] will exact vengeance from the latter.

B. "Just as, in Egypt, it was with blood, so with Edom it will be the same: *I will show wonders in the heavens and in the earth, blood, and fire, and pillars of smoke* (Job 3:3).

C. "Just as, in Egypt, it was with frogs, so with Edom it will be the same: *The sound of an uproar from the city, an uproar because of the palace, an uproar of the Lord who renders recompense to his enemies* (Is. 66:6).

D. "Just as, in Egypt, it was with lice, so with Edom it will be the same: *The streams of Bosrah will be turned into pitch, and the dust thereof into brimstone, and the land thereof shall become burning pitch* (Is. 34:9). *Smite the dust of the earth that it may become lice* (Ex. 8:12).

E. "Just as, in Egypt, it was with swarms of wild beasts, so with Edom it will be the same: *The pelican and the bittern shall possess it* (Is. 34:11).

F. "Just as, in Egypt, it was with pestilence, so with Edom it will be the same: *I will plead against Gog with pestilence and with blood* (Ez. 38:22).

G. "Just as, in Egypt, it was with boils, so with Edom it will be the same: *This shall be the plague wherewith the Lord will smite all the peoples that have warred against Jerusalem: their flesh shall consume away while they stand upon their feet* (Zech. 14:12).

H. "Just as, in Egypt, it was with great stones, so with Edom it will be the same: *I will cause to rain upon Gog...an overflowing shower and great hailstones* (Ez. 38:22).

I. "Just as, in Egypt, it was with locusts, so with Edom it will be the same: *And you, son of man, thus says the Lord God: Speak to birds of every sort...the flesh of the mighty shall you eat...blood shall you drink...you shall eat fat until you are full and drink blood until you are drunk* (Ez. 39:17-19).

J. "Just as, in Egypt, it was with darkness, so with Edom it will be the same: *He shall stretch over Edom the line of chaos and the plummet of emptiness* (Is. 34:11).

K. "Just as, in Egypt, he took out their greatest figure and killed him, so with Edom it will be the same: *A great slaughter in the land of Edom, among them to come down shall be the wild oxen* (Is. 34:6-7).

L. Said R. Meir, "[The letters of the word for *wild* (*reemim*) may be read as *Rome*, thus,] 'Among them to come down shall be Rome.'"

The elaborate proof makes a familiar point, which is the proposition of the entire pisqa: the Exodus from Egypt is the paradigm for the coming redemption from Rome. The passage is cogent, beginning to end, since No. 1 is essential, and No. 2 forms the bridge to No. 3.

VII:XII

1. A. *For behold darkness shall cover the earth, and thick darkness the peoples; but the Lord will arise upon you, and his glory will be seen upon you. [And nations shall come to your light, and kings to the brightness of your rising]* (Is. 60:2-3):

   B. R. Levi bar Zechariah in the name of R. Berekhiah: *"Darkness and thick darkness* affected Egypt for three days. What verse of Scripture indicates it? *And there was darkness, thick darkness* (Ex. 10:22).

   C. "But emptiness and void have never yet affected this world.

   D. "But where [and when] will they come to pass?

   E. "They will envelope the great city of Rome: *He will stretch over it the line of chaos and the plummet of emptiness* (Is. 34:11)."

   F. Rabbis say, "As to the nations of the world, who never accepted the Torah which was given in darkness, concerning them Scripture says, *For behold darkness shall cover the earth, and thick darkness the peoples....*

   G. "But as to Israel, which accepted it in darkness, concerning them Scripture says, *...but the Lord will arise upon you, and his glory will be seen upon you."*

The closing statement underlines the foregoing, the contrast between Israel's coming glory, because of its acceptance of the Torah, and the nations' humiliation.

Pisqa Eight

[When you enter the land which I give you and reap its harvest, you shall bring]
the first sheaf *[of your harvest to the priest. He shall present the sheaf as a
special gift before the Lord on the day after the sabbath so as to gain acceptance
for yourselves]*
(Lev. 23:11).

VIII:I

1. A. [With reference to the passage that follows: *The Lord spoke to Moses
and said, Speak to the Israelites in these words: When you enter the land
which I give you and reap its harvest, you shall bring the first sheaf of
your harvest to the priest. He shall present the sheaf as a special gift
before the Lord on the day after the sabbath so as to gain acceptance for
yourselves. On the day you present the sheaf, you shall prepare a perfect
yearling ram for a whole offering to the Lord...You shall eat neither
bread nor grain parched or fully ripened during that day, the day on which
you bring your God his offering; this is a rule binding on your
descendants for all time wherever you live. From the day after the
sabbath, the day on which you bring your special gift, you shall count
seven full weeks. The day after the seventh sabbath will make fifty days,
and then you shall present to the Lord a grain-offering from the new crop*
(Lev. 23:9-16):] [we consider the following:] *What does man gain by all
the toil at which he toils under the sun? [A generation goes, and a
generation comes, but the earth remains forever]* (Qoh.1:3).
   B. Said R. Benjamin b. R. Levi, "Sages proposed to hide away the scroll of
Qohelet, for they found in it[s teachings] matters that tended toward
heresy.
   C. "They said, 'Lo, is this the whole of Solomon's wisdom, which he came
along to teach: *What does man gain by all the toil at which he toils
under the sun?* May one then suppose that that is the case even for the
[man's] toil over Torah?'
   D. "They retracted and ruled, 'He did not phrase matters as "all the toil" but
"all the toil for his own benefit." [The meaning of Solomon therefore
must be] for the toil that pertains to oneself, he does not profit, thus
[implying] one does profit from the toil that pertains to the Torah.'"

2. A. Said R. Samuel b. R. Isaac, "Sages proposed to hide away the scroll of
Qohelet, for they found in it[s teachings] matters that tended toward
heresy.
   B. "They said, 'Lo, is this the whole of Solomon's wisdom, which he came
along to teach: *Rejoice, O young man, in your youth, and let your heart
cheer you in the days of your youth; walk in the ways of your heart and*

*the sight of your eyes. [But know that for all these things, God will
bring you into judgment]* (Qoh. 11:9)?

C.   "Moses stated, *...not to follow after your own heart and your own eyes,
[which you are inclined to go after wantonly]'* [Num. 15:39], and yet
[Solomon] has said, *Walk in the ways of your heart and the sight of your
eyes!*

D.   "'[Accordingly, he would imply] there is neither justice nor a Judge, so
the penalty of flogging has been annulled!'

E.   "But when [Solomon further] stated, *But know that for all these things,
God will bring you judgment* (Qoh. 11:9), they stated, 'Well has
Solomon spoken.'"

3. A.   R. Yudan said, "[He means the toil that one does in study of Torah only]
under the sun [after sunrise] does not [yield gain], but [what he studies]
before the sun [has risen] does yield [gain]."

   B.   [With regard to the statement, *What does man gain by all the toil at
which he toils under the sun?* (Qoh. 1:3)], R. Huna and R. Aha in the
name of R. Ilpai: "[Solomon means] one toils under the sun but lays up
treasures above the sun [in Heaven]."

4. A.   R. Levi and rabbis:

   B.   R. Levi said, "[God says,] 'What do people gain as a reward who
accumulate treasures of religious actions and good deeds? It is sufficient
for them that I make the light [of the sun] to shine on them: *The sun
rises and the sun sets* (Qoh. 1:5).'"

   C.   Rabbis say, "What do people gain as a reward who accumulate treasures
of religious actions and good deeds? It is sufficient for them that the
Holy One, blessed be He, in the age to come is going to renew the light
of their faces to shine like the orb of the sun.

   D.   "That is in line with the following verse of Scripture: *But those who
love him are as the sun when it goes forth in its strength* (Jud. 5:31)."

5. A.   Said R. Yannai, "Under ordinary circumstances, when someone buys a
litra of meat, take note of how much trouble and effort he encounters
until he has cooked it.

   B.   "But the Holy One, blessed be He, brings up the wind and brings forth
clouds and brings down rain and brings up plants and dries them and
spreads a table before every individual.

   C.   "Should you not bring him the sheaf of the first fruits?"

6. A.   Said R. Phineas, "Under ordinary circumstances when a person washes his
garment in the rainy season, how much trouble and effort does he
encounter before he is able to dry it.

   B.   "But [God says,]: 'I bring up the wind and bring forth clouds and bring
down rain and bring up plants and dry them and spread a table before
every individual.

   C.   "'Should you not bring me the sheaf of the first fruits?'"

7. A.   Said R. Abin, "Come and take note of how much trouble and effort do the
Israelites undergo in bringing the sheaf of the first fruits!"

B. That is in line with the following Mishnah passage that we have learned (at M. Menahot 10:4): "They reaped it and put it into baskets. They brought it to the courtyard [of the Temple]. They parched it in fire, so as to carry out the requirement that it be parched with fire" [Lev. 2:14], the words of R. Meir. And sages say, "With reeds and with stems of plants do they [first] beat it [to thresh it], so that it not be crushed. And they put it into a tube, and the tube was perforated, so that the fire affect all of it." They spread it out in the courtyard, and the breeze blows over it. They put it into a grist mill and took out from it a tenth *ephah*, which is sifted through thirteen sieves. [Cf. also M. Menahot 10:3:] "How did they do it? Agents of the court go forth on the eve of [the afternoon before] the festival [of Passover]. And they make [the grain] into sheaves while it is still attached to the ground, so that it will be easy to reap. And all the villagers nearby gather together there [on the night after the first day of Passover], so that it will be reaped with great pomp."]

8. A. Said R. Levi, "You have worked, plowed, sown, weeded, pruned, hoed, reaped, made sheaves, threshed and stacked the sheaves. If [God] does not produce for you a little wind for winnowing, how will anyone live?

B. "Lo, should you not give him back a fee for the wind?"

C. *What does man gain by all the toil at which he toils under the sun?*

9. A. Said R. Levi, *"Neither do they say in their heart, let us now fear the Lord our God who has given the former rain and the latter rain in due season; [he is the one who must keep the appointed weeks of the harvest]* (Jer. 5:24).

B. *"who has given:* He has given everything to you. Do you not need him from now on?

C. "To the contrary: *...the former rain and the latter rain in due season; he is the one who must keep the appointed weeks of the harvest.*

D. "He must keep it for us from the hot wind and the harsh breezes. And what are they? They are the seven weeks between Passover and Pentecost [marked by the sheaf of first fruits]."

10. A. R. Hiyya taught on Tannaite authority, *"From the day after the sabbath, the day on which you bring your special gift, you shall count seven full weeks:*

B. "When are the weeks complete? When the priestly watches of Jeshua and Shekheniah come [to take up their duties in the cultic service of the Temple, that is, ninth and tenth in the order of the twenty-four priestly watches that divide up the year in the Temple service]."

11. A. R. Joshua b. R. Levi: "[God says,] 'I serve as your watchman [over your crop] and should you not give me the wage of my watch?'"

B. Said R. Berekhiah, "[God says, 'In making the crops possible], I serve as your chef, and should you not give me a taste of what I have cooked for you, so that I may know what [further spices] it needs? [The first cutting of the grain represents that taste].'

B. "That is in line with what David says, *Rain as a free gift pour down, O God* (Ps. 68:10).

C. "If [the crop] requires rain, then it is a matter of *a free gift.* If [the crop] requires dew, then *Pour down, O God.*

D. "...*wave down dew, with which you support your inheritance when it is weary* (Ps. 68:10)."

12. A. Said R. Benayyah, "Said the Holy One, blessed be He, to Israel, 'My children, when I gave the omer to you, I gave each one of you an omer individually, that is, *A sheaf for each head, in accord with the number of all your souls* (Ex. 16:16). When you give the sheaf, you give one for all of you.

B. "And not only so, but it is not of wheat but of barley [a cheaper grain, that you give me the sheaf].'"

C. Therefore Moses admonished Israel, saying to them, *When you come into the land which I give you and reap its harvest, you shall bring the sheaf of the first fruits of your harvest to the priest* (Lev. 23:10).

The passage is shared more or less verbatim with Leviticus Rabbah Parashah 28, because it deals with the same base-verse, namely. Lev. 23:10, on the sheaf of first grain. The composite contains two distinct materials, those at Nos. 1-4, exercises on the intersecting-verse, Qoh. 1:3, and No. 5ff., which take up the substance of the base-verse and ignore the intersecting one entirely. I assume that no explicit link between Qoh. 1:3 and Lev. 23:10 is drawn because to the exegetes it was self-evident. Once we refer to the fruit of a harvest, the negative evaluation of one's gain from all his labor will come to mind. At any rate, Nos. 1-4 labor solely on that matter, trying to explain (away) Solomon's view by harmonizing it with that of sages. At issue then is, first, the worth of study of Torah, which must be affirmed, Nos. 1 and 3. The power of Heaven to distinguish good from bad deeds, No. 2, has no bearing upon the base-verse, only on the theme introduced at 1.C. It must follow that Nos. 1 and 2 were joined together before being set whole into the present context. No. 3 then reverts to the exegesis of the intersecting-verse, and No. 4 continues the theme, but not the sentiment or problematic, of No. 3. No. 5, at the end, simply gives a reason for the commandment of Lev. 23:10. So the construction is formed of three available compositions, Nos. 1-3, 3-4, and 5. No. 6 introduces the shift in climate marked by the sheaf of first fruits. No. 6 completes the theme introduced above. The rainy season comes to an end at Passover. At that point the grain is dry and ready. God makes possible what a human being cannot do, so 6.A's contrast to 6.B. I do not see why the sizable citation of M. Men. 10:4, then 10:3, is attached. Benaiah's statement, 7.A, does not really fit in with what has gone before. It serves only as a pretext for citing the Mishnah's rules. No. 8, by contrast, reverts to the theme of No. 1, namely, justification for bringing the sheaf of the first grain. No. 9 explains why the sheaf is owing for the seven weeks from Passover to Pentecost. No. 10 adds its own point, referring to the course of priestly families, as explained at 10.B. No. 11 goes over the established point, that the omer is a minor compensation for all that God does. No. 12 then draws us back to our base-verse. But the intersecting-verse is long in the past and forgotten. No. 12 presents an exposition of the theme in its own terms. In all, we have little more than a hodgepodge of compositions relevant to the overall theme or the intersecting-verse but not to one another. Only now do we revert to the base-verse – and through an essentially formal statement, ignoring what has gone before.

VIII:II

1. A. *His harvest the hungry eat, and he takes it even without a buckler; and the thirsty pant after their wealth* (Job 5:5).
   B. *His harvest* refers to Nimrod [one of the four kingdoms of Gen. 14:1].
   C. *The hungry eat* refers to our father, Abraham.
   D. *And he takes it even without a buckler* – without a sword, without a shield, but with prayer and supplications.
   E. This is in line with the following verse of Scripture: *He led forth his trained servants [empty handed, understanding the Hebrew word RK as empty], [those born of his house, three hundred and eighteen]* (Gen. 14:14).
   F. Said R. Simeon b. Laqish, "It was Eliezer alone [whom Abraham took with him]. And how do we know? [The numerical value of the letters that make up the Hebrew name] Eliezer adds up to three hundred and eighteen."
   G. *And the thirsty pant after their wealth* – who trampled on the wealth of Nimrod?
   H. It was Abraham and all those who were allied with him.

2. A. Another interpretation: *His harvest* refers to Pharaoh.
   B. *The hungry eat* refers to Moses and Aaron.
   C. *And he takes it even without a buckler* – without a sword, without a shield, but with prayer and supplications.
   D. *And the Lord said to Moses, Why do you cry out to me?* (Ex. 14:15).
   E. *And the thirsty pant after their wealth* – who trampled the wealth of Pharaoh? It was Moses and Aaron and all those who were allied with them.

3. A. Another interpretation: *His harvest* refers to Sihon and Og.
   B. *The hungry eat* refers to Moses and Aaron.
   C. *And he takes it even without a buckler* – without a sword, without a shield, but with a [mere] word.
   D. *And the Lord said to Moses, Be not afraid of him, because I have given him into your hand* (Num. 21:34).
   E. *And the thirsty pant after their wealth* – who trampled on the wealth of Sihon and Og? It was Moses and Aaron and all those who were allied with them.

4. A. Another interpretation: *His harvest* refers to Sisera.

    B. *The hungry eat* refers to Deborah and Barak.

    C. *And he takes it even without a buckler* – without a sword, without a shield, but [solely] by means of good deeds.

    D. That is in line with the following verse of Scripture: *Was shield or spear to be seen among forty thousand in Israel?* (Jud. 5:8).

    E. *And the thirsty pant after their wealth* – who trampled on the wealth of Sisera? It was Deborah and Barak and all those who were allied with them.

5. A. Another interpretation: *His harvest* refers to Sennacherib.

    B. *The hungry* eat refers to Isaiah and Hezekiah.

    C. *And he takes it even without a buckler* – without a sword, without a shield, but [solely] through prayer.

    D. *And Hezekiah the king and Isaiah ben Amoz, the prophet, prayed concerning this matter* (2 Chron. 32:20).

    E. *And the thirsty pant after their wealth* – who trampled on the wealth of Sennacherib? It was Hezekiah and Isaiah and all those who were allied with them.

6. A. Another interpretation: *His harvest* refers to Haman.

    B. *The hungry eat* refers to Mordecai.

    C. *And he takes it even without a buckler* – without a sword, without a shield, but solely with sack and ashes, as it is said, *Many lay in sackcloth and ashes* (Est. 4:3).

    D. *And the thirsty pant after their wealth* – who trampled upon the wealth of Haman? It was Mordecai and Esther and all those who were allied with them.

7. A. Another interpretation: *His harvest* refers to the thirty-one kings [of the Canaanites].

    B. *The hungry eat* refers to Joshua and Caleb.

    C. *And he takes it even without a buckler* – without a sword, without a shield, but with hailstones.

    D. *For the Lord said to Joshua, Rise, go, why are you here, falling on your face* (Josh. 7:10).

    E. *And the thirsty pant after their wealth* – who trampled upon the wealth of the third-one kings [of the Canaanites]? It was Joshua and Caleb and all those who were allied with them.

8. A. Now on the basis of what merit did the Israelites inherit the land of Canaan? One must say that it was on the basis of the religious duty of offering the sheaf of first grain.

    B. Therefore Moses admonished the Israelites, saying to them, *When you come into the land which I give you and reap its harvest, you shall bring the sheaf of the first fruits of your harvest to the priest* (Lev. 23:10).

The sole point of difference between the present version and that at Leviticus Rabbah 28 is moving Joshua, No. 7, to the end. In Leviticus Rabbah Joshua's pericope is right where it should be, in the sequence of salvific events, before Sisera. But the compositor here wishes to make the point important for the sheaf of first grain, and he has done what he had to do. The construction rigidly follows a self-evident pattern in interpreting the sequence of clauses of the intersecting-verse. The sheaf is interpreted as a means of securing the land. Where do we find the connection between the intersecting-verse and the base-verse? It seems to me there is none. We have a theme – God's handing the kingdoms over to the Israelites – and not a detailed reading of the clauses of Job 5:5 in terms of the giving of the sheaf at Lev. 23:10. True, God fed the wealth of the enemies to the Israelites, who were hungry and ate solely by virtue of their faith and good deeds. But the real tie is merely verbal, the linking of the harvest under discussion at Job 5:5 to the harvest to which Lev. 23:10 refers. The common word choice then allows the established, exegetical tradition for Job 5:5, independent of No. 8, to be reframed in terms of the substance of Lev. 23:10 by No. 8. If that is the case, then the entire exegetical tradition on the intersecting-verse had taken shape prior to the focusing of that tradition upon the sheaf of first fruits to which Lev. 23:10 alludes.

VIII:III

1. A. *And he shall wave the sheaf before the Lord* (Lev. 23:11).
   B. How did one wave [the sheaf]?
   C. R. Hama b. R. Uqba in the name of R. Yose b. R. Hanina: "Forward and backward, upward and downward:
   D. "Forward and backward, so as to counteract damaging winds, upward and downward so as to counteract destructive dew."
   E. R. Simon in the name of R. Joshua b. Levi said, "[Forward and backward, upward and downward.]
   F. "Forward and backward – to him to whom the entire earth belongs.
   G. "Upward and downward – to him to whom both the upper world and the lower world belong."
   H. Said R. Abin, "That is the view of R. Judah and R. Nehemiah."
   I. R. Jacob bar Abba in the name of R. Judah b. R. Simon, "That is the view of R. Yohanan and R. Simeon b. Laqish."

The amplification of the cited verse consists in the provision of relevant information rather than in citation of an intersecting-verse. T. Men. 7:19D contains the same formula as C.

VIII:IV

1. A. R. Jacob bar Abayye in the name of R. Judah bar Simon, R. Yohanan, and R. Simeon b. Laqish:
   B. R. Yohanan said, "The religious duty concerning the waving of the sheaf of first grain should not be a minor matter in your view. For it was on account of the merit of that religious duty that Abraham, our father, inherited the land.

C. "That is in line with the following verse of Scripture: *And I shall give to you and to your seed after you the land of your sojourning* (Gen. 17:8).

D. "That is on the following condition: *And God said to Abraham, And you will keep my covenant* (Gen. 17:9)."

2. A. R. Simeon b. Laqish said, "The religious duty concerning the waving of the sheaf of first grain should never be a minor matter in your view. For it is on account of the merit of that religious duty that peace is restored between a man and his wife.

B. "That is in line with the following verse of Scripture: *Then the man shall bring his wife to the priest, and bring the offering required of her, a tenth of an ephah of barley meal; he shall pour no oil upon it and put no frankincense on it, [for it is a cereal offering of jealousy]* (Num. 5:15). [Further: *And the priest shall take the cereal offering of jealousy out of the woman's hand and shall wave the cereal offering before the Lord* (Num. 5:25).]

C. "[Lev. R. adds:] And to what religious duty [does this refer]? To the sheaf of the first fruits that requires waving. [Accordingly,] it is on account of the merit of the flour of barley [used for both the woman's jealousy offering and the sheaf of first grain] that peace is restored between a man and his wife."

3. A. R. Abbahu stated the matter, [as did] R. Joshua b. Levi, R. Samuel bar Nahman, and rabbis.

B. R. Joshua b. Levi said, "It [the merit accruing to the religious duty of waving the sheaf of first grain] is what stood up for [the Israelites] in the time of Gideon.

C. "For it is written: *When Gideon came, behold, a man was telling a dream to his comrade, and he said, Behold, I dreamed a dream, and lo, a cake of barley bread tumbled into the camp of Midian and [came to the tent and struck it so that it fell]* (Jud. 7:13)."

D. What is the meaning of the word for cake, *selil?*

E. R. Levi said, "It is written, 'Bare, *salul.*' For that entire generation was bare of righteous men. Then on what account were they redeemed? It was on account of the merit accruing to the cake of barley bread. And what was it? It was the religious duty of waving the sheaf of first grain [made up of barley]."

F. R. Samuel bar Nahman said, "It [the merit accruing to the religious duty of waving the sheaf of first grain] is what stood up for [the Israelites] in the time of Hezekiah.

G. "For it is said, *And every stroke of the staff of punishment which the Lord lays upon them will be to the sound of timbrels and lyres; battling with battles of waving he will fight with them* (Is. 30:32). Now was there such a thing as 'battles of waving' at that time?

H. "To what then is reference made? It is to the religious duty of offering the sheaf of first grain, which requires waving."

I. Rabbis say, "It [the merit accruing to the religious duty of waving the sheaf of first grain] is what stood up for [the Israelites] in the time of Ezekiel.

J. "For it is said, *And you, take wheat and barley, beans and lentils, millet and spelt, and put them into a single vessel, and make bread of them* (Ez. 4:9).

K. [Since this was a mixture of grain, how can it be called only a barley cake, as at Ez. 4:12: *And you shall eat it as a barley cake?*] R. Hama bar Haninah said, "He put in more barley [than the other grains]."

L. R. Samuel bar Nahman said, "[He put in] things that clear the bowels [as barley does]."

M. Samuel said, "There [in Babylonia] they make it into a dried cake, which [even] a dog will not taste."

N. [Referring to Ezekiel's trial,] a noble lady asked R. Yose b. Halapta, "How much distress did that righteous man suffer! How many man slaves and woman slaves he owned, and they all rejected the food and drink [that he gave them]!"

O. He said to her, "[That tale] is to tell you that so long as the Israelites are in distress, the righteous suffer distress along with them."

4. A. R. Levi said, "It [the merit accruing to the religious duty of waving the sheaf of first grain] is what stood up for [the Israelites] in the time of Haman.

B. "You find that when Mordecai saw that Haman was coming to meet him leading a horse in hand, [he was afraid], thinking, 'It appears that that wicked man is coming to kill me.'

C. "[He was in session, with his disciples before him. He] said to them, 'Flee for yourselves, so that you will not be burned by the coals with which that wicked man is coming to kill me.'

D. "They said to him, 'Whether we shall be among the dead or the living, we are with you.'

E. "What did he do? He cloaked himself in his cloak and stood up to pray. [Leviticus Rabbah: "He said to them, 'If so, let us arise for prayer and perish while we are praying.']

F. "That wicked man came up and went into session with them. He said to them, 'What are you working on?'

G. "They said to him, 'The religious duty of offering the sheaf of first grain, which [the Israelites] used to offer in the sanctuary.'

H. "He said to them, 'And as to that sheaf, what is it, gold or silver?'

J. [Leviticus Rabbah:] "They said to him, 'It is neither gold nor silver, nor even wheat, but merely barley.'

K. "He said to them, 'And how much was it worth, ten *centenaria* [= 3,000 *manehs*]?'

L. "They said to him, 'Much less, ten *manehs*.'

M. "He said to them, "Arise, for your ten *manehs* have conquered my ten thousand talents of silver."

N. "When Mordecai had finished his prayer, Haman came to him, saying to him, 'Elder, put on this purple garment, [for your sheaf of first grain, worth ten *manehs*, has vanquished the ten thousand *centenaria* of mine which I paid to the king for the right to kill you].'

N. "[Mordecai] said to him, 'Why do you despise the royal status? [Leviticus Rabbah:] Is that man [you] not a fool? Do you not see [before you] a man who is unwashed, [in sackcloth and in fasting? For what do I need to put on a royal robe of purple and to adorn myself?]'

O.   "[Leviticus Rabbah:] [Haman] said to him, 'What do you then want?'

P.   "[Leviticus Rabbah:] [Mordecai] said to him, 'To wash first.'

Q.   "Haman went to find a bathhouse keeper, but he did not succeed, [Leviticus Rabbah:] for Queen Esther had given orders that no bathhouse keeper should open his establishment on that day on which that Jew [Mordecai] was going to be hanged.

R.   "[Haman] went and heated an oven and drew the bathwater and washed him. When he had washed him, he dressed him in the purple robe. He then said to him, 'Elder, set this wreath [on your head], [for your sheaf of first grain, worth ten *manehs,* has vanquished the ten thousand *centenaria* of mine.]'

S.   "[Mordecai] said to him, 'Why do you despise the royal status? [Leviticus Rabbah:] [Mordecai] said to him, 'Is that man not a fool? Can someone put on a royal wreath without first getting a haircut? [Leviticus Rabbah:] Do you not see that my hair is overgrown?'

T.   "[Leviticus Rabbah:] [Haman] said to him, 'What do you then want?'

U.   "[Leviticus Rabbah:] [Mordecai] said to him, 'To get a haircut first.'

V.   "Haman went to find a barber, but he did not succeed. He went home and brought a pair of scissors from his house and gave him a haircut. After he had given him a haircut, he began to sigh.

W.   "[Mordecai] said to him, 'Why are you sighing?'

X.   "[Haman] said to him, 'Is it not a woe for that man, who used to appoint the minister in charge of all matters, the minister in charge of the king's appointments, now is turned into a bathhouse keeper and a barber!'

Y.   "[Mordecai] said to him, 'And what question is there! But don't I know that your father came from Kepar Qirynos, and was a barber and a bathhouse keeper? And he prepared women's make-up, and these are his very shears!'

Z.   "[Leviticus Rabbah:] After he had given him a haircut, he dressed him in the wreath. He said to him, 'Elder, ride on this horse, [Leviticus Rabbah:] for your sheaf of first grain, worth ten *manehs,* has vanquished the ten thousand *centenaria* of mine!'

AA. "[Mordecai] said to him, '[Leviticus Rabbah:] Is that man not a fool? Do you not see that I am an old man? Can I ride on a horse?'

BB. "[Haman] said to him, 'And am I too not an old man?' [Leviticus Rabbah:] What is it that you want?'

CC. "[Mordecai] said to him, 'And are you not the one who caused this to happen to yourself?' Bend your back down for me, so that I can ride, and I'll ride.'

DD. "He bent his back down for him, and he mounted up.

EE. "This was meant to fulfill the following verse of Scripture: *And your enemies will dwindle away before you and you shall tread on their high places* (Deut. 33:29).

FF. "While he was riding, he began to praise the Holy One, blessed be He: *I will extol you, O Lord, for you have drawn me up, and have not let my foes rejoice over me. O Lord my God, I cried to you for help, and you have healed me. O Lord, you have brought up my soul from Sheol, and restored me to life among those gone down to the pit* (Ps. 30:1-3).

GG. "His disciples said, *Sing praises to the Lord, O you his saints and give thanks to his holy name. For his anger is but for a moment, and his favor is for a lifetime. Weeping may tarry for the night, but joy comes with the morning* (Ps. 30:4-5).

HH. "That wicked man [Leviticus Rabbah:] Haman said, *As for me, I said in my prosperity, I shall never be moved. By your favor, O Lord, you had established me as a strong mountain. You hid your face, I was dismayed* (Ps. 30:6-7).

II. "Esther said, *To thee, O Lord, I cried, and to the Lord I made supplication; what profit is there in my death, if I go down to the pit? Will the dust praise you? Will it tell of your faithfulness?* (Ps. 30:8-9).

JJ. "The congregation of Israel said, *Hear, O Lord, and be gracious to me! O Lord, be my helper. You have turned for me my mourning into dancing, you have loosed my sackcloth and girded me with gladness* (Ps. 30:10-11).

KK. "[Leviticus Rabbah:] And the holy spirit says, *That glory may praise you and not be silent. O Lord, my God, I will give thanks to you forever* (Ps. 30:12)."

LL. [Commenting on E-F, above], said R. Phineas, "It was with the recitation of the *Shema* that he had been occupied, and he did not interrupt the recitation at all: *That glory may praise you and not be silent. O Lord my God, I will give thanks to you forever* (Ps. 30:12)."

This anthology of materials on the importance of the religious duty of waving the sheaf of first grain begins with a matched pair, Nos. 1-2. The formal base is blatant. No. 3 then assigns to the same matter power to save and redeem Israel, citing passages in which a barley cake figures in a salvific tale, Gideon, Hezekiah, Ezekiel. No. 4 proceeds with a separate example. It is wholly Levi's version, since, as we see at the end, Phineas would not have regarded the story of Haman and Mordecai as relevant to the reward for waving the sheaf of first grain. 4.F accounts for the inclusion of the entire matter. But that is no minor detail, since it is part of the recurrent triad of action, M, R, Z. Accordingly, those who selected the composition for inclusion here made a good choice. I cannot then imagine how to revise the tale to conform to Phineas' picture, but the exegesis of Ps. 30 will not change much.

Pisqa Nine

When a bull or sheep or goat *[is born, it shall remain seven days with its mother, and from the eighth day on, it shall be acceptable as an offering by fire to the Lord]*

(Lev. 22:27).

IX:I

1. A. [Concerning the verse: *When a bull or sheep or goat is born, it shall remain seven days with its mother; and from the eighth day on it shall be acceptable as an offering by fire to the Lord* (Lev. 22:27):] *Your righteousness is like the mountains of God, your judgments are like the great deep; [man and beast you save, O Lord]* (Ps. 36:6).
   B. R. Ishmael and R. Aqiba:
   C. R. Ishmael says, "With the righteous, who carry out the Torah, which was given *from the mountains of God* the Holy One, blessed be He, does righteousness *like the mountains of God. Your righteousness is like the mountains of God.*
   D. "But with the wicked, who do not carry out the Torah, which was given 'from the mountains of God,' the Holy One, blessed be He, seeks a strict accounting, unto *the great deep. Your judgments are like the great deep.*
   E. R. Aqiba says, "All the same are these and those: the Holy One, blessed be He, seeks a strict accounting with [all of] them in accord with strict justice.
   F. "He seeks a strict accounting with the righteous, collecting from them the few bad deeds that they do in this world, in order to pay them an abundant reward in the world to come.
   G. "And he affords prosperity to the wicked and gives them a full reward for the minor religious duties that they successfully accomplished in this world, in order to exact a full penalty from them in the world to come."

2. A. Rabbi [Judah the Patriarch] [Leviticus Rabbah: Meir] says, "The righteous are comparable to their abode [like the mountains of God] and the wicked are comparable to their dwelling [like the great deep].
   B. "The righteous are comparable to their abode: *I will feed them in a good pasture, and upon the high mountains of Israel will be their fold* (Ez. 34:14).
   C. "The wicked are comparable to their abode: *Thus said the Lord in the day when he went down to the netherworld, I caused the deep to mourn and cover itself for him* (Ez. 31:15)."
   D. R. Judah b. Rabbi said, "'I caused to mourn (H'BLTY)' is written, 'I brought down (HWBLTY).'"

- 135 -

E. "By way of parable: they do not make a cover for a bowl of silver, gold, copper, iron, tin, or lead [Num. 31:22] but only [for one] of clay, for it is a material of the same sort [as the bowl].

F. "So said the Holy One, blessed be He, 'Gehenna is dark, and the wicked are dark, and the deep is dark. Let the dark come and cover the dark,'

G. "[as it is said], *For [the wicked] comes in vanity and departs in darkness and his name is covered with darkness* (Qoh 6:4)."

3. A. R. Jonathan in the name of R. Josiah would rearrange the elements of this verse: *"Your righteousness over your judgments [prevails] like the mountains of God over the great deep.*

    B. "Just as these mountains conquer the great deep, so that it may not rise up and flood the entire world, so the deeds of the righteous overcome punishment, keeping it from spreading over the world.

    C. "Another interpretationof the verse, *our righteousness over your judgments [prevails] like the mountains of God over the great deep:* Just as these mountains have no end, so the reward of the righteous in the world to come will know no end.

    D. *"Your judgments are like the great deep* (Ps. 36:6):

    E. "Just as there is no searching out the great deep, so there is no searching out the punishment that is coming upon the wicked in the age to come."

4. A. Another interpretation: *Your righteousness is like the mountains of God:* Just as the mountains are [readily] visible, so the deeds of the righteous are [readily] visible.

    B. That is in line with the following verse of Scripture: *May they fear you in the sun* (Ps. 72:5).

    C. *Your judgments are like the great deep* : Just as the deep is hidden [from view], so the deeds of the wicked are hidden [from view].

    D. That is in line with the following verse of Scripture: *Whose deeds are in the dark* (Is. 29:15).

5. A. Another interpretation: *Your righteousness is like the mountains of God:* Just as these mountains are sown and bring forth fruit, so the deeds of the righteous bring forth fruit.

    B. That is in line with the following verse of Scripture: *Tell the righteous that it shall be well with them, for they shall eat the fruit of their deeds* (Is. 3:10).

    C. *Your judgments are like the great deep:* Just as the great deep is not sown and does not bring forth fruit, so the deeds of the wicked do not bear fruit.

    D. That is in line with the following verse of Scripture: *Woe to the wicked. It shall be ill with him, for what his hands have done shall be done to him* (Is. 3:11).

6. A. Another interpretation: *Your righteousness is like the mountains of God:*

    B. [Said] R. Judah b. R. Simon, "The act of righteousness which you did with Noah in the ark is *like the mountains of God.*

    C. "That is in line with the following verse of Scripture: *And the ark rested...on the mountains of Ararat* (Gen. 8:4).

D. *["Your judgments are like the great deep:]* The judgments which you meted out to his generation you exacted from them even to the great deep.

E. "That is in line with the following verse of Scripture: *And on that day the springs of the great deep broke open* (Gen. 7:11).

F. "And not only so, but, when you remembered him, it was not him alone that you remembered, but him and everyone that was with him in the ark.

G. "That is in line with the following verse of Scripture: *And God remembered Noah and all the living creatures* (Gen. 8:1)."

7. A. [Leviticus Rabbah adds:] Another interpretation of *Your righteousness is like the mountains of God:*

B. R. Joshua b. Levi went to Rome. There he saw marble pillars covered with tapestries, so that in the hot weather they should not crack from expansion and in the cold weather they should not crack from contraction.

C. When he went out, he met a poor man with a mat of reeds underneath him and a mat of reeds on top of him.

D. Concerning the marble pillars he recited the following verse of Scripture: *Your righteousness is like the mountains of God.*

E. He said, "Where you give, you give lavishly."

F. Concerning the poor man he recited this verse: *Your judgments are like the great deep.*

G. "Where you smite, you pay close attention to every little detail."

8. A. Alexander of Macedonia went to the king of Kasia, beyond the mountains of darkness. He came to a certain town, called Cartagena, and it was populated entirely by women.

B. They came out before him and said to him, "If you make war on us and conquer us, word will spread about you that you destroyed a town of women. But if we do battle with you and conquer you, word will spread about you that you made war on women and they beat you. And you'll never again be able to hold up your head among kings."

C. [Leviticus Rabbah adds: At that moment he turned away and left.] After he went away, he wrote on the door of the gate of the city, saying, "I, Alexander the Macedonian, a king, was a fool until I came to the town called Cartagena, and I learned wisdom from women."

D. He came to another town, called Africa. They came out and greeted him with apples made out of gold, golden pomegranates, and golden bread.

E. He said, "Is this gold what you eat in your country?"

F. They said to him, "And is it not this way in your country, that you have come here?"

G. He said to them, "It is not your wealth that I have come to see, but it is your justice that I have come to see."

H. While they were standing there, two men came before the king for justice.

I. [Leviticus Rabbah adds: This one kept himself far from thievery, and so did that.] One of them said, "I bought a rubbish heap from this man. I dug it open and found a jewel in it. I said to him, 'Take your jewel. I bought a rubbish heap. A jewel I didn't buy.'"

J. The other said, "When I sold the rubbish heap to that man, I sold him the rubbish heap and everything that is in it."

K. The king called one of them and said to him, "Do you have a male child?"

L. He said to him, "Yes."

M. The king called the other and said to him, "Do you have a daughter?"

N. He said to him, "Yes."

O. Then the king said to them, "Let this one marry that one, and let the two of them enjoy the jewel."

P. Alexander of Macedonia began to express surprise.

Q. He said to him, "Why are you surprised? Did I not give a good judgment."

R. He said to him, "Yes, you did."

S. He said to him, "If this case had come to court in your country, how would you have judged it?"

T. He said to him, "We should have cut off the head of this party and cut off the head of that party, and the jewel would have passed into the possession of the crown."

U. He said to him, "Does rain fall on you?"

V. He said to him, "Yes."

W. "And does the sun rise for you?"

X. He said to him, "Yes."

Y. He said to him, "Are there small cattle in your country?"

Z. He said to him, "Yes."

AA. "Woe to you! It is on account of the merit of the small cattle that you are saved."

BB. That is in line with the following verse of Scripture: *Man and beast you save, O Lord* (Ps. 36:7).

CC. Man on account of the merit of the beast do you save, O Lord."

9. A. So did the Israelites say before the Holy One, blessed be He: "Lord of the world, we are mere men. Save us like a beast, for we are drawn after you like beasts."

B. [That is in line with the following verse of Scripture:] *Draw me, we will run after you, like a beast, we are drawn to you.* (Song of Songs 1:4).

C. And whither *[are we drawn after you]?* A member of the household of Rabbi said, "To the Garden of Eden."

D. For it is written, *They feast on the abundance of your house, and you give them drink from the river of your delights* (Ps. 36:9).

E. Said R. Eleazar b. R. Menahem, "'Your delight' is not written here, but rather, *Your delights.* On the basis of that fact we may conclude that every righteous person has an Eden unto himself."

10. A. Said R. Isaac, "*Judgment* is stated with regard to man, and *judgment* is stated with regard to beast.

B. "The *judgment* stated with regard to a man: *And on the eighth day, he shall be circumcised* (Lev. 12:3).

C. "And the judgment stated with regard to the beast: *[When a bull or sheep or goat is born, it shall remain seven days (with its mother);] and from the eighth day on, it shall be acceptable [as an offering by fire to the Lord]* (Lev. 22:26).

The intersecting-verse is worked out in reference to the righteous, compared to the mountains of God, and the wicked – those subject to judgment – compared to the great deep. This general approach links Nos. 1-7. Once people read the verse in this way, the range of conclusions they propose is fairly standard. There are a few secondary developments, but in the main a single pattern is followed, for example, at Nos. 3-6. The only connection I can see between the Alexander fables and the intersecting-verse is the reference to the "mountains of darkness." No. 9 is added because of the conclusion of No. 8. No. 10, however, is entirely germane to our base-verse. But it is tacked on, since the connection to the preceding is tenuous. It too relies on Ps. 36:6. But it has no relationship to the earlier reading of the verse.

IX:II

1. A. R. Tanhuma commenced discourse by citing this verse: *Who has given me anything beforehand, that I should repay him? Whatever is under the whole heaven is mine* (Job 41:3 [Heb. 41:11]).

    B. R. Tanhuma interpreted the verse to speak of a bachelor who was living in a town and who [though he had no children and owed nothing] gave wages for scribes and Mishnah teachers: "Said the Holy One, blessed be He, 'It is my responsibility to pay him back for his goodness and to give him a male child.'

    C. [Leviticus Rabbah:] *"That is in line with the following verse of Scripture: He who is kind to the poor lends to the Lord], and he will repay him for his deed* (Prov. 19:17)."

2. A. Said R. Jeremiah b. Eleazar, "An echo is going to proclaim on the tops of the mountains, saying, 'Whoever has worked with God' shall come and collect his reward.'

    B. "That is in line with the following verse of Scripture: *In time it will be said to Jacob and to Israel, What has God worked* (Num. 23:23).

    C. "Whoever has worked with God now let him come and collect his reward."

    D. "And the Holy Spirit says, *'Who has given me anything beforehand? I shall repay him'* (Job. 41:3).

    E. "'Who praised me before I gave him a soul, who was circumcised in my name before I gave him a male child, who made a parapet for me before I gave him a roof, who made a *mezuzah* for me before I gave him a house, who made a *sukkah* for me before I gave him a place [for it], who made a *lulab* for me before I gave him money, who made show fringes for me before I gave him a cloak, who separated *peah* for me before I gave him a field, who separated heave offering for me and tithe before I gave him a harvest, who separated dough offering for me before I gave him dough, who separated an offering for me before I gave him a beast!'

    F. *"When a bull or a sheep or a goat [is born]* (Lev. 22:7)."

One who does his religious duties before he is obligated to do so is praised, in line with the cited verse of Job. That is the point of No. 1, and it is made still more explicit at No. 2. But one can do religious duties only if through God's grace he gets the opportunity: "Whatever is under the whole heaven is mine," so 2:E. The intersecting-verse recovers the base-verse because the latter speaks of when a bull or sheep is born – that is, by God's grace. Only then can one make an offering (Margulies).

IX:III

1. A. R. Jacob b. R. Zabedi in the name of R. Abbahu opened [discourse by citing the following verse:] *"And it shall never again be the reliance of the house of Israel, [recalling their iniquity, when they turn to them for aid. Then they will know that I am the Lord God]* (Ez. 29:16).

    B. "It is written, *Above him stood the seraphim: each had six wings, [with two he covered his face, and with two he covered his feet,] and with two he flew'* (Is. 6:2).

    C. *"[With two he flew]* – singing praises.

    D. *"With two he covered his face* – so as not to gaze upon the Presence of God.

    E. *"And with two he covered his feet* – so as not to let them be seen by the face of the Presence of God.

    F. "For it is written, *And the soles of their feet were like the sole of a calf's foot* (Ez. 1:7).

    G. "And it is written, *They made for themselves a molten calf* (Ex. 32:8).

    H. "[Leviticus Rabbah adds:] So [in covering their feet, they avoided calling to mind the molten calf,] in accord with the verse, *And it shall never again be the reliance of the house of Israel, recalling their iniquity* (Ez. 29:16)."

2. A. There we have learned in the Mishnah (M. R.H. 3:2): **All [horns] are suitable except for that of a cow.**

    B. Why except for that of the cow? Because it is the horn of a calf.

    C. [Leviticus Rabbah adds:] And it is written, *They made for themselves a molten calf* (Ex. 32:8).

    D. So [in not using the horn of a cow, they avoid calling to mind the molten calf, in accord with the verse], *And it shall never again be the reliance of the house of Israel, recalling their iniquity* (Ez. 29:16).

3. A. There we have also learned: *And you shall kill the woman and the beast [that lay with her]* (Lev. 20:16). If a human being has sinned, what sin did the beast commit?

    B. But since through that beast a disaster has come upon a human being, the Torah has said that it should be stoned.

    C. Another consideration: That a beast should not walk through the market and people should say, "That is the beast on account of which So-and-so was stoned to death."

    D. This is in line with the verse of Scripture: *And it shall never again be the reliance of the house of Israel, recalling their iniquity* (Ez. 29:17).

4. A. It has been taught: On what account does a wife accused of infidelity not drink from a cup used by another woman [the water that brings a curse]? So that people should not say, "Out of this cup another woman drank the water and died."

   B. This is in line with the verse of Scripture: *And it shall never again be the reliance of the house of Israel, recalling their iniquity* (Ez. 29:17).

5. A. And so too here: *When a bull or a sheep or a goat is born* (Lev. 22:27).

   B. Now is it born as a *bull* and not as a *calf*? But because it is said, *They made for themselves a molten calf,* therefore the Scripture refers to it as a *bull* and not as a calf: *When a bull, a sheep, a goat is born.*

Here is a classic example of the systematic exposition of an intersecting-verse, leading, at the climax, to a new insight into the meaning of the base-verse. The same point is made again and again, so that, when we reach the base-verse, we readily grasp the pertinence of the intersecting-verse. That diverse materials have been assembled is self-evident. What is striking is how they have been put together to make a single, entirely cogent point, five times over and fully spelled out. The question that is answered, concerning our verse, is why the author refers to a bull, when, at birth, the beast is hardly a bull but only a calf. The answer is, to avoid calling to mind the sin of the golden calf. The same syllogism, in all its particularity, is then expressed through other examples of the matter.

IX:IV

1. A. *That which is already has been, that which is to be already has been. [God seeks that which is pursued]* (Qoh. 3:15).

   B. R. Judah and R. Nehemiah:

   C. R. Judah says, "If someone should say to you that had the first Adam not sinned and eaten from that tree, he would have lived and endured even to this very day, tell him, *It already has been.* Elijah, of blessed memory, who did not sin, does not live forever.

   D. "'*That which is to be already has been:*' If someone should tell to you, it is possible that the Holy One, blessed be He, in the future is going to resurrect the dead, say to him, *It already has been.* He has already resurrected the dead through Elijah, Elisha, and Ezekiel in the valley of Dura."

   E. And R. Nehemiah says, "If someone should say to you that it is possible that to begin with the world was entirely made up of water in water, say to him, *It already has been,* for the ocean is full of diverse water.

   F. "*That which is to be already has been:* If someone should say to you, the Holy One, blessed be He, is going to dry the sea up, say to him, *It already has been.* Has he not already done so through Moses: *And the children of Israel walked on dry land through the sea* (Ex. 14:29)."

2. A. R. Aha in the name of R. Simeon b. Halapta: "Whatever the Holy One, blessed be He, is destined to do in the age to come in some small measure already has he done through the righteous in this world.

B.   "The Holy One, blessed be He, has said that he is going to resurrect the dead: he has already resurrected the dead through Elijah, Elisha, and Ezekiel.

C.   "The Holy One, blessed be He, has said that he is going to bring [people] through water on to dry land: [Leviticus Rabbah:] *When you pass through water, I am with you* (Is. 43:2). He has already brought Israel through [water] with Moses: *And the children of Israel walked on dry land through the sea* (Ex. 14:29).

D.   [Leviticus Rabbah:] *"And through rivers they shall not overwhelm you* (Is. 43:2). This he has already accomplished through Joshua: *On dry land the Israelites crossed the Jordan* (Josh. 4:2).

E.   [Leviticus Rabbah:] *"When you walk through fire you shall not be burned* (Is. 43:2). This he has already accomplished through Hananiah, Mishael, and Azariah.

F.   [Leviticus Rabbah:] *"And the flame shall not consume you* (Is. 43:2). This he has already accomplished: *[The fire had not had any power over the bodies of those men] no smell of fire had come upon them* (Dan. 3:27).

G.   [Leviticus Rabbah:] "The Holy One, blessed be He, has said that he will sweeten bitter water, he has already accomplished through Moses: *The Lord showed him a tree, and he threw it into the water, and the water became sweet* (Ex. 15:25).

H.   [Leviticus Rabbah:] "The Holy One, blessed be He, has said that God will sweeten what is bitter through something bitter, he has already accomplished through Elisha: Then he went to the spring of water and threw salt into it and said, Thus says the Lord, I have made this water wholesome (2 Kgs. 2:21).

I.   [Leviticus Rabbah:] "The Holy One, blessed be He, has said that he blesses what is little [and makes it much], he already has accomplished through Elijah and Elisha: *For thus says the Lord, the God of Israel, "The jar of meal shall not be spent, and the cruse of oil shall not fail, [until the day that the Lord sends rain upon the earth]* (1 Kgs. 17:14).

J.   [Not in Leviticus Rabbah:] The Holy One, blessed be He, has said that he will *open the eyes of the blind* (Is. 35:5). *Has he not already done so: And God opened the eyes of the youth* (2 Kgs. 6:17)?

K.   "The Holy One, blessed be He, has said that he will visit barren women, but he has already accomplished it [Leviticus Rabbah adds: through Sarah, Rebecca, Rachel, and Hannah]: *And the Lord visited Sarah* (Gen. 21:1).

L.   [Leviticus Rabbah adds:] *"The wolf and the lamb will pasture together* (Is. 65:25), he has already accomplished through Hezekiah: *The wolf shall dwell with the lamb* (Is. 11:6).

M.   The Holy One, blessed be He, has said, *"And kings will be your tutor* (Is. 49:23. Has he not has already accomplished it through Daniel: *Then the king Nebuchadnezzer fell upon his face and worshipped Daniel* (Dan. 2:46)."

3.   A.   *God seeks what has been driven away* (Qoh. 3:15):

B.   R. Huna in the name of R. Joseph said, "The Holy One, blessed be He, is destined to avenge the blood of the pursued through punishing the pursuer.

C. "[You find that] when a righteous man pursues a righteous man, *God seeks what has been driven away.*

D. "When a wicked man pursues a wicked man, *God seeks what has been driven away.*

E. "All the more so when a wicked man pursues a righteous man, *God seeks what has been driven away.*

F. "[The same principle applies] even when you come around to a case in which a righteous man pursues a wicked man, *God seeks what has been driven away.*'"

4. A. [Leviticus Rabbah adds:] R. Yose b. R. Yudan in the name of R. Yose b. R. Nehorai says, "It is always the case that the Holy One, blessed be He, demands an accounting for the blood of those who have been pursued from the hand of the pursuer.

    B. "You may know that this is the case, for lo, Abel was pursued by Cain, *God seeks what has been driven away* [and God sought an accounting for the pursued]: *And the Lord looked [favorably] upon Abel and his meal offering* (Gen. 4:4).

    C. "Noah was pursued by his generation, *God seeks what has been driven away: Noah found favor in the eyes of God* (Gen. 6:8). [Leviticus Rabbah adds: *You and all your household shall come into the ark'* (Gen. 7:1). And it says, *For this is like the days of Noah to me, as I swore [that the waters of Noah should no more go over the earth]* (Is. 54:9).]

    D. "Abraham was pursued by Nimrod, *God seeks what has been driven away: You are the Lord, the God who chose Abram and brought him out of Ur* (Neh. 9:7).

    E. "Isaac was pursued by the Philistines [Leviticus Rabbah: Ishmael], *God seeks what has been driven away. And they said, We have certainly seen that the Lord is with you* (Gen. 26:28) [Leviticus Rabbah: *For through Isaac will seed be called for you* (Gen. 21:12)].

    F. "Jacob was pursued by Esau, *God seeks what has been driven away. For the Lord has chosen Jacob, Israel for his prized possession* (Ps. 135:4).

    G. "Joseph was pursued by his brothers, *God seeks what has been driven away. The Lord was with Joseph, and he was a successful man* (Gen. 39:2).

    H. "Moses was pursued by Pharaoh, *but Moses, the man God had chosen, threw himself into the breach to turn back his wrath lest it destroy them* (Ps. 106:23).

    I. [Leviticus Rabbah adds:] "David was pursued by Saul, *God seeks what has been driven away. And he chose David, his servant* (Ps. 78:70).

    J. "Israel is pursued by the nations, *God seeks what has been driven away. And you has the Lord chosen to be a people to Him* (Deut. 14:2).

    K. R. Judah bar Simon in the name of R. Yose bar Nehorai, "And the rule applies also to the matter of offerings. A bull is pursued by a lion, a sheep is pursued by a wolf, a goat is pursued by a leopard.

    L. "Therefore the Holy One, blessed be He, has said, 'Do not make offerings before me from those animals that pursue, but from those that are pursued: *When a bull, a sheep, or a goat is born* (Lev. 22:27).

The intersecting-verse of **IX:IV**.1, 2 is thoroughly explained through Scriptural examples, all of which make the point that whatever people believe will happen already has happened. The rather extensive illustration of that proposition occupies the entire passage. I have inserted Margulies' materials of Leviticus Rabbah into the version before us, noting at each point what is not in Mandelbaum's Pesiqta deRav Kahana. The base-verse is reached in the next passage, **IX:IV**.3-4. Now, at **IX:IV**.3-4, the intersecting-verse leads right back to the base-verse and makes its point in a powerful way. God favors the persecuted over the persecutor, the pursued over the pursuer. This point is made in an abstract way at No. 1, and then through a review of the sacred history of Israel at No. 2. The intent of the whole is established at the outset, so we have a unitary composition. Still, 2.A-C speak of an accounting for blood, and 2.D-K resort to slightly different rhetoric.

IX:V

1. A. *O my people, what have I done to you, in what have I wearied you? Testify against me* (Mic. 6:3).
    B. Said R. Aha, *"Testify against me* and receive a reward, but *Do not bear false witness* (Ex. 20:13) and face a settlement of accounts [Leviticus Rabbah adds:] in the age to come."

2. A. Said R. Samuel b. R. Nahman, "On three occasions the Holy One, blessed be He, came to engage in argument with Israel, and the nations of the world rejoiced, saying, 'Can these ever [dare] engage in an argument with their creator? Now he will wipe them out of the world.'
    B. "One was when he said to them, *Come, and let us reason together, says the Lord* (Is. 1:18). When the Holy One, blessed be He, saw that the nations of the world were rejoicing, he turned the matter to [Israel's] advantage: *If your sins are as scarlet, they shall be white as snow* (Is. 1:18).
    C. "Then the nations of the world were astonished, and said, 'This is repentance, and this is rebuke? He has planned only to amuse himself with his children.'
    D. "[A second time was] when he said to them, *Hear, you mountains, the controversy of the Lord* (Mic. 6:2), so the nations of the world rejoiced, saying, 'How can these ever [dare] engage in an argument with their creator? Now he will wipe them out of the world.'
    E. "When the Holy One, blessed be He, saw that the nations of the world were rejoicing, he turned the matter to [Israel's] advantage: *O my people, what have I done to you? In what have I wearied you? Testify against me* (Mic. 6:3). *Remember what Balak king of Moab devised* (Mic. 6:5).
    F. [Leviticus Rabbah adds:] "Then the nations of the world were astonished, saying, 'This is repentence, and this is rebuke, one following the other? He has planned only to amuse himself with his children.'
    G. "[A third time was] when he said to them, *The Lord has an indictment against Judah, and will punish Jacob according to his ways* (Hos. 12:2), the nations of the world rejoiced, saying, 'How can these ever [dare] engage in an argument with their creator? Now he will wipe them out of the world.'

H. "When the Holy One, blessed be He, saw that the nations of the world were rejoicing, he turned the matter to [Israel's] advantage. That is in line with the following verse of Scripture: *In the womb he [Jacob = Israel] took his brother [Esau = other nations] by the heel [and in his manhood he strove with God. He strove with the angel and prevailed, he wept and sought his favor]* (Hos. 12:3-4)."

3. A. [Leviticus Rabbah adds: Said R. Yudan b. R. Simeon,] "The matter may be compared to a widow who was complaining to a judge about her son. When she saw that the judge was in session and handing out sentences of capital punishment [Leviticus Rabbah adds:] punishment by fire, pitch, and lashes, she said, 'If I report the bad conduct of my son to that judge, he will kill him now.' She waited until he was finished. When he had finished, he said to her, 'Madam, this son of yours, how has he behaved badly toward you?'

B. "She said to him, 'My lord, when he was in my womb, he kicked me.'

C. "He said to her, 'Now has he done anything wrong to you?'

D. "She said to him, 'No.'

E. "He said to her, '[Leviticus Rabbah adds: Go your way], there is nothing wrong in the matter [that you report].

F. [Leviticus Rabbah adds:] "So, when the Holy One, blessed be He, saw that the nations of the world were rejoicing, he turned the matter to [Israel's] advantage:

G. [Leviticus Rabbah adds:] *"In the womb he took his brother by the heel* (Mic. 12:3)

H. "Then the nations of the world were astonished, saying, 'This is repentence and this is rebuke, one following the other? He has planned only to amuse himself with his children.'"

4. A. Said R. Berekhiah [Leviticus Rabbah: Isaac], "The matter may be compared to the case of a king who sent his proclamation to a city. What did the inhabitants of the city do? They stood up and bared their heads and read the proclamation in awe, trembling, fear, and trepidation.

B. "So the Holy One, blessed be He, said to Israel, 'The proclamation of the *Shema* is my proclamation [that I sent you]. I did not impose on you by telling you to read [the *Shema*] either standing on your feet or having bared your heads, but only [at your convenience: merely] *When you sit in your house and when you walk by the way* (Deut. 6:7).'" [Leviticus Rabbah supplies the following: *And how have I wearied you?* (Mic. 6:3). Said R. Berekhiah, "The matter may be compared to the case of a king, who sent three messengers to a certain city, and the inhabitants of the city stood up before them and paid them service] in awe, trembling, fear, and trepidation. So the Holy One, blessed be He, said to Israel, 'I sent you three messengers, Moses, Aaron, and Miriam. Now did they eat any of your food? Did they drink any of your drink? Did they impose upon you in any way? Is it not through their *merit* that you are maintained? The mana was through the merit of Moses, the well through the merit of Miriam, and the clouds of glory through the merit of Aaron.'"]

5. A. Another teaching concerning the verse, *And how have I wearied you:*

B. Said R. Judah b. R. Simon, "Said the Holy One, blessed be He, 'I handed over ten clean beasts to you [as suitable food for you and for me], three in your domain [under your control, as domesticated beasts], and seven not in your domain.

C. "The three in your domain: *the ox, sheep, and the goat* (Deut. 14:4).

D. "'The seven not in your domain: *the hart, gazelle, roebuck, wild goat, ibex, antelope, and mountain sheep* (Deut. 14:5).

E. "'I did not trouble you, and I did not tell you to go up into the mountains and to tire yourselves in the fields to [hunt and so to] bring me an offering of those beasts that are not within your domain.

F. "'I asked only for those that are in your domain, the ones that grow at your crib: *Ox, sheep or goat that is born* (Lev. 22:27).'"

The systematic exposition of the intersecting-verse, Mic. 6:3, establishes a basic point, that God really does not trouble Israel, which leads us to the intersecting-verse as climactic evidence of that point. God does not demand that the Israelites go to a great deal of trouble to find for the sacrifices animals not readily at hand. But before we reach that simple point, we work through a somewhat more complicated message. Whenever God begins a process of inquiry against Israel, the reaction of the nations of the world is such as to warn God off and to make him turn the process into an affirmation of God's love for Israel. This point comes in a number of versions, all of them following a single pattern of rhetoric and argument. There is a secondary motif, that, as Micah says, God does not impose inconvenience on Israel.

IX:VI

1. A. R. Levi opened [discourse by citing the following verse of Scripture:] *"Behold you are nothing, and your work is nought; [an abomination is he who chooses you]* (Is. 41:24).

    B. *"Nothing* – from nil, from a foul secretion.

    C. *"Nought* (M'P') – from the hundred (M'H) outcries (P'YWT) that a woman cries out when she is sitting on the birth stool, ninety-nine are for death, and one for life."

2. A. *An abomination is he who chooses you.*

    B. Even though the infant emerges from his mother's belly filthy and soiled, covered with secretions and blood, everybody caresses and kisses him.

    C. And even more so if it is a male.

3. A. Another interpretation: *Behold, you are nothing:*

    B. Said R. Berekhiah, "The word 'behold' (HN) is Greek, 'hina,' meaning one.

    C. "Said the Holy One, blessed be He, 'I have only one nation among the nations of the world.'

    D. *"Nothing*: This refers to those about which it is written, *The nations are nothing before Him* (Is. 40:17)."

    E. *And your work is nought* (Is. 41:24):

F.   Said R. Levi, "All the good and comforting works that the Holy One, blessed be He, is going to do for Israel are only on account of a single exclamation (P'YYH) which you made before Me at Sinai, when you said, *Everything that the Lord has said we shall do and we shall hear* (Ex. 24:7)."

G.   *An abomination is he who chooses you* (Is. 41:24):

H.   That abomination concerning which it is written, *They made for themselves a molten calf* (Ex. 32:4), is the same abomination [that] they shall bring to me as an offering:

I.   *Bull or sheep or goat* (Lev. 22:27).

The intersecting-verse, Is. 41:24, bears two distinct interpretations. In the first – Nos. 1-3 – the verse is made to refer to the condition of the newborn child. In the second, No. 4, it refers to Israel, its redemption and God's forgiveness of Israel's sin with the golden calf. The stress then is on the sacrificial system as a mode of overcoming and expiating the idolatry of the people in the wilderness. The issue of the golden calf, already familiar, evidently strikes the exegetes as important in explaining the verse at hand. We shall now see further instances of the same concern.

IX:VII

1.   A.   *By their wickedness they make the king glad, and the princes by their adultery* (Hos. 7:3).

B.   Now why was the bull recognized to be designated as the first of all of the offerings [*bull, sheep, goat* (Lev. 22:27)]?

C.   Said R. Levi, "The matter may be compared to the case of a highborn lady who got a bad name on account of [alleged adultery with] one of the lords of the state.

D.   "The king looked into the matter and found nothing. What did the king do? He made a banquet and sat the [accused] man at the head of the guests.

E.   "Why so? To show that the king had looked into the matter and found nothing.

F.   "So the nations of the world taunt Israel and say to them, 'You made the golden calf!'

G.   "The Holy One, blessed be He, looked into the matter and found nothing. Accordingly, the bull was made the first among all the offerings: *Bull, sheep, goat* (Lev. 22:27)."

No. 1 carries forward the familiar line of thought that the sin of the calf had long since been found to be null. The intersecting text provokes 1.C.

IX:VIII

1.   A.   R. Huna, R. Idi in the name of R. Samuel b. R. Nahman: "The [true] Israelites were saved from that act. For if the Israelites had themselves made the calf, they ought to have said, 'These are *our* gods, O Israel.' It was the proselytes who came up with Israel from Egypt [who made the calf]: *And also a mixed multitude came up with them* (Ex. 12:38).

B.   "They are the ones who made the calf. They taunted them, saying to them, *These are* your *gods, O Israel* (Ex. 32:8)."

2.   A.   Said R. Judah b. R. Simon, "It is written, *An ox knows its owner, and an ass its master's crib, [but Israel does not know]* (Is. 1:3).
   B.   "Did they really not know? Rather, they trampled under heel [God's commandments]. [They did not pay adequate attention and sinned by inadvertence (Margulies).]"
   C.   "Along these same lines: *For my people is foolish. Me they have not known* (Jer. 4:22). Did they not know? Rather, they trampled under heel.
   D.   "Along these same lines: *And she did not know that it was I who gave her the grain, [wine, and oil]* (Hos. 2:8). Did she not know? Rather, she trampled under heel."

No. 1 then explains that the true Israelites did not commit the sin at all. I am puzzled by No. 2; I do not see its relevance to the passage at hand, nor does it relate to what follows. Margulies proposes that it carries forward the view that the prophets exaggerated Israel's guilt, but in fact Israel was not deliberately sinning at all. It is not that they were worse than the beasts but rather that they paid no attention and so sinned through inadvertence. This seems to me implausible.

IX:IX

1.   A.   *[A bull, a sheep, or a goat (Lev. 22:27):]*
   B.   *A bull* on account of the merit of Abraham, as it is said: *[And Abraham ran to the herd and took a calf]* (Gen. 18:7).
   C.   *A sheep* on account of the merit of Isaac, as it is written, *And he looked, and behold, a ram caught by its horns* (Gen. 22:13).
   D.   *A goat* on account of the merit of Jacob, as it is written in his regard, *Now go to the flock and get me two good kid goats* (Gen. 27:9).

2.   A.   What is the meaning of "good"?
   B.   R. Berekhiah in the name of R. Helbo: "Good for you, good for your children.
   C.   "Good for you, for on their account you will receive blessings.
   D.   "Good for your children, for on their account you will have atonement on the Day of Atonement: *For on this day atonement will be made for you* (Lev. 16:30), [including the atonement of the sacrifice of the goat (Lev. 16:9)]."

The exegesis of the verse is clear as specified. The several beasts now are related to the patriarchs, a fairly standard approach to the amplification of Scripture. The secondary development of Gen. 27:9 presents no problems.

IX:X

1.   A.   *It shall remain seven days with its mother* (Lev. 22:27).
   B.   [Leviticus Rabbah adds:] Why for seven days?

C. R. Joshua of Sikhnin in the name of R. Levi said, "The matter may be compared to the case of a king who came into a town and made decrees, saying, 'None of the residents who are here will see me before they first see my lady.'

D. "Said the Holy One, blessed be He, 'You will not make an offering before me until a Sabbath shall have passed over [the animal that is to be offered], for seven days cannot pass without a Sabbath, and [for the same reason] the rite of circumcision [takes place on the eighth day] so that it cannot take place without the advent of a Sabbath.

E. *"And from the eighth day on it shall be acceptable [as an offering by fire to the Lord]* (Lev. 22:27)."

2. A. Said R. Isaac, "A rule is written with regard to a man, and the same rule is written with regard to a beast:

B. "The rule with regard to a man: *And on the eighth day the flesh of his foreskin will be circumcised* (Lev. 12:3).

C. "The same rule with regard to a beast: *And from the eighth day on, it shall be acceptable* (Lev. 22:27)." [Leviticus Rabbah adds: *[When a bull or sheep or goat is born,] it shall remain seven days with its mother; [from the eighth day on it shall be acceptable as an offering by fire to the Lord]* (Lev. 22:27). Why for seven days? So that the beast may be inspected, for if the dam should have gored it, or if some disqualifying blemish should turn up on it, lo, it will be invalid and not be suitable for an offering. For we have learned (M. Nid. 5:1): **That which goes forth from the side [delivered by Caesarean section] – they do not sit out the days of uncleanness and the days of cleanness [Lev. 12:1ff.] on its account, and they are not liable on its account for an offering. R. Simeon says, "Lo, this is like one that is born [naturally] [so that the rules of Lev. 12:1ff. do apply]."**

We continue the exegesis of the base-verse, with a brilliant inquiry into the specification of the eighth day. No. 1 introduces the matter of the Sabbath, which any reference to eight days should provoke.

IX:XI

1. A. *And whether the mother is a cow or a ewe, [you shall not kill] both her and her young [in one day]* (Lev. 22:28).

B. R. Berekhiah in the name of R. Levi: "It is written, *A righteous man has regard for the life of his beast, [but the mercy of the wicked is cruel]* (Prov. 12:10).

C. *"A righteous man has regard for the life of his beast* refers to the Holy One, blessed be He, in whose Torah it is written, *You will not take the mother with the young* (Deut. 22:6).

D. *"But the mercy of the wicked is cruel* refers to Sennacherib, the wicked one, concerning whom it is written, *The mother was dashed into pieces with her children* (Hos. 10:14)."

2. A. Another interpretation: *A righteous man has regard for the life of his beast* refers to the Holy One, blessed be He, in whose Torah it is written,

*And whether the mother is a cow or a ewe, you shall not kill both her
and her young in one day* (Lev. 22:28).

B. *But the mercy of the wicked is cruel* refers to the wicked Haman,
concerning whom it is written, *To destroy, to slay, to obliterate all Jews
young and old children and women, on a single day* (Est. 3:13).

3. A. Said R. Levi, "Woe for the wicked, who make conspiracies against Israel,
each one saying, 'My plan is better than your plan.'

B. "Esau said, 'Cain was a fool, since he killed his brother while his father
was yet alive. Did he not know that his father would continue to be
fruitful and multiply? That is not how I am going to do things.' Rather:
*The days of mourning for my father are approaching; [only upon his
death] will I kill my brother Jacob* (Gen. 27:41).

C. "Pharaoh said, 'Esau was a fool. For he said, *The days of mourning for
my father are approaching.* But did he not know that his brother would
continue to be fruitful and multiply in the lifetime of his father? That is
not how I am going to do things. But while they are still little, under
their mother's belly, I will strangle them.' That is in line with the
following verse of Scripture: *Every son that is born you shall cast into
the river* (Ex. 1:22).

D. "Haman said, 'Pharaoh was a fool, for he said, *Every son that is born and
let the daughter live.* Did he not realize that the daughters would marry
husbands and be fruitful and multiply with them? That is not how I am
going to do things. Rather: *To destroy, to slay, to obliterate all Jews*
(Est. 3:13)."

E. Said R. Levi, "So, too, Gog, in time to come, is going to say the same,
'The ancients were fools, for they made conspiracies against Israel and
did they not know that they have a patron in Heaven? That is not how I
am going to do things. First I shall seek a confrontation with their
patron, and afterward I shall seek a confrontation with them.' That is in
line with the following verse of Scripture: *The kings of the earth set
themselves, and the rulers take counsel together, against the Lord and
against his anointed* (Ps. 2:2).

F. "Said to him the Holy One, blessed be He, 'Wicked man! Do you seek a
confrontation with me? By your life, I shall make war with you.' That
is in line with the following verse of Scripture: *The Lord will go forth as
a mighty man, like a fighter, he whips up his rage, He yells, He roars
aloud* (Is. 42:13).

G. *"And the Lord will go forth and fight against those nations* (Zech. 14:3).

H. "[Leviticus Rabbah adds:] And what is written there? *The Lord will be
king over all the earth* (Zech. 14:9)."

The exegeses of Lev. 22:27ff., **IX:VIII-XI** reach a climax and conclusion
with an eschatological motif. The first two units treat Prov. 12:10 in an
entirely appropriate way, tying it closely to the substance of the base-verse. But
it is not a construction built on the basis of the intersecting-verse. Nos. 1 and 2
make essentially the same point, one with Sennacherib, the other with Haman.
Levi's systematic picture of Cain, Esau, and Haman then is tacked on because of
the prior allusion to Sennacherib and Haman. Nothing in No. 3 alludes to the
base-verse. And yet the theme still resonates: the cruelties of the wicked, now

the ever-increasing, but ever-more-futile, folly of the wicked who conspire against Israel. The cruelty of each is what joins No. 3 to Nos. 1-2. Nonetheless, it is difficult to deny that No. 3 was framed for its own purpose, prior to its serving to amplify the reference to Haman at No. 2.

IX:XII

1. A. *And when you sacrifice a thanksgiving sacrifice to the Lord sacrifice it so that it may be acceptable in your favor* (Lev. 22:29):

    B. R. Phineas and R. Levi and R. Yohanan in the name of R. Menahem of Gallia: "In time to come all offerings will come to an end, but the thanksgiving-offering will never come to an end.

    C. "All forms of prayer will come to an end, but the thanksgiving-prayer will never come to an end.

    D. "That is in line with that which is written, *The voice of joy and the voice of gladness, the voice of the bridegroom and the voice of the bride, the voice of them that say, Give thanks to the God of Hosts, for the Lord is good, his kindness is everlasting* (Jer. 33:11). This refers to the thanksgiving-prayer.

    E. *"Who bring a thanksgiving-offering to the house of the Lord* (Jer. 33:11). This refers to the thanksgiving-offering.

    F. "And so did David say, *Your vows are incumbent upon me, O God I shall render [thanksgivings to you]* (Ps. 56:13).

    G. "'I shall render thanksgiving [in the singular] to you' is not written here, but rather, *I shall render thanksgivings [plural] to you* (Ps. 56:13). The reference [of the plural usage] then is to both the thanksgiving-prayer and the thanksgiving-offering."

The passage serves the next verse in sequence, Lev. 22:29. But it treats the theme, rather than the particular statement at hand.

Pisqa Ten

[Year by year] you shall set aside a tithe *[of all the produce of your seed, of everything that grows on the land. You shall eat it in the presence of the Lord your God in the place which he will choose as a dwelling for his name – the tithe of your corn and new wine and oil, and the firstborn of your cattle and sheep, so that for all time you may learn to fear the Lord your God]*

(Deut. 14:22).

X:I

1. A. *The miser is in a hurry to grow rich, never dreaming that want will overtake him* (Prov. 28:22):
   B. R. Haninah interpreted the verse to speak of Ephron. [The reference is to the following verse: *"No, my lord, hear me, I give you the field, and I give you the cave that is in it; in the presence of the sons of my people I give it to you; bury your dead. Then Abraham bowed down before the people of the land. And he said to Ephron in the hearing of the people of the land, 'But if you will, hear me; I will give the price of the field; accept it from me, that I may bury my dead there.' Ephron answered Abraham, 'My lord, listen to me; a piece of land worth four hundred shekels of silver, what is that between you and me? Bury your dead.' Abraham agreed with Ephron; and Abraham weighed out for Ephron the silver which he had named in the hearing of the Hittites, four hundred shekels of silver, according to the weights current among the merchants"* (Gen. 23:11-16)]:
   C. Said R. Haninah, "All references to shekels in the Torah speak of *selas*, in the Prophetic books speak of *litras*, and in the Writings, speak of a *centenarium .*"
   D. Said R. Judah b. R. Pazzi, "Except for the shekels paid out to Ephron, which were *centenarii*, as it is written, *I will give the price of the field; accept it from* me (Gen. 23:9)
   E. "Because he was jealous of the wealth of Abraham, Scripture removed a vav, in line with the following verse: *'My lord, listen to me; a piece of land worth four hundred shekels of silver, what is that between you and me?...*
   F. "'If you want to pay me four hundred *centenarii* of silver out of the mere horseshit of your household, you can pay me [since that means nothing to a rich man like you].'
   G. "Because he was jealous of the wealth of Abraham, Scripture removed a *vav*, in line with the following verse: *Abraham agreed with Ephron; and Abraham weighed out for Ephron...* The second reference to Ephron is written without the O [i.e., the *vav*]."
2. A. R. Ammi interpreted the verse *[The miser is in a hurry to grow rich, never dreaming that want will overtake him* (Prov. 28:22)] to speak of a

- 153 -

borrower who was too much of a miser to rent two oxen [at one and the same time], but would borrow one and rent one:

B. "But he did not realize *that want will overtake him.*

C. "For it is written, If the master is not with him, he will surely pay [damages for any loss done to the borrowed oxen. So in saving money by borrowing, he placed himself at risk.]"

3. A. R. Isaac interpreted the verse *[The miser is in a hurry to grow rich, never dreaming that want will overtake him* (Prov. 28:22)] to speak of one who lent money to Israelites at usurious terms, who was too much of a miser to lend money not on usury:

B. "In lending money at usurious terms, he did not realize *that want will overtake him.*

C. "For it is written, *He who augments his wealth by interest and increase gathers it for him who is kind to the poor* (Prov. 28:8).

D. "Now who is the one who is *kind to the poor?*

E. "It is the wicked Esau.

F. "But is it not the case that the wicked Esau oppresses the poor, as in the case of the bureaucrats who go out into the villages and plunder sharecroppers and then go into the city and announce, 'Bring together the poor for we want to carry out a religious duty with them.'

G. "The saying refers to such as these:'She screws for apples and hands them out to the poor.'"

4. A. R. Levi intepreted the cited verse *[The miser is in a hurry to grow rich, never dreaming that want will overtake him* (Prov. 28:22)] to speak of those who do not set aside the required tithes as is proper.

B. For R. Levi said, "There is the case of one who would set aside his required tithes as was proper.

C. "Now the man had one field, which produced a thousand measures of grain. He would separate from it a hundred measures for tithe. From the field he would derive his livelihood all his days, and from it he would nourish himself all his life. When he was dying, he called his son and said to him, 'My son, pay attention to this field. Such and so has it produced, such and so I would separate from the crop for tithe, and from that field I derived my livelihood all my days, and from it I nourished myself all my days.'

D. "In the first year [following the father's death], the son sowed the field and it produced a thousand measures of grain, from which the son set aside a hundred measures for tithe. In the second year the son became niggardly and deducted ten measures, and the field produced a hundred measures less, and so he deducted ten and it produced a hundred less, until the field yielded only the amount that had originally been set aside as tithe.

E. "When the man's relatives realized it, [as a sign of rejoicing] they put on white garments and cloaked themselves in white and assembled at his house. He said to them, 'Why have you come to rejoice over that man who has been afflicted?'

F. "They said to him, 'God forbid! We have come only to rejoice with you. In the past you were the householder, and the Holy One, blessed be He, was the priest [collecting the tithes as his share of the crop]. Now you have been turned into the priest, and the Holy One, blessed be He, has become the householder [keeping back the larger share of the crop, nine tenths of the former yield, for himself]. [So we are rejoicing at your rise in caste status!]'"

G. Said R. Levi, "After he had deducted [the priests' share] year by year, yearly the field reduced its yield."

H. Therefore Moses admonished Israel, saying to them, *[Year by year] you shall set aside a tithe [of all the produce of your seed, of everything that grows on the land. You shall eat it in the presence of the Lord your God in the place which he will choose as a dwelling for his name – the tithe of your corn and new wine and oil, and the firstborn of your cattle and sheep, so that for all time you may learn to fear the Lord your God]* (Deut. 14:22).

The intersecting-verse is appropriate in its theme, since its main point is that the miserly person pays a penalty. One should not be niggardly in setting aside tithe, but should pay off the entire ten per cent. But the exposition of the intersecting-verse as usual goes its own way, first of all speaking of Ephron. Nos. 2, 3 then treat the miser in the setting of the law of the Torah, first of all, the one who borrows, saving the fee of renting the ox, but losing on the liabilities; then the one who lends at interest. Finally, at No. 4, we come to the theme at hand. There is no exposition of the verse, rather a story makes the point. H is tacked on as the formal conclusion to the whole.

X:II

1. A. *Trust in the Lord and do good, so you will dwell in the land and enjoy faithfulness* (Ps. 37:3):
   B. R. Haggai in the name of R. Isaac transposed the elements of this verse, as follows: *Do good and trust in the Lord.*
   C. "The matter may be compared to the case of a market inspector, who went forth to inspect the weights and measures. Someone saw him and began to avoid him. He said to him, 'Why are you avoiding me? Inspect your measures and do not fear.'
   D. "That is in line with the verse, *Do good and trust in the Lord.*"
2. A. *...so you will dwell in the land:* [Mandelbaum:] Make [the land] suitable as a dwelling, by sowing and planting it.
   B. *...and enjoy faithfulness:* enjoy the faithfulness of the patriarchs:
   C. *My eyes are on the faithful of the land* (Ps. 101:6).
3. A. R. Joshua of Sikhnin in the name of R. Levi: "It is on account of the merit of two matters that the Israelites are purified before the Omnipresent.
   B. "It is on account of the merit attained by keeping the Sabbath, and it is on account of the merit attained by setting aside the required tithes.
   C. "How on the basis of Scripture do we know that it is on account of the merit of keeping the Sabbath?
   D. *"If you turn back your foot from the sabbath, from doing your business on my holy day, and call the Sabbath a delight, an the holy day of the Lord honorable* (Is. 58:13). What is written immediately following? *Then you shall take delight in the Lord and I will make you ride upon the heights of the earth* (Is. 58:14).'

E.   "How on the basis of Scripture do we know that it is on account of the merit attained by setting aside the required tithes?

F.   "*And you shall rejoice in all the good which the Lord your God has given to you and to your house, you and the Levite and the sojourner who is among you* (Deut. 26:11).   What is written immediately following? When you have finished paying all the tithe of your produce in the third year, which is the year of tithing... (Deut. 26:14)."

G.   Therefore Moses admonishes Israel, saying to them, *[Year by year]* you shall set aside a tithe *[of all the produce of your seed, of everything that grows on the land. You shall eat it in the presence of the Lord your God in the place which he will choose as a dwelling for his name – the tithe of your corn and new wine and oil, and the firstborn of your cattle and sheep, so that for all time you may learn to fear the Lord your God]* (Deut. 14:22).

The exposition of the intersecting-verse is completed at No. 1. No. 2 is tacked on; it has no pertinence to the matter in hand. But what that means is that the intersecting-verse is never referred back to the base-verse, since when, at No. 3, we move on to the base-verse, the intersecting-verse has been forgotten, not only formally, but also in its proposition. It follows that No. 1+2 essentially ignores our redactional context.

X:III

1.   A.   *Honor the Lord with your substance [and with the first fruits of all your produce; then your barns will be filled with plenty, and your vats will be bursting with wine]* (Prov. 3:9-10):

     B.   For if you are good-looking, do not chase skirts, so that people should not say, "Mr. So-and-so is good-looking and does not restrain himself."

     C.   This is in line with the verse: *Honor the Lord with your substance,* [Mandelbaum: reading the letters of the word for substance as though the indicated the word for charm].

2.   A.   Another matter: *Honor the Lord with your substance [and with the first fruits of all your produce then your barns will be filled with plenty, and your vats will be bursting with wine]* (Prov. 3:9-10):

     B.   For if you have a lovely voice, recite the Shema and go before the ark [to sing the prayers for the conregation].

     C.   This is in line with the verse: *Honor the Lord with your substance,* [reading the letters of the word for substance as though the indicated the word for charm].

3.   A.   R. Hiyya bar Addah, son of the sister of Bar Qappara, had a nice voice. Bar Qappara would say to him, "Now, my son, recite the Shema and go before the ark.

     B.   "This is in line with the verse: *Honor the Lord with your substance,* meaning, honor the Lord with that with which he has favored you."

4.   A.   Another matter: *Honor the Lord with your substance, [and with the first fruits of all your produce; then your barns will be filled with plenty, and your vats will be bursting with wine]* (Prov. 3:9-10):

     B.   Do [what you should] by your own will and intention, before you have to do things not in accord with your own will and intention [when you have become senile] [Mandelbaum, p. 165].

5. A. [Illustrating the foregoing:] there is the case of one who would collect his wine and oil, without appropriately setting aside the tithes that he owed.

   B. What did the Holy One, blessed be He, do? He put into the man a wandering spirit, and he took his staff and began to break the jugs. His household member rebuked him. What did he do to him? He took the staff and broke his skull.

   C. He said to the dependent, "Instead of helping me, you rebuke me."

   D. He said to him, "Then give me a staff, and I'll break jugs too."

   E. He gave him a staff, and he went around breaking jugs, one by one, while the other broke them two by two.

   F. What made this happen? It was because [he collected his wine and oil,] without appropriately setting aside the tithes that he owed.

6. A. For R. Levi said, "There was the case of one who would appropriately set aside the tithes that he owed.

   B. He had a field, and the Holy One gave him the thought of turning half of it into a sown field, leaving the other half as an area for reservoirs of water.

   C. In a year of want, people set the price, announcing, "A *seah* of wheat is going for a *sela*, a *seah* of water is going for three *selas*."

   D. He went and announced, "Who wants a *seah* of water?"

   E. And it yielded for him the same return as three *seahs* of wheat.

   G. Now what caused this [good fortune] for him? It was because he who would appropriately set aside the tithes that he owed.

   H. Therefore Moses admonishes Israel, saying to them, *[Year by year] you shall set aside a tithe [of all the produce of your seed, of everything that grows on the land. You shall eat it in the presence of the Lord your God in the place which he will choose as a dwelling for his name – the tithe of your corn and new wine and oil, and the firstborn of your cattle and sheep, so that for all time you may learn to fear the Lord your God]* (Deut. 14:22).

The systematic exposition of the intersecting-verse works on the word for *substance*, Nos. 1, 2, 3, 4, interpreted to mean gift of grace. No. 5 is tacked on to illustration No. 4, and that accounts for the insertion of the whole. No. 6 goes over familiar grounds, but that composition in no way takes up the intersecting-verse, though one might make a case that No. 6 continues No. 6. Then at 6.H we have the redactional *finis*.

X:IV

1. A. *She is not afraid of snow for her houshold, for all her household are clothed in scarlet* (Prov. 31:21):

   B. Hezekiah said, "The judgment meted out to the wicked is to spend twelve months in Gehenna. For six months it is in the heat, and for six months in the cold. In the beginning the Holy One, blessed be He, puts an itch on them, and brings them into the hot part of Gehenna. [Getting relief from the itch through the heat,] they say, 'That is the Gehenna of the Holy One, blessed be He.'

C. "So then he brings them into the cold, and they say, 'This is the cold of the Holy One, blessed be He.'

D. "To begin with they say 'Ah,' but in the end, 'Oh.'

E. "And that is what David says: *He drew me up from the desolate pit, out of the miry bog, [and set my feet upon a rock making my steps secure]* (Ps. 40:2).

F. "What is the meaning of the words, *miry bog*? It is from a place in which [using the letters that occur in the cited words] people say, 'Ah, Oh.'"

G. And where do they finish out [the torment to] their souls?

H. Judah b. Rabbi says, "In snow."

I. "That is in line with this verse of Scripture: *When the Almighty scattered kings there, snow fell on Zalmon* (Ps. 68:14).

J. "The snow is their place of darkness [a play on the word, see Mandelbaum, *ad loc.*]

K. "But can one suppose that that is how it is for Israel?

L. "Scripture says, *She is not afraid of snow for her houshold, [for all her household are clothed in scarlet]* (Prov. 31:21).

M. "...*for all her household are clothed in scarlet* (Prov. 31:21): that is in the rite of circumcision, including the rite of the cutting off of the foreskin, the rite of wearing show-fringes on the garments, and the rite of wearing phylacteries."

2. A. *[If your brother, a Hebrew man or a Hebrew woman, is sold to you, he shall serve you six years, and in the seventh year you shall let him go free from you. And when you let him go free from you, you shall not let him go empty-handed;] you shall furnish him liberally [out of your flock, out of your threshing floor, and out of your wine press, as the Lord your God has blessed you, you shall give to him]* (Deut. 14:12-14). [The cited verb is duplicated.]

    B. *You shall give to him freely [and your heart shall not be grudging when you give to him]* (Deut. 14:10). [Again, the cited verb is duplicated.]

    C. *You shall open wide your hand.[to your brother, to the needy and to the poor in the land]* (Deut. 14:11). [Again, the cited verb is duplicated.]

    D. Tithing, you will tithe (Deut. 14:22). [Again, the cited verb is duplicated.]

    E. Therefore Moses admonishes Israel, saying to them, *[Year by year]* you shall set aside a tithe *[of all the produce of your seed, of everything that grows on the land. You shall eat it in the presence of the Lord your God in the place which he will choose as a dwelling for his name – the tithe of your corn and new wine and oil, and the firstborn of your cattle and sheep, so that for all time you may learn to fear the Lord your God]* (Deut. 14:22).

I simply cannot account for the inclusion of No. 1, which seems to me utterly out of phase with our base-verse. But No. 2 shows us what is at issue. The word for scarlet in the base-verse may be translated to mean, *a second time,* or, *again and again.* No. 2 then draws attention to the duplication of the verb at a number of contiguous verses, including ours. That, sum and substance, accounts for the redactor's choice of No. 1. I cannot see No. 2 as a secondary expansion of No. 1. It is simply juxtaposed for the reason given. What follows is that we deal with an exposition of the base-verse, even though, formally, we appear to have an intersecting-verse/base-verse composition.

X:V

1. A.   *The earth lies polluted under its inhabitants, [for they have transgressed the Torahs, violated the statutes, broken the everlasting covenant]* (Is. 24:5):

    B.   Said R. Isaac, "If you imagine polluting it, it will pollute you. It will give you the spectacle of standing grain, but it will not then show you grain in sheaves. It will show you grain in sheaves, but it will not show you a threshing floor. It will show you the threshing floor, but it will not show you a pile of winnowed grain.

    C.   "Why so? Because *for they have transgressed the Torahs.*

    D.   "That is, two Torahs, the Torah in writing, the Torah in memory.

    E.   *"...violated the statutes:* they have violated the statute governing the requirement to set aside tithes.

    F.   *"...broken the everlasting covenant:* they have violated the covenant made by the patriarchs."

    G.   Therefore Moses admonishes Israel, saying to them, *[Year by year] you shall set aside a tithe [of all the produce of your seed, of everything that grows on the land. You shall eat it in the presence of the Lord your God in the place which he will choose as a dwelling for his name – the tithe of your corn and new wine and oil, and the firstborn of your cattle and sheep, so that for all time you may learn to fear the Lord your God]* (Deut. 14:22).

The exegesis of the intersecting-verse is far more germane to the base-verse. The reason is that the intersecting-verse refers to the earth, which has been polluted. The main point, B, is that the earth retaliates for mistreatment, and then in the later clauses of the intersecting-verse we are able to find an appropriate reference to our topic. This seems to me a fine model for the present formal exercise.

X:VI

1. A.   *My son, keep your father's commandment, and do not forsake your mother's teaching* (Prov. 6:20):

    B.   Said R. Hunah, "The original patriarchs set aside both the priestly ration ["heave-offering"] and tithes.

    C.   "Abraham set aside the principal priestly ration ["great heave-offering"]: *I have raised my hands to God, the Lord* (Gen. 14:22). The word raising up refers only to the priestly ration ["heave-offering"] as it is said, And you will raise up from it the priestly ration that belongs to the Lord (Num. 18:26).

    D.   "Isaac set aside second tithe: *And Isaac sowed in that land and found in that same year a hundredfold* (Gen. 26:12)."

    E.   [Explaining how the cited verse proves the matter,] said R. Abbah bar Kahana, "Is it not the case that a blessing falls not on a crop that is measured or weighed or countered? Why then did he measure the yield at

all? It weas so as to tithe the crop. That is in line with the statement of
Scripture: *And the Lord blessed him* (Gen. 26:12)."

F.   "Jacob set aside first tithe, in line with this verse of Scripture: *And of*
everything that you will give me, tithing, I shall tithe it to you (Gen.
28:22)."

2. A.   A Samaritan asked R. Meir, saying to him, "Do you not maintain that
Jacob was a truthteller?"

B.   He said to him, "Indeed so, for it is written, *You give truthfulness to*
Jacob (Micah 7:20)."

C.   He said to him, "And did he not say this: *And of all that you give me I*
will give the tenth to you?"

D.   He said to him, "[Yes.] He separated the tribe of Levi as one of the ten."

E.   He said to him, "Then should he not have separated a tenth of the other
two tribes?"

F.   He said to him, "You maintain that they were twelve tribes, but I say that
they were fourteen, as it is said, *Ephraim and Manasseh even as Reuben*
and Simeon shall be mine (Gen. 48:5)."

G.   He said to him, "All the more so. You support my case. You add more
flour, so I'll add more water."

H.   He said to him, "Do you not concede that there were four matriarchs?"

I.   He said to him, "Yes."

J.   He said to him, "Deduct the four firstborn of each of the patriarchs from
the fourteen, for the firstborn is not tithed. Why? Because he is already
holy, and what is already consecrated cannot serve to exempt what is
consecrated [and that leaves ten, hence Levi was enough]."

K.   He said to him, "Happy is your nation on account of what is within it."

3. A.   *[My son, keep your father's commandment,] and do not forsake your*
mother's teaching (Prov. 6:20):

B.   [Reading the consonants for mother with vowels that yield the word
nation, we interpret:] *[do not forsake] your nation's teaching.*

C.   That is in line with what David says: *My desire is to do your will, O*
God, and your Torah is in my intestines [in the great assembly I have
proclaimed what is right] (Ps. 40:8-9).

D.   Said R. Aha bar Ulla, "Is there such a thing as a Torah in the intestines?

E.   "Is it not written, *I shall write it on their heart* (Jer. 31:32)?

F.   "But this is the sense of what David said, 'May a curse come upon me if
anything shall descend into my intestines before I have tithed it!'

G.   "That is in line with this verse of Scripture [indicating the authorities
responsible for tithing]: *Asmoth son of diel was in charge of the king's*
stores; Jonathan son of Uzziah was in charge of the stores in the
country, in the cities, in the villages,nd in the foretresses (I Chr.
27:25)."

H.   Therefore Moses admonishes Israel, saying to them, *[Year by year] you*
shall set aside a tithe *[of all the produce of your seed, of everything that*
grows on the land. You shall eat it in the presence of the Lord your God
in the place which he will choose as a dwelling for his name — the tithe
of your corn and new wine and oil, and the firstborn of your cattle and
sheep, so that for all time you may learn to fear the Lord your God]
(Deut. 14:22).

The intersecting-verse in both of its clauses addresses the theme of tithing. The commandment of the patriarchs was to tithe, so Hunah, No. 1. No. 2 is tacked on because it is pertinent in theme. No. 3 then moves on to the second clause of the intersecting-verse, with equally satisfactory results. The movement back to the theme seems somewhat protracted at No. 3, but the main point is to link David, as much as Abraham, Isaac, and Jacob, to the tradition of tithing.

X:VII

1. A. *If my land has cried out against me, and its furrows have wept together; [if I have eaten its yield without payment, and caused the death of its owners, let thorns grow instead of wheat, and foul weeds instead of barley]* (Job 31:38-40).

   B. They said to Job, "Do you have any right to the land more than three cubits [of burial ground] when you die, that you say, *If my land has cried out against me?* Is it then yours?"

   C. R. Hiyyah the Elder said, "The matter may be compared to the case of someone who was selling a cloak in the market. Someone came by and saw it and said, 'It's mine.'

   D. "He said to him, 'Put it on. If it fits, it's yours, and if not, it's not yours.'

   E. "So said the Holy One, blessed be He, to Job, 'Am I not he concerning whom it is written, "Do I not fill the heavens and the earth?" (Jer. 23:24) And yet you say, *"If my land has cried out against me, and its furrows have wept together; if I have eaten its yield without payment, and caused the death of its owners, let thorns grow instead of wheat, and foul weeds instead of barley "!* Is it then yours? [Is it your property?]'"

   F. And R. Simeon b. Halputa said, "The matter may be compared to the case of someone who was selling a slave-girl in the market. Someone came by and saw her and said, 'She's mine.'

   G. "He said, to him, 'Rebuke her. If she pays attention to you, she's yours, and if not, she's not yours.'

   H. "So said the Holy One, blessed be He, to Job, 'Am I not he concerning whom it is written, *"...who looks at the land and it trembles, touches the mountains and they smoke"* (Ps. 104:33). And yet you say, *"If my land has cried out against me, and its furrows have wept together; if I have eaten its yield without payment, and caused the death of its owners, let thorns grow instead of wheat, and foul weeds instead of barley"!* Is it then yours? [Is it your property?]'"

   I. At that moment said Job before the Holy One, blessed be He, "Lord of the ages, I have not made that statement before you. But this is the language in which I made that statement: *'If my land has cried out against me, [and its furrows have wept together; if I have eaten its yield without payment, and caused the death of its owners, let thorns grow instead of wheat, and foul weeds instead of barley].'*

   J. "[May I be cursed] if I have not appropriately removed the tithes owing from it."

   K. *"...and its furrows have wept together:* [May I be cursed] if I have planted it with mixed seeds.

   L. *"...if I have eaten its yield without payment:* this refers to second tithe, as it is written, *And you will hand over money and bind up the coins [and take the coins, instead of the produce set aside as second tithe, for use in Jerusalem]* (Deut. 14:25).

M.   *"...and caused the death of its owners:* this refers to the tithe set aside for the poor.

N.   "And if I have not done so, then *let thorns grow instead of wheat, and foul weeds instead of barley. Here end the words of Job."*

2. A.   [Reverting to the verse *let thorns grow instead of wheat, and foul weeds instead of barley,]* R. Hoshaiah taught, "The Torah has here taught you appropriate procedure.

B.   "A field which produces thorns is good for sowing wheat, one that produces foul weeds is good for growing barley.

C.   "What verse of Scripture indicates it? *let thorns grow instead of wheat, and foul weeds instead of barley."*

3. A.   *[...Here end the words of Job:]*

B.   From this point forward [in the book of Job] he goes on and prophesies a number of times, and yet you say, *Here end the words of Job?*

C.   But this is what Job said, "If I have not done [what I have said I did,] then let it be the case that *Here end the words [of Job].*

D.   "And let me not have an opening to say before you, *I have removed what is holy from the household* (Deut. 26:13)."

E.   Therefore Moses admonishes Israel, saying to them, *[Year by year]* you shall set aside a tithe *[of all the produce of your seed, of everything that grows on the land. You shall eat it in the presence of the Lord your God in the place which he will choose as a dwelling for his name – the tithe of your corn and new wine and oil, and the firstborn of your cattle and sheep, so that for all time you may learn to fear the Lord your God]* (Deut. 14:22).

The intersecting-verse is systematically worked out in accord with our theme. Job is made to claim that he has faithfully set aside the required tithes and offerings. The model of the foregoing is followed.

X:VIII

1. A.   *To you, O Lord, belongs righteousness, but to us confusion of face, as at this day [to the men of Judah to the inhabitants of Jerusalem and to all Israel, those that are near and those that are far away, in all the lands to which you have driven them, because of the treachery which they have committed against you]* (Daniel 9:7):

B.   Said R. Judah bar Ilai, "An idol passed through the sea with the Israelites.

C.   "What verse of Scripture indicates it? *They shall pass through the sea of distress [and the waves of the sea shall be smitten, and all the depths of the Nile dried up]* (Zech. 10:11).

D.   "The word for *distress* refers only to an idol, for it is written, *The molten thing was a distress in the gathering [of waters as in a heap]* (Is. 28:20)."

2. A.   Said R. Yudan, "It is written, *And the house of Joseph, they too, went up to Beth El, and the Lord was with them* (Judges 1:22).

B.   "They were going to serve an idol, and yet you say, And *the Lord was with them!*

C.   "[Now with reference to the verse, *To you, O Lord, belongs righteousness, but to us confusion of face*], can there be a greater act of 'righteousness' than that?

D.   "One has therefore to say that *To you, O Lord, belongs righteousness, but to us confusion of face.*"

3.   A.   Said R. Judah bar Simon, "It is written, *Thus they carried off the things Micah had made and the priest he had acquired and attacked Laish, whose people were quiet and carefree* (Judges 18:27).

B.   "...*the things Micah had mad* refers to an idol.

C.   "...*the priest he had acquired* refers to a priest who served idolatry.

D.   "...*and attacked Laish* that is Paneas [Mendelbaum].

E.   "...*whose people were quiet and carefree:* they were contented worshipping an idol, which brought them success.

F.   "And yet you say, ...*were quiet and carefree*? Can there be a greater act of 'righteousness' than that?

G.   "One has therefore to say that *To you, O Lord, belongs righteousness, but to us confusion of face.*"

4.   A.   Said R. Samuel bar Nahman, "You find that on the day on which Haman attacked Israel, on that day the Israelites worshipped idols.

B.   "And not only so, but they took [an offering] from him and offered it up to their idol.

C.   "That is in line with this verse: *You took the food I had given you, the flour, the oil, and the honey, with which I had fed you, and set it before them as an offering of soothing odor and so it was* (Ez. 16:19)."

D.   What is the meaning of the word, *and so it was*?

E.   Said R. Judah, "It is in line with the expression, 'And so it was for the morrow.'"

F.   [Reverting to Samuel's statement,] "And nonetheless you did not hold back your mana from them! Can there be a greater act of 'righteousness' than that?

G.   "One has therefore to say that *To you, O Lord, belongs righteousness, but to us confusion of face.*"

5.   A.   Said R. Eleazar, "When Hananiah, Mishael, and Azariah came up out of the fiery furnace, they proclaimed this verse *[To you, O Lord, belongs righteousness, but to us confusion of face, as at this day to the men of Judah to the inhabitants of Jerusalem and to all Israel, those that are near and those that are far away, in all the lands to which you have driven them, because of the treachery which they have committed against you* (Daniel 9:7)].

B.   "You find that when Hananiah, Mishael, and Azariah came up out of the fiery furnace, all the kinds of the nations of the world gathered against them. This is in line with this verse: *The satraps, the prefects, the governors, and the king's ministers gathered together, seeing that these men, that the fire had no power over their bodies* (Dan. 3:27).

C.   "And all the nations of the world said to them, 'You knew that your God had power to do all these miracles for you, and yet you caused him to destroy his house and to send his children into exile.

D.   "And all the nations of the world spit in their faces until they had made them a block of spit.

E.   "And Hananiah, Mishal, and Azariah raised their faces upward and said, *To you, O Lord, belongs righteousness, but to us confusion of face, as at*

*this day to the men of Judah to the inhabitants of Jerusalem and to all
Israel, those that are near and those that are far away, in all the lands to
which you have driven them, because of the treachery which they have
committed against you* (Daniel 9:7)."

6. A. Said R. Joshua bar Nehemiah, *"To you, O Lord, belongs righteousness*
refers to the acceptance of God's judgment [stated by the three]:

   B. "'For we have angered you so much, but you have been patient with us.'"

7. A. It was taught on Tannaite authority in the name of R. Nehemiah, "Under
ordinary conditions if someone has a field, he gives it out for
sharecropping on terms of half, or a third, or a fourth of the crop.

   B. "But the Holy One, blessed be He, is not that way. The Holy One, who
brings the winds and produces clouds and brings down rain and makes
dew fructify the field and nurtures the seeds and fattens the produce has
asked us to separate only one out of ten portions of the crop."

   C. Therefore Moses admonishes Israel, saying to them, *[Year by year] you
shall set aside a tithe [of all the produce of your seed, of everything that
grows on the land. You shall eat it in the presence of the Lord your God
in the place which he will choose as a dwelling for his name – the tithe
of your corn and new wine and oil, and the firstborn of your cattle and
sheep, so that for all time you may learn to fear the Lord your God]*
(Deut. 14:22).

I assume that the relevance of the intersecting-verse is at No. 7. But then it
is not spelled out. God asks so little, yet the Israelites do not do even that. So
God is righteous, and Israel gets shame. The first six cases prepare the way for
the seventh and, overall, provide ample instantiation for the intersecting-verse.
But the established theme scarcely plays a role, and when it does enter in, we are
left to compose for ourselves the appropriate point.

X:IX

1. A. *What is written just prior to this matter [that is, before the base-verse,
[Year by year] you shall set aside a tithe [of all the produce of your seed,
of everything that grows on the land. You shall eat it in the presence of
the Lord your God in the place which he will choose as a dwelling for his
name – the tithe of your corn and new wine and oil, and the firstborn of
your cattle and sheep, so that for all time you may learn to fear the Lord
your God]* (Deut. 14:22)]?

   B. *You shall not eat anything that dies of itself; you may give it to the
alien who is within your towns, that he may eat it, or you may sell it to
a foreigner; for you are a people holy to the Lord your God. You shall
not boil a kid in its mother's milk* (Deut. 14:21):

   C. R. Azariah and R. Jonathan b. Haggai and R. Isaac bar Merion in the
name of R. Yose bar Haninah said, "[The juxtaposition of the two topics
indicates that] one who eats his produce prior to their being properly
tithed is like one who eats meat that has died or itself or that has been
torn.

   D. "What scriptural evidence supports that statement?

   E. *"You shall not eat anything that dies of itself."*

F. R. Abba bar Huna in the name of Rab: "He who eats his produce prior to their being properly tithed as to the removal of the tithe that is owing to the poor is liable to the death penalty."

2. A. Said R. Isaac, "In three passages in scripture it is written, *You shall not boil a kid in its mother's milk.*

B. "One statement serves to state the rule on its own, the second states the rule for purposes of Torah-study, and the third states it for the purposes of joining it to the issue of tithing.

C. "As to the original statement, what is written in that context? *You shall bring the choicest first fruits of your soil to the house of the Lord your God. You shall not boil a kid in its mother's milk* (Ex. 23:19). And thereafter: *And now I send an angel before you to guard you on your way and to bring you to the place I have prepared* (Ex. 23:20).

D. "As to the matter of Torah-study: *You shall bring the choicest first fruits of your soil to the house of the Lord your God. You shall not boil a kid in its mother's milk* (Ex. 34:26). Thereafter: *The Lord said to Moses, Write these words down, because the covenant I make with you and with Israel is in these words* (Ex. 34:27).

E. "Said the Holy One, blessed be He, to him, 'Moses, when the sandal is on your foot, crush the thorn' [so Mandelbaum]. [A further version has it that the angels wanted to receive the Torah for themselves. God told them that they were not fit to receive the Torah, because they ate milk and meat when they visited Abraham. Therefore the verse about not seething the kid in its mother's milk is juxtaposed to the verse about writing down the words of the Torah (Mandelbaum, *ad loc.*)].

F. "After writing down the verse, *You shall not boil a kid in its mother's milk* (Ex. 34:26), write the verse, *The Lord said to Moses, Write these words down, because the covenant I make with you and with Israel is in these words* (Ex. 34:27).

G. "As to the matter of tithing, *[Year by year] you shall set aside a tithe of all the produce of your seed, of everything that grows on the land. You shall eat it in the presence of the Lord your God in the place which he will choose as a dwelling for his name – the tithe of your corn and new wine and oil, and the firstborn of your cattle and sheep, so that for all time you may learn to fear the Lord your God]* (Deut. 14:22)], and then it is written, *You shall not eat anything that dies of itself; you may give it to the alien who is within your towns, that he may eat it, or you may sell it to a foreigner; for you are a people holy to the Lord your God. You shall not boil a kid in its mother's milk* (Deut. 14:21):

H. "Said the Holy One, blessed be He, 'Do not cause me to make the kernels ripen while they are still in their pods [Hebrew: their mother's wombs]. For if you do not properly produce your tithes, I shall send a certain east wind, which will blight them."

I. "That is in line with this verse: *The grain will thus be blasted before it is ripe* (2 Kgs. 19:26)."

The syllogism covers a point relevant to our theme but transcends the issue. The mode of exegesis – interpreting juxtapositions – yields a single approach to diverse items, with a good result for our point of interest.

X:X

1. A. *[Year by year]* you shall set aside a tithe *[of all the produce of your seed, of everything that grows on the land. You shall eat it in the presence of the Lord your God in the place which he will choose as a dwelling for his name – the tithe of your corn and new wine and oil, and the firstborn of your cattle and sheep, so that for all time you may learn to fear the Lord your God]* (Deut. 14:22): [the duplication of the verb, yielding tithing, you shall tithe] allows for the play on words utilizing the same letters, for one instance, *tithing, you shall tithe* – so that you will not lose out.

   B. ...*tithing, you shall tithe* – so that you will get rich.

   C. Said the Holy One, blessed be He, "Give a tithe of what is mine, and I shall enrich what is yours."

2. A. *[Year by year you shall set aside a tithe]* of all *[the produce of your seed, of everything that grows on the land. You shall eat it in the presence of the Lord your God in the place which he will choose as a dwelling for his name – the tithe of your corn and new wine and oil, and the firstborn of your cattle and sheep, so that for all time you may learn to fear the Lord your God]* (Deut. 14:22):

   B. Said R. Abba bar Kahana, "Scripture thereby gives an indication that people in trade and in commerce overseas should set aside a tenth of their gain for those who labor in the Torah."

3. A. *[Year by year you shall set aside a tithe of all]* the produce of your seed, of everything that grows on the land. *[You shall eat it in the presence of the Lord your God in the place which he will choose as a dwelling for his name – the tithe of your corn and new wine and oil, and the firstborn of your cattle and sheep, so that for all time you may learn to fear the Lord your God]* (Deut. 14:22):

   B. If [by tithing] you attain merit, in the end you will go forth to sow seed in your field, and if not, the one who goes forth into the field will make war on you. And who is that? It is the wicked Esau, concerning whom it is written, *A hunter, a man of the field* (Gen. 25:27).

4. A. Another interpretation of the clause, *[Year by year you shall set aside a tithe of all]* the produce of your seed, of everything that grows on the land. *[You shall eat it in the presence of the Lord your God in the place which he will choose as a dwelling for his name – the tithe of your corn and new wine and oil, and the firstborn of your cattle and sheep, so that for all time you may learn to fear the Lord your God]* (Deut. 14:22):

   B. If [by tithing] you attain merit, in the end you will go forth to your field and see that the world needs rain and pray and be answered. But if not, in the end the (enemies of) Israel will go forth to bury their children in the field.

5. A. Year by year *[you shall set aside a tithe of all]* the produce of your seed, of everything that grows on the land. *[You shall eat it in the presence of the Lord your God in the place which he will choose as a dwelling for his name – the tithe of your corn and new wine and oil, and the firstborn of your cattle and sheep, so that for all time you may learn to fear the Lord your God]* (Deut. 14:22):

   B. "People may not set aside tithe from the produce of one year to cover that of another year," the words of R. Aqiba.

6. A. *[Year by year you shall set aside a tithe of all the produce of your seed, of everything that grows on the land.]* You shall eat it in the presence

of the Lord your God *[in the place which he will choose as a dwelling for his name – the tithe of your corn and new wine and oil, and the firstborn of your cattle and sheep, so that for all time you may learn to fear the Lord your God]* (Deut. 14:22):

B. If [by tithing] you attain merit, it is your grain, and if not, [the grain not having been tithed,] it is my grain.

C. That is in line with this verse: *And I shall take my grain in its due season* (Hos. 2:11).

7. A. *[Year by year you shall set aside a tithe of all the produce of your seed, of everything that grows on the land. You shall eat it in the presence of the Lord your God in the place which he will choose as a dwelling for his name]* – the tithe of your corn *[and new wine and oil, and the firstborn of your cattle and sheep, so that for all time you may learn to fear the Lord your God]* (Deut. 14:22):

B. If [by tithing] you attain merit, it is your new wine, and if not, it is mine.

C. That is in line with this verse: *And my new wine in its due time* (Hos. 2:11).

8. A. Said R. Simeon b. Laqish, "Said the Holy One, blessed be He, 'I have instructed you to separate your tithes from the choicest of the harvest. How so? If a son of a Levite comes to you, if you have given him from the choicest of the crop, so I have what to give you out of the choicest: *May the Lord open to you his good treasury* (Deut. 28:12).

B. "'But if you have given to him out of the dessicated portions of the crop or from the inferior part, so I have what to give you out of the dessicated or inferior parts of the crop: *The Lord will send the rain of your land as power and dust* (Deut. 28:24).'"

9. A. *[At the end of every third year you shall bring out all the tithe of your produce for that year and leave it in your settlements]* so that the Levites, *who have no holding or patrimony among you, and the aliens, [orphans, and widows in your settlements] may come [and eat their fill. If you do this, the Lord your God will bless you in everything to which you set your hand]* (Deut. 14:28-29):

B. Said R. Luliani of Rome in the name of R. Judah bar Simon, "Said the Holy One, blessed be He, 'As for you, you are responsible for four categories of dependents of your household, and as for me, I am responsible for four such categories. You are responsible for four categories of household dependents, your son, your daughter, your slave-boy, and your slave-girl, and I am responsible for four categories, the Levites, the strange, the orphan, and the widow, and all of them are included in a single verse of Scripture.

C. "'That verse is as follows: *You will rejoice in your festival [of Tabernacles], you, your son, your daughter, your slave boy and your slave girl, the Levite, the stranger, the orphan, and the widow who are in your midst* (Deut. 16:14).'

D. "Said the Holy One, blessed be He, 'I have instructed you to give joy to mine and to yours on the festival days that I have assigned to you. If you do so, I for my part will give joy to both yours as well as mine.

E. "To both these and those I shall give joy in the chosen house: *These I will bring to my holy mountain and make them joyful in my house of prayer; their burnt-offerings and their sacrifices will be accepted on my altar, for my house shall be called a house of prayer for all peoples* (Isaiah 56:7).'"

We conclude with a systematic exegesis of the base-verse in its own terms and also with the expected eschatological climax. Nos. 1, 2 play on the word for tithing. No. 3 proceeds to the next clause, and No. 4, 6, and 7 work on the same approach, that is, tithing brings merit – but that point is implicit. No. 5 introduces an explanation for the cited language. No. 8 sets the stage for what is coming: the reciprocal relationship between the householder's treatment of God's dependents, and God's treatment of the householder's dependents. This yields the eschatological climax of No. 9.

Pisqa Eleven

Now it came to pass that when Pharaoh let the people go, *[God did not guide them by the road towards the Philistines, although that was the shortest; for he said, "The people may change their minds when they see war before them, and turn back to Egypt." So God made them go round by way of the wilderness towards the Red Sea, and the fifth generation of Israelites departed from Egypt]*
(Exodus 13:17-18).

XI:I

1. A. *When a man's ways please the Lord, even his enemies are at peace with him* (Prov. 16:7):
   B. R. Meir says, "This [*his enemies*] refers to a dog."
   C. R. Joshua b. Levi says, "This [*his enemies*] refers to a snake."
   D. R. Meir says, "This refers to a dog. There was a herdsman who milked a cow. A snake came and drank from the milk. A dog saw it. The [herdsman and his family] sat down to eat. The dog began to bark at them, but they paid no attention to it. So the dog went and lapped up some of the milk and died. They buried him and set up a gravestone, and even now it is called 'the dog's gravestone.'"
   E. R. Joshua b. Levi said, "It refers to a snake. There was a man who ground up garlic. A wild snake came along and ate of it. The house-snake saw this. They sat down to eat. The house-snake began to spit dirt at them, but they did not pay attention. In the end the snake threw itself into the garlic-mush [and died]."

2. A. R. Abbahu went to Caesarea. He happened by a certain person's house. The householder placed the dog by the visitor. He [Abbahu] said to him, "Do I owe you all this humiliation [that you inflict on me? Have I earned it?]"
   B. He said to him, "My lord, I pay you only the greatest respect. On one occasion kidnappers came to town, and one of them came and wanted to drag off my wife. The dog went and bit off the man's balls."

3. A. R. Yohanan said, *"When a man's ways please the Lord, even his enemies are at peace with him:* The reference to one's enemies speaks, in fact, of one's wife, as it is written, *A man's enemies are the people of his own house* (Mic. 7:6). This refers to one's wife."
   B. For R. Yohanan said, "The wife of a thug is like a thug."
   C. There was the case of a woman who complained against her husband to the government, and they found him guilty and cut off his head.
   D. After a time the judge found grounds to bring an indictment against her and put her to death.

F. R. Samuel bar Nahman said, *"When a man's ways please the Lord, even his enemies are at peace with him:* the cited verse refers to the impulse to do good."

G. *"...even his enemies are at peace with him:* refers to the impulse to do evil.

H. "Under ordinary circumstances if someone grows up with a fellow for two or three years, he develops a close tie to him. But the impulse to do evil grows with someone from youth to old age, and, if one can, someone strikes down the impulse to do evil even when he is twenty, he overthrows it. If he can, he strikes it down even at seventy or even at eighty."

4. A. They said concerning Yohanan, the high priest, that he served for eighty years in the high priesthood, but at the end he turned into a Sadducee.

B. That is the sense of what David said, *All my bones shall say, "Lord, who is like unto you, who delivers the poor from him who is too strong for him, [yes, the poor and the needy from him who spoils him]"* (Ps. 35:10).

C. This refers to the impulse to do good's saving one from the impulse to do evil.

D. *...yes, the poor and the needy from him who spoils him:*

E. [Gen. R. LIV:I.3 adds: Said R. Aha,] "And is there a greater thief than this one?"

F. R. Berekhiah would recite in connection with such a one: *"If your enemy be hungry, give him bread to eat* (Prov. 25:21). The meaning is, *If your enemy is hungry, feed him* with the bread of the Torah [which will help a person resist the enemy that is the impulse to do evil], as it is said, *Come, eat of my bread* (Prov. 9:5).

G. *"If he is thirsty give him water to drink* (Prov. 25:21), that is, the water of the Torah, as it is said, *Ho, everyone who is thirsty come for water* (Is. 55:1)."

H. *For you pour coals on his head and the Lord will repay you* (Prov. 25:22).

I. And R. Berekhiah said, "When the cited verse refers to '...*also* his enemies' (Prov 16:7), the word *also* encompasses the insects of the house, vermin, flies and the like."

5. A. And rabbis say, *When a man's ways please the Lord, [even his enemies are at peace with him]* (Prov. 16:7) refers to Israel, for it is written, *And every man of Israel* (1 Sam. 17:24).

B. *...even his enemies are at peace with him* refers to Pharaoh.

C. *The enemy said, I will pursue, I will overtake; I will divide the spoil, [I will glut my appetite upon them; I will draw my sword, I will rid myself of them]* (Ex. 15:9).

D. You find that, when Moses came to Pharaoh and said to him, *Thus said the Lord, Send out my people, that they may serve me* (Ex. 8:16), that wicked man said, *Who is the Lord that I should listen to his voice? I do not know the Lord, and furthermore I shall not send forth Israel* (Ex. 5:2).

E.   The very mouth that said, *Who is the Lord that I should listen to his voice?* is the mouth that said, *the Lord is righteous, while Pharaoh and his people are wicked* (Ex. 9:27).

F.   The very mouth that said, *I do not know the Lord, and furthermore I shall not send forth Israel* made the rounds of the Israelites' homes and said, "Go forth to peace, go in peace."

G.   That is why it is said, when Pharaoh let the people go, *[God did not guide them by the road towards the Philistines, although that was the shortest; for he said, "The people may change their minds when they see war before them, and turn back to Egypt." So God made them go round by way of the wilderness towards the Red Sea, and the fifth generation of Israelites departed from Egypt]* (Exodus 13:17-18).

The intersecting-verse calls up the possibility of God's forcing a person's enemies to show him favor, which is precisely what, in the end, Pharaoh had to do. The exposition is stunningly apt, and the point of the exegete, that God's favor makes all the difference, finds ample illustration in the case of our base-verse. The intervening exposition, for its part, covers a variety of other enemies, none of them of a historical character, specifically, the snake and the dog. No. 2 quite correctly contradicts the choice of the dog as enemy of the human being. No. 3 invokes yet another possibility, the wife, then the evil impulse. No. 4 ignores our setting and develops the matter of the evil impulse in essentially its own terms, and No. 5 then draws us back to the main point – a highly successful compositon.

XI:II

1.   A.   *Say unto God, How fearful are your works! Your foes cower before the greatness of your strength. [All men on earth fall prostrate in your presence and sing to you, sing psalms in honor of your name. Come and see all that God has done, tremendous in his dealings with mankind. He turned the waters into dry land so that his people passed through the sea on foot, there did we rejoice in him]* (Ps. 66:3-6):

B.   Said R. Yohanan, "They say to a competent worker, Well done."

C.   *How fearful are your works!:* How awesome are your actions!

D.   Those who are slain slay their own murders, those who are crucified crucify their crucifiers, those who are drowned drown those who drowned them.

E.   The mouth that said, *Every son that is born should you toss into the river* (Ex. 1:22) was itself thrown into the sea: *The chariots of Pharaoh and his host sunk into the sea* (Ex. 15:4).

F.   The remainder of the passage is in accord with the preceding, [which is as follows: *The enemy said, I will pursue, I will overtake; I will divide the spoil, [I will glut my appetite upon them; I will draw my sword, I will rid myself of them]* (Ex. 15:9). You find that, when Moses came to Pharaoh and said to him, *Thus said the Lord, Send out my people, that they may serve me* (Ex. 8:16), that wicked man said, *Who is the Lord that I should listen to his voice? I do not know the Lord, and furthermore I shall not send forth Israel* (Ex. 5:2). The very mouth that said, *Who is the Lord that I should listen to his voice?* is the mouth that

said, *the Lord is righteous, while Pharaoh and his people are wicked* (Ex.
9:27). The very mouth that said, *I do not know the Lord, and
furthermore I shall not send forth Israel* made the rounds of the Israelites'
hovels and said, "Go forth to peace, go in peace." That is why it is said,
Now when Pharaoh let the people go, *[God did not guide them by the
road towards the Philistines, although that was the shortest; for he said,
"The people may change their minds when they see war before them, and
turn back to Egypt." So God made them go round by way of the
wilderness towards the Red Sea, and the fifth generation of Israelites
departed from Egypt]* (Exodus 13:17-18).]

The expository pattern established at **XI:I.5** is continued.

XI:III

1. A. *A reproof is felt by a man of discernment more than a hundred blows by
        a stupid man* (Prov. 17:10):

    B. It was taught on Tannaite authority by R. Ishmael, "The matter may be
        compared to the case of a king who said to his servant, 'Go and bring me
        a fish from the market place.' The man went and brought a rotten fish.

    C. "He said to him, 'By your life! One of these three punishments you are
        not going to avoid. Either you will are going to eat the rotten fish, or
        you are going to receive a hundred strokes, or you are going to pay be
        the value of the fish.'

    D. "He said to him, 'I'll eat the rotten fish.' He had scarcely begun to eat it
        when it turned his stomach. He said, 'I'd rather take the stripes.' He had
        scarcely received fifty stripes before he said, 'I'd rather pay the money.'

    E. "The man turned out to eat the rotten fish, to be beaten, and to pay
        money.

    F. "So said the Holy One to the wicked Pharaoh, 'By your life, either you
        are going to be smitten with ten stripes, or you are going to have to part
        with your money, or you will have to send out the Israelites.'

    G. "'...you are going to be smitten with ten stripes': this refers to the ten
        plagues.

    H. "'...or you are going to have to part with your money': *And they
        despoiled the Egyptians* (Ex. 12:36).

    I. "'...or you will have to send out the Israelites': *Now it came to pass that
        when Pharaoh let the people go, [God did not guide them by the road
        towards the Philistines, although that was the shortest; for he said, 'The
        people may change their minds when they see war before them, and turn
        back to Egypt.' So God made them go round by way of the wilderness
        towards the Red Sea, and the fifth generation of Israelites departed from
        Egypt]* (Exodus 13:17-18)."

The exposition encompasses our base-verse in a larger construction that
makes the point invited by the intersecting-verse: the stupid man received the
hundred blows, whereas a man of discernment would have corrected his error
right away. The movement from intersecting-verse through parable and back to
our base-verse makes the point with great power.

XI:IV

1. A. *Has God struck him down as he struck others down? Has the slayer been slain as he slew others?* (Is. 27:7):

   B. R. Judah and R. Nehemiah:

   C. R. Judah said, "With the staff with which the Egyptians had smitten Israel were they themselves beaten [thus: *God struck him down as he struck others down*]."

   D. R. Nehemiah said, "With the sword with which the Egyptians smote the Israelites, they themselves were smitten."

   E. [Following Braude and Kapstein, p. 204:] *When in full measure before you would let Israel go, you contended* (Is. 27:8): measure for measure.

   F   It was taught in the name of **R. Meir, "With the measure with which one metes out to others, one's own measure is meted out"** [M. Sot. 1:7].

   G. ...*before you would let Israel go, you contended:* he was smitten, and then he sent Israel out.

   H. Therefore it is said, *Now it came to pass that when Pharaoh let the people go, [God did not guide them by the road towards the Philistines, although that was the shortest; for he said, "The people may change their minds when they see war before them, and turn back to Egypt." So God made them go round by way of the wilderness towards the Red Sea, and the fifth generation of Israelites departed from Egypt]* (Exodus 13:17-18).

The main point, which repeats the foregoing, is clear: the Egyptians were punished before they sent the Israelites out. But the base-verse does not make that point; it goes over another matter entirely. The exegete wishes to underline that God had his own purpose, which is to punish the Egyptians. That purpose was realized in his leading the Israelites the long way.

XI:V

1. A. *Cease your proud boasting, let no word of arrogance pass your lips; [for the Lord is a God of all knowledge, he governs all that men do]* (1 Sam. 2:3):

   B. R. Eleazar, R. Joshua b. Levi, and rabbis:

   C. One of them said, "As you made others fall, so you were made to fall, as you measured out [what was coming to others], so they measured out for you."

   D. The other said, "With the recipe by which you prepared food for others, your food was cooked, as it is said, *And Jacob made a mess of pottage* (Gen. 25:29)."

   E. And rabbis said, In accord with the plan that you framed for others, the plan for you was worked out, as it is said, *If a man deliberately conspire against his fellow* (Ex. 21:14)."

2. A. ....*who executes judgment for the oppressed, who gives bread to the hungry* (Ps. 146:7):

   B. ...*who executes judgment for the oppressed:* this refers to Israel. *Thus said the Lord of hosts, the children of Israel and the children of Judah are oppressed together* (Jer. 3:33).

C. The one who redeems them is powerful, the Lord of hosts is his name, he will most certainly undertake their complaint.

D. The mouth that said, *Every son who is born you will toss into the river* (Ex. 1:22).

E. The remainder of the passage is in accord with the preceding, [which is as follows: *The enemy said, I will pursue, I will overtake; I will divide the spoil, [I will glut my appetite upon them; I will draw my sword, I will rid myself of them]* (Ex. 15:9). You find that, when Moses came to Pharaoh and said to him, *Thus said the Lord, Send out my people, that they may serve me* (Ex. 8:16), that wicked man said, *Who is the Lord that I should listen to his voice? I do not know the Lord, and furthermore I shall not send forth Israel* (Ex. 5:2). The very mouth that said, *Who is the Lord that I should listen to his voice?* is the mouth that said, *the Lord is righteous, while Pharaoh and his people are wicked* (Ex. 9:27). The very mouth that said, *I do not know the Lord, and furthermore I shall not send forth Israel* made the rounds of the Israelites' hovels and said, "Go forth to peace, go in peace." That is why it is said, Now when Pharaoh let the people go, *[God did not guide them by the road towards the Philistines, although that was the shortest; for he said, "The people may change their minds when they see war before them, and turn back to Egypt." So God made them go round by way of the wilderness towards the Red Sea, and the fifth generation of Israelites departed from Egypt]* (Exodus 13:17-18).]

The main point made by the succession of intersecting-verses is that what others planned to do to Israel was done to them. I follow the sense, but not the wording, of Braude and Kapstein as indicated. Otherwise the passage poses no problems.

XI:VI

1. A. *My sister, my bride is a garden close-locked, a garden close-locked, a fountain sealed* (Song 4:12):

    B. R. Judah bar Simon in the name of R. Joshua b. Levi: "The matter may be compared to the case of a king who had pubescent daughters, whom he had not yet married off. He went overseas, and the daughters for their part went and took care of their own needs and were married to husbands. And each one of them took the ring of her husband and his seal.

    C. "After some days the king return from overseas and heard the report that people were gossiping about his daughters, saying that the king's daughters had acted like whores.

    D. "What did he do? He made an announcement saying, 'Everybody to the piazza.' He then called up the first husband and said to him, 'Who are you?'

    E. "He said to him, 'I am your son-in-law.'

    F. "He produced his ring and said to him, 'To whom does this belong?'

    G. "He said to him, 'To me.'

    H. "He produced his seal and said to him, "To whom does this belong?'

    I. "He said to him, 'To me.'

    J. "And so he did with the second and the third.

K. "The king then said, 'My daughters have gone and taken care of their own needs and married husbands. And yet people gossip, saying that the king's daughters have acted like whores!

L. "So too, since the nations of the world counted the Israelites and said to them that they are in fact children of the Egyptians, who ruled the lives of the Israelites, all the more so their wives, [people thought that the Israelites were sired by Egyptians. But that was not so, and we shall now see what God did about it.]"

M. Said R. Hoshaiah, "At that moment the Holy One, blessed be He, called the angel who was assigned authority over conception and said to him, 'Go and form the shape of the offspring in accord with the face of the father.'

N. "That is in line with the verse: *Reuben, of the Reubenite family, Simeon of the Simeonite family* (Num. 26:7, 14)."

O. Said R. Marinus bar Hoshaiah, "[That is not the sense of the verse. These are merely family names (Mandelbaum).] It is like the case of the families of the Varonians, the Severians, the Saconians."

P. Said R. Addi, "If there is an *H* at the beginning of the word, and a *Y* at the end, it indicates that these are the sons of their fathers." [Mandelbaum, from Rashi: The *he* as the initial letter and the *yod* as the concluding letter in the Tribal family names spell the name of YH, Lord, and thus bear witness concerning Israelites that they were indeed their Tribe Fathers' sons.]

Q. What is the scriptural evidence for that fact? *There the tribes went up, the tribes of the Lord, a testimony to Israel* (Ps. 122:4) – a testimony that they are their fathers' sons.

2. A. Another explanation of the verse, *My sister, my bride is a garden close-locked, a garden close-locked, a fountain sealed* (Song 4:12) – this refers to the virgins.

    B. *...a garden close-locked* – this refers to those women who have had sexual relations.

    C. *...a fountain sealed* – this refers to the males.

3. A. It was taught on Tannaite authority in the name of R. Nathan, "It says two times: *a garden close-locked, a garden close-locked.*

    B. "One refers to [chastity as to] sexual relations in the routine position, the other to sexual relations not in the routine position."

4. A. R. Hunia in the name of R. Hiyyah bar Ba: "Sarah went down to Egypt and kept herself fenced off from fornication, and on her merit all women were kept fenced off."

    B. Said R. Hiyya bar Bah, "That act of restraint from fornication on its own was worthy of providing sufficient merit for the Israelites to be redeemed."

5. A. R. Huna in the name of Bar Qappara, "On account of the merit of four matters the Israelites were redeemed from Egypt:

B. "because they did not change their names [for Egyptian ones], because
    they did not change their language [for Egyptian], because they did not
    gossip about one another, and because they did not practice fornication;
C. "because they did not change their names [for Egyptian ones]: they were
    Reuben and Simeon when they went down, Reuben and Simeon when they
    came up;
D. "because they did not change their language [for Egyptian]: *for it is my
    mouth that is speaking to you* (Gen. 45:12), he was speaking in the
    Holy Language [to them];
E. "because they did not gossip about one another: *Speak, please, in the
    ears of the people, that they ask...* (Ex. 11:2), which indicates that the
    matter was left with them all those twelve months and not a single one
    of them ratted on his fellow;
F. "and because they did not practice fornication: you may know that that
    was the case, for there was only one who did so, and Scripture made the
    matter public: *the name of his mother was Shelomit, daughter of Dibri,
    of the tribe of Dan* (Lev. 24:11)."

6. A. R. Phineas in the name of R. Hiyya bar Ba: "On account of the merit
        that, when the Israelites went down to Egypt, they fenced themselves off
        from fornication, on account of that merit: *Your shoots [are an orchard
        full of pomegranates]* (Song 4:13). [The letters for the word for *shoots*
        may be read] *your being sent forth.*
    B. On that account it is said, *Now it came to pass when Pharaoh let the
        people go, [God did not guide them by the road towards the Philistines,
        although that was the shortest; for he said, "The people may change their
        minds when they see war before them, and turn back to Egypt." So God
        made them go round by way of the wilderness towards the Red Sea, and
        the fifth generation of Israelites departed from Egypt]* (Exodus 13:17-18).

The link is somewhat tortured, but it makes an important point. The
Israelites in Egypt preserved their purity in various ways, and therefore they were
sent forth from Egypt. No. 6 accomplishes the connection by moving from
Song 4:12 to Song 4:13, as though that verse were always in mind. So the
main point is that because, Song 4:12, the sister is a garden close-locked, the
sister was sent forth, Song 4:13. No. 1 introduces the question at hand: were the
Israelites really Israelites and not bastard Egyptians. They were indeed; the
physical parentage of their tribal fathers is affirmed. 1.Off. then present a
secondary exposition of the proof-text, but that discussion does not obscure the
main point. No. 2, buttressed by No. 3, reaffirms that Israelite virgins, married
women, and men all preserve the same purity. Nos. 4, 5 are set-piece
compositions that are added because of their general thematic pertinence, not
because they contribute to the particular discourse at hand. Then, as I said, No.
6 completes the composition and endows the whole with cogency.

XI:VII

1. A. *Now it came to pass [when Pharaoh let the people go, God did not guide
        them by the road towards the Philistines, although that was the shortest;*

*for he said, "The people may change their minds when they see war
before them, and turn back to Egypt." So God made them go round by
way of the wilderness towards the Red Sea, and the fifth generation of
Israelites departed from Egypt]* (Exodus 13:17-18).

B. [Examining the proposition, Any passage in which the words, *and it
came to pass*, appear is a passage that relates misfortune, Leviticus
Rabbah XI:VII.1.B, with the notion that the letters for *and it came to
pass* spell out the word for woe, we ask:] Who cried, "Woe"?

C. The Egyptians cried, "Woe."

D. It was taught on Tannaite authority by R. Simeon b. Yohai, "The matter
may be compared to the case of someone who received by inheritance a
property overseas. But the heir was slothful, so he went and sold it for a
paltry price. The buyer went and excavated the property, and uncovered a
treasure, and built a palace on the proceeds. The purchaser would go
around the market place with slaves in front and slaves behind. The
seller began to choke, saying, 'Woe is me! What have I lost!'

E. "So when the Israelites were camping at the sea shore, they looked like a
royal horde. The Egyptians choked, saying, 'Woe! What have we sent
forth from our land!'"

2. A. Said R. Yose, "The matter may be compared to the case of someone who
received as inheritance a field of a *kor's* size, consisting of a pit. But
the heir was slothful, so he went and sold it for a paltry price. The buyer
went and excavated the property, and uncovered a spring, and he turned
the area into fields and orchards.

B. "So when the Israelites were camping at the seashore, they looked like a
royal horde. The Egyptians choked, saying, 'Woe! What have we sent
forth from our land!'"

3. A. Said R. Nathan, "The matter may be compared to the case of someone
who received as inheritance the trunk of a cedar. But the heir was
slothful, so he went and sold it for a paltry price. The buyer went and
made it into tables, chairs, and benches.

B. "So when the Israelites were camping at the seashore, they looked like a
royal horde. The Egyptians choked, saying, 'Woe! What have we sent
forth from our land!'"

The three parables make the same point. But while the focus now is on the
narrative, that is, the Egyptian pursuit, the base-verse still governs, since we
take up the first element of it: *and it came to pass,* with the question, "who has
cried woe and why." We shall now continue the exposition of the components
of the base-verse.

XI:VIII

1. A. Now it came to pass when Pharaoh let the people go, *[God did not guide
them by the road towards the Philistines, [although that was the shortest;
for he said, "The people may change their minds when they see war
before them, and turn back to Egypt." So God made them go round by
way of the wilderness towards the Red Sea, and the fifth generation of
Israelites departed from Egypt]* (Exodus 13:17-18).

B. This [phrase, *he did not guide them by the road,* yields the meaning, *in accord with accepted practice,* hence it] teaches that he did not lead them in the ordinary and accepted manner.

C. R. Levi in the name of R. Hama bar Haninah stated eight instances [of variation from the normal procedure:]

D. "Ordinarily, water comes from above and bread from below, but here the bread came from above and water from below. The bread came from above: *Lo, I shall rain bread for you from heaven* (Ex. 16:4), and water from below: *Then Israel sang this song, Rise up well, sing to it* (Num. 21:17).

E. "Ordinarily, the disciple holds the lantern and goes before the master, but here, *the pillar of cloud did not depart by day* (Ex. 13:22).

F. "Ordinarily, the disciple goes first and the master follows, but here, *And the Lord went before them by day* (Ex. 13:21).

G. "Ordinarily, the disciple washes the master, but here, *And I washed you in water* (Ez. 16:9).

H. "Ordinarily, the disciple dresses the master, but here, *And I dressed you in weaving* (Ez. 16:10)."

I. R. Simai said, "This refers to purple."

J. Aqilas translated it, "Multicolored."

K. "Ordinarily, a disciple puts on the master's shoe for him, but here, *And I shod you with sealskin* (Ez. 16:10).

L. "Ordinarily, the disciple bears the master, but here, *And I carried you on wings of eagles* (Ex. 19:4).

M. "Ordinarily, the master sleeps and the disciples wakes and watches, but here, *Lo, the guardian of Israel neither slumbers nor sleeps* (Ps. 121:4)."

The exegesis of the signified words is fully worked out, and with great force.

XI:IX

1. A. Now it came to pass when Pharaoh let the people go, *[God did not guide them by the road towards the Philistines, although that was the nearest [shortest], [for he said, "The people may change their minds when they see war before them, and turn back to Egypt." So God made them go round by way of the wilderness towards the Red Sea, and the fifth generation of Israelites departed from Egypt]* (Exodus 13:17-18).

   B. *Near* is the punishment that is coming on the wicked Pharaoh, which he will exact from them.

2. A. Another explanation of the word, *Near:*

   B. *Near* is the punishment that is coming on the Egyptians, which he will exact from them.

3. A. Another explanation of the word, *Near:*

   B. *Near* is the full recompense for the act of kindness which the Canaanites did for our father, Jacob [on account of which they were permitted to remain in the land a while longer].

   C. That is in line with this verse of Scripture: *And the inhabitants of the land, the Canaanites, saw the mourning* (Gen. 50:11).

D. [And what were the acts of kindness that they performed for our father, Jacob?] R. Eleazar said, "[When the bier was brought up there,] they unloosened the girdle of their loins."

E. R. Simeon b. Laqish said, "They untied the shoulder-knots."

F. Rabbis said, "They stood upright."

G. R. Judah said, "They pointed with their finger."

H. Now is it not an argument *a fortiori:* now if these, who did not do a thing with their hands or feet, but only because they pointed their fingers, were saved from punishment, our brethren, Israel, who perform an act of kindness [for the dead] with their adults and with their children, and with their sages [Gen. R. adds: with their hands and with their feet], how much the more so [will they enjoy the merit of being saved from punishment]!

4. A. Another interpretation of the word, *Near:*

B. Near is the time for the total fulfillment of the oath that Abimelech had imposed on our father, Abraham.

C. That is in line with this verse of Scripture: *And now take an oath to me by God, if you deal falsely with me, my son or my grandson* (Gen. 21:23).

D. How many generations were covered by the oath? Three generations were subject to the oath: *with me, my son or my grandson* .

E. That is, with me, my son, and my grandson.

5. A. *Abraham set seven ewe lambs of the flock apart* (Gen. 21:28):

B. R. Joshua of Sikhnin in the name of R. Levi: "Said the Holy One, blessed be He, to him, 'You have given him seven ewe lambs. By your life, matching them my ark will spend seven months in the fields of the Philistines.' That is in line with this verse of Scripture: *He delivered his strength into captivity [and his beauty into the enemy's hand]* (Ps. 78:61).

C. *"He delivered his strength into captivity* refers to the ark of the covenant.

D. *"And the ark of the Lord spent seven months in the field of the Philistines* (1 Sam. 6:1).

E. *"...and his beauty into the enemy's hand* refers to the high priestly garments.

F. *"And you shall make holy garments for Aaron your brother, for honor and for beauty* (Ex. 28:2)."

G. R. Joshua of Sikhnin in the name of R. Levi: "Said to him the Holy One, blessed be He, 'You have given him seven ewe lambs. By your life matching them his descendants [the Philistines] will kill seven righteous men among your descendants, and these are they: Saul and his three sons, and Eli, Hophni, and Phineas.'"

H. And some say that on the list belongs Samson and not Eli.

I. R. Joshua of Siknin in the name of R. Levi: "Said to him the Holy One, blessed be He, 'You have given him seven ewe lambs. By your life, matching them the seven sanctuaries of your descendants will be destroyed, namely, the tent of meeting, the altars at Gilgal, Nob, Gibeon, Shiloh, and the two eternal houses of the sanctuary.'"

The sense of *near* is dual, first, near is punishment, then, more distant is the conquest of the land. The point of interest from No. 3 to the end is why God has taken the longer road, and the sense is that God wishes to postpone the conquest of the Land by Israel. Nos. 1, 2 then concentrate on the former, that is, to whom is *near* applicable, as is clearly stated. The rest is fully exposed.

XI:X

1. A. *...for he said, "The people may change their minds when they see war before them, [and turn back to Egypt." So God made them go round by way of the wilderness towards the Red Sea, and the fifth generation of Israelites departed from Egypt]* (Exodus 13:17-18).
   B. And who are these?
   C. Rabbis say, "These are the children of Ephrain, the sons of Shuthelah.
   D. "It was because they erred in calculating the end-time [of redemption] by a factor of eighty years. One hundred and eighty thousand of them fell.
   E. "That is in line with this verse of Scripture: *The children of Ephraim, armed and carrying bows, turned back on the day of battle* (Ps. 78:9)."

The exposition of the base-verse continues, clause by clause.

XI:XI

1. A. *So God made them go round by way of the wilderness towards the Red Sea, [and the fifth generation of Israelites departed from Egypt]* (Exodus 13:17-18).
   B. This teaches that the way of the wilderness encompassed them.

2. A. *...and the fifth generation of Israelites departed from Egypt:*
   B. [Reading the letters of the word for *fifth generation* to mean armed,] the verse teaches that they were armed with five kinds of armament.

3. A. *...and the fifth generation of Israelites departed from Egypt:*
   B. [Reading the letters of the word for *fifth generation* to mean *counted out by fives*,] this teaches that only one out of five succeeded [in joining the exodus].
   C. Some say, "Only one out of fifty."
   D. Others say, "Only one out of five hundred."
   E. Said R. Nehorai, "By the Temple service! Even one out of five hundred did not succeed [in joining the exodus]."

4. A. R. Yose said, "*...and the fifth generation of Israelites departed from Egypt* means that it was after five generations that they went up."

5. A. *And the children of Israel were fruitful and swarmed and multiplied and became very mighty* (Ex. 1:7):
   B. There were two Amoras.
   C. One of them said, "If it is to the largest among all swarming things that you compare them, lo, the mouse, which produces six at once.

D. "If it is to the smallest of swarming things that you compare them, then
    lo, it is the scorpion, which produces sixty at once."

We proceed to the interpretation of further clauses in the base-verse, working
our way to the end. No. 1 takes up the language translated, *go around,* and Nos.
2ff. go on to the word for fifth/five/armed. We now move on to the second verse
in sequence beyond our base-verse.

XI:XII

1. A. *And Moses took the bones of Joseph with him* (Ex. 13:19):
    B. This tells you how praiseworthy was Moses.
    C. For all the Israelites were occupied in despoiling Egypt, while Moses was
        occupied with the bones of Joseph.
    D. That is in line with this verse of Scripture: *And Moses took the bones of
        Joseph with him* (Ex. 13:19).
    E. *With him,* said R. Yohanah, refers to *with him* in the camp.

2. A. Who told Moses were Joseph was born? They say as follows:
    B. Serah, daughter of Asher, was in that generation, and she told Moses,
        "Moses, it is in the River Nile that Joseph is buried."
    C. Moses went and stood at the bank of the Nile River and said, "Joseph,
        Joseph, the hour has come for the Holy One, blessed be He, to redeem
        his children.
    D. "The Presence of God is held up for you, the Israelites are held up for
        you, the clouds of glory are held up for you.
    E. "If you now show yourself, well and good, but if not, lo, we are free of
        the oath that you have imposed on us."
    F. At that moment the ark of Joseph floated upward to the surface.
    G. And some say that he took a sherd and wrote the Ineffable Name of God
        on it, and tossed it into the wwater.
    H. At that moment the ark of Joseph floated upward to the surface.

3. A. There were two dogs, conjured by magicians, who began to bark at
        Moses. Moses said, "People, you will see [what these are]. Real dogs
        do not bark, fake dogs bark."
    B. Said R. Yudan, "It was because that dog snarled, while, *And to all the
        children of Israel a dog did not show its tongue* (Ex. 11:7) [that Moses
        knew these were fake dogs]."

4. A. There were two arks that went with the Israelites in the wilderness, the
        ark of Joseph and the ark of the Life of the Ages.
    B. And the nations of the world said, "What sort of things are these two
        arks?"
    C. And the Israelites replied, "One is the ark of Joseph, who is deceased,
        and the other is the ark of the Life of the Ages."
    D. Then everyone began ridiculing the Israelites, saying to them, "Now how
        is it that the ark of God should be going along with the ark of a corpse!"
    E. Then the Israelites replied, "This corpse, resting in this ark, carried out
        all that is written down [in the Torah that is] in that ark."

The exposition of the next verse in sequence proceeds apace, with the introduction of the story about the preservation of Joseph's bones. The elements are clear as given and produce no problems.

XI:XIII

1. A. R. Yohanan was in session expounding how the water was turned into a wall for the Israelites.
   B. Explained R. Yohanan, "It was like a lattice."
   C. Serah, daughter of Asher, looked down and said, "I was there, and it was only like a windows opened for illumination [Mandelbaum, *ad loc.*, *emphomata*]."

2. A. R. Yohanan was in session, expounding, "*All the persons belonging to Jacob who came into Egypt, who were his own offspring, [not including Jacob's sons' wives, were sixty-six persons in all: and the sons of Joseph, who were born to him in Egypt, were two; all the persons of the house of Jacob that came into Egypt were seventy]* (Gen. 46:26-27):
   B. "Lo, they were lacking one." [Gen. R. 94:9.1.B adds: R. Levi in the name of R. Samuel bar Nahman, "Have you ever seen someone give his friend sixty-six glasses and go and give him three more, and then the other counts them and comes up with seventy?]
   C. R. Levi in the name of R. Hama bar Hanina: "[But the seventieth] is Jochebed, [who completed the number of Israel in Egypt. She was born by the gates of Egypt.]"
   D. Some say, "It was Serah, daughter of Asher, who completed the full count of Israel. That is in line with this verse: *She said to him, 'I am of them that are peaceable and faithful in Israel'* (2 Sam. 20:19). I am the one who completed the number of Israel in Egypt [so that they reached the number of seventy]. I am the one who delivered the faithful one to the faithful one, [namely, Joseph to Moses]."
   E. Said R. Tanhum bar Hanilai, "The Holy One, blessed be He, came down in all his glory with them.
   F. "What verse of Scripture so indicates? *He is your glory abnd he is your God* (Deut. 10:21), followed by, *Your fathers went down to Egypt with threescore and ten* (Deut. 10:22)."

The exposition moves along thematic lines, with a general interest in the story of the Exodus. But No. 2 does bring us close to the materials just now covered, that is, the ark of Joseph's bones.

XI:XIV

1. A. *To David: To you, O Lord my God, I lift up my heart, [in you I trust, do not put me to shame, let not my enemies exult over me]* (Ps. 25:1-2):
   B. The word for *lift up* is so written that it may be read, *bend low* [Mendelbaum].
   C. Said David before the Holy One, blessed be He, "Lord of the ages, my soul is bent low because of those who are destined to give up their lives in the sanctification of God's name."

D. "And who is this? It is the entire generation of the persecution [of Hadrian, following Bar Kokhba's war].

E. Said the Holy One, blessed be He, to him, "And did they lose on that account? Is their share not in [eternal] life? *Their share is in eternal life. That which is laid up for you will fill their belly* (Ps. 17:14).

F. Said David before the Holy One, blessed be He, "Lord of the ages, do I have my share with them?"

G. He said to him, "What is written is not *that which is laid up for* them *will fill their belly*, but rather, *That which is laid up for* you *will fill their belly* (Ps. 17:14) – what is yours and what is theirs.

H. Said David before the Holy One, blessed be He, "Lord of the ages, these and those come about on account of the power accruing for studying the Torah and doing good deeds, but, as for me, *Only through righteousness may I see your face* (Ps. 17:15)."

I. Said R. Hiyya bar Ba, "If someone should say to you, 'Give your life for the sanctification of God's name,' say to him, 'I shall give it up, on condition that they cut off my head right away.'

J. "But let it not be done as was done in the generation of the persecution, when they would put fiery iron balls in their armpits and sharpened reeds under their fingernails.:"

I cannot explain the inclusion of this discussion, which has nothing to do with our theme, let alone our base-verse(s).

XI:XV

1. A. There was this incident. R. Yudan bar Goria, R. Isaac, and R. Jonathan went to listen to the exposition by R. Simeon b. Yohai of a passage of the Torah concerning the drink-offerings. They stayed for three days. They said, "We have to take our leave of him."

B. One of them went up and interpreted the verse, *I have set my bow in the cloud* (Gen. 9:13).

C. Said R. Simeon b. Yohai, "That refers to a sign given to the world."

D. The second went up and interpreted the verse, *And the bow appeared in a cloud* (Gen. 9:14)..

E. Said R. Simeon b. Yohai, "That refers to a sign given to the world."

2. A. R. Hezekiah in the name of R. Jeremiah: "If R. Simeon b. Yohai said, 'Valley, valley, fill up with golden denars,' it would fill up."

B. R. Hezekiah in the name of R. Jeremiah: "Elijah of blessed memory and R. Joshua b. Levi were in session, interpreted verses of Scripture. A tradition in the name of R. Simeon b. Yohai came to hand. R. Simeon b. Yohai himself came by. They said, 'Here comes the master of the teaching at hand, let us go and present a question concerning it to him.'

C. "They went and asked him about it. [Simeon] said to [Elijah], 'Who is this with you?'

D. "He said to him, 'It is R. Joshua b. Levi, and he is the greatest authority of his generation.'

E. "He said to him, "And has a rainbow appeared in his lifetime?'

F. "He said to him, 'Yes.'

G. "He said to him, 'If a rainbow has appeared in his lifetime, he is not worthy of seeing my face.'"

3. A. R. Hezekiah in the name of R. Jeremiah: "Thus did R. Simeon b. Yohai say, 'The Holy One, blessed be He, took an oath to our father Abraham that there would never be in the world less than thirty righteous men like him.'
   B. "What verse of Scripture proves it? *And Abraham will surely be* (Gen. 18:18). The word for *will surely be* contains letters, the numerical value of which adds up to thirty.
   C. "[And Simeon continued], 'And if there is only one, it is I.'"

4. A. R. Hezekiah in the name of R. Jeremiah: "Thus did R. Simeon b. Yohai say, 'Let Abraham draw the people from his time to mine near [to God], and I shall draw those from my time to the coming of the king-messiah.
   B. "'But if not, let Ahijah the Shilonite join together with me, and we shall bring the whole world near [to God].'"

5. A. [Reverting to 1.E:] The third went and interpreted the verse, *Go, sell the oil* (2 Kgs. 4:7).

The inclusion of this rather disjointed passage, with its vast interpolation at Nos. 2-4, is nearly incomprehensible. The parallel at Gen. R. 35:3 includes the following, however, which explains why, in complete and full form, the passage can have impressed a redactor as appropriate for the present composition:

When [Simeon b. Yohai] recognized that these were men of such well-established learning, he sent with them a pair of disciples to find out what they were discussing on the way. One of them gave this exposition: *And the angel of God, who went before the camp of Israel, left and went behind* (Ex. 14:19). Then why is it further stated, *And the pillar of cloud went from before them and stood behind them* (Ex. 14:19)? What it means is that measure of strict justice that the Holy One, blessed be He, had originally stretched out against Israel did he reverse himself and stretched forth against the Egyptians.

It seems to me that there is a solid thematic tie to our topic.

XI:XVI

1. A. There was this incident: R. Simeon b. Yohai spent thirteen years in hiding in a cave, along with his son, R. Eleazar, eating dried carobs, so that their bodies produced sores. In the end he went out and sat at the mouth of the cave. He saw a hunter trapping birds.
   B. When the hunter spread the net the first time, he heard an echo say [from heaven], "Pardoned" [in Latin, *dimissio*, as given here], the bird escaped, but when he spread the net the second time, the echo shouted, "Death" [in Latin: *specula*, as given here], and the bird was trapped.
   C. He said, "Without the intervention of heaven, even a bird is not trapped, [all the more so the soul of a mortal], yet we are sitting here!"

D.   When he heard that the difficulties had abated, he said, "Let us go down and immerse and find healing in the hot springs at Tiberias. His son said to him, "We have to express thanks, as our fathers did, for they set up markets [in places in which they received hospitality,] and sold produce at cheap prices." So he set up a market and sold produce at low prices. They said, "[We have derived so much benefit from Tiberias,] should we not [also] purify it from corpse-uncleanness?"

E.   [What did he do?] He took radishes, cut them up, and [in order to locate the presence of corpse-matter and to remove it, so the town would be free of cultic uncleanness deriving from corpse-matter] threw down the pieces, and a corpse would rise and they carried the corpse outside of the town, so they thus removed all the corpse-uncleanness from Tiberias.

F.   A Samaritan saw it and said, "Should I not go and ridicule this sage of the Jews?" What did he do? He took a corpse and hid it away in a market place which he had purified [so restoring the cultic uncleanness from which the town had suffered before].

G.   [In the morning] he said, "Did you purify such-and-such a market place [in Tiberias]?

H.   He said to him, "Yes."

I.   He said to him, "If I produce a corpse behind you [what will you say?]"

J.   He said to him, "Go, show me."

K.   R. Simeon b. Yohai realized through the Holy Spirit that there was a corpse placed there, and he said, "I now decree concerning those above, that they go down, and concerning those below, that they go up." And so it happened [that the man dropped dead and the corpse came back to life].

I.   When he left, he passed by the synagogue of Magdela and heard the voice of a teacher of Magdela, saying [Mendelbaum: sarcastically], "Lo, Bar Yohai has purified Tiberias."

J.   He said to him, "Were you not with us when the vote was taken? [You had no right to make such a statement.]"

K.   He laid his eyes on him and looked at him and the man immediately turned into a hill of bones.

I assume that the long sequence of Simeon b. Yohai-stories travels in a train, which is why the present materials are in hand.

XI:XVII

1.   A.   R. Simeon bar Yohai was going [through the valley of Beth Tofah] in the sabbatical year [during which one is not supposed to gather crops]. He saw someone standing there and collecting the aftergrowth of crops that had grown in the Seventh Year [when sowing was forbidden]. He said, "Isn't this the aftergrowth of produce of the seventh year? [How come you're gathering it?]"

B.   The man said, "But you yourself have declared it permitted [for use]."

C.   He said to him, "But is it not the case that my colleagues differed from my view?"

D.   He recited in his regard the verse, *One who breaks down a fence will be bitten by a snake* (Qoh. 10:8).

E.   And that is what happened to him.

The established program continues.

XI:XVIII

1. A. R. Eleazar bar Simeon: ass-drivers came to his town, wanting to buy fodder for their asses. They saw him sitting before an oven. His mother brought him food and he ate, his mother brought him food and he ate, until he had eaten all of the loaf of bread.
   B. They said, "Woe! There is a wicked snake living in that man's belly."
   C. He heard what they said.
   D. What did he do to them? He took their asses and brought them up to the top of the roof. They went and told his father. He said to them, "Is it possible that you have pronounced something bad?"
   E. They said to him, "We saw him sitting before an oven. His mother brought him food and he ate, his mother brought him food and he ate, until he had eaten all of the loaf of bread. And we said, 'Woe! There is a wicked snake living in that man's belly.'"
   F. He said to them, "Now was he eating what is really yours? The One who created him also created food for him. Nonetheless, go and speak to him in my name, and he will let them [the asses] down for you."
   G. They went and spoke with him.
   H. The latter miracle was more difficult than the former. When he had taken them up, he did it one by one, but when he let them down, he did it two by two.

The line of tales continues, a composition wholly independent of our setting.

XI:XIX

1. A. R. Eleazar bar Simeon was appointed chief tax-collector. He put people to death who were guilty of crimes subject to the death penalty, and R. Joshua b. Qorha called him, "Vinegar son of wine."
   B. He said to him, "Whom do you call vinegar son of wine? Have I not merely removed thorns? Were they not people who were subject to the death penalty, whom I have put to death?"
   C. He said to him, "Could you not have fled to Laodicea [to avoid having to make this severe decree]?"
   D. He said to him, "You should have fled to the other side of the world, and left it for the master of the garden to come and remove his own thorns."

The line of stories continues, now returning to his gluttony.

XI:XX

1. A. R. Eleazar bar Simeon went to R. Simeon bar Yose bar Laqonia, his father-in-law.
   B. He slaughtered an ox for him, baked a troughful of bread, and cracked open a cask of wine.
   C. As he [the father-in-law] mixed the wine, he [Eleazar] drank it, as he mixed the wine, he drank it.

D. He said to him, "Is it possible that you have ever heard from your father how much is the measure of a cup of wine?"

E. He said to him, "As is, one [gulp suffices], chilled, two, hot, three. But the evaluation of sages [as to how many gulps are needed] does not apply to a cup such as yours, which is niggardly, nor to wine such as yours, which is good, nor for a belly such as mine, which is enormous."

The stories of Eleazar's prodigious appetite unfold.

XI:XXI

1. A. R. Eleazar bar Simeon asked R. Simeon bar Yose bar Laqonia, his father-in-law, saying to him, "What is the meaning of the verse of Scripture, *The clothes on your backs did not wear out, [nor did your feet swell all these forty years]* (Deut. 8:4)? [How could such a thing be so?] Is it possible that weavers' gear went along with the Israelites in the wilderness [to keep their garments in good repair]?"

    B. He said to him, "Clouds of glory enfolded them, and they did not wear *out.*"

    C. He said to him, "What it says is *The clothes on your backs did not wear out.*"

    D. "But didn't [the younger ones] grow up [and need larger sizes]?"

    E. He said to him, "Take the case of a snail. While it grows, its shell grows along with it."

    F. "Didn't they need to launder their clothing?"

    G. He said to him, "The clouds of glory would clean them [with fire]. And do not find that surprizing, for asbestos linen is cleaned only with fire."

    H. "Didn't the clothes stink because of sweat?"

    I. He said to him, "They would deodorize them with the herbs around the well: *The smell of your garments is like the smell of Lebanon* (Song 4:11)."

The father-in-law line of stories leads us to the present item.

XI:XXII

1. A. R. Eleazar bar Simeon was appointed to impress men and beasts into forced labor [in the corvée]. One time Elijah, of blessed memory, appeared to him in the guise of an old man. He said to him, "Get me a beast of burden."

    B. He said to him, "What do you have as a cargo [to load on the beast]?"

    C. He said to him, "This old skin-bottle of mine, my cloak, and me as rider."

    D. He said, "Take a look at this old man! I [personally] can take him and carry him to the end of the world, and he says to me to get a beast ready!"

    E. What did he do? He loaded him on his back and carried him up mountains and down valleys and over fields of thorns and fields of thistles.

    F. In the end [Elijah] began to bear down on him. He said to him, "Old man, old man! Make yourself lighter, and if you don't, I'll toss you off."

G. [Elijah] said to him, "Now do you want to take a bit of a rest?"

H. He said to him, "Yes."

I. What did he do? He took him to a field and set him down under a tree and gave him food and drink. When he had eaten and drunk, he [Elijah] said to him, "All this running about – what is in it for you? Would it not be better for you to take up the vocation of your fathers?"

J. He said to him, "And can you teach it to me?"

K. He said to him, "Yes."

L. And there are those who say that for thirteen years Elijah of blessed memory taught him until he could recite even Sifra [the exegesis of Leviticus, which is particularly difficult].

M. But once he could recite that document, [he had so lost his strength that] he could not lift up even a cloak.

2. A. The household of Rabban Gamaliel had a member who could carry forty *seahs* [of grain] to the baker [on his back].

B. He said to him, "All this vast power do you possess, and you do not devote yourself to the study of Sifra."

C. When he could recite that document, they say that even a single seah of grain he was unable to bear.

D. There are those who say that if someone else did not take it off him, he would not have been able to take it off himself.

These stories about how a mark of the sage is physical weakness are included only because they form part of the (in this instance, secondary) composition on Eleazar b. Simeon.

XI:XXIII

1. A. R. Eleazar bar Simeon, when he grew weaker [as he lay dying], his arm came to be exposed. He saw his wife both laughing and weeping. He said to her, "By your life, I know exactly why you are laughing and also why you are weeping.

B. "You are laughing, because you are thinking, 'How good it has been for me! How excellent has been my portion in this world. How good it has been for me, that I have cleaved to the body of that righteous man!'

C. "You are weeping, because you are thinking, 'Woe for that body that is going to the worms.'

D. "And that is true: I am dying. But the worm – God forbid! – will never rule over me. But there is one worm that is destined to chew on the back of my ears, for one time I was going into the synagogue, and heard a voice of a man who was blaspheming, and I had the power to do something about it and I did not do so."

2. A. When he died, he was buried in Gush Halab. R. Simeon b. Yohai appeared to the people of Meron [where he was buried] and said to them, "The right eye that I had – do I not have the merit of having him buried near me?"

B. The people of Meron went to bring him. But the people of Gush Halab went out after them with sticks and spears. [They would not give up the body.]

C. One time, on the eve of the Great Fast [of the Day of Atonement], they said, "This is the right time to bring him, while they are filling up [with food before the fast]."

D. When they were outside of the town, two snakes of fire went before them. They said, "It is the right time for us to bring him."

E. When they reached the cave [in which he was buried], the two snakes of fire set themselves up [as a guard] at the entrance. They said, "Who will go in to bring him out?"

F. Said his wife, "I shall go in and bring him out, for I know the mark [that will tell me which body is his]."

G. She went in and wanted to bring him out, and found the worm nibbling on the back of his ear.

H. She wanted to take away [the worm], but heard an echo saying, "Let the Creditor collect his debt."

I. They brought out the body and set it next to the body of his father.

J. They say that from that time R. Simeon b. Yohai never again appeared to the people of Meron.

The story now reaches the death scene and the reunification of father and son. But the order of the entries into the story does follows the life of Eleazar, as we shall now see, which suggests that, in some redactional circles, the biography of a sage formed the redactional structure of a contemplated composition.

XI:XXIV

1. A. When R. Eleazar bar Simeon would go into the meeting room, the face of Rabbi would glower, and his father would say to him, "Do you see this one? He is a lion, son of a lion, while as to you, you are a lion but merely son of a fox."

B. When he died, he sent and sought his widow in marriage.

C. She sent to him, "Should a utensil which has been used for sacred purposes now be used for merely secular purposes?"

D. She said to her, "What did he ever do that I do not do?"

E. She said to him, "When he would work in Torah-study, having completed all that he could do, he would go to lie down, and say, 'May all the sorrows of Israel come upon me,' and they would come upon him [so that, in atonement for all Israel, he would suffer].

F. "And when the time would come again for him to labor in Torah-study, he would say, 'May each and every one of you return to its place,' and they would go their way."

G. He said to her, "I too can do that."

H. He called them and they came. He wanted them to go their way, but they did not go their way.

I. There are those who say that for thirteen years he suffered from a toothache.

J. She sent and said to him, "I have heard that people may ascend the ladder
of holiness but not descend [on which account I shall not marry you]."

The biography now comes to an end, the whole simply parachuted into our
composition. Who thought the document appropriate to the present theme and
why I cannot say.

XI:XXV

1. A. *[Moses took the bones of Joseph with him,] because Joseph had exacted
an oath from the Israelites: ["Some day," he said, "God will show his
care for you and then, as you go, you must take my bones with you"]*
(Ex. 131:19):
   B. Why did he impose two oaths [for in the Hebrew the verb, *exacting an
oath*, is stated twice]?
   C. This teaches that Joseph imposed an oath on his brothers, and his
brothers on their sons, and their sons on yet another generation.

2. A. *God will show his care for you* (Ex. 13:19):
   B. Why does the verb for *show his care* appear two times?
   C. One refers to the expression of care in Egypt, the other at Sinai.
   D. There is likewise a display of care in Nisan and one in Tishre.
   E. This is to indicate that there is one in this world, one in the world to
come.

3. A. *[as you go,] you must take my bones with you:*
   B. Is it possible to imagine that this was meant to be done just then?
   C. Scripture says, *...as you go.*
   D. R. Meir says, *"...as you go* teaches that each tribe was to take up the
bones of the head of the tribe along."

We conclude with attention to the continuation of the base-verse.

Pisqa Twelve

In the third month [after Israel had left Egypt, they came to the wilderness of Sinai. They set out from Rephidim and entered the wilderness of Sinai, where they encamped, pitching their tent opposite the Mountain. Moses went up the mountain of God, and the Lord called to him from the mountain and said, "Speak thus to the house of Jacob and tell this to the sons of Israel: You have seen with your own eyes what I did to Egypt and how I have carried you on eagles' wings and brought you here to me. If only you will now listen to me and keep my covenant, then out of all peoples you shall become my special possession; for the whole earth is mine. You shall be my kingdom of priests, my holy nation"]

(Exodus 19:1-6).

XII:I

1. A. R. Judah bar Simon commenced discourse by citing the following verse: *"Many daughters show how capable they are, but you excel them all. [Charm is a delusion and beauty fleeting; it is the God-fearing woman who is honored. Extol her for the fruit of her toil and let her labors bring her honor in the city gate]* (Prov. 31:29-31):

   B. "The first man was assigned six religious duties, and they are: not worshipping idols, not blaspheming, setting up courts of justice, not murdering, not practicing fornication, not stealing.

   C. "And all of them derive from a single verse of Scripture: *And the Lord God commanded the man, saying, 'You may freely eat of every tree of the garden, [but of the tree of the knowledge of good and evil you shall not eat, for in the day that you eat of it you shall die]'* (Gen. 2:16).

   D. *"And the Lord God commanded the man, saying:* this refers to idolatry, as it is said, *For Ephraim was happy to walk after the command* (Hos. 5:11).

   E. *"The Lord:* this refers to blasphemy, as it is said, *Whoever curses the name of the Lord will surely die* (Lev. 24:16).

   F. *"God:* this refers to setting up courts of justice, as it is said, *God [in context, the judges] you shall not curse* (Ex. 22:27).

   G. *"the man:* this refers to murder, as it is said, *He who sheds the blood of man by man his blood shall be shed* (Gen. 9:6).

   H. *"saying:* this refers to fornication, as it is said, *Saying, will a man divorce his wife...* (Jer. 3:1).

   I. *"You may freely eat of every tree of the garden:* this refers to the prohibition of stealing, as you say, *but of the tree of the knowledge of good and evil you shall not eat.*

   J. "Noah was commanded, in addition, not to cut a limb from a living beast, as it is said, *But as to meat with its soul – its blood you shall not eat* (Gen. 9:4).

K. "Abraham was commanded, in addition, concerning circumcision, as it is said, *And as to you, my covenant you shall keep* (Gen. 17:9).

L. "Isaac was circumcised on the eighth day, as it is said, *And Abraham circumcised Isaac, his son, on the eighth day* (Gen. 21:4).

M. "Jacob was commanded not to eat the sciatic nerve, as it is said, *On that account the children of Israel will not eat the sciatic nerve* (Gen. 32:33).

N. "Judah was commanded concerning marrying the childless brother's widow, as it is said, *And Judah said to Onen, Go to the wife of your childless brother and exercise the duties of a levir with her* (Gen. 38:8).

O. "But as to you, at Sinai you received six hundred thirteen religious duties, two hundred forty-eight religious duties of commission [acts to be done], three hundred sixty-five religious duties of omission [acts not to be done],

P. "the former matching the two hundred forty-eight limbs that a human being has.

Q. "Each limb says to a person, 'By your leave, with me do this religious duty.'

R. "Three hundred sixty-five religious duties of omission [acts not to be done] matching the days of the solar calendar.

S. "Each day says to a person, 'By your leave, on me do not carry out that transgression.'"

2. A. *Charm is a delusion and beauty fleeting; [it is the God-fearing woman who is honored. Extol her for the fruit of her toil and let her labors bring her honor in the city gate]:*

B. *Charm is a delusion:* the charm of Noah was a *delusion: Noah found favor* (Gen. 6:8).

C. *...and beauty fleeting:* the beauty of the first man was fleeting.

D. The round part of the First Man's heal outshone the orb of the sun.

E. "And do not find that fact surprising, for in ordinary practice a person makes for himself two salvers, one for himself and one for a member of his household. Which of the two is the finer? Is it not his own?

F. "So the first Man was created for the service of the Holy One, blessed be He, while the orb of the sun was created only for the service of the created world.

G. "Is it not an argument *a fortiori* that the round part of the first Man's heal outshone the orb of the sun.

H. "And the countenance of his face all the more so!"

3. A. *...it is the God-fearing woman who is honored:*

B. this refers to Moses [who received the commandments of the Torah and was totally God-fearing].

4. A. *Extol her for the fruit of her toil and let her labors bring her honor in the city gate:*

B. Said R. Yose bar Jeremiah, "On what account does Scripture compare prophets to women? Just as a woman is not ashamed to demand from her husband what her household needs, so the prophets are not ashamed to demand before the Holy One, blessed be He, the needs of Israel.

C. "Said the Holy One, blessed be He, to Israel, 'My children, read this passage every year, and I shall credit it to you as if you were standing before me at Mount Sinai and receiving the Torah."

D. "When is that the case?

E. *"In the third month after Israel had left Egypt, [they came to the wilderness of Sinai. They set out from Rephidim and entered the wilderness of Sinai, where they encamped, pitching their tent opposite the Mountain. Moses went up the mountain of God, and the Lord called to him from the mountain and said, 'Speak thus to the house of Jacob and tell this to the sons of Israel: You have seen with your own eyes what I did to Egypt and how I have carried you on eagles' wings and brought you here to me. If only you will now listen to me and keep my covenant, then out of all peoples you shall become my special possession; for the whole earth is mine. You shall be my kingdom of priests, my holy nation']* (Exodus 19:1-6).

The climax at No. 4 shows how apt is the choice of the intersecting-verse. For it allows us to review the religious duties assigned to the successive figures, the first man, Noah, the patriarchs, finally Israel. That, after all, is the centerpiece of the pisqa, the revelation of the Torah at Sinai, meaning, of the religious duties assigned to Israel in particular. No. 1 therefore leads us directly and by a straight road right to No. 4. No. 2 disposes of the figures in No. 1 whom the compositor wishes to dismiss, and No. 3 leads us right to No. 4. I cannot imagine a more successful example of the genre.

XII:II

1. A. R. Yohanan commenced discourse by citing the following verse of Scripture: *"He rescued me from my enemies, strong as they were, from my foes when they grew too powerful for me. [They confronted me in the hour of my peril, but the Lord was my buttress. He brought me out into an open place, he rescued me because he delighted in me]* (Ps. 18:17-18).

   B. *"He rescued me from my enemies:* this refers to Pharaoh, *Said the enemy, I shall pursue* (Ex. 16:19).

   C. *"from my foes when they grew too powerful for me:* this refers to the Egyptians.

   D. *"They confronted me in the hour of my peril:* from what Pharaoh planned, from what Amalek planned.

   E. "And of them all: *the Lord was my buttress.*

   F. *"He brought me out into an open place:* for he gave me the Torah" [which is called an "open place" (Job 11:19)—Mendelbaum] .

2. A. *"...he rescued me because he delighted in me:*

   B. Said R. Yohanan, "His trust [Mendelbaum, p. 204n.] is what drew him to give me the Torah.

   C. "When did this take place?

   D. *"In the third month [after Israel had left Egypt, they came to the wilderness of Sinai. They set out from Rephidim and entered the wilderness of Sinai, where they encamped, pitching their tent opposite*

the Mountain. Moses went up the mountain of God, and the Lord called
to him from the mountain and said, 'Speak thus to the house of Jacob and
tell this to the sons of Israel: You have seen with your own eyes what I
did to Egypt and how I have carried you on eagles' wings and brought
you here to me. If only you will now listen to me and keep my
covenant, then out of all peoples you shall become my special
possession; for the whole earth is mine. You shall be my kingdom of
priests, my holy nation'] (Exodus 19:1-6)."

The movement to the base-verse does not seem to me so inexorable as in
the preceding, but the main point is that after God has saved the Israelites from
Pharaoh and the Egyptians, he gave them the Torah as a mark of exceptional
love.

XII:III

1. A. R. Isaac commenced his discourse by citing the following verse: *"Refresh*
   me with raisins, [he revived me with apricots, for I was faint with love.
   His left arm was under my head, his right arm was around me] (Song 2:5).
   B. "[Reading the letters for the word for *raisins* to yield the sound for the
   word for *fire*, we interpret as follows]: Refresh me with two fires, the fire
   of Abraham [whom Nimrod threw into the fiery furnace] and the fire of
   Hananiah, Mishael, and Azariah."

2. A. Another interpretation: *"Refresh me with raisins, [he revived me with*
   apricots, for I was faint with love. His left arm was under my head, his
   right arm was around me] (Song 2:5).
   B. "[Reading the letters for the word for *raisins* to yield the sound for the
   word for *fire*, we interpret as follows]: Refresh me with two fires, the fire
   of Moriah and the fire of Sinai.

3. A. Another interpretation of the verse: *Refresh me with raisins, [he revived*
   me with apricots, for I was faint with love. His left arm was under my
   head, his right arm was around me] (Song 2:5).
   B. [Reading the letters for the word for *raisins* to yield the sound for the
   word for *well construed*, we interpret as follows]: Refresh me with laws
   that are well construed.
   C. *...revived me with apricots:* this refers to words of Torah, which have a
   fragrance as pleasant as apricots.

4. A. *...for I was faint with love:*
   B. Said R. Isaac, "In olden times, when a penny was commonplace, a person
   would hunger for a teaching of the Mishnah or of Talmud. Now that a
   penny is uncommon, and all the more so as we are sick of the rule of the
   kingdoms, a person hungers to hear a teaching of Scripture and of lore."

5. A. *...for I was faint with love:*
   B. Said R. Levi, "The matter may be compared to the case of a prince, who
   had fallen ill but recovered. Said the teacher, 'Let the boy go to school.'
   Said the king, 'His robust health has not yet returned after his illness,

and should he go to school? But let my son enjoy three months of food and drink, and then he can go to school.'

C.   "Thus when the Israelites went forth from Egypt, they were fit to receive the Torah, but among them were injured people on account of the hard labor with mortar and bricks. Said the Holy One, blessed be He, 'The robust health of my children has not yet been restored from the effects of the hard labor with mortar and bricks, and should they receive the Torah? Let my children enjoy three months of the water of the well and the manna and quail, and then they can receive the Torah.

D.   "When? *In the third month [after Israel had left Egypt, they came to the wilderness of Sinai. They set out from Rephidim and entered the wilderness of Sinai, where they encamped, pitching their tent opposite the Mountain. Moses went up the mountain of God, and the Lord called to him from the mountain and said, 'Speak thus to the house of Jacob and tell this to the sons of Israel: You have seen with your own eyes what I did to Egypt and how I have carried you on eagles' wings and brought you here to me. If only you will now listen to me and keep my covenant, then out of all peoples you shall become my special possession; for the whole earth is mine. You shall be my kingdom of priests, my holy nation']* (Exodus 19:1-6).

The intersecting-verse once more yields an insight into the purpose of the three months' delay between the Exodus and the revelation of the Torah. The movement is direct and inexorable as before.

XII:IV

1. A.   R. Yohanan opened his discourse by citing this verse of Scripture: *So I got her back for fifteen pieces of silver, [a homer of barley, and a measure of barley; and I said to her, 'Many a long day you shall live in my house and not play the wanton and have no intercourse with a man, nor I with you. For the Israelites shall live many a long day without king or prince, without sacrifice or sacred pillar, without image or household gods, but after that they will again seek the Lord their God and David their king and turn anxiously to the Lord for his bounty in days to come']* (Hos. 3:2-5).

    B.   Said R. Yohanan, "*So I got her back* for me, *for fifteen pieces of silver*: this refers to the fifteenth day of Nisan [Passover].

    C.   "*...and for a homer of barley*, lo, thirty.

    D.   "*...and a measure of barley*, lo, forty-five.

    E.   "And where are the other five [to reach the number of fifty days after Passover, on which Pentecost, celebrating the giving of the Torah, is reached]?

    F.   *"and I said to her, 'Many a long day you shall live in my house.'"*

2. A.   [As to the verse, *and I said to her, 'Many a long day you shall live in my house'],* it was taught on Tannaite authority by R. Hiyya, "*Many* refers to two days, *long* to three – lo, the fifty days of the counting of the sheaf of first grain.

    B.   "From that point we refer to the Ten Commandments."

3. A. ...and not play the wanton:

   B. You will not make for yourself graven images (Lev. 26:1).

   C. ...and have no intercourse with a man:

   D. You will have no other gods (Ex. 20:3).

   E. And if you have done so, nor I with you.

   F. When? In the third month [after Israel had left Egypt, they came to the
       wilderness of Sinai. They set out from Rephidim and entered the
       wilderness of Sinai, where they encamped, pitching their tent opposite
       the Mountain. Moses went up the mountain of God, and the Lord called
       to him from the mountain and said, 'Speak thus to the house of Jacob and
       tell this to the sons of Israel: You have seen with your own eyes what I
       did to Egypt and how I have carried you on eagles' wings and brought
       you here to me. If only you will now listen to me and keep my
       covenant, then out of all peoples you shall become my special
       possession; for the whole earth is mine. You shall be my kingdom of
       priests, my holy nation'] (Exodus 19:1-6).

The somewhat intricate interpretation of the intersecting-verse is meant to
bring us back to the base-verse, with the former referring to the Exodus from
Egypt, the latter the giving of the Torah fifty days later. No. 1 goes over the
movement from Passover to Pentecost. No. 2 makes the same point in a
different way. No. 3 interweaves the intersecting-verse with the Ten
Commandments, and then tacks on the base-verse.

XII:V

1. A. R. Abun commenced his discourse by citing the verse: Here have I not
       written out for you three-fold sayings, full of knowledge and wise advice,
       [to impart to you a knowledge of the truth, that you may take back a true
       report to him who sent you] (Prov. 22:20-21)."

   B. Bar Hoté said, "The word that we read as three-fold in three-fold sayings
       of full of knowledge and of wise advice yields 'the day before yesterday'
       [Mendelbaum: the word for 'three-fold' is related to the word for 'day
       before']."

   C. Said R. Eleazar, "It is so that the words of the Torah should not appear to
       you like a dated decree, but they should appear to you like a new one
       which everyone is running to read.

   D. "That is in line with this verse of Scripture: On this very day the Lord
       your God is commanding you to do... (Deut. 26:16)."

2. A. R. Samuel bar Nahman said, "The word that we read as three-fold in three-
       fold sayings, full of knowledge and wise advice yields officers,

   B. "as in the following verse of Scripture: and officers over all of them (Ex.
       14:7)."

   C. Said R. Samuel bar Nahman, "Words of Torah are compared to a weapon.
       Just as a weapon protects its owner, so words of Torah protects those
       who work on them as much as is needed.

   D. "What verse of Scripture indicates it? Let the high praises of God be on
       their lips, and a two-edged sword in their hand [to wreak vengeance on
       the nations and to chastise the heathen] (Ps. 149:6)."

3 . A.   [With reference to the verse, *Let the high praises of God be on their lips, and a two-edged sword in their hand [to wreak vengeance on the nations and to chastise the heathen]* (Ps. 149:6), R. Judah, R. Nehemiah, and rabbis [make statements, as follows:]

   B.   R. Judah says, "The word for *double-edged sword* yields the duplication of the word for *mouth*, hence meaning two Torahs, one in writing, the other oral."

   C.   R. Nehemiah says, "The word for *double-edged sword* yields the duplication of the word for *mouth*, hence meaning a sword which consumes on both edges, giving life in this world and in the world to come."

   D.   And rabbis say, *"For there were sacred officers and officers of God* (1 Chr. 24:5).

   E.   "They make a decree concerning the beings of the upper world, and they carry it out, concerning the beings of the lower world, and they carry it out."

4 . A.   Said R. Aha, "[Since the word that we read as thirty in *three-fold sayings, full of knowledge and wise advice* yields heroes, we may interpret as follows:] Words of Torah are heroic in exacting a penalty from him who does not work hard in them as is required."

5 . A.   Said R. Abun, "Words of Torah are compared to a sweet mixed wine. Just as a sweet mixed wine contains wine and also honey and spices,

   B.   "so words of Torah contain wine: *For your kisses are better than wine* (Song 1:2).

   C.   "They also contain honey: *They are sweeter than honey* (Ps. 19:11).

   D.   "They also contain spices: *Your saying is most refined* (Ps. 119:140)."

The interpretation of the intersecting-verse is fully exposed in its own terms and never returns – even as a formality – to the base-verse at all. No. 1 seems to me most apt. The giving of the Torah, celebrated in the passage of the Torah before us, should always appear current. The interpretation of the word three-fold then occupies the rest of the passage, at each point being assigned a meaning in connection with words of the Torah.

XII:VI

1 . A.   *I myself have made it known and I saved and declared it, I and no alien god amongst you, and you are my witnesses, says the Lord. I am God; [from this very day I am He. What my hand holds, none can snatch away; what I do none can undo]* (Is. 43:12-14):

   B.   *I myself have made it known:* in Egypt, *And Moses told Aaron all the words of the Lord* (Ex. 4:28).

   C.   *And I saved:* at the Red Sea, *And on that day the Lord saved...* (Ex. 14:30).

   D.   *...and declared it:* at Sinai, *From the heaven I declared the judgment* (Ps. 76:9).

   E.   *...and no alien...amongst you:* this refers to Jethro.

   F.   *...and you are my witnesses, says the Lord. I am God:*

G. It was taught on Tannaite authority by R. Simeon b. Yohai, "If *you are my witnesses, says the Lord, then I am God*, and if you are not my witnesses, then, as it were, it is as if I am not the Lord."

I take it that the point of contact is simply the theme of the revelation of God at the Exodus and Sinai.

XII:VII

1. A. *For everything its season, [and for every activity under heaven its time]* (Qoh. 3:1):
    B. There was an appropriate time for the first Man to enter the Garden of Eden, *And the Lord God took the Man and put him in the Garden of Eden* (Gen. 2:15).
    C. And a time for him to leave: *And he drove out the Man* (Gen. 3:24).
    D. There was a time for Noah and his sons to enter the ark: *Come, you and all your household, into the ark* (Gen. 7:11).
    E. And a time for him to leave: *Go forth form the ark* (Gen. 8:16).
    F. There was a time for our father, Abraham, to be assigned the rite of circumcision: *And you will keep my covenant* (Gen. 17:9).
    G. And there was a time for the rite to fall away from his sons on two occasions, once in Egypt, the other time in the Wilderness [in line with Joshua 5:5 (Mandelbaum)]. [The tribe of Levi was the only tribe that was circumcised at the time of the Exodus, and the passage of Joshua indicates that in the wilderness the rite was not practiced at all.]

2. A. *...and for every activity under heaven its time* (Qoh. 3:1):
    B. Said R. Bibi, "Something which was higher than heaven was assigned to Moses from heaven. And what is it? It is the Torah.
    C. "When? *In the third month [after Israel had left Egypt, they came to the wilderness of Sinai. They set out from Rephidim and entered the wilderness of Sinai, where they encamped, pitching their tent opposite the Mountain. Moses went up the mountain of God, and the Lord called to him from the mountain and said, 'Speak thus to the house of Jacob and tell this to the sons of Israel: You have seen with your own eyes what I did to Egypt and how I have carried you on eagles' wings and brought you here to me. If only you will now listen to me and keep my covenant, then out of all peoples you shall become my special possession; for the whole earth is mine. You shall be my kingdom of priests, my holy nation']* (Exodus 19:1-6)."

The specification of the date in the base-verse calls to mind the intersecting-verse, which notes that there is a proper time for all things. The established sequence – Adam, Noah, Abraham, Moses – is followed in the exemplification of the matter. The whole seems rather conventional.

XII:VIII

1. A. *I follow the course of virtue, my path is the path of justice; [I endow with riches those who love me and I will fill their treasuries]* (Prov. 8:20-21):

B. The Torah speaks [in the cited verse], "In what path am I to be found? It is in the path of those who do righteousness: in *the path of justice.*"

C. Said R. Huna, "The matter may be compared to the chariot that belongs to a noble lady. When the woman goes through the market place, [the guards] clear the path with sword and weapon both before her and after her.

D. "So is the case of the Torah: there are laws specified before [the account of the giving of the Torah] and afterward.

E. "There are laws specified before the account of the giving of the Torah: *There he made for them a statute and an ordinance* (Ex. 15:25).

F. And afterward as well: *These are the ordinances which you shall set before them* (Ex. 21:1)."

The juxtaposition of subject matter both prior to the account of the revelation of the Torah and following it is explained by the parable at hand. It should be clear that the pattern is not a construction of intersecting- and base-verse; our base-verse does not make an appearance at all, nor, indeed, does even its theme appear here.

XII:IX

1. A. *The heart knows its own bitterness, and a stranger has no part in its joy. [The house of the wicked will be torn down, but the home of the upright flourishes]* (Prov. 14:10-11):

    B. Said R. Jonathan, "Why does a person smell the stench of brimstone and his soul recoils? Because the soul knows that it is destined to be judged in that: *Upon the wicked he will pour coals, fire and brimstone* (Ps. 11:6)."

    C. R. Samuel bar Nahman in the name of R. Jonathan, "It is like the double cup [of wine] that is drunk after the bath [in line with the verse: *and afterwards a double cup of scalding wind will be their drink* (Ps. 11:6)]."

2. A. Another interpretation of the verse: *The heart knows its own bitterness, [and a stranger has no part in its joy. The house of the wicked will be torn down, but the home of the upright flourishes]* (Prov. 14:10-11):

    B. *[The heart knows its own bitterness]* speaks of Israel.

    C. *...and a stranger has no part in its joy* refers to Jethro: *And Moses sent his father in law, Jethro, and he went to his land* (Ex. 18:27).

    D. What is written thereafter? *In the third month [after Israel had left Egypt, they came to the wilderness of Sinai. They set out from Rephidim and entered the wilderness of Sinai, where they encamped, pitching their tent opposite the Mountain. Moses went up the mountain of God, and the Lord called to him from the mountain and said, 'Speak thus to the house of Jacob and tell this to the sons of Israel: You have seen with your own eyes what I did to Egypt and how I have carried you on eagles' wings and brought you here to me. If only you will now listen to me and keep my covenant, then out of all peoples you shall become my special possession; for the whole earth is mine. You shall be my kingdom of priests, my holy nation']* (Exodus 19:1-6).

It is only by a circuitous route that the intersecting-verse reaches the base-verse. The exegete treats the juxtaposition of thematic materials, explaining why it is only after the departure of Jethro that the Torah was given.

XII:X

1. A. *Like an apricot tree among the trees of the wood, so is my beloved among boys. [To sit in its shadow was my delight, and its fruit was sweet to my taste. He took me into the wine garden and gave me loving glances]* (Song 2:3-4):

   B. R. Huna, R. Aha in the name of R. Yose b. Zimra, "Just as in the case of an apricot tree, everyone avoids it, because it yields no shade, so the nations of the world fled before the Holy One, blessed be He, on the day of the giving of the Torah.

   C. "Is it possible that the Israelites were the same way?

   D. "Scripture says, *To sit in its shadow was my delight, and its fruit was sweet to my taste.*

   E. Said R. Ahvah bar Zeorah, "Just as an apricot produces its buds before its leaves, so the Israelites gave precedence to doing over hearing at Sinai."

   F. Said R. Azariah, "Just as an apricot produces ripened fruit only in Sivan, so the Israelites produces a good fragrance in the world only in Sivan.

   G. "When? *In the third month [after Israel had left Egypt, they came to the wilderness of Sinai. They set out from Rephidim and entered the wilderness of Sinai, where they encamped, pitching their tent opposite the Mountain. Moses went up the mountain of God, and the Lord called to him from the mountain and said, 'Speak thus to the house of Jacob and tell this to the sons of Israel: You have seen with your own eyes what I did to Egypt and how I have carried you on eagles' wings and brought you here to me. If only you will now listen to me and keep my covenant, then out of all peoples you shall become my special possession; for the whole earth is mine. You shall be my kingdom of priests, my holy nation']* (Exodus 19:1-6)."

The thematic exercise deftly returns us to our base-verse. The several exegeses move in the same direction throughout.

XII:XI

1. A. *In the third month [after Israel had left Egypt, they came to the wilderness of Sinai. They set out from Rephidim and entered the wilderness of Sinai, where they encamped, pitching their tent opposite the Mountain. Moses went up the mountain of God, and the Lord called to him from the mountain and said, 'Speak thus to the house of Jacob and tell this to the sons of Israel: You have seen with your own eyes what I did to Egypt and how I have carried you on eagles' wings and brought you here to me. If only you will now listen to me and keep my covenant, then out of all peoples you shall become my special possession; for the whole earth is mine. You shall be my kingdom of priests, my holy nation']* (Exodus 19:1-6).

   B. It is when the third month came.

   C. The matter may be compared to the case of a king who betrothed a noble lady. He specified a particular time for her [for the wedding to be

consummated]. When the time came, they said, "Lo, the time has come
for her to enter the marriage canopy.'

D. So when the time of the Torah to be given had come, they said, "Lo, the
time for the giving of the Torah to Israel has come."

2. A. R. Levi in the name of R. Samuel b. Halputah: 'The matter may be
compared to the case of a king, whose son was kidnapped. He cloaked
himself in vengeance and went and redeemed his son. He said, 'You
should count the years of my rule from the date of the redemption of my
son.'

B. "So said the Holy One, blessed be He, 'You should count my reign from
the time of the Exodus from Egypt.'"

3. A. R. Hama bar Hanina: 'The matter may be compared to the case of a king
who was marrying off his daughter and said, 'You should count the days
of my reign from the time of my daughter's marriage.'

B. "So said the Holy One, blessed be He, 'You should count my reign from
the time of the giving of the Torah.'"

4. A. ...*they came to the wilderness of Sinai.* [*They set out from Rephidim and
entered the wilderness of Sinai, where they encamped, pitching their tent
opposite the Mountain. Moses went up the mountain of God, and the
Lord called to him from the mountain and said, "Speak thus to the house
of Jacob and tell this to the sons of Israel: You have seen with your own
eyes what I did to Egypt and how I have carried you on eagles' wings and
brought you here to me. If only you will now listen to me and keep my
covenant, then out of all peoples you shall become my special
possession; for the whole earth is mine. You shall be my kingdom of
priests, my holy nation"*] (Exodus 19:1-6).

B. Said R. Joshua b. Levi, "The matter may be compared to the case of the
son of a king who was walking in the market, and was met by an ally of
the king, who filled his pockets with precious stones and pearls.

C. "Said the king, 'Open up the gates of my treasuries, so that my son
should not say, "Were it not for father's ally, he would not have
anything to give to me.'"

D. "So said the Holy One, blessed be He, to Moses, 'So that the Israelites
should not say, if it were not for the fact that Jethro came and taught you
the laws, you would not have had the power to give the Torah to us.
Therefore I shall give them the Torah, wholly made up of laws: *And these
are the judgments which you shall lay before them* (Ex. 21:1)."

5. A. Said R. Levi, "The matter may be compared to the case of a king who
wanted to marry a woman of good family, of honored genealogy.

B. "He said, 'I do not lay claim on you for nothing. Once I have done a
number of good deeds for you, then I shall lay claim on you.'

C. "He [God] saw her [Israel] naked and clothed her: *And I clothed you in
ornamented garments* (Ez. 16:10).

D. "He saw her at the sea and brought her across: *And the children of Israel
walked on dry land through the sea* (Ex. 14:29).

E. "He saw kidnappers come against her and saved her, referring to the Amalekites."

6. A. Said R. Eleazar, "The matter may be compared to the case of a king who wanted to marry a woman of good family, of honored genealogy.

   B. "He said, 'I do not lay claim on you for nothing. Once I have done a number of good deeds for you, then I shall lay claim on you.'

   C. "He [God] saw her [Israel] at the baker and filled her arms with cakes of bread, at the storekeeper and provided spiced wine for her, at the spice dealer and filled her arms with spices, at the [Braude and Kapstein:] store of the one who force feeds birds and filled her arms with force-fed birds.

   D. "...at the baker and filled her arms with cakes of bread: *Lo, I rain down for you bread from heaven* (Ex. 16:4).

   E. "...at the storekeeper and provided spiced wine for her: *Then sang Israel this song, Rise O spring and reply* (Num. 21:17).

   F. "...at the spice dealer and filled her arms with spices: *And He made him suck honey out of the crag* (Deut. 32:13).

   G. "...at the [Braude and Kapstein:] store of the one who force feeds birds and filled her arms with force-fed birds: *And quail flew in from the sea* (Num. 11:31)."

7. A. Said R. Abba bar Yudan, "The matter may be compared to the case of a king who was marrying off his daughter, and he had made a decree against marrying overseas, saying, 'The sons of Rome will not acquire wives in Syria, and the sons of Syria will not come up to Rome for that purpose.'

   B. "But when he had married off his daughter, he released the decree [that he had made prohibiting intermarriages of this sort].

   C. "So before the Torah was given, *the heavens are the heavens of the Lord, and the earth belongs to the children of men* (Ps. 115:16).

   D. "But once the Torah was given from heaven, *Moses went up the mountain of God, and the Lord called to him from the mountain [and said, 'Speak thus to the house of Jacob and tell this to the sons of Israel: You have seen with your own eyes what I did to Egypt and how I have carried you on eagles' wings and brought you here to me. If only you will now listen to me and keep my covenant, then out of all peoples you shall become my special possession; for the whole earth is mine. You shall be my kingdom of priests, my holy nation']* (Exodus 19:1-6). *And the Lord came down upon Mount Sinai* (Ex. 19:20)."

The power of the exegesis of Nos. 1-3 is to link the giving of the Torah, celebrated in our base-verse, to the marriage of Israel. Nos. 1, 3 make that point. No. 2 is equally a propos. So the entire composition, which marks the beginning of the exegesis of the base-verse in its own terms, bears its own power. No. 4 reverts to the explanation of the meaning of the juxtaposition of the several stories at hand. No. 5 again exploits the comparison of Israel to the bride. No. 6 carries forward the same line of thought. No. 7 then proceeds to the base-verse and makes a solid point of its own.

XII:XII

1. A. *In the third month after Israel [had left Egypt, they came to the wilderness of Sinai. They set out from Rephidim and entered the wilderness of Sinai, where they encamped, pitching their tent opposite the Mountain. Moses went up the mountain of God, and the Lord called to him from the mountain and said, 'Speak thus to the house of Jacob and tell this to the sons of Israel: You have seen with your own eyes what I did to Egypt and how I have carried you on eagles' wings and brought you here to me. If only you will now listen to me and keep my covenant, then out of all peoples you shall become my special possession; for the whole earth is mine. You shall be my kingdom of priests, my holy nation']* (Exodus 19:1-6).

   B. This is in line with the following verse of Scripture: *Have I not written for you three-fold sayings full of knowledge and wise counsel [to show you what is right and true, that you may give a true answer to those who sent you?]* (Prov. 22:20-21).

   C. If you wish to take counsel from the Torah, take it.

   D. Said David, "When I wanted to take counsel in the Torah, I would look into the Scripture and take counsel."

   E. So it is said, *I will meditate on your precepts and fix my eyes on your ways, [I will delight in your statutes and I will not forget your word]* (Ps. 119:15-16).

2. A. And it is said, *Through your precepts I get understanding* (Ps. 119:104).

   B. Said Ben Hoté, "If you want to build [a ship] and do not know how to proportion its height, look into the Torah and you will learn. What is written? *With lower, second, and third decks you shall make it* (Gen. 6:16).

   C. "Thus: *Through your precepts I get understanding* (Ps. 119:104)."

3. A. Another interpretation of the verse, *Here have I not written out for you three-fold sayings, [full of knowledge and wise advice, to impart to you a knowledge of the truth, that you may take back a true report to him who sent you]* (Prov. 22:20-21)."

   B. Said R...., "It is so that the words of the Torah should not appear to you like a dated decree, but they should appear to you like a new one, two or three days old.

   C. "That is in line with the verse, *Here have I not written out for you three-fold sayings, [full of knowledge and wise advice, to impart to you a knowledge of the truth, that you may take back a true report to him who sent you]* (Prov. 22:20-21). The word for thirty may be read as *the day before yesterday*."

4. A. Ben Azzai says, "Not like a proclamation that is two or three days old, but like a proclamation issued that very day. You may know that that is so, for what is written? *In the third month after Israel had left Egypt, on this day they came to the wilderness of Sinai* (Exodus 19:1-6). What is written is not, *on that day*, but, *on this day they came to Sinai.*

   B. "And so it is written, *On this very day the Lord your God is commanding you to do [these laws and statutes]* (Deut. 26:16)."

We go over familiar material to take up the interpretation of a clause in our base-verse that speaks of *this* day, rather than *that* day. The stress then is on the freshness of the teachings of the Torah, their immediacy and relevance. No. 1 goes over the simple ground that the Torah contains correct counsel, and No. 2 repeats that point and prepares the way for the introduction of the intersecting-verse. Nos. 3, 4 then make the main point.

XII:XIII

1. A. Another interpretation of the verse, *In the third month after Israel had left Egypt, [they came to the wilderness of Sinai. They set out from Rephidim and entered the wilderness of Sinai, where they encamped, pitching their tent opposite the Mountain. Moses went up the mountain of God, and the Lord called to him from the mountain and said, 'Speak thus to the house of Jacob and tell this to the sons of Israel: You have seen with your own eyes what I did to Egypt and how I have carried you on eagles' wings and brought you here to me. If only you will now listen to me and keep my covenant, then out of all peoples you shall become my special possession; for the whole earth is mine. You shall be my kingdom of priests, my holy nation']* (Exodus 19:1-6).

   B. The Torah is tripartite, the fathers too, the [name of the] tribe to which the Torah was given is the third, and the month is the third.

   C. How do we know that the Torah is in three parts?

   D. Said R. Abun the Levite, son of Rabbi, "How do we know that the Torah is called tripartite? It is because it may be compared to three things, wine, honey, and spices.

   E. "As to wine: *Come, eat of my bread and drink of the wine which I have mixed* (Prov. 9:5).

   F. "As to honey: *They are sweeter than honey* (Ps. 19:11)."

   G. As to spices, said R. Abun the Levite, son of Rabbi, "[Proof derives from this verse] *Every word of God is refined* (Prov. 30:5), with reference to spices.

   H. "On this basis, then the Torah is divided into three."

2. A. Each item associated with the events of that day is divided into three.

   B. The Torah is divided into three: Torah, Prophets, Writings.

   C. The letters of the Torah are divided into three: A, B, C.

   D. And Israel is divided into three: Priests, Levites, Israelites.

   E. The patriarchs are three: Abraham, Isaac, and Jacob.

   F. Moses was the third [and intermediary between God and Israel, a triad]: *I stand between the Lord and you* (Deut. 5:5).

   G. The letters of the name of Moses are three: M, S, H.

   H. And he comes from the third tribe in order: Reuben, Simeon, Levi [he was a Levite].

   I. And the letters of the name of that tribe are three: L, V, Y.

   J. And there were three siblings: Moses, Aaron, Miriam.

   K. He was watched over, after birth, for three months: *And she watched him for three months* (Ex. 2:2).

   L. It was the third day: *For on the third day the Lord came down before the eyes of all the people* (Ex. 19:11).

M. It was the third month: *In the third month [after Israel had left Egypt, they came to the wilderness of Sinai]* (Ex. 19:1-6).

The amplification of the triads works itself out in two units, the second of which leads us back to our base-verse.

XII:XIV

1. A. That is in line with the following verse of Scripture: *Her ways are ways of pleasantness, and all her paths are peace. [She is a tree of life to those who lay hold of her; those who hold her fast are called happy]* (Prov. 3:17-18):

    B. *Her ways are ways of pleasantness*: the Holy One, blessed be He, planned to give his Torah to Israel when the Israelites went forth from Egypt. But they contended with one another, saying, *Let us appoint a head and return to Egypt* (Num. 14:4).

    C. What is written? *They [severally] journeyed from Sukkot and they [severally] encamped at Etham* (Ex. 13:20), meaning, they journeyed in strife and they encamped in strife.

    D. But as soon as they came to Rephidim, they became of one mind and formed a single united group, as it is said, *They set out from Rephidim and entered the wilderness of Sinai, [where they encamped, pitching their tent opposite the Mountain]*.

    E. Now how do we know that they became of one mind and formed a single united group?

    F. What is written is not, The Israelites [in the plural, hence, severally] encamped there, but, *Israel* [in the singular, hence jointly] *encamped...opposite the Mountain.*

    G. Said the Holy One, blessed be He, "The Torah is wholly a message of peace. To whom shall I give it? To the nation that holds fast to peace."

    H. That is in line with this verse: *Her ways are ways of pleasantness, and all her paths are peace. [She is a tree of life to those who lay hold of her; those who hold her fast are called happy]* (Prov. 3:17-18)

The focus of the exegesis is not on our base-verse, which contributes only a minor detail to the main point. The passage of course is appropriately included here, but the composition derived from an authorship with its own interests. The anthological character of this part of the *pisqa* defines what follows as well.

XII:XV

1. A. *In the third month after Israel had left Egypt, [they came to the wilderness of Sinai. They set out from Rephidim and entered the wilderness of Sinai, where they encamped, pitching their tent opposite the Mountain. Moses went up the mountain of God, and the Lord called to him from the mountain and said, 'Speak thus to the house of Jacob and tell this to the sons of Israel: You have seen with your own eyes what I did to Egypt and how I have carried you on eagles' wings and brought you here to me. If only you will now listen to me and keep my covenant, then out of all peoples you shall become my special*

possession; for the whole earth is mine. You shall be my kingdom of priests, my holy nation'] (Exodus 19:1-6).

B. This is in line with the following verse of Scripture: *Through sloth the roof sinks in, and through indolence the house leaks* (Qoh. 10:18).

C. What brought it about that this woman menstruates a great deal [and her period is prolonged]? [Thus: *If a woman has a discharge of blood for many days, not at the time of her impurity* (Lev. 15:25)].

D. It is because this woman is indolent about examining herself during her menstrual period, to find out whether she is unclean or not.

E. Why so? Our rabbis have taught: **In the case of a hand that is used a great deal to make inspections of the genitals, in the case of women it is praiseworthy, in the case of men, it is to be cut off [M. Nid. 2:1].**

2. A. There is the case of the slave girl of Rabban Gamaliel, who was moving from one room to another utensils and jugs that were in a state of cultic cleanness. She examined herself prior to touching each and every jug. At the end, she examined herself and turned out to be unclean.

B. Rabban Gamaliel was concerned, saying, "Is it possible that all of the objects preserved in a state of cultic cleanness have now been made unclean?"

C. Rabban Gamaliel called to her and said to her, "Were you not examining yourself [as you worked]?"

D. She said to him, "My lord, by your life! I was examining myself prior to touching each and every jug, and it was only at the end, when touching this last one, that I turned out to be unclean."

E. Said Rabban Gamaliel, "If this one had been indolent, all of the objects preserved in a state of uncleanness would have become unclean."

3. A. *Through sloth the roof sinks in* (Qoh. 10:18).

B. It is because this woman is indolent about examining herself during her menstrual period that this woman menstruates a great deal [and her period is prolonged]. [Thus: *If a woman has a discharge of blood for many days, not at the time of her impurity* (Lev. 15:25)].

C. For *the roof sinks in* is to be interpreted thus: the word for *roof* means only blood, as it is said, *[And he shall uncover her nakedness, he has made naked her fountain,] and she has uncovered the fountain of her blood [– both of them shall be cut off from among their people]* (Lev. 20:18).

D. ...*and through indolence the house leaks* (Qoh. 10:18):

E. *If a woman has a discharge of blood for many days, not at the time of her impurity* (Lev. 15:25).

4. A. Another interpretation of the verse, *Through sloth the roof sinks in, [and through indolence the house leaks]* (Qoh. 10:18):

B. The passage speaks of Israel when they came to Rephidim.

C. For what is written in that regard? *They set out from Rephidim and entered the wilderness of Sinai, [where they encamped, pitching their tent opposite the Mountain].*

D. Why was the name of that place called Rephidim? Because their hands were "slothful" about committing transgression ["slothful" in Hebrew is similar to Rephidim].

5. A. *Through sloth the roof sinks in:*
   B. *The Lord came down to Mount Sinai, to the top of the mountain* (Ex. 19:20).
   C. *...and through indolence the house leaks:*
   D. Because the Israelites were "slothful" about committing transgressions, *the house leaked.*
   E. What is written thereafter? *The earth shook, also the heaven opened up, and also the clouds dripped water* (Judges 5:4).
   F. When did all these things take place?
   G. It was on the day of the giving of the Torah.
   H. *In the third month [after Israel had left Egypt, they came to the wilderness of Sinai. They set out from Rephidim and entered the wilderness of Sinai, where they encamped, pitching their tent opposite the Mountain. Moses went up the mountain of God, and the Lord called to him from the mountain and said, 'Speak thus to the house of Jacob and tell this to the sons of Israel: You have seen with your own eyes what I did to Egypt and how I have carried you on eagles' wings and brought you here to me. If only you will now listen to me and keep my covenant, then out of all peoples you shall become my special possession; for the whole earth is mine. You shall be my kingdom of priests, my holy nation']* (Exodus 19:1-6).

The interpretation of the intersecting-verse moves from one construction of the words to a quite different one. At the outset we interpret the intersecting-verse in its obvious sense that there is a connection between sloth and the condition of "the house," in the opening instances, Nos. 1-3, the woman householder. Nos. 4, 5 go over the same ground, with No. 4 setting the stage for No. 5. The connection to the base-verse is somewhat shaky, but it does hold.

XII:XVI

1. A. What is written prior to the matter at hand? It is the passage that deals with Jethro, specifically spelling out what he taught Moses.
   B. *You shall seek out able men out of the people* (Ex. 18:21), then: *In the third month [after Israel had left Egypt, they came to the wilderness of Sinai]* (Exodus 19:1-6).
   C. Said Solomon, *The heart knows its own bitterness.*
   D. Therefore: *...and a stranger has no part in its joy. [The house of the wicked will be torn down, but the home of the upright flourishes]* (Prov. 14:10-11).
   E. Said the Holy One, blessed be He, "The Israelites were enslaved to mortar and bricks in Egypt, while Jethro was dwelling in his house at peace and in security. Now he has come to witness the rejoicing over the Torah with my children?"

F. Therefore: *And Moses sent his father-in-law, Jethro, and he went to his land* (Ex. 18:27).

G. And thereafter: *In the third month [after Israel had left Egypt, they came to the wilderness of Sinai]* (Exodus 19:6).

2. A. Another interpretation: why so? Moses composed an argument a fortiori:

B. He said, "Now if when the Holy One, blessed be He, came to give a single religious duty, namely, the religious duty concerning the Passover, he said, *No son of an alien shall eat of it* (Ex. 12:43), now that he is giving the entirety of the Torah to Israel, should Jethro be here and see us?"

C. Therefore: *And Moses sent his father-in-law, [Jethro, and he went to his land]* (Ex. 18:27).

D. And thereafter: *In the third month [after Israel had left Egypt, they came to the wilderness of Sinai* (Exodus 19:6).

The same point is made twice, and it is the familiar one resting on the interpretation of the juxtaposition of discrete pericopae of the scriptural narrative.

XII:XVII

1. A. [With reference to *the third month after Israel had left Egypt,*] why in the third month and not the second or the fourth?

B. Said R. Hoshaia, "R. Hiyya the Elder taught me as follows:

C. "A female convert, a woman taken captive and returned, and a freed slave girl should not get married or betrothed until three months have passed [to ascertain that they are not pregnant].

D. "As to Israel, then, they are called converts: *for you were converts in the land of Egypt* (Lev. 19:43).

E. "...captives: *They shall take as captives those who had taken them captive* (Is. 14:32).

F. "...and freed slaves: *I the Lord your God, who has taken you out of the land of Egypt so that you should not be slaves* (Lev. 26:13).

G. "Said the Holy One, blessed be He, 'Let us wait for them for three months, and then I shall give them the Torah.'"

H. *In the third month [after Israel had left Egypt, they came to the wilderness of Sinai]* (Exodus 19:1).

The interpretation of the detail about the third month proceeds apace, now with a powerful and fresh message.

XII:XVIII

1. A. [With reference to *the third month after Israel had left Egypt,*] said R. Aibu, "[The sense of *in the third month* may be gained by reading the same letters to mean, *here,*] *the month has come.*

B. "When the Holy One, blessed be He, revealed himself to Moses, he stipulated with him, saying to him, *When you bring the people out of Egypt, you shall serve God on this mountain* (Ex. 3:12).

C. "And Moses was watching for the day, saying, 'When will it come?'

D. "But it did not come about. When the end had come, the Holy One, blessed be He, said to him, 'The month has come for which you were waiting.

E. Thus: ...*the third month [after Israel had left Egypt]* (Exodus 19:1).

The exegesis of the same words yields yet another point.

XII:XIX

1. A. [With reference to *the third month after Israel had left Egypt,*] it does not say in the third moon, as it calls other months, e.g., *in the moon of Ziv* (1 Kgs. 6:37), *in the moon of Bul* (1 Kgs. 6:38), *in the moon of Etanim* (1 Kgs. 8:2), but rather, *in the third month?*

B. Said R. Judah bar Simon, "Said the Holy One, blessed be He, to them, '[Since the letters for the word for month yield the word for innovation,] I am going to do a new thing and I am going to make you new.'

C. "The matter may be compared to the case of a king who had a son, and the son reached maturity. The king wanted to marry him off, but he did not have a new silver setting. Said the king, 'It is not appropriate to the honor owing to my son to have matters in this way. If we wait until a new silver setting is made for him, I shall postpone my son's occasion for rejoicing.'

D. "What did the king do? He brought smiths and metal workers who polished the copper utensils [he had in hand], and he brought wood carvers, who made patterns on the wooden utensils [then in hand], so the king turned out to marry off his son using a setting that was old but appeared new.

E. "So the Holy One, blessed be He, when the Israelites went forth from Egypt wanted to give them the Torah. But in their midst were blind and crippled and mute people. Said the Holy One, blessed be He, "The Torah itself is wholly complete and unblemished, as it is said, *The Torah of the Lord is unblemished* (Ps. 19:8). Shall I then give it to this generation, in which are people who bear blemishes? But if we should wait until their children grow up, I shall postpone the rejoicing over the Torah.'

F. "What did the Holy One, blessed be He, do? He healed them and then he gave them the Torah.

G. "And how do we know that he healed them?

H. "One who was blind was made to see, as it is said, *And the entire people saw the voices* (Ex. 20:18).

I. "One who was deaf he made to hear, as it is said, *Everything that the Lord has spoken we shall do and we shall hear* (Ex. 24:7).

J. "One who was crippled he made whole, as it is said, *And they stood at the foot of the mountain* (Ex. 19:17).

K. "That then shows the meaning of the statement, 'I am going to do a new thing and I am going to make you new.'

L. "for 'I shall make you a paradigm of the world to come.'

M. "Just as in the world to come, *Then will the eyes of the blind be opened* (Is. 356:5), so here: *And the entire people saw the voices* (Ex. 20:18).

N. "Just as in the world to come, *the ears of the deaf will be opened* (Is. 35:6), so here, *Everything that the Lord has spoken we shall do and we shall hear* (Ex. 24:7).

O. "Just as in the world to come, *Then the lame one will leap like a lamb* (Is. 35:6), so here, *And Moses brought the people out to meet God, and they stood at the foot of the mountain* (Ex. 19:17).

P. "Just as in the world to come, *The tongue of the dumb shall sing* (Is. 35:6), so here: *Then the people all answered together, saying* (Ex. 19:8)."

This sustained and cogent statement develops the point at B, the interest in the use of the word that yields not only month but also new thing. That new thing is then spelled out, first of all through a parable, then through a sustained inquiry into the pertinent verses, and finally through a restatement in eschatological terms. The upshot then is to specify that new thing promised at the outset, in a stunningly successful and sustained statement.

XII:XX

1. A. [With reference to] *the third month [after Israel had left Egypt,]* why in the third month?

    B. It was so as not to give the nations of the world an opening to say, "If he had given the Torah also to us, we should have carried it out."

    C. Said to them the Holy One, blessed be He, "See in what month I am giving the Torah. It is the third month, under the star of the twins [standing for Jacob and Esau], so that if the wicked Esau should want to become a proselyte and to repent and to come and study the Torah, he may come and study it and I shall accept him."

    D. Therefore he gave it in the third month [to allow time for Esau to come and accept the Torah, which he failed to do].

2. A. And why was it given *in the wilderness of Sinai*?

    B. It is to teach you that if a person does not treat himself as utterly lacking in all ownership [and freely available to others] like this wilderness, he will not have the merit to master teachings of the Torah.

    C. Just as the wilderness is without end, so the Torah is without end, as it is said, *The measure thereof is longer than the earth and wider than the sea* (Job 11:9).

    D. And just as it has no end, so there is no end to the reward that is given on its account, as it is said, *How great is your good, which you have laid out for those who fear you* (Ps. 31:20).

The exegesis takes up two clauses of our base-verse, *the third month* and *the wilderness at Sinai*. The details are turned into occasions for a paradigmatic statement.

XII:XXI

1. A. *[In the third month after Israel had left Egypt], on that day they came to the wilderness of Sinai:*

    B. Did they come on that day in particular? [Hardly!] [Rather, it is as if God said this to them,] "But when you study my words, let them not appear to you as though there were old, but rather as though the Torah was given today."

C. What is written here is not *that day* but *this day*. [God says,] "In this world I gave you the Torah, and individuals work hard at it, but in the world to come, I shall personally teach it to *all* Israel, and they will study it and not forget."

D. For it is said, *For this is the covenant which I shall make with the house of Israel after those days, says the Lord, I shall put my Torah in their heart and I shall write it on their heart, and I shall be for them as God and they shall be for me as a people* (Jer. 31:32).

E. "And not only so, but I shall bring encompassing peace among them," as Isaiah said, *And all your children will be taught by God and great will be the peaced of your children* (Is. 54:13).

This exposition of the base-verse moves toward a wholly eschatological reading of the matter. The first point, B, has already been made. The rest is new and moves us far from our base-verse.

XII:XXII

1. A. *I am the Lord your God who brought you out of the land of Egypt* (Ex. 20:2):

   B. This is in line with the following verse of Scripture: *With mighty chariotry, twice ten thousand, thousands upon thousands, the Lord came from Sinai into the holy place* (Ps. 68:17).

   C. Said R. Abdima of Haifa, "I have learned in my repetition [of tradition] that twenty-two thousand ministering angels came down with the Holy One, blessed be He, to Sinai."

   D. Said R. Berekhiah the Priest, son of Rabbi, "It was equivalent to the camp of the Levites.

   E. "For the Holy One, blessed be He, foresaw that in their time only the tribe of Levi would endure in their faith. Therefore twenty-two thousand ministering angels came down, equivalent to the camp of the Levites: *With mighty chariotry, twice ten thousand, thousands upon thousands, [the Lord came from Sinai into the holy place]* (Ps. 68:17)."

2. A. Another matter concerning *With mighty chariotry, twice ten thousand, thousands upon thousands, [the Lord came from Sinai into the holy place]* (Ps. 68:17):

   B. With the Holy One, blessed be He, came down twenty-two thousand chariots. And on every chariot, such as Ezekiel saw, God was mounted.

   C. [The italicized words are a speculative guess:] *In a tradition* that came up from Babylonia they said that with the Holy One, blessed be He, came down twenty-two thousand chariots, so did Elijah, of blessed memory, teach.

3. A. *With mighty chariotry, twice ten thousand, thousands upon thousands, [the Lord came from Sinai into the holy place]* (Ps. 68:17):

   B. Said R. Tanhum bar Hanilai, "[Following Braude and Kapstein, p. 244:] "There were thousands multiplied by thousands, myriads multiplied by myriads, to a number which only a mathematician can calculate."

4. A. *With mighty chariotry, twice ten thousand, thousands upon thousands,*
        [the Lord came from Sinai into the holy place] (Ps. 68:17):
    B. Said R. Eleazar b. Pedat, "And all of them came down armed to destroy
        [delete: the enemies of] Israel.
    C. "For if the Israelites had refused to accept the Torah, they would have
        annihilated them."
    D. Said R. Levi, "But they saw the face of the Holy One, blessed be He, and
        whoever has seen the face of the king will not die, as it is said, *In the*
        light of the face of the king they live (Prov. 16:15)."

5. A. Another interpretation of the verse: *With mighty chariotry, twice ten*
        thousand, thousands upon thousands, [the Lord came from Sinai into the
        holy place] (Ps. 68:17):
    B. Said R. Eleazar b. Pedat, "What is the meaning of the clause *twice ten*
        thousand? It refers to the ones that were the most attractive and
        praiseworthy among them.
    C. "Nonetheless, *the Lord is among them*, meaning, outshining them all."
    D   "Said the community of Israel, *My beloved is all radiant and ruddy,*
        [distinguished among ten thousand] (Song 5:10).
    E. "If a mortal king goes forth to the piazza, how many are as elegant as he
        is, how many are as powerful as he is, how many have well groomed here
        as he does, how many are as handsome as he is.
    F. "But the Holy One, blessed be He, is not that way. But when he came to
        Sinai, he took with him the most elegant and praiseworthy ministering
        angels that were among them."
    G. Said R. Judah bar Simon, "What verse of Scripture makes that point?
        [The Lord came from Sinai and dawned from Seir upon us, he shone forth
        from Mount Paran, he] came from the ten thousands of holy ones, [with
        flaming fire at his right hand] (Deut. 33:2).
    H. "And he was himself the noteworthy sign among the myraids of holy
        ones. That must be at the moment that he came to Sinai."

6. A. Another interpretation of the verse: *With mighty chariotry, twice ten*
        thousand, thousands upon thousands, the Lord came from Sinai into the
        holy place (Ps. 68:17):
    B. Said R. Eleazar b. Pedat, "When there is a big crowd, there is pressing,
        but at Sinai, when the Holy One, blessed be He, came down, there
        descended with him thousands of thousands and myriads of myriads: *twice*
        ten thousand.
    C. "And nonetheless, there was plenty of room for all of them.
    D. "That is in line with this verse: *Moab has been comfortable from his*
        youth (Jer. 48:11)."

7. A. R. Eleazar b. Azariah and R. Eliezer the Modite:
    B. One of them says, "Could the mountain hold them all? But the Holy
        One, blessed be He, said to [the mountain], 'Get longer, get wider, and
        receive the children of your Lord.'"
    C. The other of them says, "When the Holy One, blessed be He, will return
        to Jerusalem, he will bring back into its midst the exiles. For it is said,

Behold, these shall come from far, and lo, these from the north (Is. 49:12).

D. "Now can the city contain them all?

E. "But the Holy One, blessed be He, will say to it, *Enlarge the place of your tent* (Is. 54:2)."

8. A. *...the Lord is among them* (Ps. 68:17):

B. Said R. Simeon b. Laqish, "There is a plaque on the heart of every angel, and the name of the Holy One, blessed be He, is joined thereon with the name of that angel, e.g., Micha/el, Gabri/el, Rapha/el."

9. A. *The Lord is among them* (Ps. 68:17):

B. The word is written as *my lord*, meaning, *my lordship* [dominion] is among them.

C. It is so that one should not say that the dominion of the ministering angels alone [was at hand], but even when he came to give his Torah, it was in this language that it was given to Israel, and in that language that he commenced: *I am the Lord your God* (Ex. 20:2).

We have essentially moved on to a new theme, namely, the giving of the Ten Commandments. The base-verse is left behind, and there is no further interest in expounding any of its elements. Now the intersecting-verse leads us to Ex. 20:2, with stress on God's presence at Sinai, on God's delivering the Ten Commandments on his own, accompanied to be sure by angels. That fact is indicated by the introduction at 1.A of the new base-verse, a remarkable initiative, which we have not seen before, of dismissing one base-verse and dealing with another. The first point is that twenty-two thousand angels came down, which is explained at No. 1 and accounts also for the intersecting-verse. I cannot claim to have done justice to No. 2. No. 3 is clear and repeats the familiar point that it was quite a large number that came down. No. 4 then moves us on to the matter of accepting the Torah. No. 5 then introduces the point stressed from there to the end, that God was chief among all who had descended from heaven. Not only so, but there was ample space at Sinai, so No. 6, No. 7. No. 8 seems to me aimless, but No. 9 leads us to the climax: the revelation of the Ten Commandments.

XII:XXIII

1. A. That is in line with what Scripture says: *Hear O my people and I will speak, O Israel, I will testify against you. I am God, your God* (Ps. 50:7).

B. Said R. Phineas b. Hama, *"Hear O my people and I will speak:* [hear in the sense of obey the Ten Commandments,] so that I may have an opening to indict the princes [that is, the angels who oversee] the nations of the world."

2. A. *Hear O my people and I will speak:*

B.   Said R. Judah bar Simon in the name of R. Joshua b. Levi, "[God says,]
     'In the past, *Israel* was your name, that is, before you had received the
     Torah, [so your name was] equivalent to the names of the nations of the
     world, e.g., *Sheba, Havilah, Sabeta, Raama* (Gen. 10:7). Along these
     same lines, your name was *Israel.*

C.   "But once you have accepted the Torah, it is *my people: Hear O my
     people and I will speak.*'

D.   "For people give testimony only to one who is listening: *Hear O my
     people and I will speak, O Israel, I will testify against you.*

3. A.   *...I am God, your God* (Ps. 50:7):

   B.   R. Yohanan and R. Simeon b. Laqish:

   C.   R. Yohanan said, *"I am God* means *I am judge. Your God* means *your
        patron am I, who defends you."*

   D   R. Simeon b. Laqish said, *"I am God your God* means *your patron am I.*

   E.   "Just as a patron can help in a case, so *I am God your God.*

4. A.   R. Phineas b. Hamah said, *"I am God your God* – to whom does he
        speak?

   B.   "It is to Moses that he speaks, saying to him, 'It is [necessary to make
        this statement] because I have called you God,' as it is said, *Lo, I have
        set you as God to Pharaoh* (Ex. 7:1).

   C.   "But, in fact, *I am God your God."*

5. A.   Another interpretation of the verse: *I am God your God:*

   B.   Our rabbis say, "He speaks of the judges. He said to them, 'It is
        [necessary to make this statement] [delete: not] because I have called you
        divinities, as it is said, *The God* [in context: the judges] *you shall not
        curse* (Ex. 22:27). Rather: *I am God your God."*

6. A.   Said R. Judah the Levite, son of R. Shallum, "It is concerning Israel that
        he speaks. He said to them, 'It is [necessary to make this statement]
        [delete: not] because I called you God, as it is said, *I said, You are God*
        (Ps. 82:6). Rather: *I am God your God."*

The interpretation of the theme of the Ten Commandments produces a new
intersecting-verse. But the point of contact is difficult to locate, since my
reading of No. 1 is solely for the purpose of underlining the sense of hear as
obey. No. 2 speaks in general terms of the receiving of the Torah, not of the
specific circumstance of the Ten Commandments, required by the conclusion of
the preceding composition. No. 3 hardly helps, and Nos. 4-6 form a subset to
make their own point. So I assume that the one point of entry into the
intersecting-verse is the use of the same word for I, *anokhi,* as occurs in the
opening sentence of the base-verse introduced at **XII:XXII** above. That that is
certain is shown by what follows.

XII:XXIV

1. A. *I [anokhi] am the Lord your God who brought you out of the land of Egypt* (Ex. 20:2):

   B   What is the meaning of the word *anokhi/I*?

   C. Rab said, "[God speaks:] 'You should not treat the Torah which I have given to you. The word *anokhi* generates a set of words through its letters, a, n, k, and y, yielding the sense, 'I (a) myself (n) have written (k) [and] given (y) [it].'"

2. A. Another interpretation: the same letters are to be read in reverse order, that is, y, k, n, a, yielding the sense, "[The Torah that is] given in writing – pleasant are its words."

3. A. Said R. Berekhiah the Priest, "[The letters a n k y] mean that] said the Holy One, blessed be He, 'I am your light, your glory, your beauty.'

   B. "When will this be so? When you accept the Ten Commandments.

   C. "'*I [anokhi] am the Lord your God who brought you out of the land of Egypt*' (Ex. 20:2)."

4. A. R. Aha said, "For twenty-six generations the letter A made complaint before the Holy One, blessed be He, saying to him, 'Lord of the world! I am the first among all the letters of the alphabet, yet you did not create your world by starting with me, but you used a B instead, aas it is said, *In the beginning* (BR'SYT) *God created ...* (Gen. 1:1)!'

   B. "Said the Holy One, blessed be He, to the A, 'By your life! I shall make it up to you. The Torah was created before me two thousand years before the creation of the world, and when I come and give my Torah to Israel at Sinai, and I shall begin only with you: *I [beginning with the A] am the Lord your God* (Ex. 20:1).'"

5. A. Said R. Nehemiah, "What is the meaning of the word for I, *anokhi*?

   B. "It is the Egyptian word for I.

   C. "To what is the matter likened? To the case of a mortal king whose son was taken captive and spent quite some time among the kidnappers. His father put on his cloak of vengeance and went to him and brought him back, and he came to converse with him in the language of the kidnappers.

   D. "So it was with the Holy One, blessed be He: the Israelites had spent so much time in Egypt that they were used to carry on their conversations in Egyptians. When, therefore, the Holy One, blessed be He, redeemed them and came to give the Torah to them, they did not know how to understand.

   E. "Said the Holy One, blessed be He, 'Lo, I shall talk with them in the Egyptian language.'

   F. "So the Holy One, blessed be He, began, *Anok*, [that is, I in Egyptian], so the Holy One, blessed be He, commenced his discourse in their language:

   G. "*I [anokhi] am the Lord your God who brought you out of the land of Egypt* (Ex. 20:2)."

6. A. Because the Holy One, blessed be He, had appeared to them at the sea like a heroic soldier, doing battle, appeared to them at Sinai like a teacher, teaching the repetition [of traditions], appeared to them in the time of Daniel like a sage, teaching Torah, appeared to them in the time of Solomon like a younger man,

   B. [it was necessary for] the Holy One, blessed be He, to say to them, "You see me in many forms. But I am the same one who was at the sea, I am the same one who was at Sinai, *I [anokhi] am the Lord your God who brought you out of the land of Egypt* (Ex. 20:2)."

7. A. Said R. Hiyya the Elder, "It is because through every manner of deed and every condition he had appeared to them [that he made that statement, namely:]

   B. "he had appeared to them at the sea as a heroic soldier, carrying out battles in behalf of Israel,

   C. "he had appeared to them at Sinai in the form of a teacher who was teaching Torah and standing in awe,

   D. "he had appeared to them in the time of Daniel as an elder, teaching Torah, for it is appropriate for Torah to go forth from the mouth of sages,

   E. "he had appeared to them in the time of Solomon as a youth, in accord with the practices of that generation: *His aspect is like Lebanon, young as the cedars* (Song 5:15),

   F. "so at Sinai he appeared to them as a teacher, teaching Torah: *I am the Lord your God who brought you out of the land of Egypt* (Ex. 20:2)."

The focus now is on the first word of the new base-verse, *I/anokhi*. This is beautifully spelled out in an anthology that is given point and purpose at the end. The same God who figured in diverse actions and forms in the end is that I who gave the Ten Commandments. Nos. 1-3 work on the letters of the word, No. 4 moving on to the letter A. No. 5 makes a philological comment, and Nos. 6, 7, move on to a profound theological observation.

XII:XXV

1. A. Another interpretation of *I am the Lord your God [who brought you out of the land of Egypt]* (Ex. 20:2):

   B Said R. Hinena bar Papa, "The Holy One, blessed be He, had made his appearance to them with a stern face, with a neutral face, with a friendly face, with a happy face.

   C. "...with a stern face: in Scripture. When a man teaches his son Torah, he has to teach him in a spirit of awe.

   D. "...with a neutral face: in Mishnah.

   E. "...with a friendly face: in Talmud.

   F. "...with a happy face: in lore.

   G. "Said to them the Holy One, blessed be He, 'Even though you may see all of these diverse faces of mine, nonetheless: *I am the Lord your God who brought you out of the land of Egypt* (Ex. 20:2)."

2. A. Said R. Levi, "The Holy One, blessed be He, had appeared to them like an icon that has faces in all directions, so that if a thousand people look at it, it appears to look at them as well.

   B. "So too when the Holy One, blessed be He, when he was speaking, each and every Israelite would say, 'With me in particular the Word speaks.'

   C. "What is written here is not, I am the Lord, your [plural] God, but rather, *I am the Lord your [singular] God who brought you out of the land of Egypt* (Ex. 20:2)."

3. A. Said R. Yose bar Hanina, "And it was in accord with the capacity of each one of them to listen and understand what the Word spoke with him.

   B. And do not be surprised at this matter, for when the manna came down to Israel, each and every one would find its taste appropriate to his capacity, infants in accord with their capacity, young people in accord with their capacity, old people in accord with their capacity.

   C. "...infants in accord with their capacity: just as an infant sucks from the tit of his mother, so was its flavor, as it is said, *Its taste was like the taste of rich cream* (Num. 11:8).

   D. "...young people in accord with their capacity: as it is said, *My bread also which I gave you, bread and oil and honey* (Ez. 16:19).

   E. "...old people in accord with their capacity: as it is said *the taste of it was like wafers made with honey* (Ex. 16:31).

   F. "Now if in the case of manna, each and every one would find its taste appropriate to his capacity, so in the matter of the Word, each and every one understood in accord with capacity.

   G. "Said David, *The voice of the Lord is [in accord with one's] in strength* (Ps. 29:4).

   H. "What is written is not, *in accord with his strength in particular*, but rather, *in accord with one's strength*, meaning, in accord with the capacity of each and every one.

   I. "Said to them the Holy One, blessed be He, 'It is not in accord with the fact that you hear a great many voices, but you should know that it is I who [speaks to all of you individually]: *I am the Lord your God who brought you out of the land of Egypt* (Ex. 20:2)."

4. A. In this world the Israelites were redeemed from Egypt and then taken into captivity in Babylonia, then from Babylonia to Media, from Media to Greece, from Greece to Edom.

   B. But from Edom the Holy One, blessed be He, will redeem them, and they will not be again taken into captivity.

   C. For it is said, *But Israel has been delivered by the Lord, delivered for all time to come, they shall not be confounded or put to shame for all eternity* (Is. 45:17).

The theological initiative begun above is carried forward with startling success in Nos. 1-3 of this concluding and powerful unit. The eschatological conclusion is tacked on. It has no relevance to anything that has gone before.

Pisqa Thirteen

The words of Jeremiah *[son of Hilkiah, one of the priests at Anathoth in Benjamin. The word of the Lord came to him in the thirteenth year of the reign of Josiah son of Amon, king of Judah; also during the reign of Jehoiakim, son of Josiah, king of Judah, until the eleventh year of Zedekiah son of Josiah, king of Judah, was completed. In the fifth month the people of Jerusalem were carried away into exile]*

(Jer. 1:1-3).

XIII:I

1. A. R. Abba bar Kahana opened his discourse by citing this verse: *"Cry aloud, O daughter of Gallim [waves]! Hearken, O Laishah! Answer her, O Anathoth! [Madmenah is in flight, the inhabitants of Gebim flee for safety. This very day he will halt at Nob, he will shake his fist at the mount of the daughter of Zion, the hill of Jerusalem]* (Is. 10:30-32):
   B. *"Cry aloud:* Raise your voice.
   C. *"...daughter of Gallim:* just as waves stand out in the sea, so your patriarchs stood out in the world."

2. A. Another interpretation of *O daughter of Gallim:* read the word for *waves* as though its vowels yields, *daughter of exiles,* daughter of those who went into exile,
   B. Daughter of Abraham, concerning whom it is written, *And the Lord said to Abram, Go from your land* (Gen. 12:1).
   C. Daughter of Isaac, concerning whom it is written, *And Isaac went to Abimelech, king of the Philistines, to Gerar* (Gen. 26:1).
   D. Daughter of Jacob, concerning whom it is written, *And Jacob obeyed his father and his mother [and went to Paddan Aram]* (Gen. 28:7).

3. A. *Hearken, O Laishah:* Hearken to my commandments, harken to the words of the Torah, hearken to the words of prophecy.
   B. If not, then *Laishah:* lo, a lion will come down upon you.
   C. This refers to Nebuchadnezzar, the wicked man, concerning whom it is written, *A lion has gone up from its thicket* (Jer. 4:7).

4. A. *Answer her:* [reading the letters for answer her with vowels that yield poor,] poor in righteous ones, poor in words of the Torah, poor in religious duties and good deeds.

5. A. And if not, *[Answer her,] O Anathoth:* lo, a man who comes from Anathoth will come and prophecy against you words of rebuke.

B. Therefore Scripture had to state The words of Jeremiah *[son of Hilkiah, one of the priests at Anathoth in Benjamin. The word of the Lord came to him in the thirteenth year of the reign of Josiah son of Amon, king of Judah; also during the reign of Jehoiakim, son of Josiah, king of Judah, until the eleventh year of Zedekiah son of Josiah, king of Judah, was completed. In the fifth month the people of Jerusalem were carried away into exile]* (Jer. 1:1-3).

The intersecting-verse demands attention because of its explicit reference to Anathoth. The point, then, is that the failure to respond to Isaiah's prophecy made it necessary for Jeremiah of Anathoth to declare his message. It seems to me that the entire passage points to this conclusion, first with reference to the examples of the patriarchs, then with reference to study of Torah and practice of religious deeds.

XIII:II

1. A. R. Aha opened his discourse by citing the following verse: *How long, O simple ones, will you love being simple? How long will scoffers delight in their scoffing [and fools hate knowledge? Give heed to my reproof, behold I will pour out my thoughts to you, I will make my words known to you. Because I have called and you refused to listen, have stretched out my hand and no one has heeded, and you ignored all my counsel and would have none of my reproof, I also will laugh at your calamity]* (Prov. 1:22-26):
   B. Said R. Simeon b. Nezirah, "Under ordinary circumstances, if someone eats garbage for two or three days, it turns his stomach on that account.
   C. "But as for you, how many years have you served idols, concerning whom it is written, *Go, say to it,* (Is. 30:22), which we may read to mean, *Call it shit.*
   D. "And yet, you are not nauseated on that account."

2. A. Said R. Yudan, "Two men prophesied concerning scoffing, and these are they: Solomon and Isaiah.
   B. "Solomon said, *How long will scoffers delight in their scoffing.*
   C. "And Isaiah said, *Now therefore do not be scoffers, lest your bands be made strong [extermination wholly determined have I heard from the Lord, the God of hosts]* (Is. 28:22)."

3. A. R. Phineas, R. Jeremiah in the name of R. Simeon bar R. Isaac: "Scoffing is a hard matter, for at the outset it brings punishment and at the end utter extermination.
   B. "At the beginning, it brings punishment: *lest your bands be made strong.*
   C. "And at the end extermination: *extermination wholly determined have I heard from the Lord, the God of hosts.*"

4. A. ...*Give heed to my reproof, behold I will pour out my thoughts to you, I will make my words known to you. [Because I have called and you refused to listen, have stretched out my hand and no one has heeded, and*

*you ignored all my counsel and would have none of my reproof, I also
will laugh at your calamity]* (Prov. 1:22-26):

B. *...behold I will pour out my thoughts to you:* This was through Ezekiel:
The word of the Lord came to Ezekiel son of Buzi, the priest (Ez. 1:3).

C. But if not, *I will make my words known to you:* This was through
Jeremiah.

D. Therefore Scripture had to state The words of Jeremiah *[son of Hilkiah,
one of the priests at Anathoth in Benjamin. The word of the Lord came
to him in the thirteenth year of the reign of Josiah son of Amon, king
of Judah; also during the reign of Jehoiakim, son of Josiah, king of
Judah, until the eleventh year of Zedekiah son of Josiah, king of Judah,
was completed. In the fifth month the people of Jerusalem were carried
away into exile]* (Jer. 1:1-3).

The connection to the base-verse is reached only at the end of the
intersecting-verse, as we see. But the general theme – Israel's failure to obey the
prophets, its scoffing of the prophets, is of course entirely appropriate. Nos. 1,
2, and 3 thus fit in quite well, but only No. 4 leads us to the climactic
intersection with the base-verse.

XIII:III

1. A. R. Aha opened discourse by citing this verse: *Your fathers, where are
they? And the prophets, do they live for ever? [But my words and my
statutes, which I commanded my servants the prophets, did they not
overtake your fathers? So they repented and said, As the Lord of hosts
purposed to deal with us for our ways and deeds, so has he dealt with us]*
(Zech. 1:5-6):

B. Said R. Aha, "Said the Holy One, blessed be He, to Israel, 'My children,
your fathers, who sinned before me, where are they?'

C. "They said to him, 'Lord of the ages, *And the prophets, do they live for
ever?'*

D. "He said to them, 'Nonetheless, even though they have died, does their
prophecy not endure? Moses died, but does not his prophecy endure? So
too Jeremiah, who lived, and whose words endure!'"

E. Therefore Scripture had to state The words of Jeremiah *[son of Hilkiah,
one of the priests at Anathoth in Benjamin. The word of the Lord came
to him in the thirteenth year of the reign of Josiah son of Amon, king
of Judah; also during the reign of Jehoiakim, son of Josiah, king of
Judah, until the eleventh year of Zedekiah son of Josiah, king of Judah,
was completed. In the fifth month the people of Jerusalem were carried
away into exile]* (Jer. 1:1-3).

The main point is a simple one. Though the propehts died, their prophecy
endures. Jeremiah then is given as a principal example, after Moses, of that fact.

XIII:IV

1. A. R. Joshua of Sikhnin in the name of R. Levi commenced discourse by
citing this verse: *A slave who deals wisely will rule over a son who acts
shamefully and will share the inheritance as one of the brothers. [The*

crucible is for silver and the furnace is for gold, and the Lord tries the hearts] (Prov. 17:2-3).

B. *"A slave who deals wisely* refers to Jeremiah.

C. *"...will rule over a son who acts shamefully* refers to the Israelites, who shamed themselves through idolatry."

2. A. Said R. Abba bar Kahana, "It is written, *Yet you were not like a harlot, because you scorned hire* (Ez. 16:31).

B. "Let the son of the women who was in a state of utter disarray but corrected her ways and rebuke the son of the one who was in order and who then corrupted her ways.

C. "You find that whatever is written with respect to Israel in a negative spirit is written as a matter of praise for Rahab.

D. "In regard to Rahab it is written, *And now, take an oath, I ask, to me, by the Lord, that I have done mercy with you* (Joshua 2:12). And in respect to Israel: *Therefore they take an oath in vain* (Jer. 5:2).

E. "In regard to Rahab it is written, *And you will keep alive my father and my mother* (Joshua 2:13). And in respect to Israel: *In you have they ridiculed father and mother* (Ez. 22:7).

F. "In regard to Rahab it is written, *And she brought them up to the roof* (Joshua 2:6). And in connection with Israel: *Those who bow down on the roofs to the host of the heaven* (Zeph. 1:5).

G. "In regard to Rahab it is written, *And she hid them in the stalks of flax* (Josh. 2:6). And in connection with Israel: *Who say to a piece of wood, You are my father* (Jer. 2:27).

H. "In regard to Rahab it is written, *And she said, Go to the mountain* (Josh. 2:16). And in connection with Israel: *They sacrifice on the tops of the mountains* (Hos. 4:13).

I. "In regard to Rahab it is written, *You will give me a true token* (Josh. 2:13). And in connection with Israel: *Truth they will not speak* (Jer. 9:4).

J. "Thus whatever is written with respect to Israel in a negative spirit is written as a matter of praise for Rahab."

3. A. *...and will share the inheritance as one of the brothers. [The crucible is for silver and the furnace is for gold, and the Lord tries the hearts]* (Prov. 17:2-3):

B. This refers to Jeremiah, concerning whom it is written, *And Jeremiah went forth from Jerusalem to go [into the land of Benjamin to receive his portion there in the midst of his brethren]* (Jer.. 37:12).

C. Rab said, "It was to take a part of his share that he went forth."

D. R. Benjamin b. Levi said, "It was to divide up prophecies there."

E. "What is written is not, the word of Jeremiah, but rather, *the words of Jeremiah.*"

F. Therefore Scripture had to state *The words of Jeremiah [son of Hilkiah, one of the priests at Anathoth in Benjamin. The word of the Lord came to him in the thirteenth year of the reign of Josiah son of Amon, king of Judah; also during the reign of Jehoiakim, son of Josiah, king of Judah, until the eleventh year of Zedekiah son of Josiah, king of Judah, was completed. In the fifth month the people of Jerusalem were carried away into exile]* (Jer. 1:1-3).

The base-verse is assigned to Jeremiah, beginning to end. The opening unit is rather general, but No. 2 makes matters quite precise. The sons of Rahab may rebuke the Israelites, because she corrected her ways, while the sons of the Israelites had corrupted theirs. The relevance of the Rahabites then is because Jeremiah is held to be Rahab's grandson, as we shall see in the next pericope. But that connection is not made explicitly. No. 3 then draws us back to Jeremiah in a direct way.

XIII:V

1. A. R. Samuel bar Nahman commenced discourse by citing this verse: "*But if you do not drive out the inhabitants of the land from before you, [then those of them whom you let remain shall be as pricks in your eyes and thorns in your sides, and they shall trouble you in the land where you dwell. And I will do to you as I thought to do to them]* (Num. 33:55-56).
   B. "Said the Holy One, blessed be He, to Israel, 'I said to you, *You shall utterly destroy them: the Hittite and the Amorite* (Deut. 209:17).
   C. "'But instead of doing so, you did this: *Rahab the harlot and her father's household and all she had did Joshua save alive* (Josh. 6:25).
   D. "'Lo, Jeremiah comes from the grandchildren of Rahab the whore, and he is the one who serves as *pricks in your eyes and thorns in your sides.*'"
   E. Therefore Scripture had to state *The words of Jeremiah [son of Hilkiah, one of the priests at Anathoth in Benjamin. The word of the Lord came to him in the thirteenth year of the reign of Josiah son of Amon, king of Judah; also during the reign of Jehoiakim, son of Josiah, king of Judah, until the eleventh year of Zedekiah son of Josiah, king of Judah, was completed. In the fifth month the people of Jerusalem were carried away into exile]* (Jer. 1:1-3).

Now the connection to Jeremiah is drawn explicitly. The faith that Joshua kept with Rahab now is presented as disobedience to God.

XIII:VI

1. A. R. Judah bar Simon opened discourse by citing this verse: "*I will raise up for them a prophet like you from among their brethren; [and I will put my words in his mouth, and he shall speak to them all that I command him. And whoever will not give heed to my words which he shall speak in my name, I myself will require it of him]* (Deut. 18:18-19).
   B. "It is written, There arose no prophet again in Israel like Moses (Deut. 34:10), and yet you say, *a prophet like you!*
   C. "But the sense is, *like you in giving rebuke.*
   D. "You find that whatever is written about this one [Moses] is written about that one [Jeremiah].
   E. "This one prophesied for forty years and that one prophesied for forty years.
   F. "This one prophesied concerning Judah and Israel, and that one prophesied concerning Judah and Israel.

G.   "As to this one, the members of his tribe opposed him, and as to that
     one, the members of his tribe opposed him.

H.   "This one was throne into the river, and that one was thrown into a pit.

I.   "This one was saved by a slave girl, and that one was saved by a slave
     boy.

J.   "This one came with words of rebuke, and that one came with words of
     rebuke."

K.   Therefore Scripture had to state *The words of Jeremiah [son of Hilkiah,
     one of the priests at Anathoth in Benjamin. The word of the Lord came
     to him in the thirteenth year of the reign of Josiah son of Amon, king
     of Judah; also during the reign of Jehoiakim, son of Josiah, king of
     Judah, until the eleventh year of Zedekiah son of Josiah, king of Judah,
     was completed. In the fifth month the people of Jerusalem were carried
     away into exile]* (Jer. 1:1-3).

The completion of the intersecting-verse/base-verse construction leads us
back to the exposition of the theme. The topic of Jeremiah as prophet
immediately directs our attention to Moses as the base for comparison, and the
rest follows.

XIII:VII

1.   A.   R. Tannuma said it, R. Eleazar in the name of R. Meir, R. Menahama,
          and R. Bibi:

     B.   R. Eleazar in the name of R. Meir: "Every passage in which it is said,
          the words, words of, or *words* – the intent is to deliver curses, and
          rebukes.

     C.   "It is written, *These are the words which Moses spoke to all Israel* (Deut.
          1:1), and what, further, is written there? *The wasting of hunger and the
          devouring of the fiery bolt* (Deut. 32:24).

     D.   "It is written, *The word of the Lord that come to Hosea the son of Beeri*
          (Hos. 1:1), and what further is written there? *You are not my people*
          (Hos. 1:9).

     E.   "It is written, *The words of Jeremiah* (Jer. 1:1-3), and what further is
          written there? *Such as are for death to death, [and such as are for
          captivity to captivity]* (Jer. 32:11).

The syllogism encompasses our base-verse, but of course is not built upon
it.

XIII:VIII

1.   A.   Said R. Tanhum bar Hanilai, "In three passages the Holy One, blessed be
          He, complains against the wicked Nebuchadnezzar, in the book of
          Jeremiah, in the book of Kings, and in the book of Chronicles.

     B.   "It is like a man who says to his fellow, 'Look what that guy did, may
          his bones rot!'

     C.   "So said the Holy One, blessed be He, 'See what the Babylonian shrimp
          has done to me.'"

2. A. Another interpretation [of the name] Jeremiah *[The words of Jeremiah* (Jer. 1:1-3)]:
   B. It is the lamentation of desolation [that is coming] [Braude and Kapstein, p. 257: In another comment, the name *Jeremiah* is constructed as derived from the Greek *eremos*, 'void, destitute,' and is taken to bespeak the lamentations of Jeremiah in such verses as, etc.]
   C. [Thus:] *How does the city sit solitary* (Lam. 1:1). *How in his anger has he covered himself with a cloud* (Lam. 2:1). *How is the gold become dim* (Lam. 4:1).

3. A. [Commenting on the clause, *the words of*, in *The words of Jeremiah* (Jer. 1:1-3), and reading the letters that spell out *words* as though their vowels produced the word for *pestilence*, we interpret:] the pestilence that produces death [brought by] Jeremiah:
   B. *Such as are for death to death, [and such as are for captivity to captivity]* (Jer. 32:11).

4. A. Another matter concerning *The words of Jeremiah:* Said the Holy One, blessed be He, to Jeremiah, "Go, say to Israel, 'Repent, and if not, lo, I shall destroy the house of my sanctuary."
   B. They said, "If he destroys it, is he not destroying what is his own?"
   C. So thus did the Holy One, blessed be He, say, "Lo, I shall destroy my sanctuary, and my words will be carried out by Jeremiah."

5. A. Another matter concerning *The words of Jeremiah:* [reading the phrase, *the words of*, construed as *my word* through, hence *my word through Jeremiah*:] Said the Holy One, blessed be He, to Jeremiah, "Jeremiah, I have been seeking of them [that they carry out] my words.
   B. "I said to them, *I am the Lord your God* (Ex. 20:2), but they did not act in accord with that statement, but rather, *Saying to a piece of wood, You are my father* (Jer. 2:27).
   C. "I said to them, *You shall have no other gods before me* (Ex. 20:2), but they did not act in accord with that statement, but rather, *...worshipping the host of heaven on the roofs* (Zeph. 1:5).
   D. "I said to them, *You shall not take the name of the Lord your God in vain* (Ex. 20:7), but they did not act in accord with that statement, but rather, *Surely they swear falsely* (Jer. 5:2).
   E. "I said to them, *Remember the Sabbath day to keep it holy* (Ex. 20:8), but they did not act in accord with that statement, but rather, *You have despised my holy things and you have profaned my sabbaths* (Ez. 22:8).
   F. "I said to them, *Honor your father and your mother* (Ex. 20:12), but they did not act in accord with that statement, but rather, *In you have they made light of father and mother* (Ez. 22:7).
   G. "I said to them, *You shall not murder you shall not commit adultery, you shall not steal* (Ex. 20:13), but they did not act in accord with that statement, but rather, *You steal, murder, and commit adultery* (Jer. 7:9).
   H. "I said to them, *You shall not bear false witness against your neighbor* (Ex. 20:13), but they did not act in accord with that statement, but rather, *They bend their tongue their bow to falsehood* (Jer. 9:2).

I. "I said to them, *You shall not covet* (Ex. 20:14), but they did not act in accord with that statement, but rather, *They covet fields and seize them, houses and take them away* (Mic. 2:2)."

No. 1 starts out with a general comment on the topic of the book as a whole, explaining why more than a single document covers the same subject. No. 2 then gives an interpretation of the name of Jeremiah. The several treatments of the word words of systematically develop the potential meanings, specifically, No. 3 takes the word DBR and reads it *dever*, pestilence; No. 4, sanctuary (*debir*), meaning, the message of desolation concerning my sanctuary, No. 5, *my word*, meaning, God's, with enormous effect.

XIII:IX

1. A. Another matter: *The words of Jeremiah:*
   B. Said the Holy One, blessed be He, to Jeremiah, "Either you go down with them to Babylonia and I shall stay here, or you stay here and I shall go down with them [to Babylonia]."
   C. Said Jeremiah before the Holy One, blessed be He, "Lord of the ages, if I go down with them, what good can I do for them? But let their Creator go down with them, because He can do them some good."

2. A. Three statements did Nebuchadnezzar command to Nebuzaradan concerning Jeremiah, saying to him, *Take him and watch over him, do not do any bad thing to him* (Jer. 39:2).
   B. When Jeremiah would see a band of youths chained in neck-collars, he would go and place his hand among them [joining them].
   C. When Jeremiah would see a band of elders chained in neck-collars, he would go and place his hand among them [joining them].
   D. Said to him Nebuzaradan, "One of three judgments applies to you. Either you are a false prophet, or you reject [just] punishment, or you shed blood.
   E. "Either you are a false prophet: for lo, for so many years you prophesied over this hovel that it would be destroyed, and now that I destroy it, the act is wrong in your view.
   F. "...or you reject [just] punishment: for I do not want to give you distress, and there is no prohibition contemplated against you.
   G. "...or you shed blood: for if the king hears what you are doing and doing, while I do nothing to you, he will send and remove the head of that person [me].
   H. "But *if it is good to you to come with me to Babylonia, come, and I will take good care of you, [but if it seems bad to you to come with me to Babylonia, desist]* (Jer. 40:4)."
   I. *But he would not go back* (Jer. 40:5) until the Holy One, blessed be He, so instructed him.
   J. That is in line with this verse of Scripture: *The word which came to Jeremiah from the Lord after Nebuzaradan sent him* (Jer. 40:1).

3. A. *...and he was imprisoned in chains* (Jer. 40:1):
   B. What is the meaning of *and he?*

C. Said R. Aha, "It is as if to say, *and both he and He.*"

4. A. [With reference to *The word of the Lord came to him* ,] what is that word [that is announced at the base-verse, since it is not then specified]?

    B. R. Eleazar and R. Yohanan:

    C. R. Eleazar said, *He who scattered Isrqel will gather him and keep him as a shepherd keeps his flock* (Jer. 31;10)

    D. R. Yohanan said, *The Lord will redeem Jacob and save him from the hand of him that is stronger than he* (Jer. 31:11).

5. A. When he was returning [after being sent back by Nebuzaradan,] he saw the fingers and toes that had been cut off and thrown by the side of the road.

    B. He would collect them and kiss and caress them and put them into his cloak, saying to them, "My children, did I not say to you: *Give glory to the Lord your God, before it grows dark and before your feet stumble* (Jer. 13:16), meaning before the words of Torah grow dark for you, before the words of prophecy grow gloomy."

We continue at No. 1 the inquiry into the meaning of *words of.*   Nos. 2, 4, with the former glossed at No. 3, then move on to a separate matter, Jeremiah's colloquy with Nebuzaradan. These lead us directly to Nos. 4, 5, which resume the explication of the meanings of word/words, begun at **XIII:VIII.**

XIII:X

1. A. *I will take up weeping and wailing for the mountains, and a lamentation for the pastures of the wilderness, [because they are laid waste so that no one passes through, and the lowing of cattle is not heard; both the birds of the air and the beasts have fled and are gone. I will make Jerusalem a heap of ruins, a lair of jackals, aand I will make the cities of Judah a desolation, without inhabitant]* (Jer. 9:10-11):

    B. For the high mountains which have been turned into a wilderness I take up weeping.

    C. *...because they are laid waste so that no one passes through, and the lowing of cattle is not heard:*

    D. It is not enough for you that you did not listen to his voice, but even that of the cattle.

    E. [Reading the letters for the word *cattle* with vowels that yield the word for *provoke,* we interpret:] They provoked me with their idolatry.

2. A. *...both the birds of the air and the beasts have fled and are gone.*

    B. Said R. Yose bar Halputa, "For fifty-two years no bird was seen to fly over the land of Israel, to carry out the verse, *both the birds of the air and the beasts have fled and are gone.*"

    C. Said R. Haninah, "Forty years before the Israelites went into exile in Babylonia, they planted date treats in Babylonia, for the Israelites loved the sweetness that readies the tongue for Torah-study."

    D. It was taught on Tannaite authority in the name of R. Judah, "For seven years the decree was carried out on the land: *The whole land is brimstone and salt and a burning* (Deut. 29:22). This is on the count of the following [Braude and Kapstein, p. 260]: *The covenant shall cause the many enemies to prevail for a week of years* (Dan. 9:27)."

E.   As to the Samaritans that remained in the land, what did they do? The land burned up in patches, so if they sowed here, the crop burned up, and they would saw there, and the crop burned up.

3. A.   Said R. Zeira, "Come and take note of the impudence of the Land of Israel, which produced crops."

B.   And why did it produce crops?

C.   Two Amoras:

D.   One of them said, "Because [the Samaritans] manured it."

E.   The other of them said, "Because they turned over the land, like someone who turns over the ground, so that what is on top is set below, and what is on the bottom is set on top."

F.   There was the story of someone who was ploughing in the valley of Arbel, and his ploughshare dug deep, so the hot soil that came up burned the seed.

4. A.   Said R. Haninah son of R. Abbahu, "There are seven hundred species of fish that are clean, eight hundred species of locusts that are clean, and birds without number, and all of them went into exile with the Israelites to Babylonia.

B.   "And when they came back, all of them came back with them except for the fish called the shibuta-fish."

C.   But how did fish swim into exile?

D.   R. Hunah in the name of R. Yose: "They went via the path in the great deep, and they came back via the path in the great deep."

We now focus on the exile itself, a theme introduced in the preceding. Nos. 1, 2 deal with the cited verse by clarifying its details. No. 3 then pursues the theme of the condition of the land during the exile, and No. 4 is tacked on. I do not see how this item is cogent with what has gone before. We now continue the exegesis of that opening sentence in the book of Jeremiah.

XIII:XI

1. A.   Another matter concerning *The words of Jeremiah:*

B.   The name [referring to the letters r m y h] means, *the Lord went up.*

2. A.   In ten upward stages the Presence of God departed: from the cherub to the cherub, from the cherub to the threshold of the temple-building; from the threshold of the temple to the two cherubim; from the two cherubim to the eastern gate of the sanctuary; from the eastern gate of the sanctuary to the [wall of the] temple court; from the [wall of the] temple court to the altar; from the altar to the roof; from the roof to the city wall, from the city wall to the city, from the city to the Mount of Olives.

B.   ...from the ark cover to the cherub: *And he rode upon a cherub and flew* (2 Sam. 22:11).

C. ...from the cherub to the cherub: *And the glory of the Lord mounted up from the cherub to the threshold of the house* (Ez. 10:45).

D. ...from the threshold of the temple to the two cherubim: *And the glory of the Lord went forth from off the threshold of the house and stood over the cherubim* (Ez. 10:18). Lo, it was necessary to say only, *And the glory of the Lord came...*

E. They drew a parable: to what may the matter be compared? To the case of a king who was leaving his palace. He kissed the walls and embraced the columns and said, "May you remain whole, O my house, may you remain whole, O my palace." So the Presence of God kissed the walls and embraced the columns and said, "May you remain whole, O my house, may you remain whole, O my palace."

F. ...from the two cherubim to the eastern gate of the sanctuary: *The cherubs raised their wings and flew above the earth before my eyes* (Ez. 10:9).

G. ...from the eastern gate of the sanctuary to the [wall of the] temple court: *And the courtyard was filled with the splendor of the glory of the Lord* (Ez. 10:4).

H. ...from the [wall of the temple] court to the altar: *I saw the Lord standing beside the altar* (Amos 9:1).

I. ...from the altar to the roof: *It is better to dwell on the corner of the roof* (Prov. 21:9).

J. ...from the roof to the city wall: *Lo, he showed me, and behold, the Lord was standing on the wall made by a plumb line* (Amos 7:7).

K. ...from the city wall to the city: *A voice cries, The Lord into the city* (Mic. 6:9).

L. ...from the city to the Mount of Olives: *And the glory of the Lord went up from the midst of the city and stood on the mountain* (Ez. 11:23).

3. A. Said R. Jonathan, "For three and a half years the Presence of God stayed on the Mount of Olives, declaring three times a day, saying, *Return, wandering children, I shall heal your backslidings* (Jer. 3:22).

B. "But when they did not repent, the Presence of God began to fly in the air, reciting this verse of Scripture: *I will go and return to my place until they confess their guilt and seek my face, in their trouble they will seek me earnestly* (Hos. 5:15)."

No. 1 resumes the interpretation of the name of Jeremiah, and then No. 2 simply presents but not at all verbatim Avot deR. Nathan **XXXIV:IX.1**. No. 3 complements No. 2.

XIII:XII

1. A. Another matter concerning the name *Jeremiah:*

B. It is because in his time the house of the sanctuary was made desolate (Greek: *erimon*, Hebrew: *eremos*).

2. A. Another matter concerning the name *Jeremiah:*

B. Because in his time the divine attribute of justice [as against mercy and forgiveness] was exalted.

3. A. *...son of Hilkiah:*
   B. Said R. Judah bar. Simon, "From the tribe concerning which is it written, *I am your share* [which uses the letters of the word Hilkiah] *and your inheritance* (Num. 18:20)."

4. A. Said R. Samuel bar Nahman, "There are four who come from a blighted family, and these are they: Phineas, Uriah, Ezekiel, and Jeremiah.
   B. "Phineas: In the case of Phineas, you find that when he came to inspect the genealogies of Israel, they said to him, 'Do you come to inspect our genealogies? To whom was Eleazar married? It was to the daughter of Putiel [an Egyptian priest]. Is it not written, *And Eleazar son of Aaron took for him a wife from the daughters of Putiel* (Ex. 6:256). And do you come to inspect our genealogy?'
   C. "When the Holy One, blessed be He, noted that they were humiliating him, he began to assign him a more distinguished genealogy: *Phineas son of Eleazar son of Aaron the priest* (Num. 25:11), that is, a priest son of a priest. A zealot son of a zealot.
   D. "Uriah: The Israelites were ridiculing him, saying, 'Is he not a Gibeonite? *And also there was a man who was prophesying in the name of the Lord, Uriah ben Shemayahu of Qiriat Yearim* (Jer. 26:20). And it is written, *Gideon and Chepirah and Bearot and Qiriat Yearim* (Josh. 9:17) [thus proving that he was a Gibeonite].
   E. "Accordingly, it was necessary for Scripture to supply him with a genealogy: *And I called to testify for me faithful witnesses, Uriah the priest* (Is. 8:2).
   F. "Ezekiel: The Israelites were ridiculing him, saying, 'Is this one not one of the gradnchildren of the whore, Rahab?'
   G. "Accordingly, it was necessary for Scripture to supply him with a genealogy: *The word of the Lord came to Ezekiel ben Buzzi the priest* (Ez. 1:3).
   H. "...and Jeremiah: The Israelites were ridiculing him, saying, 'Is this one not one of the gradnchildren of the whore, Rahab?'
   I. "Accordingly, it was necessary for Scripture to supply him with a genealogy: *son of Hilkiah, one of the priests at Anathoth in Benjamin.*"

The syllogism encompasses Jeremiah and draws on our base-text for its own purposes.

XIII:XIII

1. A. *...one of the priests at Anathoth [in Benjamin. The word of the Lord came to him in the thirteenth year of the reign of Josiah son of Amon, king of Judah; also during the reign of Jehoiakim, son of Josiah, king of Judah, until the eleventh year of Zedekiah son of Josiah, king of Judah, was completed. In the fifth month the people of Jerusalem were carried away into exile]* (Jer. 1:1-3):
   B. Said R. Berekhiah, "Said Jeremiah, 'My name is disgraced among the priests. In the time of Moses [the priests said,] *...the Lord bless you and keep you* (Num. 6:25). But in my times: *of them shall be taken up a curse* (Jer. 29:22).

C. "'In the time of Moses [the priests said,] ...*the Lord make his face to shine on you* (Num. 6:25). But in my times: ...*such as are for death, to death* (Jer. 15:2).

D. "'In the time of Moses [the priests said,] ...*and be gracious to you* (Num. 6:25). But in my times: *He has made me live in dark places, like whose who have been dead for a long time* (Lam. 3:6).

E. "'In the time of Moses [the priests said,] ...*the Lord lift up his face to you and give you peace* (Num. 6:25). But in my times: *I will show you no favor* (Jer. 16:13).

F. "'In the time of Moses [the priests said,] ...*the Lord lift up his face to you* But in my times: *A nation of fierce countenance, that will not regard the person of the old or show favor to the young* (Deut. 28:50).

G. "'In the time of Moses [the priests said,] ...*and give you peace* But in my times: *I have taken away my peace from this people, says the Lord, even mercy and compassion* (Jer. 16:25).'"

The contrast between the priestly benediction and the statements concerning Jeremiah and his times is aptly drawn.

XIII:XIV

1. A. ...*in the land of Benjamin:*

   B. [Following Mandelbaum:] His share was assigned in the land of Benjamin.

   C. Just as in the case of Benjamin, the meaning of the blessing that our father, Jacob, would produce twelve tribes was not clarified until Benjamin was born, so among all the prophets who prophesied concerning Jerusalem, the full meaning of the prophecy of none of them was clarified until Jeremiah came along.

2. A. Further, just as in the case of Benjamin, so long as he was in his mother's belly, she did not die, but when he came forth from her, she died, as it is written, *And when her soul expired, for she was dying* (Gen. 35:18),

   B. so too, as long as Jeremiah was in Jerusalem, it was not destroyed, but when he left it, it was destroyed, in line with what Jeremiah says, *You have enticed me and I was enticed...* (Jer. 20:7).

   C. "You set out to entice me, O Lord, and I was enticed, you have removed me from its midst and it was destroyed.

   D. "Yesterday you said to me, *Lo, Hanamel, son of Shallum, your uncle, will come to you saying, Buy my field* (Jer. 32:7), and so ...*you have overcome me and prevailed* (Jer. 20:7).

3. A. Further: just as Benjamin was the last among all the tribes, so Jeremiah was the last among all the prophets.

   B. But did not Haggai, Zechariah, and Malachi prophecy after him?

   C. R. Eleazar and R. Samuel bar Nahman:

   D. R. Eleazar said, "Their prophecy was cut short."

   E. R. Samuel bar Nahman said, "The prophecy [that they later on delivered] was already put in storage in their possession [in the time of Jeremiah]."

4. A. R. Eleazar and R. Yohanan:
   B R. Eleazar said, "All the prophets began their works with words of rebuke but ended with words of comfort, except for Jeremiah, who concluded also with words of rebuke, saying, *Thus shall Babylonia sink and shall not rise again* (Jer. 51:64)."
   C. Said R. Yohanan, "He too concluded with words of consolation, for he went and prophesied concerning the destruction of the house of the sanctuary. Now is it possible that it was concerning the house of the sanctuary that he concluded? Scripture says, *Thus far are the words of Jeremiah* (Jer. 51:64). He thus concluded with the fall of those who had destroyed it."
   D. And did Isaiah not conclude with words of rebuke? And is it not written, *They shall be an abhorring to all flesh* (Is. 66:24)?
   E. He is dealing with the gentiles.
   F. [Reverting to Jeremiah:] and is it not written, *For you have rejected us* (Lam. 5:22)? *Restore us because you have rejected us* (Lam. 5:21-22) [is the sense of the passage].

The comparison to Benjamin yields apt observations on the role of Jeremiah among the prophets. Nos. 2, 3 make this point with great force. No. 4 surely belongs for the same reason.

XIII:XV

1. A. *The word of the Lord came to him in the thirteenth year of the reign of Josiah son of Amon, king of Judah; also during the reign of Jehoiakim, son of Josiah, king of Judah, until the eleventh year of Zedekiah son of Josiah, king of Judah, was completed. In the fifth month the people of Jerusalem were carried away into exile* (Jer. 1:1-3):
   B. Said R. Abun, "A lion came up under the sign of the lion and destroyed the lion of God [=Ariel] [that is, Jerusalem].
   C. "...the lion came up: this is Nebuchadnezzar the wicked, concerning whom it is written, *The lion has come up out of its thicket* (Jer. 4:7).
   D. "...under the sign of the lion: *In the fifth month the people of Jerusalem were carried away into exile.*
   E. "...and destroyed the lion of God: *Oh, Ariel, Ariel, the city where David encamped* (Is. 29:1).
   F. "It was so that the lion should come up in the sign of the lion and rebuild the lion of God [Ariel, Jerusalem].
   G. "...the lion should come up: thus is the Holy One, blessed be He, of whom it is written, *The lion has roared, who will not tremble* (Amos 3:8).
   H. "...in the sign of the lion: *And I shall change their time of mourning to rejoicing* (Jer. 31:13).
   I "...and rebuild the lion of God: *the Lord builds Jerusalem, the scattered ones of Israel he will bring back together* (Ps. 147:2)."

The conclusion works on the tripartite image, handsomely articulated.

Pisqa Fourteen

Hear *[the word of the Lord, O House of Jacob, and all the families of the House of Israel. Thus says the Lord: "What wrong did your fathers find in me that they went far from me and went after worthlessness and became worthless? They did not say, 'Where is the Lord who brought us up from the Land of Egypt, who led us in the wilderness, in a land of deserts and pits, in a land of drought and deep darkness, in a land that none passes through, where no man dwells?'"]*

(Jer. 2:4-6).

XIV:I

1. A. *Therefore hear me you men of understanding, far be it from God that he should do wickedness, and from the almighty that he should do wrong. [For according to the work of a man he will requite him, and according to his ways he will make it befall him]* (Job 34:10-11):

    B. R. Azariah, R. Jonathan bar Haggai in the name of R. Samuel bar R. Isaac, "[With reference to the verse, *Then Jacob became angry and upbraided Laban. Jacob said to Laban, 'What is my offense? What is my sin, that you have hotly pursued me? Although you have felt through all my goods, what have you found of all your household goods? Set it here before my kinsmen and your kinsmen that they may decide between us two'* (Gen. 31:36-37),] "Better the captiousness of the fathers than the irenic obsequiousness of the sons.

    C. "[We learn the former from this verse:] *Then Jacob became angry and upbraided Laban. Jacob said to Laban, ["What is my offense? What is my sin, that you have hotly pursued me?]* [Gen. R. 74:10 adds: You might imagine that, in consequence, there would be a brawl. But in fact there was nothing but an effort at reconciliation. Jacob made every effort to reconcile his father-in-law: *Although you have felt through all my goods, what have you found of all your household goods? Set it here before my kinsmen and your kinsmen that they may decide between us two.]*

    D. "[We learn about] the irenic obsequiousness of the sons from the case of David:

    E. *"And David fled from Naioth in Ramah and came and said before Jonathan, What have I done? What is my iniquity? and what is my sin before your father, that he seeks my life?* (1 Sam. 20:1).

    F. "Even while he is trying to reconcile with the other, he mentions bloodshed.

    G. Said R. Simon, "Under ordinary circumstances, when a son-in-law is living with his father in law and then proceeds to leave the household of his father in law, is it possible that the father-in-law will not find in his possession even the most minor item? But as to this [Jacob], even a shoelace, even a knife, was not found in his possession.

H. "That is in line with this verse of Scripture: *Although you have felt through all my goods, what have you found of all your household goods? Set it here before my kinsmen and your kinsmen that they may decide between us two.*

I. "Said the Holy One, blessed be He, 'By your life! In the very language by which you have rebuked your father-in-law, I shall rebuke your children: *What wrong did your fathers find in me that they went far from me and went after worthlessness and became worthless?*"

The intersecting-verse is simply ignored, but the exegesis is remarkable for its power to link to unrelated situations and to show their profound connection. I take it that the exegete may have in mind the clause, *For according to the work of a man he will requite him, and according to his ways he will make it befall him.* Then the ways of the father, Jacob, explain the language used to the descendants. But if that is the connection, it seems tenuous, and, of more consequence, needless, since the link is direct and through the language shared by the passage of Jeremiah and the passage of Genesis. We have therefore to classify the composition as other than an intersecting-verse/base-verse one.

XIV:II

1. A. [*For the simple are killed by their turning away, and the complacence of fools destroys them;*] *but he who listens to me will dwell secure, and will be at ease, [without dread of evil]* (Prov. 1:33):

    B. There are four categories of hearing.

    C. There is one who listens and loses, there is one who listens and gains, one who does not listen and loses, one who does not listen and gains.

    D. There is one who listens and loses: this is the first Man: *And to Man he said, Because you listened to the voice of your wife* (Gen. 3:17).

    E. What did he lose? *For you are dust and to dust you will return* (Gen. 3:19).

    F. ...who listens and gains: this is our father, Abraham: *Whatever Sarah says to you, Listen to her voice* (Gen. 21:12).

    G. How did he gain? *For through Isaac will you have descendents* (Gen. 21:12)

    H. ...who does not listen and gains: this refers to Joseph: *And he did not listen to her, to lie with her* (Gen. 39:11).

    I. How did he gain? *And Joseph will place his hand over your eyes* (Gen. 46:4).

    J. ...who does not listen and loses: this refers to Israel: *They did not listen to me and did not pay attention* (Jer. 7:26).

    K. What did they lose? *Him to death, to death, and him to the sword, to the sword* (Jer. 15:2).

2. A. Said R. Levi, "The ear is to the body as the kiln to pottery. Just as in the case of a kiln, when it is full of pottery, if you kindle a flame under it, all of the pots feel it,

B. "so: *Incline your ear and go to me and listen and let your souls live* (Is. 55:3)."

Neither composition pays attention to the base-verse nor introduces an intersecting-verse.

XIV:III

1. A. *If you are willing and listen, you shall eat the good of the land; but if you refuse and rebel, [you shall be devoured by the sword; for the mouth of the Lord has spoken]* (Is. 1:19-20):
   B. *[...you shall eat the good of the land:]* You shall eat carobs.
   C. Said R. Aha, "When an Israelite has to eat carobs, he will carry out repentance.
   D. Said R. Aqiba, "As becoming is poverty for a daughter of Jacob as a red ribbon on the breast of a white horse."

2. A. Said R. Samuel bar Nahman, "Even while a palace is falling, it is still called a palace, and even when a dung heap rises, it is still called a dung heap.
   B. "Even while a palace is falling, it is still called a palace: *Hear the word of the Lord, O House of Jacob, and all the families of the House of Israel* (Jer. 2:4-6). When while they are declining, he still calls them *the House of Israel*.
   C. "...and even when a dung heap rises, it is still called a dung heap: *Behold the land of the Chaldeans – this is the nation that was nothing* (Is. 23:13) – would that they were still nothing!"

3. A. Said R. Levi, The matter may be compared to the case of a noble woman who had two family members at hand, one a villager, the other a city-dweller. The one who was a villager, [when he had occasion to correct her,] would speak in words of consolation: 'Are you not the daughter of good folk, are you not the daughter of a distinguished family?'
   B. "But the one who was a city-dweller, [when he had occasion to correct her,] would speak in words of reprimand: 'Are you not the daughter of the lowest of the poor, are you not the daughter of impoverished folk?'
   C. "So too in the case of Jeremiah, since he was a villager, from Anathoth, he would go to Jerusalem and speak to Israel in words of consolation [and pleading,] *Hear the word of the Lord, O House of Jacob, [and all the families of the House of Israel. Thus says the Lord: "What wrong did your fathers find in me that they went far from me and went after worthlessness and became worthless? They did not say, "Where is the Lord who brought us up from the Land of Egypt, who led us in the wilderness, in a land of deserts and pits, in a land of drought and deep darkness, in a land that none passes through, where no man dwells?"]* (Jer. 2:4-6).
   D. "'These are the improper deeds which your fathers did.'
   E. "But Isaiah, because he was a city dweller, from Jerusalem, would speak to Israel in terms of reprimand: *Hear the word of the Lord, you rulers of Sodom, attend, you people of gomorrah, to the instruction of our God* (Is. 1:10).

F.   "'Do you not come from the mold of the people of Sodom?'"

4. A.   Said R. Levi, "Amoz and Amaziah were brothers, and because Isaiah was
         the son of the king's brother, he could speak to Israel in such terms of
         reprimand,

   B.   "in line with this verse: *A rich man answers impudently* (Prov. 18:23)."

The relevance of No. 1 is not obvious to me. No. 2, by contrast, leads us
directly into our base-verse, commenting on the language that is used. No. 3, 4
then amplify that point by comparing Jeremiah and Isaiah.

XIV:IV

1. A.   Said R. Levi, "The matter may be compared to the case of a noble lady
         who [as her dowry] brought into the king two myrtles and lost one of
         them and was distressed on that account.

   B.   "The king said to her, 'Take good care of this other one as if you were
         taking care of the two of them.'

   C.   "So too, when the Israelites stood at Mount Sinai, they said, *Everything
         that the Lord has spoken we shall do and we shall hear* (Ex. 24:7). They
         lost the *we shall do* by making the golden calf.

   D.   "Said the Holy One, blessed be He, be sure to take care of the *we shall
         listen* as if you were taking care of both of them.'

   E.   "When they did not listen, the Holy One, blessed be He, said to them,
         *Hear the word of the Lord, O House of Jacob, [and all the families of the
         House of Israel. Thus says the Lord: "What wrong did your fathers find
         in me that they went far from me and went after worthlessness and
         became worthless? They did not say, "Where is the Lord who brought us
         up from the Land of Egypt, who led us in the wilderness, in a land of
         deserts and pits, in a land of drought and deep darkness, in a land that
         none passes through, where no man dwells?"]* (Jer. 2:4-6)."

2. A.   [A further comment on the verse, *Hear the word of the Lord* (Jer. 2:4-6):]
         before you have to listen to the words of Jeremiah.

   B.   Listen to the words of the Torah, before you have to listen to the words
         of the prophet.

   C.   Listen to the words of prophecy before you have to listen to words of
         rebuke.

   D.   Listen to words of rebuke before you have to listen to words of
         reprimand.

   E.   Listen to words of reprimand before you have to listen to *the sound of
         the horn and the pipe* (Dan. 3:15).

   F.   Listen in the land before you have to listen abroad.

   G.   Listen while alive, before you have to listen when dead.

   H.   Let your ears listen before your bodies have to listen.

   I.   Let your bodies listen before your bones have to listen: *Dry bones, hear
         the word of the Lord* (Ez. 37:4).

3. A.   R. Aha in the name of R. Joshua b. Levi, "Nearly eight times in Egypt
         the Israelites [Braude and Kapstein, p. 270:] stood shoulder to shoulder.

B. "What is the scriptural verse that indicates it? *Come, let us take counsel against* him (Ex. 1:10).

C. "On that account [God] took the initiative for them and redeemed them: *And I came down to save* him *from the hand of the Egyptians* (Ex. 3:8)."

4. A. R. Abin, R. Hiyya in the name of R. Yohanan: "It is written, *My mother's sons were displeased with me, they sent me to watch over the vineyards; so I did not watch over my own vineyard* (Song 1:6).

B. "What brought it about that I watched over the vineyards? It is because *I did not watch over my own vineyard.*

C. "What brought it about that in Syria I separate dough-offering from two loaves? It is because in the Land of Israel I did not properly separate dough-offering from one loaf.

D. "I thought that I should receive a reward on account of both of them, but I receive a reward only on account of one of them.

E. "What brought it about that in Syria I observe two days for the festivals? It is because in the Land of Israel I did not properly observe one day for the festivals.

F. "I thought that I should receive a reward on account of both of them, but I receive a reward only on account of one of them."

G. R. Yohanan would recite the following verse of Scripture in this connection: *And I also gave them ordinances that were not good* (Ez. 20:25).

No. 1 presents a powerful comment on our base-verse. No. 2 moves in its own direction, but its contrast between listening to A so that you will not have to listen to B makes its point with great power as well. The relevance of Nos. 3, 4 is hardly self-evident. Speculation that these items illustrate entries on the catalogue of No. 3 is certainly not groundless.

XIV:V

1. A. It is written, *Thus said the Lord, What wrong did your fathers find in me that they went far from me and went after worthlessness and became worthless?* (Jer. 2:5)

B. Said R. Isaac, "This refers to one who leaves the scroll of the Torah and departs. Concerning him, Scripture says, *What wrong did your fathers find in me that they went far from me.*

C. "Said the Holy One, blessed be He, to the Israelites, 'My children, your fathers found no wrong with me, but you have found wrong with me.

D. "'The first Man found no wrong with me, but you have found wrong with me.'

E. "To what may the first Man be compared?

F. "To a sick man, to whom the physician came. The physician said to him, 'Eat this, don't eat that.'

G. "When the man violated the instructions of the physician, he brought about his own death.

H. "[As he lay dying,] his relatives came to him and said to him, 'Is it possible that the physician is imposing on you the divine attribute of justice?'

I. "He said to them, 'God forbid. I am the one who brought about my own death. This is what he instructed me, saying to me, 'Eat this, don't eat that,' but when I violated his instructions, I brought about my own death.

J. "So too all the generations came to the first Man, saying to him, 'Is it possible that the Holy One, blessed be He, is imposing the attribute of justice on you?'

L. "He said to them, 'God forbid. I am the one who has brought about my own death. Thus did he command me, saying to me, *Of all the trees of the garden you may eat, but of the tree of the knowledge of good and evil you may not eat* (Gen. 2:17). When I violated his instructions, I brought about my own death, for it is written, *On the day on which you eat it, you will surely die* (Gen. 2:17).'

M. "[God's speech now continues:] 'Pharaoh found no wrong with me, but you have found wrong with me.'

N. "To what may Pharaoh be likened?

O. "To the case of a king who went overseas and went and deposited all his possessions with a member of his household. After some time the king returned from overseas and said to the man, 'Return what I deposited with you.'

P. "He said to him, 'I did not such thing with you, and you left me nothing.'

Q. "What did he do to him? He took him and put him in prison.

R. "He said to him, 'I am your slave. Whatever you left with me I shall make up to you.'

S. "So, at the outset, said the Holy One, blessed be He, to Moses, *Now go and I shall send you to Pharaoh* (Ex. 3:10).

T. "That wicked man said to him, *Who is the Lord that I should listen to his voice? I do not know the Lord* (Ex. 2:5).

U. "But when he brought the ten plagues on him, *The Lord is righteous and I and my people are wicked* (Ex. 9:27).

V. "[God's speech now continues:] 'Moses found no wrong with me, but you have found wrong with me.'

W. "To what may Moses be compared?

X. "To a king who handed his son over to a teacher, saying to him, 'Do not call my son a moron."

Y. What is the meaning of the word moron?

Z. Said R. Reuben, "In the Greek language they call an idiot a moron."

AA. [Resuming the discourse:] "One time the teacher belittled the boy and called him a moron. Said the king to him, 'With all my authority I instructed you, saying to you, Do not call my son a fool,' and yet you have called my son a fool. It is not the calling of a smart fellow to go along with fools. [You're fired!]'

BB. "Thus it is written, *And the Lord spoke to Moses and to Aaron and commanded them concerning the children of Israel* (Ex. 6:13).

CC. "What did he command them? He said to them,'Do not call my sons morons.' But when they rebelled them at the waters of rebellion, Moses said to them, *Listen, I ask, you morons* (Num. 20:10).

DD. "Said the Holy One, blessed be He, to them, 'With all my authority I instructed you, saying to you, Do not call my sons fools,' and yet you have called my sons fools. It is not the calling of a smart fellow to go along with fools. [You're fired!]'

EE. "Therefore, what is written is not *You* [singular] *therefore shall not bring,* but *you* [plural] *therefore shall not bring* (Num. 20:12). [For God said,] 'Neither you nor your brother nor your sister will enter the Land of Israel.'

FF. "[God's speech now continues:] Said the Holy One, blessed be He, to Israel, 'Your fathers in the wilderness found no wrong with me, but you have found wrong with me.'

GG. "'I said to them, *One who makes an offering to other gods will be utterly destroyed* (Ex. 22:19), but they did not do so, but rather, *They prostrated themselves to it and worshipped it* (Ex. 32:8).

HH. "After all the wicked things that they did, what is written, *And the Lord regretted the evil that he had considered doing to his people* (Ex. 32:14)."

2. A. Said R. Judah bar Simon, "Said the Holy One, blessed be He, to Israel, 'Your fathers in the wilderness found no wrong with me, but you have found wrong with me.'

B. "'I said to them, *For six days you will gather [the manna] and on the seventh day it is a Sabbath, on which there will be no collecting of manna* (Ex. 16:26).

C. "'But they did not listen, but rather: *And it happened that on the seventh day some of the people went out to gather manna and did not find it* (Ex. 16:27).

D. "Had they found it, they would have gathered it [and violated his wishes, so he did not give mana on the seventh day, therefore avoiding the occasion of making them sin].'"

The sustained and powerful story amplifies the statement, *What wrong did your fathers find in me.* The point is that the fathers found no fault with God, which makes the actions of Jeremiah's generation all the more inexplicable. The movement from the first Man to Pharaoh, then Moses and Aaron, leads then to Israel, and the complaint is remarkably apt: it has to do with the forty years in the wilderness, to which Jeremiah makes reference! So the storyteller has dealt with both parts of the complaint. First, the fathers found no fault with their punishment, that is, the forty years they were left to die in the wilderness, and, second, the forty years were a mark of grace. So complaining against God is without rhyme or reason. I cannot imagine a better example of a sustained amplification, through exegesis of intersecting-verses, parables, and syllogisms, of the basic proposition.

XIV:VI

1. A. ...*they went far from me and went after worthlessness and became worthless?* (Jer. 2:5).

B. Said R. Phineas in the name of R. Hoshaiah, "For they would drive out those who did return to God.

C. "That is in line with this verse of Scripture: *Therefore I chased him away from me* (Neh. 13:28), [Braude and Kapstein, p. 272 add: they chased away and made go far from me those who would have returned to me]."

The exegesis of a clause of the base-verse imparts to the message a still deeper dimension.

XIV:VI

1. A.   *...and went after worthlessness and became worthless?* (Jer. 2:5):

    B.   Said R. Isaac, "The matter may be compared to the case of a banker, against whom a debit was issued, and he was afraid, saying, 'Is it possible that the debit is for a hundred gold coins or two hundred gold coins.'

    C.   "Said the creditor to him, 'Do not fear, it covers only a kor of bran and barley, and in any event it's already been paid off.'

    D.   "So said the Holy One, blessed be He, to Israel, My children, as to the idolatry after which you lust, *it is nothing of substance, but they are nought, a work of delusion* (Jer. 10:15).

    E.   "But not like these is *the portion of Jacob, for he is the creator of all things, Isarael are the tribes of his inheritance; the Lord of hosts is his name* (Jer. 10:16)."

The conclusion turns the final clause on its head. Since the Israelites went after what was worthless, it is easy for God to forgive them, and God does forgive them.

Index

BROWN JUDAIC STUDIES SERIES

BROWN JUDAIC STUDIES SERIES